ST. NORBERT COLLEGE
301.3609561 D22p
Danielson, Michael N.
The politics of rapid urbanization

3 5109 0011 4019 1

D0559002

The Politics of Rapid Urbanization

DATE DUE

301.3609561
D22p

864013

The Politics of Rapid Urbanization

Government and Growth in Modern Turkey

Michael N. Danielson
Ruşen Keleş

HOLMES & MEIER
NEW YORK   LONDON

First published in the United States of America 1985 by
Holmes & Meier Publishers, Inc.
30 Irving Place
New York, NY 10003
Great Britain:
Holmes & Meier Publishers, Ltd.
Hillview House
One Hallswelle Parade
London NW11 ODL, England

Copyright © 1985 by Michael N. Danielson and Ruşen Keleş
All rights reserved

Library of Congress Cataloging in Publication Data
Danielson, Michael N.
  The politics of rapid urbanization: Government and
growth in modern Turkey.
  Bibliography: p.
  Includes index.
  1. Urban policy—Turkey. 2. Urbanization—Turkey.
3. City planning—Turkey. 4. Ankara (Turkey)—City
planning. 5. Istanbul (Turkey)—City planning.
I. Keleş, Ruşen. II. Title.
HT147.T9D36 1985   307.7'6'09561   84-12819
ISBN 0-8419-0951-2
ISBN 0-8419-0952-0 (pbk.)

Manufactured in the United States of America
Book design by Stephanie Greco

King

For
Birgen and Pat
with fond memories of idyllic days
at the Villa Serbelloni

CONTENTS

LIST OF FIGURES   xi
LIST OF TABLES   xiii
GLOSSARY OF TURKISH TERMS   xv
ACKNOWLEDGMENTS   xvii

1—GOVERNMENT AND URBAN DEVELOPMENT   3
   The National Urban Setting   5
   Modern Turkey   7
      The Democratic Tradition   8
      Centralized Government and the Ottoman Legacy   9
      The Goal of Modernization   10
      A Mixed Economy   11
   The Role of Government   12
      The Importance of Government   13
      Varieties of Influence   15
   Governments and Their Sources of Influence   17
      Areal Scope   18
      Functional Scope   19
      Concentrating Resources   21
   Framework of the Study   24

2—RAPID URBANIZATION   27
  Migration and Urban Growth   29
  Rural-Urban Differences   31
  Regional Disparities   34
  Urbanization and Industrialization   38
  A Dual Urban Society   40
  Migrants and the City   43
  The Slowing of Urban Growth   46

3—THE METROPOLITAN CENTERS   49
  The Advantages of the Larger Cities   50
  The Primate City   53
    Imperial Capital   53
    Economic Center   56
    The Contemporary Metropolis   58
  The Planned City   59
    The New Capital   59
    Explosive Growth   61
  The Turkish Metropolis   63
    Spreading Cities   63
    Differentiated Cities   65
    Benefits and Costs of Concentrated Development   68

4—CITIES AND CENTRALIZED GOVERNMENT   71
  The Centralized State   72
  Local Government   75
    Provincial Government   76
    City Government   77
  The Means of Central Control   81
    Administrative Tutelage   82
    Control of Revenues   83
    State Assistance and Investments   86
  The Strands of Central Control   89
    Functional Instruments of Central Power   89
    Orchestras without Conductors   91
  Adapting to Urban Change   93
    Lost Opportunities   94
    Military Government and the Cities   95

5—POLITICAL INTERESTS AND URBAN DEVELOPMENT   99

Political Participation and Urbanization   100

Political Parties and the Cities   102

Centralized Parties and Urban Politics   103

National Politics and Urban Constituencies   104

The Quest for Urban Votes   105

The Party of the Cities   109

Parties and City Politics   111

Political Dynamics of City-Center Relations   112

Growth of City Influence   113

City-Center Conflict   114

Political Interests in Turkish Cities   117

Merchants Associations   117

Other Economic Interests   119

Labor Unions   120

Municipal Employees   121

The Middle Class   123

Squatters   124

The Changing Urban Order   127

The Politics of Assimilation   128

The Politics of Disorder   130

6—PROVIDING URBAN SERVICES   133

Adequacy of City Services   135

Distribution of Urban Services   137

Lack of Services in Squatter Settlements   137

Political Pressures and Municipal Services   138

Organizing Public Services   141

Urban Services and the İller Bankası   143

Centralizing Major Urban Services   145

Complex Problems—The Case of Transporation   147

The Congested City   148

Agencies in Search of Policy   152

The Failure to Concentrate Resourc   155

7—GOVERNMENT AND HOUSIN   157

Housing in Urban Turl   159

Squatter Housing   162

Houses "Which Land in the Night"   165

Nature of Gecekondu Housing   167

The Quest for Home Ownership   168
Gecekondus in Transition   169
Coping with Squatter Housing   170
The Failure of Prohibition   171
The Hope of Alternative Housing   174
The Gecekondu Law of 1966   175
Successes and Failures   177
Increasing the Housing Supply   180
Housing for the Middle Class   180
The Housing Law of 1981   183
City Initiatives in Housing   186

8—SHAPING URBAN DEVELOPMENT   191
Government and Urban Land   192
Soaring Land Costs   193
Building and Zoning Controls   195
Urban Planning   198
Municipal Planning   199
Metropolitan Planning   201
Development Strategies and Urbanization   204
Modernization and Urbanization   205
Regional Development and Urban Concentration   208
Rural Development and Urban Growth   212
Development Planning in Perspective   214

9—GOVERNMENT AND THE METROPOLIS   217
Urbanization and the Political System   219
Influencing Urban Development   224
Government and the Future Metropolis   228

NOTES   235

BIBLIOGRAPHY   261

INDEX   277

LIST OF FIGURES

1–1   Government Influence on Development   16
1–2   Governmental Units Classified by Areal and Functional
      Scope   20
2–1   Population Growth: 1927–1980   30
2–2   Regions and Major Cities: 1980   36
3–1   Istanbul's Geographic Setting   54
3–2   Districts of Izmir by Social Rank: 1968   67
7–1   Squatter Settlements in Istanbul: 1980   163
7–2   Squatter Settlements in Ankara: 1980   164

LIST OF TABLES

2-1 Urban and Rural Population: 1927–1980   28
2-2 Annual Rate of Population Change: 1927–1980   29
2-3 Average Family Income: 1968 and 1973   32
2-4 Urban-Rural Differences in Household Facilities and
       Conveniences: 1973   33
2-5 Urban Growth by Region: 1950–1980   37
2-6 Industrialization and Urbanization in Large Cities:
       1950–1967   38
2-7 Sectoral Distribution of the Economically Active Population
       in Major Cities: 1970   39
2-8 Occupations of Heads of Families in Squatter Settlements in
       Istanbul: 1971 and 1978   40
2-9 Unemployment Rates in Squatter Areas of Selected Large
       Cities: 1966   41
2-10 Squatter Housing: 1945–1980   42
2-11 Satisfaction with City Life Among Squatters in Istanbul   44
2-12 Cost of Living in Turkey and Istanbul: 1970–1979   47
3-1 The Growth of Turkey's Five Largest Cities: 1950–1980   50
3-2 Distribution of the Urban Population by City Size Groups:
       1927–1980   51
3-3 Availability of Electricity and Water by City Size: 1973   52
3-4 Average Family Income by City Size: 1973   53
3-5 City and Suburban Growth in Istanbul and Izmir: 1950–1980   64

3–6   Income Distribution in Istanbul: 1968 and 1980   65
3–7   Income Distribution by Districts in Istanbul: 1980   66
4–1   Number of Municipalities by Size: 1981   76
4–2   Municipal Economic Enterprises: 1980   78
4–3   Municipal Revenues in Ankara: 1976   84
4–4   Deficits of the Municipality of Istanbul: 1968–1976   86
4–5   Debts of Municipalities to Central Agencies: 1978   88
5–1   Voter Turnout by Area in 1969 National Election   101
5–2   Party Support by Type of Urban Community in the 1965
        National Election   107
5–3   Party Support by Type of Urban Community in the 1969
        National Election   108
5–4   Party Support by Type of Urban Community in the 1973
        National Election   109
5–5   Party Support in Major Cities in National Elections:
        1969–1977   110
5–6   Municipal Employment: 1950–1980   122
5–7   Violence and Socioeconomic Change: 1974–1980   131
6–1   Municipal Service Agencies in Istanbul   142
6–2   Responsibilities for Public Services in Urban Areas   144
6–3   Investments in Municipal Services by the İller Bankası:
        1946–1976   145
6–4   Share of Investments of the İller Bankası Financed through
        the Central Budget: 1972–1976   145
6–5   Increases in Buses and Population in Ankara: 1935–1978 150
6–6   Trips by Mode of Public Transportation in Istanbul: 1970 150
6–7   Trips by Mode in Ankara: 1979   150
7–1   Housing Construction Costs: 1963–1980   160
7–2   Licensed Housing Production in Terms of Housing Need:
        1963–1977   162
7–3   Squatter Housing in Ankara: 1950–1980   166

GLOSSARY OF TURKISH TERMS

Allah devlete zeval vermesin—"May God preserve the state"; popular maxim expressing positive attitude toward the state by ordinary citizens in Turkey.

Belediye Encümeni—standing committee; municipal body composed of agency heads and council members and chaired by the mayor. It performs legislative and executive functions.

Belediye Şubesi—municipal subdistricts; units of decentralized administration in the largest cities.

Belediyeler Bankası—Bank of Municipalities; central agency that assisted local service provision between 1933 and 1945.

Danıştay—High Administrative Court; a central agency that reviews governmental actions.

Devlet Baba—"father state"; the concept of the state as a benevolent *paterfamilias*.

Devrimci Belediyeler Derneği—Association of Progressive Municipalities; organization of larger cities under the control of mayors belonging to the Republican People's Party; formed in 1974 and disbanded in 1978.

Dolmuş—group taxi.

Emlak Kredi Bankası—Real Estate Bank, public credit agency responsible for housing finance in the Ministry of Reconstruction and Settlement.

Esnaf—associations or guilds of small merchants and craftsmen.

Gecekondu—squatter housing; literally, "housing built overnight."

Gecekondu Güzelleştirme Derneği—societies for settlement improvement; literally, "gecekondu beautification associations."

İl—province; the main territorial subdivision of the central government.

İlçe—county; territorial subdivision of the province.

İller Bankası—Bank of Local Authorities, or literally, "the Bank of the Provinces"; agency in the Ministry of Reconstruction and Settlement with broad responsibilities for intergovernmental financial relations.

Kalfa—craftsman-contractor.

Lonca—guilds; local organizations that provided public services in Ottoman cities.

Mahalle—neighborhood organizations, responsible for fire protection and local security in Ottoman cities.

Muhtar—headman; leader of the *mahalle*.

Pasha—provincial governor during the Ottoman Empire.

Sosyal Sigortalar Kurumu—Social Insurance Agency, which has an important role in financing social housing.

Tapu—land deed.

Vakıf (or *Waqf*)—foundations; communal organizations that provided health and social services in the Ottoman city.

Vali—provincial governor under the Republic of Turkey.

Yerel Hükümet—local government, in the sense of municipalities with considerable autonomy from central government.

Yerel Yönetim—local administration, in the sense of municipal government acting primarily as the agent of the central authorities.

A NOTE ON THE USE OF TURKISH NAMES: In general, we have used the Turkish alphabet for all Turkish names appearing in the text, footnotes, and bibliography. The only exceptions are names commonly used in English, such as Ataturk, Istanbul, and Izmir. But we employ the Turkish spelling of these names when they appear in Turkish references in the notes and bibliography.

ACKNOWLEDGMENTS

The collaboration that produced this volume had its origins in the summer of 1975 when the authors met on the campus of Boğaziçi University in Istanbul. The occasion was an exploratory meeting by a group of social scientists from Ankara University, Boğaziçi University, Middle East Technical University, and Princeton University, all with a common interest in Turkey's political economy. Out of this conference came the Turkey component of the Income Distribution Project of the Research Program in Development Studies at the Woodrow Wilson School of Public and International Affairs at Princeton University.

Our work on urbanization, centralization, and income distribution in Turkey was published, along with the other papers in the Turkey project, in *The Political Economy of Income Distribution in Turkey* (New York: Holmes & Meier, 1980), edited by Ergun Özbudun and Aydın Ulusan. Parts of this study have been adapted from our papers in the Özbudun-Ulusan volume.

Among those associated with the Income Distribution Project, we owe special thanks to two close friends and colleagues, Professor Ergun Özbudun of Ankara University and Professor Henry Bienen of Princeton University. Professor Özbudun also provided many helpful suggestions for improving the manuscript. In addition, Professor John Lewis was highly supportive in his capacity as director of the Research Program in Development Studies at Princeton at the outset of the project. Kemal Derviş, formerly of Middle East Technical University and now on the staff of the

World Bank, brought to the project an enthusiasm for understanding the economic, political, and social dynamics of his native land that was infectious.

The analytical approach outlined in Chapter 1 is adapted from *New York: The Politics of Urban Regional Development* (Berkeley, Cal.: University of California Press, 1982) by Michael N. Danielson and Jameson W. Doig. We appreciate Professor Doig's assistance, as well as his careful reading of parts of the manuscript.

A critical role in bringing our research to fruition was played by the Rockefeller Foundation, whose generosity enabled us to spend October 1982 working together on this volume as fellows at the foundation's Study and Conference Center at the magnificent Villa Serbelloni high above Bellagio, Italy. The working conditions were ideal, and we accomplished more than could have been expected in the face of the diversions of good food, interesting talk, and the glorious vistas of Lake Como and the Alps.

Professor Keleş' work in the United States during the early phase of the research was supported by the Center for Middle Eastern Studies at Harvard University. Professor Danielson received generous research assistance from the Woodrow Wilson School of Public and International Affairs at Princeton University. The final stage of our collaborative effort, in the spring of 1983 in Ankara, was made possible by support from the Princeton University Committee on Research in the Humanities and Social Sciences, the Faculty of Political Science of Ankara University, the Turkish Development Research Foundation, and the United States Embassy in Ankara. Particularly helpful were Dr. Hasan Gençağa, Secretary General of the Board of Trustees of the Turkish Development Research Foundation, and Marshall Berg, the Counsellor for Public Affairs at the U.S. Embassy. We also deeply appreciate the assistance and encouragement of Professor L. Carl Brown and Professor Charles P. Issawi of the Department of Near Eastern Studies at Princeton.

Help in gathering information and illustrative material was provided by Halûk Alatan, Chairman of the Ankara Metropolitan Planning Bureau, Murat Karayalçın, President of Kent-Koop, Engin Ural, General Secretary of the Environment Foundation of Turkey, Handan Dülger of Istanbul Technical University, and the Turkish Ministry of Reconstruction and Settlement. Liz Arbeiter at the Woodrow Wilson School ensured that material flowed smoothly between Princeton and Ankara. Pat Danielson read parts of the manuscript and helped assemble the final version as it poured out of the word processor.

We, of course, are solely responsible for what has and has not been included in the pages that follow.

Michael N. Danielson
Ruşen Keleş

The Politics of Rapid Urbanization

1
GOVERNMENT AND URBAN DEVELOPMENT

Fabled Istanbul, straddling Europe and Asia at one of history's critical crossroads, spreads inexorably along both sides of the Bosphorus. Over four million people live in the great metropolis that spills far beyond the walls of ancient Constantinople. Once the capital of Byzantium and the Ottoman Empire, Istanbul is the commercial, industrial, and intellectual capital of modern Turkey. Three hundred miles to the east is Ankara, the Anatolian town that Kemal Ataturk made the capital of the new Turkish republic in 1923. Cockpit of a highly centralized political system, Ankara has experienced dizzying growth. Two and a half million people crowd a city whose designers expected only 300,000. Almost two-thirds of Ankara's residents are squatters, part of the flood of migrants from the impoverished countryside that poured into Turkey's cities over the past third of a century.

Turkey, like so many other nations in the twentieth century, has been transformed by rapid urbanization. As is the case everywhere, urbanization in Turkey is an inherent component of the process of modernization. "Any systematic effort to transform traditional societies into modern societies," as Lucien W. Pye emphasizes, "must envisage the development of cities and modern urban societies."[1] Migration, the growth of urban economies, and rapid expansion of cities are integral features of the set of structural changes we call modernization. Urbanization, however, is not merely a synonym for modernization or industrialization. Instead, urbanization refers to a particular element of the development process— the concentration of population in relatively large settlements. Concen-

3

trating people into large settlements is associated with distinctive economic, social, and political changes, such as specialization of the labor force, alterations in family structure, and changes in the political attitudes of urban dwellers.

Urbanization generates a wide range of new tasks and conflicts that must be faced by political systems.[2] Public services have to be provided for increasingly interdependent urban populations. Governmental agencies need to be created to supply water, collect garbage, direct traffic, and perform other urban services. Costs and benefits for public facilities and services must be distributed. Migration, housing, transportation, and land use pose difficult policy questions. The growth of cities complicates the allocation of power between central government and local units, as well as among the multitude of public authorities that spring up in expanding cities.

Inevitably, urbanization stirs conflicts as interests compete for jobs, services, land, and other rewards controlled by the political system. Urban land, for example, is the focus of unending conflicts over use, cost, and the proper role of government in shaping urban development. Industrialists seek to develop land with scant regard for pollution and other environmental effects. Housing developers want as little governmental interference as possible in their profitable activities. Excluded from normal housing markets by their poverty, urban newcomers seize land for squatter settlements. And public officials struggle to secure increasingly costly land for roads, water lines, schools, hospitals, and inexpensive housing.

Intensifying this competition for scarce resources is the nature of urbanization, which both multiplies the number of people with stakes and brings varied groups with diverse stakes into close proximity in crowded cities. Growing populations are one element in this equation; so are rising expectations. Migrants come to the city in search of a better life, and their demands complicate the tasks of government. Almost always, migrants clash with more-established city dwellers, who are not eager to share public resources with unwelcome newcomers. In one way or another, the political system must respond to these demands and mediate the inevitable conflicts. Public officials also must attempt to balance the long-run interests of society against the short-term goals of most city dwellers, which leads to governmental efforts to control the forces of urban growth and change.

The interplay between urbanization and politics in the context of modern Turkey is our primary concern. In the chapters that follow, we explore both the consequences of urbanization for the Turkish political system and the impact of government on the pattern of urban development, particularly in Ankara and Istanbul. Studies of urbanization and politics in developing nations tend to be preoccupied with the effects of urban change on the political system, typically giving short shrift to the effects of political factors on urbanization. The political system usually is portrayed as overwhelmed by urbanization and incapable of influencing rapid urban growth. Reality is more complicated; as Turkey's experience indicates, the impact of government on urban development is often subtle, with results that can be unplanned and unexpected.

In examining the interaction between politics and urbanization, our concern is with urban development broadly conceived rather than more narrowly focused on squatters or the urban poor, as is the case in many urban studies in Turkey and developing countries more generally.[3] The preoccupation with the urban poor in the literature is understandable. In Turkey, squatters account for more than half the population of the largest cities, and problems associated with migration and squatter settlements tend to crowd other issues off the urban agenda. Because of the importance of the urban poor, we devote considerable attention to migration and squatters, to the impact of low-income city dwellers on government and politics in Turkey, and to governmental policies affecting housing and services for urban newcomers. We do so, however, in a broader context, examining entire cities rather than just squatter areas, and looking at the many components of the urban population instead of focusing on the poor. We also consider a sizable spectrum of governmental activities, not just those policies that affect migrants. In casting our net widely, we seek to put the critical problems of migration and the urban poor into the larger perspective of urban and political development in Turkey.

The National Urban Setting

One of the prime attractions of urbanization for political analysis is the similarity of many aspects of urban growth and change in different nations.[4] Migration to cities has the same general features in scores of societies. Traffic congestion, water supply, and housing pose common problems for public officials in cities everywhere. As a result, urban development generates similar pressures, issues, conflicts, and choices in different political systems. These shared characteristics are important because they facilitate analysis of political variables, either comparatively or in the context of a single political system such as that of Turkey.[5]

Urbanization, however, is not the same everywhere. Substantial differences exist in its nature, extent, rate, and timing, and these variations have significant political consequences. A number of political systems are almost completely urbanized, others have sizable urban and rural populations, while some urbanizing nations remain largely rural. In some larger

ntries, a complex network of major urban centers, secondary cities,
 market towns is common. In many nations, by contrast, urban development is heavily concentrated in a single city. Rates of urbanization
vary widely and tend to be closely associated with the stage of urbanization. Cities typically grow most rapidly in the early stages of urban development when rural-urban migration is the primary source of new city
dwellers.

Another important difference involves the relative importance of economic and demographic forces within a particular nation. Urbanization in
most highly developed nations resulted primarily from industrialization,
with migrants attracted to the cities by an expanding factory economy.
Industrial growth has been less significant in the explosive growth of cities
in developing countries. Instead, soaring populations have fueled urbanization, with rural overpopulation spurring migration to cities and high
urban birthrates accelerating growth. As a consequence of these demographic patterns, cities in Africa, Asia, Latin America, and the Middle
East grow at much faster rates than industry, and widespread unemployment and poverty exist among urban newcomers in much of the world.[6]
Urban politics is strongly shaped in most developing nations by "the
combination of rapid growth, weak economic bases, and large migrant
populations"; the common product is "politics characterized by severely
limited resources and intense demands for jobs, land, and urban services."[7]

In many respects, Turkey provides a classic case of rapid urbanization.
Between 1950 and 1980, Turkey's urban population grew fivefold, from 4
million to 20 million.[8] Overall population more than doubled during the
same years, from 20 million to 45 million. Even with massive migration to
the cities, high birthrates increased the rural population from 17 million to
25 million. Despite vigorous industrial expansion, development of the
modern economic sector could not keep pace with urban population increases. As a result, unemployment in metropolitan centers exceeded the
national average in recent years, and large numbers of urban newcomers
have been employed in marginal service occupations.

Rapid urbanization in Turkey has occurred within a complex network of
cities that evolved over the past half century. At the beginning of the
modern period, Istanbul dominated Turkish urban life. With the founding
of the Turkish republic came development of a new national capital at
Ankara whose spectacular growth has been strongly stimulated by
governmental policy. A third major city, Izmir, has also expanded steadily; and together the three major urban centers encompass 36 percent of
Turkey's urban dwellers. An additional 27 percent of the urban population
lives in the remaining cities with 100,000 or more inhabitants, and in

recent years this group of cities has been growing more rapidly than have the three largest urban centers.

Urban politics has been strongly influenced by the distinctive features of Turkey's pattern of urbanization. Rapid growth has generated heavy demands on the political system for services, facilities, and jobs, particularly from migrants, whose needs have been enormous. Public resources have been woefully inadequate to pay the escalating costs of urbanization, especially those resulting from the massive influx of poor migrants. Complicating government's task in allocating resources has been the variety of urban contexts—huge metropolitan complexes, rapidly growing regional centers, and a host of smaller urban communities—each with its own problems and priorities. Urban demands also must be weighed against the enormous needs of rural Turkey, where a majority of the population lives, and where public services are far more primitive than in the cities. And looming behind every policy choice is the close link between conditions in the villages and urban growth—a link that guarantees that failure to narrow the disparities between city and village will push more rural dwellers off the land and into the spreading squatter settlements of Istanbul, Ankara, Izmir, and other urban centers.

MODERN TURKEY

Even more than urban patterns. political systems are shaped by particular national settings. Political arrangements that distribute governmental authority, establish control over resources, and determine priorities vary substantially from nation to nation. Political responses to urbanization are influenced by distinctive national environments, historical experiences, social and economic patterns, and political cultures.

Turkey provides a fascinating national context for examining the interplay of rapid urbanization and political development. Modern Turkey is a relatively large and homogeneous nation. With an area of 301,000 square miles, Turkey is half again the size of France and three times larger than West Germany. Over 90 percent of the population is Turkish speaking, and less than 1 percent is non-Moslem. Turkey's political system is highly centralized, with authority and resources heavily concentrated in Ankara. For the past three decades, democratic politics have been the norm, featuring highly competitive and broad-based political parties, frequent elections, and high rates of electoral participation. Turkey is strongly committed to modernization, and has attempted to direct change through substantial governmental intervention in the form of state enterprises and national planning.

The Democratic Tradition

In contrast with most developing countries, Turkey has been a functioning democracy for a substantial period of time. After more than two decades of one-party rule, the Republican People's Party opened the door to opposition parties in 1946. Two broad-based political parties emerged, which vigorously contested elections and alternated in power over the next third of a century. Fringe parties also developed, and those on the right played an important role in coalition politics during the 1970s.

The politics of urban development in Turkey has been strongly influenced by the existence of a democratic system. Both major parties have sought support broadly, and have responded to the interests of a wide range of groups, including those spurred by rapid urbanization. Growing city populations could not be easily ignored, even though national priorities favored industrial development over investments in housing, sewers, and other urban infrastructure. Squatters in particular have secured great leverage on the political system because of the responsiveness of the major parties to large blocs of voters. Competitive multiparty politics also has provided partisan channels for conflicts between the central government and the cities, especially during periods when one party controlled the national assembly and the other some of the major cities.

Turkey's politics is turbulent as well as democratic, and democracy has not traveled an easy road. Three times since 1960 serious breakdowns in the political system led to military intervention. The latest, in 1980, came in the wake of growing political polarization and widespread terrorism and urban violence. Each time, the military has taken over in the name of preserving democracy. New constitutions emerged from the periods of military rule in 1960–1961 and 1980–1983, and the military interludes have been followed by restoration of parliamentary government. The last period of military rule was the longest and most far-reaching, with the military government abolishing existing political parties and the constitution adopted in 1982 banning their top leaders from political life.

Despite periodic crises and military rule, democracy during its relatively short history has become tightly woven into the fabric of Turkish life. Democratic politics has persevered in the face of adverse conditions—a rapidly multiplying population, sweeping urban change, widespread poverty, mushrooming demands by an increasingly impatient electorate, economic crisis, and open warfare between extremists of the left and right. In part, support for democracy is pragmatic. Democratic institutions, as Walter F. Weiker points out, "are seen by many as a means of bargaining, through which one can advance at least a part of one's interests." But, as Weiker goes on to emphasize, "what is perhaps even more important is that for many Turks, democracy has become a *norm,* which, among other things, places Turkey in a different category from many other 'developing' countries."[9]

Centralized Government and the Ottoman Legacy

Modern Turkey inherited a tradition of governmental centralization from the Ottoman Empire. Authority is concentrated at the center, with national political leaders and bureaucrats dominating the political system. Local governments have meager resources and almost no freedom of action. Although burgeoning growth has made the major cities important participants in Turkish politics, all key urban political decisions are made at the center. For most Turks practically all the time, central government is the only government that matters.

Growing out of the highly centralized political system is the concept of the "father state" *(devlet baba).* Carried over from the Ottomans, this powerful strand in Turkish political culture depicts the state as a "sovereign and autonomous entity, almost independent of society."[10] This personification of the state as a benevolent parent symbolizes widespread trust in government, particularly on the part of the masses. And it creates expectations that the state will behave kindly to its children. "This magnanimous state," explains Kemal Karpat, "is regarded as a protector, a provider, a mystical father."[11] As a squatter seeking to keep the government land on which he has settled explains:

> We have built our dwelling on the land of our father, the state. We took it and built on it. We came and settled on this empty land which belonged to the father state. Is this a crime? Do you think that it would have been better to steal or beg instead of taking refuge on its land? The state land was empty. We decided to earn a living by using it and pay our taxes and thus make it productive.[12]

Trust in the state enhances the authority of Turkey's centralized government. Large segments of the population assume that governmental policies are wise, impartial, and fair. Public confidence in the state as an institution survives despite the shortcomings of many public services, the rigidity of much of the Turkish bureaucracy, and periodic exposés of corruption. The average Turk, however, is less charitable toward politicians than to the state, and public dissatisfaction tends to be focused on political parties and elected officials. The periodic collapse of democratic government has reinforced distrust of politicians, who are widely seen as putting their own interests ahead of the *devlet baba* and its flock.

The Goal of Modernization

Modernization was the driving force of the Turkish revolution. Ataturk's overwhelming objective was to remold Turkey into a modern nation, with Western Europe's political, economic, and social structures providing the model for the new Turkey. Ataturk shattered the traditional links with Islam and Ottoman culture, building a new secular state based on modernization and nationalism. Successive governments have rededicated the nation to the goal of modernization. In overall terms, these efforts have been highly successful. An industrial economy has expanded rapidly, supported by modern communications, transportation, and other infrastructure. Educational levels have steadily risen, health care has been extended, and other public services developed, particularly for the multiplying urban population.

From the beginning of the Turkish republic, industrialization has been the key to modernization. Ataturk wanted Turkey to industrialize as quickly as possible. Turkey's Five-Year Plans enthusiastically endorsed rapid development through industrialization, with industrial growth given priority in investment policies and in the provision of infrastructure. Almost every Turkish government has emphasized industrial expansion over agricultural development, although the proportion of the population engaged in farming far exceeds that employed by modern industries. Only in the past few years has Turkey's commitment to industrialization come into question, as a consequence of severe economic problems that sharply reduced the amount of investment capital available for new industries based on expensive modern technologies.

Urbanization has also been viewed in very positive terms until recently. In Ottoman culture, cities were perceived as the highest form of development. After the revolution, urbanization was widely equated with modernization, and cities seen as the economic and social vanguard of a modernized society. Ankara was developed to symbolize the new Turkey, a planned modern city on the model of the great European capitals. Extension of the rail system and investment in new industries stimulated the growth of many other cities, and urban facilities and services were improved throughout Turkey. Urbanization, however, was not an explicit development objective in the same sense as industrialization. Urban needs received much lower priority than industrial development in the competition for the limited resources available for public investment. And with explosive growth, masses of migrants, housing shortages, traffic jams, polluted air, fouled water, and terrorist violence, urban images in contemporary Turkey became increasingly negative.

Politically, modernization has been less divisive in Turkey than in many developing societies despite pervasive change. The goal of creating a

modern society has been widely shared by a nation that has seen industrial development and urbanization as the only alternatives to rural poverty. And the benefits of development have been spread fairly widely. As
Weiker points out, modernization has "brought the great majority of the
population into the social, economic, and political mainstream of national
life. While this has led to a great increase in demands, to dislocation and
sometimes frustration, it is also the case that a great many Turks (non-
elites as well as elites) are now *agents* of continuing modernization, not
merely objects of it."[13] Modernization also has played an important role in
the development of democracy, as the beneficiaries of better education
and economic growth—most of whom live in cities—have sought to advance their interests through more active political participation.

In many important respects, however, the goal of modernization remains at best partially filled. Most striking is the failure of decades of
efforts to reduce regional and rural-urban disparities, differences that
inflate the attractions of city life for poor villagers. Turkey's cities also
offer stark contrasts between attractive modern neighborhoods and
squalid squatter settlements. Symbolic of the gap between goals and reality are the sweeping promises made in the 1961 Constitution (and
reaffirmed in the 1982 Constitution) to provide housing, health care, education, and social security to all citizens. Limited resources and the press
of other needs have severely restricted the state's ability to meet any of
these goals. Housing, health care, and education remain inadequate for
most Turks, and social security is nonexistent for most urban dwellers and
almost all villagers.

A Mixed Economy

One of the critical factors affecting the ability of government to influence
urban development is the size of the public sector. Government's potential to shape urbanization is obviously much greater in a society like the
Soviet Union, where all economic enterprises are controlled by the state,
than in a political system in which private firms have much of the responsibility for locating plants, offices, stores, and housing, as is the case in
the United States.

In Turkey, most of the economy is in private hands, but the public
sector includes a substantial number of state industries. State economic
enterprises were initially developed as a means of spurring industrial
development during the 1930s when private capital and capitalists were in
short supply. Public investment in industrial development was funneled
primarily to state enterprises, which are particularly important in
transportation, petrochemicals, steel, cement, textiles, and mining. More
than 750,000 work in state industries, which account for about one-third

of the employment and output of large industrial plants. This substantial public industrial sector provides government with a potential lever to influence urban and regional development patterns. The state economic enterprises also represent a heavy drain on public resources, some of which might otherwise be devoted to urban needs. Governmental industrial operations have been highly bureaucratized and politicized, resulting in excessive employment, low productivity, subsidized prices, and deficits that consumed one-seventh of the national budget in the late 1970s.

During the 1950s, government policy favored private industry over state enterprises, and the private sector began to expand rapidly. Under the leadership of the more conservative of Turkey's political parties, greater reliance was placed on free markets, although public investments, subsidies, and other inducements continued to play an important role in industrial expansion. Particularly in the larger cities, private development became the main element of economic expansion, and Turkey experienced a sustained period of growth that lasted through the mid-1970s.

The political pendulum, meanwhile, had swung back toward greater public direction of the economy after the military intervention in 1960, but with emphasis on planning as well as state enterprises. Under the 1961 Constitution, overall guidance for Turkey's mixed economy was to be provided by national development plans. Central planning in Turkey has reflected the plural nature of the economy. Plans are designed to guide rather than direct investment, and have had much less influence on the private sector than on state enterprises and other public agencies. Moreover, political support for state planning has never been strong, particularly from the private sector. By the early 1980s, little more than lip service was being paid to central planning, despite a pressing need for comprehensive economic policies to deal with raging inflation, huge foreign debts, high unemployment, and a generally stagnant economy.

Despite these problems, central planning has had a significant influence on development policy, and its impact has been especially important in the formulation of urban policy. Locational questions have been a major concern of the central planners, and Turkey's Five-Year Plans have dealt explicitly with the role of cities in the modernization process. Sections of the plans treated migration, housing, and regional disparities, and almost all the urban policies developed over the past two decades originated in the national development plans.

THE ROLE OF GOVERNMENT

In the chapters that follow, we examine the particular features of urbanization in Turkey and look in detail at the salient aspects of the Turkish political system. Our goal, as indicated above, is twofold: to analyze the impact of urbanization on government, and to assess government's influence on the forces of urban growth and change.

In the first instance, we are concerned with urbanization's effect on government and politics broadly defined—on governmental structure, public finance, intergovernmental relations, bureaucracy, political participation, political parties, elected officials, interest groups, and public policy. In the second, we consider the extent to which governmental actions affect urban development—migration, settlement patterns, the location of jobs, the provision of housing, and the siting of transportation and other facilities.

The Importance of Government

In exploring these questions, particularly the second set, which deal with the influence of government on urban development, we emphasize the importance of government in modern society. Governments are those organizations that authoritatively allocate values, which make binding rules, for society. While government may share the making of binding rules with religious or other institutions, government is primarily oriented toward rule-making, and in modern society typically comes to dominate this function. Because of its authoritative role, government is the key response mechanism to the needs of a modern society, to its values, and to the demands that arise from these needs and values.

Because of its critical function, government has the potential to have great impact on urban patterns. Depending on the authority and resources available within a particular political system, government can facilitate or impede migration from rural to urban areas, direct investment toward or away from cities, tolerate or prohibit squatter settlements, and encourage or discourage private ownership of automobiles. In mixed economies, governments typically regulate land use and buildings, provide public utilities and infrastructure, and otherwise exercise controls on the locational decisions of industrialists, commercial enterprises, housing developers, and individual households.

Potential, of course, does not automatically provide influence over urban development. Capabilities must be employed, and when used may or may not have significant influence on the course of urbanization. Moreover, government is not the only element in the equation. Market choices, social preferences, demography, and technology have varying degrees of influence on urban patterns, as well as on one another. Because these forces "influence each other continuously," it is "very difficult to sort out the impact on development of any one factor."[14] Further complicating the problem of assessing governmental influence is the wide set of outcomes which together make up a particular pattern of urban development.

Much of the literature on urbanization has chosen to bypass this tangle of causal relations by assuming that government has no significant impact on urban development. Marxists view urban patterns outside the socialist world as the inevitable product of capitalist exploitation, with bourgeois governments serving the interests of their capitalist masters. Dependency theorists also dismiss the impact of government on urban development, emphasizing instead the dominating influence of colonial dependency and imperial exploitation on urbanization in developing nations.[15] Another approach, prevalent in the United States, stresses the predominance of market forces in shaping urban development in a nation with a strong private sector.[16]

Each of these approaches, in our view, throws out the baby with the bath water. Government may have negligible influence on urban development, but the question needs to be answered empirically by examining whether political systems actually have an impact on urbanization. In Turkey, development in Istanbul and Izmir in the decades before World War I was strongly influenced by colonialism.[17] Resentment against the Western imperial powers and the dominant economic role of foreign firms, however, helped fuel the Turkish revolution. Ataturk's new government turned its back on Istanbul and Izmir, moving the capital to Anatolia and reshaping the nation's urban pattern. Because of these political efforts, Istanbul lost many functions to Ankara, and urban development has been spread more widely than would have been the case if the earlier colonial pattern had not been challenged by government.

As emphasized above, assessing government's influence on urban development is complex because many factors are at work on both sides of the equation. In a responsive political system, unraveling political and economic factors is especially difficult but critically important. Individual and group preferences "underlie the actions of private economic and government units—preferences which result in a close intertwining of economic and political forces."[18] Government and the marketplace tend to respond to the same general set of preferences. To see government as merely reinforcing choices made in the marketplace is "to misinterpret the relationships. Generally, activities in both areas respond to the dominant configuration of underlying social values."[19]

The relative importance of economic and political factors varies from society to society, depending on how the particular national framework allocates functions that affect urban development. When the public sector is large, as in Turkey, the role of government in responding to underlying social values is greater than in nations that leave most economic activities to the private sector. Moreover, compared with most Western societies, government in Turkey traditionally has played a more important role than have private economic organizations. "Imagine a society," writes Şerif

Mardin of Ottoman Turkey, where "the central value, the most effective—and more avidly sought after—social lever, is political power—a system where political power affects economics not only directly through the government's control of the market mechanism but where a very large proportion of the arable land is controlled by the state."[20]

From these Ottoman roots have come a conception and a reality of powerful government. From Ataturk to the present, Turkish political leaders have believed in their ability to use the powers of the state to influence development—to transform a traditional society, build a modern economy, and shape the nation's urban pattern by creating a new capital in Anatolia. The masses have looked to the state for answers to their problems, and have used their collective political power to press political parties and elected officials for responses to their demands.

Government is not omnipotent in Turkey, certainly not with respect to urban development. Rapid urban growth is a complex phenomenon in Turkey, with an intricate intertwining of governmental and market influences, along with social and technological factors. Private decisions by individual households and private enterprises often are more influential than those of public agencies. Particularly in the central areas of the major cities, as Istanbul's chief planner emphasizes, "development has been led by market forces."[21] Large firms have played a significant role in the sprawling growth of Turkey's major industrial cities, especially Istanbul, Izmir, Izmit, and Bursa. Rarely, however, does the private sector in Turkey shape urban development unilaterally. Government is involved in the establishment of hotels, theaters, factories, bakeries, bottling plants, and a host of other urban economic enterprises. Thus, governmental determinations interact with private choices in a variety of ways—sometimes reinforcing, sometimes focusing, sometimes stimulating; and, in many instances, government in Turkey plays the key role of initiating development.

Varieties of Influence

In any urbanizing society where the private sector is important, governmental influence on urban development is best represented by a continuum, ranging as shown in Figure 1-1 from instances where government plays a negligible role to cases where government initiates development.

At one end of the continuum, government does no more than ratify decisions made elsewhere. Examples in Turkey are governmental actions that accept market decisions to build apartment blocks in some areas, or which attempt to cope with the consequences of the concentration of office employment in Istanbul's crowded center. Government also has ratified through special laws vast amounts of illegal construction, includ-

FIGURE 1-1
GOVERNMENT INFLUENCE ON DEVELOPMENT

◄---►

Government	Government	Government	Government
ratifies	focuses	modifies	initiates
decisions	demand	demand	development
made			
elsewhere			

ing housing built without local permits, apartments that violated height and density regulations, and factories that failed to conform to local building and health requirements.

Toward the middle of the continuum, government remains sensitive to market or social forces, but shapes development by its response rather than merely ratifying decisions made elsewhere. Squatter policy provides a good example of governmental attempts to focus market demand in urban Turkey. In an effort to check uncontrolled squatter development, government has sought to channel market demand for squatter housing through a variety of assistance programs. By providing cheap land, mortgage credit, and technical assistance, public agencies have tried to focus demand for squatter housing into areas deemed appropriate for such settlements. Efforts to modify demand involve potentially more substantial impacts on urban development by government. In Turkey, large-scale public-housing programs have been developed to reduce demand for squatter housing, and thus increase the amount of housing that meets minimum building and health standards.

At the other end of the continuum are the most influential governmental actions, those that initiate development and thus shape the resulting urban pattern from the outset. The most striking example of government as initiator in Turkey is the decision to build a new national capital at Ankara. Government planned modern Ankara, expropriated the land for the new capital, and nurtured the city's growth by concentrating public investments on the proud symbol of the new Turkey. More recently, Ankara's local government has taken the initiative in developing a planned community for 300,000 residents that is now under construction.

In assessing governmental influence on urban development, government's intentions need to be placed in perspective. If the test of impact is whether government achieves its initially announced objectives, public influence on urban patterns is bound to appear weak. Sweeping programs to renew older cities, or to redirect urban growth through planned new towns, or to eliminate squatter settlements almost by definition will "fail" to achieve their broadest, often grandiose, goals. Such programs, however, may well focus or modify demand significantly, and they can initiate development that otherwise would not have occurred.

Moreover, governmental actions that influence urban patterns sometimes are unintended. Skewing public investment priorities toward industrialization was not an "urban" policy in Turkey. But investment policies favoring industry stimulated rapid growth in the large cities. At the same time, funneling most resources into industrial expansion reduced public capabilities to control urban development because funds were not available for the timely provision of roads, water, sewers, and other city facilities. Turkey's highway construction program was designed to increase the army's mobility and improve the distribution of farm products, not accelerate urbanization. But roads can be used in both directions, and many villagers seeking to better their lives used the improved highway system to move from rural areas to the cities. Without the massive highway improvement program, migration would have been more difficult. Thus, governmental action had the unintended effect of amplifying movement to the cities.

The appropriate test of governmental influence on urban development is what government does and how government activities affect urbanization, not whether government is able to meet its announced goals. To be sure, governmental intentions are important in assessing public capabilities. Obviously, political systems whose principal impacts on urban development are unintended or unexpected are not likely to be able to focus or modify demand in a coherent fashion, or to be capable of initiating and sustaining major projects that have significant influence on the pattern of urbanization.

GOVERNMENTS AND THEIR SOURCES OF INFLUENCE

To this point, government has been treated as a single entity. In reality, of course, governmental systems are complex aggregations, composed of many elements. Central governments are divided into executive, legislative, and judicial institutions. The executive is subdivided into a set of policy and control functions at the top and scores of specialized agencies. Below the national level are one or more tiers of government with responsibilities for regions, provinces, metropolitan areas, and localities.

One of the principal political consequences of urbanization has been to increase the complexity of governmental systems. New units are constantly spawned to wrestle with the multiplying public needs of interdependent urban populations. Planning and coordinating agencies are created to seek order out of the chaos that usually accompanies rapid growth. Population spills beyond the boundaries of established cities, leading to formation of suburban units and efforts to form area-wide governments for the spreading metropolis.

Among the many governmental agencies with an impact on urban development in Turkey, the most important are:

(1) In the central government: the Ministry of the Interior; the General Directorate of State Highways in the Ministry of Public Works; the General Directorate of Railways in the Ministry of Transportation; the State Water Works and the Turkish Electrical Agency in the Ministry of Energy; the Ministry of Reconstruction and Settlement and its Real Estate Bank, Land Office, and Bank of the Provinces; the Ministry of Local Affairs, which was created in 1978 and eliminated two years later; and the State Planning Organization in the Prime Minister's office.

(2) In the provincial governments: governor; general assembly; standing committee; and field offices of central agencies such as the Istanbul Provincial Directorate of the Ministry of Public Works.

(3) At the municipal level: mayor; city council; standing committee; planning commission; line agencies for public works, health, and inspection; and special-purpose local authorities such as Istanbul Water and Sewerage Agency and the Ankara Electricity and Gas and Bus Agency.

Within this complex mosaic, some units have greater capabilities than others with respect to urban development. To a large degree these capabilities are determined by a particular unit's areal scope, its functional scope, and its ability to concentrate resources on specific developmental goals.[22]

Areal Scope

Areal scope refers to the territorial jurisdiction of a governmental unit. In urban Turkey, agencies of the central government have the broadest areal scope, while the suburban units that ring Istanbul are the least extensive territorially.

Governmental jurisdictions with substantial areal scope are able to deal with urban development on a broader scale, which can be both an advantage and a disadvantage. On the plus side, territorial expanse permits a unit to tackle urbanization in its broadest geographical context. Programs to regulate rural-urban migration, for example, are more feasible for central agencies than for provincial or municipal authorities whose jurisdiction does not encompass the origins and destinations of migrants. Negatively, wide areal scope increases the elements that must be considered by government—interests are more diverse, development goals may be less clear, and resources typically are dispersed over a larger number of programs.

Wide areal scope is particularly important in highly centralized political systems. In Turkey, central government retains most governmental authority, delegating relatively little to units with narrower areal scope. As a result, most governmental action relating to urbanization originates from central agencies with broad areal scope, with lesser territorial units playing subordinate roles.

Functional Scope

Functional scope involves the range of activity of a particular governmental institution. Most public agencies have restricted functional range—they specialize in a particular activity such as water supply, highways, or housing credit. Because Turkey is highly centralized, functionally narrow agencies with broad areal scope—the central ministries responsible for highways, water supply, and other urban services—tend to be particularly important participants in the politics of urban development. Also of growing importance within metropolitan areas are independent functional agencies, such as the Ankara Electricity, Gas and Bus Agency, and the newly created Istanbul Water and Sewerage Agency.

Broader functional responsibilities are lodged in a variety of political institutions. First are elected officials, the national assembly, prime minister and cabinet, city councils, and mayors. Because Turkey is both democratic and highly centralized, national elected officials are important participants in urban politics. Provincial governors, who are appointed by the central government, also exercise broad functional responsibilities. Other agencies with relatively wide functional jurisdictions are the Ministry of Reconstruction and Settlement, which is the primary central agency dealing with housing and urban development, and planning offices at the national, provincial, and municipal levels.

Typically, agencies with narrow functional scope have more influence on urban development than those with broad functional responsibilities. Limited functional jurisdiction usually permits an agency to concentrate its energies and resources on a restricted set of objectives—on the building of roads or the installation of water lines—which tend to be more easily realized than broad goals such as redirecting urbanization away from the largest cities. Narrow functional agencies are particularly effective when resources are earmarked for their activity, as is frequently the case for road-building and other public works agencies.

Governmental institutions with broad functional concerns have more difficulty focusing their resources. For those with general national responsibilities, urban development is one of many competing policy questions. In these arenas in Turkey, urban development usually has received less attention than national defense, foreign policy, trade relations, budgetary deficits, inflation, economic growth rates, industrial investments, and agricultural surpluses. Local officials with broad functional responsibilities tend to be overwhelmed by the day-to-day problems of coping with tumultuous urban growth. City officials lack the resources and authority to pursue comprehensive strategies for urban development. The more specialized agencies with broad urban responsibilities, such as the Ministry of Reconstruction and Settlement and the Greater Istanbul Master Plan

FIGURE 1-2
GOVERNMENTAL UNITS CLASSIFIED BY AREAL AND FUNCTIONAL SCOPE

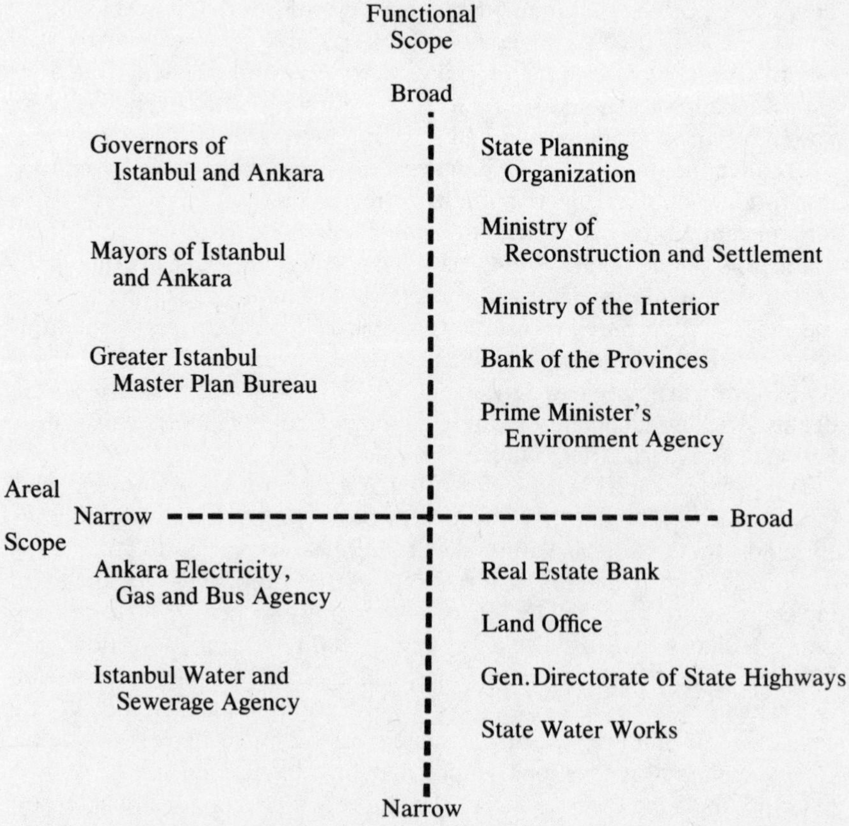

Functional Scope

Broad

Governors of Istanbul and Ankara	State Planning Organization
Mayors of Istanbul and Ankara	Ministry of Reconstruction and Settlement
	Ministry of the Interior
Greater Istanbul Master Plan Bureau	Bank of the Provinces
	Prime Minister's Environment Agency

Areal Scope   Narrow ————————————— Broad

Ankara Electricity, Gas and Bus Agency	Real Estate Bank
	Land Office
Istanbul Water and Sewerage Agency	Gen. Directorate of State Highways
	State Water Works

Narrow

Bureau, also have had difficulty concentrating resources on development objectives.

Concentrating Resources

The ability to concentrate resources "involves the focusing of public powers, funds, and skills in order to achieve specific development goals."[23] The importance of this factor lies in the complexity of urban development. Because urbanization results from the interplay of political, economic, social, and technological forces, governmental efforts to shape development must deal with the dynamism of the other forces. These efforts are most likely to succeed if public resources are concentrated effectively on specific objectives.

The ability of a governmental unit to concentrate resources depends on a number of factors. One of the most important is formal independence, "the extent to which a governmental body is formally independent of other governments in making policy, obtaining funds, and allocating funds for specific purposes."[24] In Turkey, no governmental institution is completely independent, since all are subject to constitutional restraints. Within this general framework, however, striking differences exist in the relative autonomy of governmental agencies with urban responsibilities. The central political institutions and ministries have great freedom of action, while local governments have almost none. Concentration of authority at the top of the Turkish political system enhances the development capabilities of central agencies, while severely constraining those of the city governments.

Another external factor affecting the concentration of resources is the variety and intensity of constituency demands that are placed on particular institutions. Pressures of one sort or another exist for everything that government undertakes, but different jurisdictions face different kinds of constitutency demands. Institutions with broad functional responsibilities typically deal with a greater variety of constituency demands than those with more limited mandates. Similarly, extensive areal scope increases the range of demands. The relationship between the variety of constituency pressures, areal and functional scope, and ability to concentrate resources effectively on urban objectives is subtle:

> The more narrowly focused the demands, the greater the ability of a governmental unit to affect the included area. . . . Yet the wider the range of functions with which the government is expected to deal, the wider the impact it can have on urban development . . . unless available resources are spread too thin to provide a significant counterweight to the economic, technological and other forces operating in various program areas.[25]

Concentration of resources is particularly difficult when constituency interests are in conflict. In the face of crosscutting constituency pressures, squatter policy in Turkey has zigzagged between harsh measures undertaken in response to the demands of landowners and established city dwellers and lenient actions prompted by the political efforts of urban newcomers. Intensity of demands often determines whether government will act at all, particularly when public resources are severely limited as in Turkey. Squatter housing has received more attention than other pressing urban problems, such as pollution or congestion, in part because the intensity of demands for action has been greater.

How a particular jurisdiction uses its formal authority and responds to various constituencies depends heavily on the availability of financial resources. Fiscal capability, in turn, is strongly influenced by both the degree of independence and the nature of constituency pressures since "money is likely to be diffused where multiple demands exist . . . and the ability to obtain funds . . . may be severely limited by external controls."[26] In Turkey, financial weaknesses adversely affect the ability of every type of governmental institution to influence urban development. And rising demands for action by expanding city populations have intensified the pressures on severely limited fiscal resources. Within this general framework of scarcity, local governments have been at a particular disadvantage. Almost all public revenues are monopolized by the center, with cities receiving meager allotments for various activities from national agencies.

Control over land use is particularly important to urban development. With urbanization typically comes increased public regulation of land and buildings. In mixed economies, these development controls provide a primary means of attempting to influence the locational decisions of private firms and individual households. One of the striking features of the politics of urban development in Turkey is the ineffectiveness of land-use and building controls. The pressures on land have been so great, particularly from the urban poor, and the ability of government to enforce its regulations so slight, that substantial portions of urban Turkey have been settled illegally. And many of the problems that overwhelm public agencies in Turkish cities result from the widespread inability of government to influence urban development through land-use controls.

In addition to these four factors, government's ability to concentrate resources also depends on political skill, on the ability of public officials to formulate goals clearly and employ resources effectively to achieve these objectives within the context of their units' opportunities and constraints. Political skill was a critical factor in the successful efforts of the mayors of Ankara, Istanbul, and other major cities to enlarge their role in the urban development process despite heavy dependence on the central government for authority and funds. The mayors identified with their constituents' demands, dramatized city problems, organized among themselves for collective action, engaged in well-publicized disputes with the central government over their needs, and pressed national political leaders for new urban policies.

In governmental institutions with broad functional responsibilities, subordinate units must be controlled if resources are to be concentrated. The natural inclination of functional agencies is "to define goals in terms of their own relatively narrow perspectives, to develop strong ties with their clientele, and to create functional alliances with officials at other levels of government."[27] All these tendencies are strong in Turkey, and they are reinforced by the highly centralized character of the political system. The national ministries are large, complex institutions, which operate with considerable autonomy from the Prime Minister's office and the Cabinet. Local agencies, on the other hand, are subject to close supervision by the central ministries, creating strong functional links and weakening the ability of mayors and city councils to control their subordinate units.

Planning often is seen as the principal means by which government influences urban development; and governmental success or failure frequently is measured in terms of whether plans have been followed. Planning, however, is more usefully considered as one means by which resources can be concentrated, operating in the context of other factors and subject to similar constraints. Urban planning has been defined as "the application of foresight to achieve certain preestablished goals in the growth and development of urban areas." So conceived, planning involves a "continuous process of deriving, organizing and presenting a broad and comprehensive program for urban development and renewal" which considers "immediate needs and those of the foreseeable future."[28] Planners argue that urban planning agencies should have broad areal and functional scope and that public and private decisions that shape urban development should be based on the guidelines developed by planners.

In Turkey as in most nations, there is a good deal of urban planning, but little that meets the planners' ideal, particularly with respect to guiding either public or private decisions. Urban planning has been nurtured by the central government, planning agencies exist in the larger cities, and master plans have been dutifully prepared. But little of urban Turkey bears much resemblance to the dreams of the planners, including Ankara, where unplanned growth quickly overwhelmed the grand scheme of the 1920s. Turkish planners usually have been more interested in urban design than urban development; public officials often have paid little attention to official plans; and vast amounts of private develement have occurred in defiance of city plans and regulations. As a result, urban planning has been little tested by those who would concentrate resources on development goals in urban Turkey.

The seven factors that underlie governments' ability to concentrate resources—formal independence, constituency demands, financial resources, political skill, control over land, control over subunits, and planning capabilities—are closely related. These components in turn are conditioned by areal and functional jurisdiction. All these variables are explored in detail in the chapters that follow, and their role in the politics of urban development in Turkey is elaborated.

FRAMEWORK OF THE STUDY

In examining the interplay of urbanization and politics in modern Turkey, we concentrate primarily on the third of a century that commenced in the late 1940s and ended with military intervention in 1980. Where appropriate, we examine earlier developments, such as the origins of municipal government in the late 19th century and the creation of a planned national capital at Ankara in the 1920s. We also give some attention to urban policy in the early 1980s, but do not examine government in detail during the latest interlude of military rule.

Throughout, we focus on Istanbul and Ankara, Turkey's largest and most important cities. The development of the two great metropolitan centers needs, however, to be examined in the perspective of the general process of urbanization in Turkey. Thus, we turn in Chapter 2 to the national context of rapid urban growth—examining migration to the cities and exploring the rural-urban and regional disparities that have spurred urban development. In Chapter 3, we concentrate on the largest cities, looking in detail at Istanbul's historic primacy and Ankara's emergence as the planned national capital, and at the heavy costs incurred by intensive development in the largest cities.

In Turkey, as the preceding discussion has suggested, an analysis of the politics of urban development needs to encompass the entire political system. Resources and authority are concentrated at the center, and decisions of the national government are more important than those of local units for most urban policies. In Chapter 4 we discuss the implications of this highly centralized political system for Turkey's cities. Then we move in Chapter 5 to the roles, resources, and influence of the main participants in the politics of urban development. In these chapters, the impact of urbanization on governmental structure and the political process is also examined.

With this understanding of the forces of urban growth and the centralized political system that deals with urbanization in Turkey, we turn to the interplay of urban development and the political system in some key areas of public policy. Chapter 6 looks at urban services, primarily in terms of the impact of rapid urban growth on government. In Chapter 7 we focus on housing and squatter settlements, a discussion that involves both the effect of urbanization on government and efforts by the political system to control urban development. Chapter 8 concentrates on governmental efforts to control urbanization, examining land and building regulation, urban planning, and national strategies for urban and regional development.

The last chapter appraises the interplay of urbanization and political development in Turkey, returning to many of the themes introduced in this chapter. In light of Turkey's experiences, we assess the responsiveness of the political system to urban change. We conclude by pondering an uncertain future in terms of projected urban growth and evolving public capabilities to control that unruly and wondrous beast—the modern metropolis.

2
RAPID URBANIZATION

Explosive urban growth is a recent experience for Turkey. Ataturk's republic was forged in a largely rural society. During the 1920s less than one-sixth of the population lived in cities and towns with more than 10,000 inhabitants. Aside from Istanbul with its 700,000 residents, only Izmir contained more than 100,000 people. Cities grew slowly before 1950—the urban population increased from 2.2 million to 3.9 million between 1927 and 1950, while the rural population was expanding from 11.4 million to 17.1 million.[1] Annual urban growth was 2.4 percent during this period, compared to 1.7 percent for the rural sector; and the urban share of Turkey's population advanced modestly, rising from 16.4 percent in 1927 to 18.5 percent in 1950.

After 1950, urban growth accelerated sharply. Over 3.3 million people were added to the urban population during the 1950s, more than twice as many as in the previous quarter century. Turkey became one of the most rapidly urbanizing countries in the world—between 1950 and 1980 the average annual increase of urban population was 5.7 percent. Large cities grew even faster, with cities over 100,000 experiencing yearly increases of 7 percent over the same period. Rapid urbanization also multiplied the number of major urban centers. Only five cities had more than 100,000 inhabitants in 1950; by 1980 there were twenty-nine.

Since 1950, population in urban areas has been expanding much faster than in rural Turkey. By 1980, more than five times as many people lived in cities and towns as had in 1950, compared with an increase of less than 50 percent in the villages over these years. Between 1927 and 1950, urban

TABLE 2-1
URBAN AND RURAL POPULATION: 1927–1980

	Total Population	Urban Population	Percent Urban	Rural Population	Percent Rural
1927	13,648,000	2,236,000	16.4	11,412,000	83.6
1940	17,821,000	3,234,000	18.1	14,586,000	81.9
1950	20,947,000	3,884,000	18.5	17,063,000	81.5
1960	27,755,000	7,189,000	25.9	20,566,000	74.1
1970	35,605,000	11,821,000	33.2	23,784,000	66.8
1980	44,737,000	20,330,000	45.4	24,406,000	54.6

SOURCE: State Statistical Institute, population censuses.

areas accounted for only 23 percent of Turkey's overall population growth; since 1950, cities and towns have been responsible for 69 percent of the national increase, and the urban share of the population exceeded 45 percent in 1980.

Politically, this abrupt change in Turkey's rate of urbanization is extremely significant. The relatively slow pace of urban growth before 1950 did not severely challenge the political system. Only Ankara was expanding rapidly, and the new capital was favored with the lion's share of national resources devoted to developing modern city services. Lulled by this initial experience with urbanization, the Turkish political system—indeed, the entire society—was unprepared for the swirling winds of urban change that swept across the land in the 1950s. Suddenly, urbanization was a burden as well as a blessing. On a scale never encountered before, essential services had to be provided, people and goods moved, and urban newcomers housed. City problems quickly became national issues, and the political system struggled to cope with the new realities of a rapidly enlarging urban electorate, multiplying demands for services and creating new kinds of conflicts and the need to reshape government to cope with urbanization, all within the context of severely constrained public resources and a poor rural population that continued to grow.

Despite three decades of rapid urbanization, four million more people lived in rural Turkey than in the cities in 1980. Rural population continued to expand primarily because improvements in public health reduced infant mortality and increased life expectancy. This large rural population, which exceeded 24 million in 1980, continues to feed migration to the cities, which offer more opportunities than the villages. At the same time, the rural sector competes with the cities for scarce public resources, and is far too large to be ignored by national political leaders, especially in a fiercely competitive democratic system.

MIGRATION AND URBAN GROWTH

Migration has been the prime driving force behind rapid urban growth in Turkey. Most of the 3.3 million people added to the urban population in the 1950s were migrants. By the 1980s, over 700,000 rural dwellers a year were moving to urban areas. As a result of the vast demographic tide carrying people from the village and into the cities, the proportion of people living outside their native province more than doubled after 1950. Because of migration, urban population grew five times faster than rural population over the past thirty years, despite birthrates that were 40 percent higher in the country than in the cities.[2]

Patterns of rural-urban migration vary considerably from one national setting to another. Migrants may go directly from the countryside to the largest cities, or they may move in steps, from village to town to small city and then to the metropolis. The distances involved in migration may be short or long. In Turkey, most migrants eventually settle in the larger cities, but many initially move from village to smaller city, which increases the number of settlers in the metropolitan centers who have had

TABLE 2-2
ANNUAL RATE OF POPULATION CHANGE: 1927–1980

Period	Total	Urban	Rural
1927–1940	2.1	2.8	1.9
1940–1950	1.6	1.8	1.6
1950–1960	2.9	6.4	1.9
1960–1970	2.5	5.1	1.5
1970–1980	2.3	5.6	.3
1927–1950	1.9	2.4	1.7
1950–1980	2.6	5.7	1.2

SOURCE: Calculations based on data from State Statistical Institute, population censuses.

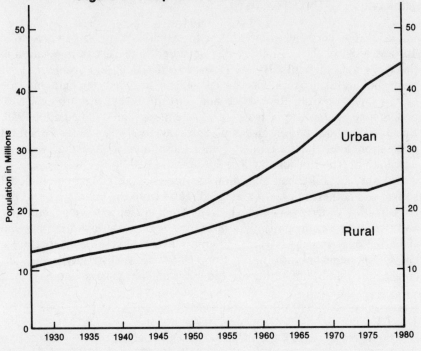

Figure 2-1. Population Growth: 1927-1980

Source: State Statistical Institute, population censuses.

some experience with urban life.[3] Because Turkey has a substantial network of cities, many migrants have moved relatively short distances and, in the process, spurred the rapid development of a number of regional growth centers.

Even more villagers would have crowded into Turkey's cities had not a million workers migrated to Western Europe during the 1960s and early 1970s. Almost half of those who went abroad were from rural areas.[4] If they had remained in Turkey, most of these rural dwellers would have joined the great march from the villages to the cities. While international migration has lessened the number of urban newcomers within Turkey, the reduction has been temporary rather than permanent for many villagers. In Europe, Turkish workers live in cities and acquire urban tastes, and upon returning home tend to settle in localities more urban than their points of departure.[5] With the sharp decline in employment opportunities for Turkish workers in Europe in the late 1970s, the number of returning workers increased, as did their impact on the growth of Turkish cities. Still, over 1.6 million workers and their families were in Europe in 1978 rather than in Istanbul, Ankara, and other urban centers.[6]

Migration in Turkey has been facilitated by governmental policies. Perhaps most important has been a benign general attitude toward the movement of millions of rural dwellers to the cities. Government has not erected barriers to migration as has been the practice in some rapidly urbanizing nations. Nor has government attempted to pursue repressive policies toward squatters, a common response to the flood of migrants in many developing nations. Instead, public policy for the most part has been permissive toward migrants once they reach the cities—providing rudimentary services to newcomers and accepting their illegal dwellings.

This perspective reflects Turkey's positive view of urbanization as an essential corollary of modernization that was noted in Chapter 1. Turkish governments have viewed urbanization as a "vehicle of economic and social development." Urban development, according to Turkey's national planners, "precedes industrialization." Government also concluded that there was "no other alternative" to "allowing massive migrations to urban areas" because "agricultural land [was] at, or near, its maximum utilization."[7]

Even if urbanization was less valued, however, negative policies toward something as attractive as movement to the cities would have been extremely difficult to sustain in a democratic political system. Growing out of these favorable attitudes toward migration, and reinforcing them, was a provision of the 1961 Constitution that guaranteed the right to free movement. The principle of freedom of travel was maintained in the 1982 Constitution, but a sentence was added permitting the state to take measures to control urban migration in order to implement large-scale resettlement plans.[8] Underlying the new constitutional provision was a more critical attitude toward rapid urbanization, a view shaped by the enormous costs imposed by an unending and unregulated flow of migrants to the cities.

RURAL-URBAN DIFFERENCES

Disparities between life in the cities and in the villages, along with a rapid increase in rural population, underlie mass migration and accelerating urbanization in modern Turkey. Rural dwellers have lower incomes, less access to public services, and fewer amenities than city residents. According to the most recent national survey, the average income of urban

TABLE 2-3

AVERAGE FAMILY INCOME: 1968 and 1973

	1968		1973	
	Income	*Index*	*Income*	*Index*
Urban	14,658	125	30,223	122
Rural	8,181	70	20,272	82
National	11,761	100	24,694	100

SOURCES: Tuncer Bulutay, Serim Timur, and Hasan Ersel, *Türkiye'de Gelir Dağılımı: 1968* (Ankara: Siyasal Bilgiler Fakültesi Yayınları, 1971); and State Planning Organization. *Gelir Dağılımı Araştırması—1973* (Ankara, 1976).

families in 1973 was 30,223 lira, about $3,000, compared with 20,272 lira, or $2,000, for rural families.[9] Thus, family income was 50 percent higher in cities than in rural areas. Five years earlier, as shown in Table 2-3, the gap was almost 80 percent.[10] Lower costs of living in the countryside narrow income differences between urban and rural areas, but not enough to offset the substantial gap in average earnings between villagers and inhabitants of cities.

Urban-rural differences are magnified when public services are considered. In 1970, fewer than one in six rural households had electricity or running water, whereas two-thirds of all urban families had water and more than three-quarters, electricity.[11] Inadequate water and electric service meant rural dwellers were less likely to have toilets, baths, refrigerators, washing machines, and other conveniences than were city residents, as shown in Table 2-4. Public investments in rural utilities reduced these disparities somewhat during the 1970s. After a decade of vigorous efforts by the Turkish Electricity Agency, a state enterprise created in 1970, half the villages had electricity by 1980. By then, however, 97 percent of municipalities had been wired.[12] Water supply was judged adequate in 63 percent of all rural settlements in 1980, compared with 94 percent of the municipalities.[13]

Education and health services are poorer in rural areas. The proportion of school-age children attending primary school in the countryside is only 61 percent of that in the cities. In the typical village, one teacher directs all the classes rather than a single grade, as is the case in most urban schools. Rural literacy rates are substantially lower than in the larger cities.[14] Hospitals and health clinics are much less accessible to rural families than to city dwellers, and infant mortality rates are considerably higher in the villages.[15]

The attractions of higher income, better schools, and more public services in the cities have been magnified by agricultural conditions in rural

Turkey. There is not sufficient arable land to support a growing rural population, and this results in widespread unemployment and underemployment among agricultural workers. Most farms are small; three-fourths of all holdings in 1970 were less than 50 decars—approximately 12 acres. Many farmers own scattered parcels of land, which makes economic operation difficult and severely limits the use of modern agricultural techniques. Because of these conditions, productivity is low and farms typically generate little income. In 1980, the 56 percent of the population engaged in agriculture accounted for only 20 percent of Turkey's gross national product. Although many migrants owned land in their villages, they departed for the city because they could not earn a living from small plots which are often eroded and lack irrigation.[16]

Social as well as agricultural conditions drive rural Turks toward the cities. High birthrates have created overcrowding in many villages, particularly in the intensively settled forest belts. Migration from these densely populated rural areas has been extensive. In addition, social conflict in the parochial world of the Turkish village has pushed people to the less confining cities. In a number of rural communities, İbrahim Şanlı observes,

> vendettas and family fights have institutionalized hostility. . . . At times, these hostilities become so intense as to induce new outbreaks of fighting. This fighting is sometimes reduced by governmental resettlement of contending forces or by one group or another (or individuals from these groups) deciding to migrate to the city.[17]

A variety of governmental policies contributed to adverse rural conditions, and these increased the city's attractions for villagers. Rural areas

TABLE 2-4
URBAN-RURAL DIFFERENCES IN HOUSEHOLD FACILITIES AND CONVENIENCES: 1973

	Percent of Households with Item	
	Urban	Rural
Toilet	63.5	26.1
Bath in house	51.4	18.5
Refrigerator	39.7	8.8
Washing machine	21.7	2.2

Source: Unpublished data from the 1973 Hacettepe Population Survey.

were largely ignored in Turkey's push to modernize, with most state investment focused on industrial development and public services in the cities. Strong governmental support of agricultural mechanization played an important role in driving people off the land. Approximately half a million agricultural workers were displaced by the introduction of more than 300,000 tractors in the years since 1950, a development strongly backed by the central government; and most of these uprooted farmers and their families became part of the exodus to the cities.

Movement of those attracted by the city and repelled by adverse rural conditions was also facilitated by substantial governmental expenditures for highways, which became the largest category of public investment in the years after World War II. Development of a modern highway system and a network of farm-to-market feeder roads greatly increased the mobility of rural dwellers. In the two decades after 1950, the mileage of paved roads was doubled, while passenger-travel volumes increased sixteen-fold.[18] Road improvements, as noted in Chapter 1, were not designed to encourage rural-urban migration. The government's aim was to strengthen national defense and provide farmers with a means of getting their produce to urban markets. But the new roads, along with the expansion of inexpensive bus service, markedly reduced the isolation of Turkey's 35,000 villages. Rural dwellers could make more frequent visits to urban centers and see for themselves the differences between life in the country and in the city. Inevitably, the highways paved the way for those who decided to start a new life in the booming urban centers.[19]

REGIONAL DISPARITIES

Migration and the pattern of urban growth in Turkey have been strongly influenced by regional disparities in wealth, industrial development, agricultural productivity, and public services. Regional differences are rooted in Turkey's geography, climate, and history. The western half of the nation has more favorable topography and rainfall than has mountainous and arid eastern Anatolia, and farming has been substantially more productive in the west than in the east. From this stronger agricultural base, and enjoying locational advantages with respect to Europe and maritime commerce, western Turkey developed a diversified economy and modernized society. The eastern provinces, by contrast, have remained physically, economically, socially, and culturally isolated from the mainstream of modern Turkish development, with a poor and illiterate population engaged primarily in subsistence agriculture.[20]

Because of these regional disparities, urban development has been heaviest in the west, and urban migrants flow westward from the impoverished eastern provinces. Most of the large cities are located west of the axis formed by Samsun and Adana, as shown in Figure 2-2. In 1980, urban centers in western Turkey accounted for 93 percent of the 12.2 million people living in cities with more than 100,000 inhabitants. Cities over 100,000 in the east are smaller—with an average population of 179,000 in 1980 compared to 500,000 in the west. Marmara in the northwest, with Istanbul and three other large cities, has been the most urbanized region through the twentieth century, and two-thirds of its population was urban in 1980. Urban growth has been particularly striking in two other regions in western Turkey—Southern Anatolia with Adana and six other rapidly growing major cities, and Central Anatolia, which includes Ankara and four additional large urban centers.[21] Between 1950 and 1980 these two regions added six million urban inhabitants. Underlying this rapid growth was massive migration from the impoverished rural areas of eastern and southeastern Anatolia.[22]

Concentration of the major cities in western Turkey affects the distribution of a wide range of activities, resources, and services, all of which in turn influence migration and urban growth patterns. Because the large cities are clustered in the west, rural areas in eastern Turkey have had little spillover benefits from urbanization compared to villages nearer cities in western Turkey. Thus, urban concentration in Marmara and the other western regions amplifies regional disparities, and in the process makes migration to the cities even more attractive in the east.

Since most industry is located in larger cities, the west has far more industrial development than the less urbanized eastern provinces. In 1975 the province of Istanbul alone accounted for 49 percent of all major industrial establishments in the nation, while less than 3 percent were located in eastern Anatolia. Wealth is also concentrated in the most heavily urbanized and industrialized provinces of the west. Incomes are substantially lower in the east, with the average family in the eastern provinces earning only two-thirds of the national average in 1973.[23] Per capita bank deposits in western Turkey were more than twenty times as great as in the eastern regions in 1980.

Public services and investments are also heavily skewed in the direction of western Turkey. Fewer families in the east are served by running water and electricity; and a smaller proportion of households than in the west have toilets, baths in the house, and electric appliances.[24] In 1980, 60 percent of all public credits were allocated to the most developed regions in the west, while eastern Anatolia received only 4 percent.[25] Roads, schools, health services, and other public facilities all fall below national norms in eastern Turkey. In the case of health care, in 1980 the most

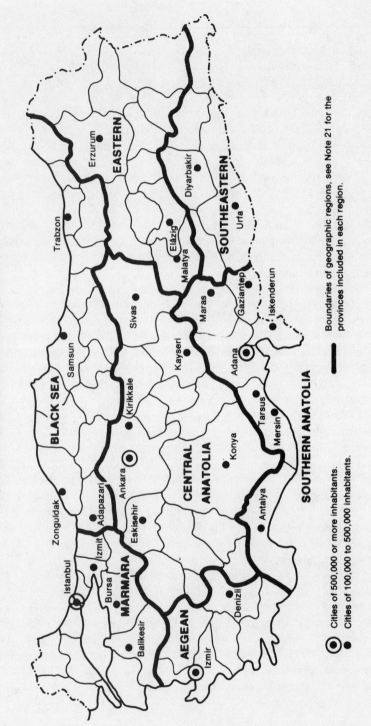

Figure 2-2. Regions and Major Cities: 1980

○ Cities of 500,000 or more inhabitants.
● Cities of 100,000 to 500,000 inhabitants.

— Boundaries of geographic regions, see Note 21 for the provinces included in each region.

EASTERN
Erzurum

SOUTHEASTERN
Diyarbakir
Urfa
Elazig
Malatya

Trabzon

BLACK SEA
Samsun

Sivas
Maras
Gaziantep
Iskenderun

Kirikkale
Kayseri
Adana

Ankara

CENTRAL ANATOLIA
Tarsus
Mersin
Konya

SOUTHERN ANATOLIA

Zonguldak
Adapazari
Eskisehir

Izmit
Istanbul

MARMARA
Bursa
Balikesir
Antalya

AEGEAN
Izmir
Denizli

36

TABLE 2-5

URBAN GROWTH BY REGION: 1950–1980

| Region | Population (000) | | Increase (000) | Percent Urban | |
	1950	1980	1950–1980	1950	1980
Marmara	1,392	6,488	5,096	36.5	68.7
Southern Anatolia	445	2,732	2,287	21.7	49.8
Aegean	532	2,243	1,711	24.1	48.6
Central Anatolia	944	4,711	3,767	19.9	47.6
Southeastern	170	1,066	896	15.1	36.5
Eastern	205	1,259	1,054	8.5	27.2
Black Sea	326	1,861	1,535	5.7	24.3

SOURCE: State Statistical Institute, population censuses.

urbanized western provinces had 57 percent of the nation's hospital beds and 70 percent of its specialists, and the least urban provinces in the east had 7 percent of the hospital beds and 3 percent of the specialists.[26]

Substantial regional disparities persist in Turkey despite governmental efforts to reduce interregional inequalities. Ankara was established as the national capital in impoverished central Anatolia. Rail lines were extended to connect provincial towns to the major cities. And many of these towns were transformed into cities through the establishment of state industries and by "making them governmental and cultural centers for their respective hinterlands and by initiating extensive municipal construction projects."[27] More recently, national development plans have tried to promote social justice through more balanced public investments among regions.

Without these governmental efforts to influence development, even greater differences would exist among regions. The early policies, as a report by the World Bank notes, "were effective in spreading industrialization throughout Turkey."[28] During the past two decades, efforts to redress regional imbalances have improved education, health care, and other public services in most backward areas, as well as spurring urbanization in eastern Anatolia. What regional development policies, which are examined in detail in Chapter 8, have not been able to deflect is the strong pull of western Turkey's major urban centers, which continue to attract the lion's share of private and public investment.

As a result, rapid urbanization has sustained substantial regional disparities despite governmental efforts to shift development eastward. These regional differences, in turn, contribute significantly to the development of a system of cities dominated by the large metropolitan complexes of western Turkey. Regional disparities also reinforce urban-rural differences, increasing the attractions of the city for the impoverished east and pushing rural Turks westward to the cities. In the process, the nation's spatial development pattern is distorted further.

URBANIZATION AND INDUSTRIALIZATION

Industrial growth spurred the rapid expansion of Turkish cities. Employment in industry rose from 250,000 in 1927 to over 2 million in 1980. Between 1948 and 1980, manufacturing's share of the gross national product almost tripled from 13 percent to 36 percent. As in most nations, Turkey's new industries were concentrated in the cities; and industrial development attracted rural dwellers to the city with the promise of jobs, higher incomes, and a better life. As indicated in Chapter 1, government played a key role in stimulating industrial development, and thus rapid urbanization, through the creation of state enterprises and the concentration of public investments in industry and supporting infrastructure.

Industrialization, however, has not been able to keep pace with urbanization. In a pattern common to the developing world, most Turkish cities have grown faster than their industrial bases, as indicated in Table 2-6,

TABLE 2-6
INDUSTRIALIZATION AND URBANIZATION IN LARGE CITIES: 1950–1967

	Industrial Index (1950 = 100)	Urbanization Index (1950 = 100)
Istanbul	240	178
Ankara	446	313
Izmir	139	174
Adana	179	246
Bursa	154	205
Eskişehir	170	194
Gaziantep	115	220
Konya	242	245
Kayseri	155	194

SOURCE: Ruşen Keleş, "Alternatif Şehirleşme Hareketlerinin Maliyeti Hakkında Ön Rapor," State Planning Organization (Ankara: 1967).

NOTE: The industrial index is based on the number of industrial workers, and the urbanization index on the population of the city.

TABLE 2-7

SECTORAL DISTRIBUTION OF THE ECONOMICALLY ACTIVE POPULATION IN MAJOR CITIES: 1970

	Industry	Percentage employed in Services	Other*
Istanbul	38.9	56.2	4.9
Ankara	20.1	69.6	10.3
Izmir	34.7	53.6	11.7
Adana	31.7	45.9	22.4
Bursa	40.4	41.1	18.5
Gaziantep	29.3	48.3	20.4
Eskişehir	30.9	53.3	15.6

SOURCE: State Statistical Institute, "Population Census, 25 October 1970 Sampling Results," Publication no. 659 (Ankara: 1972).
*Includes agriculture and unclassified occupations.

creating what has been called "overurbanization." Some of the gap between population and industrial growth has been made up by the rapid expansion of the service sector. "The structure of the service sector," as Ali Türel and Özcan Altaban point out, "is more elastic and enables a rapid response to new demands in the market.[29] Throughout urban Turkey, services account for a significantly larger share of the economically active population than does industry. Between 1950 and 1980, service employment in Turkey expanded three times as fast as industry. As a result, service jobs rather than industrial employment have absorbed a substantial portion of the rural influx, especially among the unskilled and poorly educated. Large numbers of migrants are employed, as indicated by the occupational data for squatters in Istanbul in Table 2-8, in retail trade and other services.

Failure of the urban economy to grow as fast as the labor force also results in substantial underemployment and unemployment in Turkish cities. The Ministry of Reconstruction and Settlement has estimated that the proportion of underemployed squatter dwellers in Ankara and Izmir ranged as high as 70 percent in the mid-1960s.[30] The expanding service sector accounts for most of the underemployment, as large numbers of migrants find work as street hawkers, porters, bootblacks, messengers, parking-lot attendants, caretakers, and in other marginal occupations characterized by intermittent employment and low productivity.

In part because of extensive underemployment in service trades, unemployment rates in Turkish cities were relatively low until recently. As indicated in Table 2-9, fewer than 10 percent of the squatters in major

TABLE 2-8
OCCUPATIONS OF HEADS OF FAMILIES IN SQUATTER SETTLEMENTS IN ISTANBUL: 1971 AND 1978

Occupation	Percent of total 1971	Percent of total 1978
Factory worker	35	20
Construction worker	5	3
Civil servant	18	8
Small merchant	23	24
Street vendor	6	—
Small services	7	—
Marginal	—	34
Organized business worker	—	14
Unemployed	—	6
Others	6	6
	100	100

SOURCES: For the 1971 data, see Nephan Saran, "Squatter Settlement Programs in İstanbul," in Peter Benedict, Fatma Mansur, and Erol Tümertekin, eds., *Turkey: Geographic and Social Perspectives* (Leiden: Brill, 1974), p. 343; for the 1978 data, see Tanşı Şenyapılı, *Gecekondu: Çevre İşçilerin Mekânı* (Ankara: Orta Doğu Teknik Üniversitesi, 1982), p. 97.

cities were unemployed in the mid-1960s. Unemployment, however, rose sharply in recent years as migration continued to outstrip urban economic expansion. Adding to the woes of urban Turkey's hordes of marginal workers was the onset, in the mid-1970s, of serious economic difficulties that sharply curtailed the expansion of urban employment. By 1977, 20 percent of the nonagricultural labor force was unemployed.[31] And the State Planning Organization estimated that the nonagricultural labor surplus, composed primarily of urban workers, steadily increased between 1977 and 1982, from 1.2 to 2.6 million.[32]

A DUAL URBAN SOCIETY

The interplay of these forces has produced a dual economic structure in Turkey's cities.[33] Industrialization and urbanization have given part of urban Turkey a modern industrial economy, supported by a variety of sophisticated financial and commercial services. But the inability of the modern sector to keep pace with the flood of migrants has created a second economy, often called the "informal" or "traditional" sector, characterized by small-scale service enterprises, labor intensive employment, and substantial excess labor. This second urban economy, with its ability to absorb large amounts of surplus labor, is a primary response to overurbanization, to the fact that cities in countries like Turkey attract far more migrants than can be absorbed by the growth of the modernized sector of the economy.

Duality characterizes other essential features of urban life in Turkey, as in most developing nations. Regular housing has been even less available for urban newcomers than jobs in the modern sector of the urban economy. The flood of rural dwellers generated demands for low-cost housing in the cities that could be met by neither the private market nor government. Most private housing is too expensive for the poor newcomers, and government has been unwilling to make the enormous investments that would be needed to supply housing for the millions who migrated to the cities after 1950. As in other rapidly urbanizing societies, migrants responded to the lack of housing by occupying land illegally and building squatter housing, or *gecekondu,* which literally means housing "built overnight."

Squatter settlements quickly become the main source of housing for Turkey's urban newcomers. As villagers poured into the cities, the number of gecekondus expanded rapidly, from 100,000 units in 1950 to 1.25 million in 1983. Nearly six million people lived in squatter housing in 1983, almost one-quarter of the urban population. Development of squatter settlements has been most striking in the larger cities, where migration has been the heaviest and housing shortages the most severe. Almost three-fourths of Ankara's population lived in squatter housing in 1980, while Istanbul, Izmir, Adana, Samsun, and Erzurum all housed more than

TABLE 2-9
UNEMPLOYMENT RATES IN SQUATTER AREAS OF SELECTED LARGE CITIES: 1966

City	Percent Unemployed
Bursa	6.9
Ankara	7.2
Istanbul	7.4
Eskişehir	7.5
Izmir	7.9
Adana	8.1
Gaziantep	8.9
Kayseri	8.9

SOURCE: State Statistical Institute household employment surveys.

TABLE 2-10

SQUATTER HOUSING: 1945–1980

	Number of units	Percent of housing stock	Number of Individuals	Percent of Urban Population
1945	10,000	4.0	40,000	1.4
1950	100,000	4.8	500,000	12.8
1955	170,000	6.5	850,000	13.5
1960	240,000	16.7	1,200,000	16.4
1965	430,000	22.9	2,150,000	22.9
1970	600,000	21.4	3,000,000	23.6
1980	950,000	21.1	4,750,000	23.4

SOURCE: Kent-Koop, *Konut 81* (Ankara: 1982), p. 23.

two-fifths of their residents in gecekondus. The vast majority of these gecekondu dwellers were recent migrants, with one survey indicating that 84 percent of all squatters originated in rural areas.[34]

Massive development of squatter settlements has created two different kinds of housing and neighborhoods. One has housing built according to modern standards and government regulations, the other has dwellings illegally constructed on someone else's land in violation of public building requirements. Standard housing has water and other public utilities, while gecekondus rarely have any services at the time of their construction. Over time, as the discussion of housing in Chapter 7 points out, improvements in squatter housing blur the distinction between some parts of this dual system. But the existence of an alternative form of housing, with governmental acquiescence in its establishment and willingness to invest in its improvement, has played a critical role in the rapid expansion of Turkish cities over the past three decades.

Transportation has also developed along dual lines in Turkey's burgeoning cities. Its modern sector includes private automobiles and trucks, and various public transportation services provided by local government. But, as in jobs and housing, the modern sector could not meet the transport needs of masses of migrants, particularly as journeys lengthened in the expanding city. Responding to the travel needs of the urban poor, individual entrepreneurs offered low-cost group taxi—or *dolmuş*—service along regular routes to travelers who shared the ride with others. The result, as detailed in Chapter 6, was creation of an informal public transportation system that has hauled the bulk of riders in Turkey's major urban centers, and in the process has intensified traffic congestion and air pollution.

Dual development has also generated new and often powerful political interests in the Turkish cities, organized around the distinctive activities of the informal sector of the economy, gecekondu housing, and dolmuş transportation. As Chapter 5 indicates, small merchants, dolmuş drivers and users, and, most strikingly, gecekondu residents and developers, have become influential participants in the politics of urban development, seeking to protect and improve their piece of the urban turf. And in the case of squatters, political success has had a significant impact on urbanization itself, since the improvement and legalization of gecekondus has increased the attraction of the city for villagers.[35]

The two worlds of the Turkish city, however, are not rigidly divided. Instead, they blend together in various ways, as the dynamics of urban life alter individual and collective fortunes. Some gecekondu dwellers own automobiles, while residents of conventional neighborhoods use the dolmuş taxi system. Migrants prosper and move out of gecekondus, while long-established inhabitants seek out less expensive shelter in the squatter settlements. Lack of moderately priced standard housing keeps many families in gecekondus despite rising incomes and aspirations. With private and public improvements, older squatter communities often become indistinguishable from adjacent conventional areas. And a good deal of regular housing has been constructed illegally, in violation of local land and building regulations that city governments are unable to enforce.

MIGRANTS AND THE CITY

Rapid urbanization has increased the size of cities faster than their modern economic bases, brought far more poor people into the city than could be housed conventionally, and placed severe strains on public services. Millions of urban newcomers have marginal jobs and low incomes, live in substandard squatter housing, and lack rudimentary public services. Despite these difficulties, migration has brought success to many of those who have fueled the rapid growth of Turkish cities. Employment opportunities have been better and incomes substantially higher than in the villages. Three out of four migrants questioned in a 1973 national survey claimed to be earning more in the city than they had expected.[36] Most squatters have been able to improve their homes, and a substantial portion of gecekondu dwellers now own their houses. Whatever the shortcomings of city services in the squatter settlements, access to water, electricity, education, and other public facilities has been better than in rural areas.

For the overwhelming majority of urban newcomers in Turkey, then, life has been more satisfactory in the city. They eat better food, wear nicer

TABLE 2-11

SATISFACTION WITH CITY LIFE AMONG SQUATTERS
IN ISTANBUL

	Men	Women	Unmarried
		(in percentages)	
Very satisfied	43	68	61
Reasonably satisfied	47	24	23
Very little satisfied	5	5	3
Unsatisfied	5	2	10
Other	0	1	3

SOURCE: Kemal H. Karpat, *The Gecekondu: Rural Migration and Urbanization* (Cambridge: Cambridge University Press, 1976), p. 141.

clothing, and have more varied experiences and opportunities to enjoy life. As a result, most migrants have been very positive about the city. Nine of ten squatters in Istanbul questioned by Karpat were satisfied with city life, as indicated in Table 2-11. Almost 83 percent of the urban newcomers in another survey felt that life in the city was better than in their village of origin, with only 8 percent finding the city worse than the country.[37] A more recent study in Istanbul found that only 15 percent of the residents in a gecekondu preferred village over city life.[38] Migrants measure their satisfaction by where they have come from as well as how far they have gotten. Gecekondu dwellers "are aware that their life in the city, handicapped by lack of education and social status, started at a very low level; but they believe that they have come a long way."[39]

Migrants feel strongly that their economic prospects and those of their children have been improved by moving to the city. Over 90 percent of the married respondents in Karpat's survey believed that their children would have better futures in the city.[40] Public services are seen as superior to those available in the villages. Social and psychological considerations reinforce these positive attitudes. Cities are diverse and cosmopolitan, and large cities, particularly, "can absorb people with different and even contrary beliefs."[41] Moving to the city is often closely identified with feelings of personal advancement, of becoming more modern, and of having undertaken successfully a great adventure that fundamentally changes one's life.

High levels of satisfaction with city life, at least in comparison with conditions in the villages, have made migration permanent for the vast majority of urban newcomers in Turkey. More than 90 percent of a sample of Istanbul squatters intended to stay in the city, as did 78 percent of the respondents in an Ankara gecekondu.[42] Once they become permanently established in the city, most migrants sever their economic ties with their native villages.[43] Another indication of the permanency of migration is the lack of substantial differences in the proportion of males and females who migrate to Turkish cities. Unbalanced sex ratios, with males outnumbering females, are indicative of substantial temporary and seasonal migration, whereas more balanced male-female ratios are associated with permanent settlement. In Turkey, males do not greatly outnumber females, either in major cities or within squatter areas. And, as Özbudun notes, "whatever male-female difference exists among the urban migrants . . . seems to be due to the fact that single males often migrate, while single females very seldom do."[44]

The positive attitudes toward the city of those who have migrated are shared by most Turks living in rural areas. In the 1973 national survey conducted by Hacettepe University, almost 80 percent of those living in villages with 2,000 or fewer inhabitants believed that migrants were living better in the cities than they had in the country.[45] These attitudes obviously reflect the positive experiences of the vast majority of those who have migrated. They also underscore widespread rural awareness of the substantial differences between city and village in terms of employment, income, public services, housing, and the quality of life in general. The fact that this positive view of urban life has been so widespread spurred successive waves of rural migration to Turkey's cities.

Underlying the success of migration for most of the millions of Turkey's urban newcomers has been economic growth. For the first quarter century of rapid urbanization, an accelerating economy provided jobs, rising incomes, and opportunities for occupational mobility. Personal success based on economic well-being greatly facilitated assimilation of migrants into urban society. Because of Turkey's economic vitality, rapid urbanization did not result in the creation of a large mass of desperately poor urban marginals alienated from the rest of society. The newcomers shared the middle-class aspirations of most urban Turks. They wanted their children to have access in the city to the schools that trained the future doctors, lawyers, engineers, and government officials. Thus, Turkey's relatively prosperous cities were centers of hope, drawing optimistic new urbanites who saw themselves as bettering their lives.

Social factors also played an important role in easing the assimilation of millions of rural migrants into Turkey's cities. Change of this scale inevitably generates substantial conflict among different elements in the urban population. In Turkey, these conflicts have been moderated by the absence of significant ethnic, tribal, racial, or religious differences, cleavages that typically intensify conflict between urban newcomers and more established city residents, and between the urban poor and better-off city dwellers. Migrants to Turkish cities share a common language and religion with other city dwellers, and have blended easily into the general urban milieu as they became familiar with their new surroundings.

The scale of migration in Turkey and the breathtaking pace of urbanization have resulted in a mutual transformation—both the newcomers and the city have been changed significantly by the experience. The migrants quickly become city people—better off, more informed, and alert to the opportunities and pitfalls of urban life. As we will see, they soon developed urban political interests and the means to press for governmental responses to their demands. At the same time, Turkish cities, like urban centers throughout the developing world, have been transformed by the waves of migrants and the rapid growth they induce. Sprawling squatter settlements, hordes of small traders, and other aspects of the dual urban society are part of this change. So are the social and political perspectives that the newcomers brought from the villages—"mutual help, respect for authority and obedience [to] leaders."[46]

Of course, the migrant and the city have not interacted in a vacuum. Instead, these mutual impacts have occurred within the context of the sweeping changes that urbanization itself has brought to Turkey's cities, increasing their scale and complexity, producing the development of modern industrial and commercial districts, generating traffic congestion and pollution, and creating needs for apartment buildings, public transport, and sophisticated water-supply and sewerage-treatment systems.

The Slowing of Urban Growth

Since the middle 1970s, the economic conditions that nourished 25 years of rapid urban growth in Turkey have soured. Skyrocketing oil prices dealt heavy blows to Turkey's foreign-exchange position. Efforts to overcome this problem through massive borrowing abroad further damaged the economy. By 1977 Turkey was virtually bankrupt, industrial expansion was grinding to a halt, and inflation was raging. During the winter of 1979–1980, shortages of fuel were severe—homes could not be heated and gasoline lines were endless. Pervasive shortages of imported goods closed factories, hospitals, and other facilities.

Economic adversity was particularly severe in the cities, where highly interdependent populations were especially vulnerable to inflation, rising energy costs, and mounting unemployment. Inflation, which ran higher than 100 percent annually between 1977 and 1980, was especially punishing for urban dwellers. Prices rose faster in the big cities. The difference between the cost of living in Istanbul and in the nation as a whole rose from under 7 percent in 1970 to over 11 percent at the end of the decade,

TABLE 2-12

COST OF LIVING IN TURKEY AND ISTANBUL: 1970–1979
INDEX BASED ON 1963 = 100

	Turkey	*Istanbul*	*Difference*
1970	146	156	+ 6.8 percent
1975	343	366	+ 6.7 percent
1977	492	541	+ 10.0 percent
1978	751	876	+ 11.7 percent
1979	1231	1433	+ 11.6 percent

SOURCE: Ruşen Keleş and Artun Ünsal, *Kent ve Siyasal Şiddet* (Ankara: Siyasal Bilgiler Fakültesi, 1982), pp. 45–46.

as shown in Table 2-12. Skyrocketing costs made urban living almost impossible for low- and middle-income families. An apartment in Istanbul renting for 168 lira in 1970 cost 4,100 lira in 1980, and the cost of a visit to a doctor increased from 16.50 lira to 600 lira, and a ticket to a movie theater rose from 1.75 lira to 50 lira.[47] Urban wages did not keep pace with inflation, and employment opportunities in the cities narrowed as Turkey's economy plunged.

Because Turkey's economic woes were more serious in the cities than in the country, potential migrants were less likely to move to urban centers after 1975. Agricultural policies also contributed to lessening urban-rural differences. Government price subsidies for tobacco, cotton, tea, hazelnuts, and other crops raised rural incomes while increasing the cost of living in cities. Migration was also discouraged by the contagion of violence in the major cities. Almost 500 people died in Istanbul alone between 1978 and 1980, and another 1,200 were killed in other cities.[48] In some urban areas racked by violent encounters, city dwellers fled for the relative safety of their villages.

As a result of these developments, urban growth slowed markedly between 1975 and 1980. The annual growth rate was 4 percent, compared with 7.2 percent for the preceding five years; and no five-year census period since 1950 experienced a lower rate of urban expansion. The question of whether the slowing of Turkey's phenomenal urbanization during the late 1970s marked the beginning of a new period of slower growth or merely was a pause caused by special circumstances is not easily answered in the absence of more data. What needs to be emphasized at this point is that, in the face of formidable difficulties, Turkey's cities have continued to grow at the robust annual rate of 4 percent. Istanbul alone added 171,000 annually during this period. The persistence of substantial rural-urban differences and regional disparities, as well as the very real attractions of the major urban centers, to which we turn in the next chapter, suggest that rapid urbanization has not run its course in Turkey; and this course has produced the sweeping changes that we will examine in the remainder of this volume.

3
THE METROPOLITAN CENTERS

Turkey's large cities have been the driving force behind the mush-rooming urban growth of the past three decades. Economic expansion was concentrated in existing large cities, and migrants flocked to these established urban centers. During the first fifteen years of explosive growth, more than 90 percent of all migration was to cities with 100,000 or more inhabitants.[1] The most dynamic cities were the three largest—together, Istanbul, Ankara, and Izmir added over a million residents during the 1950s, with Ankara more than doubling over the decade.

Rapid urbanization spurred the growth of other urban centers as well. Turkey's fourth largest city, Adana, increased from 118,000 in 1950 to 575,000 in 1980, while Bursa was growing from 104,000 to 445,000. As regional centers began to attract migrants in the 1960s and 1970s, the number of cities with more than 100,000 inhabitants increased rapidly, from 9 in 1960 to 29 in 1980.[2] Among the fastest-growing of the newer urban centers have been several in the east, such as Gaziantep and Diyarbakir. Some industrial cities also have been expanding very rapidly. Kırıkkale, a machinery center near Ankara, grew from 92,000 to 178,000 during the 1970s.

Because of their attractions, big cities have grown much faster than lesser ones, and their share of urban population has steadily increased. Between 1950 and 1980, cities over 100,000 had an annual growth rate of 7 percent compared to 4.2 percent for smaller cities, and the large cities increased their share of the urban population from 43.8 percent to 63.3 percent. In 1980, almost 13 million of Turkey's 20 million urban dwellers lived in larger cities.

TABLE 3-1
THE GROWTH OF TURKEY'S FIVE LARGEST CITIES: 1950–1980

	1950 (000)	1960 (000)	1970 (000)	1980 (000)	Growth Index (1950 = 100)
Istanbul	983	1,467	2,132	4,433*	451
Ankara	289	650	1,236	1,878	650
Izmir	228	361	521	1,096	481
Adana	118	232	347	575	487
Bursa	104	154	276	445	428

SOURCE: State Statistical Institute, population censuses.
*Of this total, 1.6 million was added by the incorporation of 25 suburbs into Istanbul.

As the number of major cities increased and their population expanded, the relative importance of the three largest urban centers declined somewhat. Although Istanbul, Ankara, and Izmir added 5.9 million residents between 1950 and 1980, their share of the total population of cities over 100,000 dropped from 87 percent to 57 percent. Still, more than one-third of all urban Turks live in one of the three metropolitan centers, and their share of migrants, wealth, industry, and public goods is even greater. Two-fifths of all urban newcomers during the period of accelerated growth wound up in Istanbul, Ankara, and Izmir.[3] Their combined population was 7.4 million in 1980, up from 1.5 million in 1950. And the expansion of other urban centers has not deflected sufficient growth from the biggest cities to ease their intense housing, transportation, and employment problems.

THE ADVANTAGES OF THE LARGER CITIES

Large cities in Turkey, as in most urbanizing societies, capture the lion's share of growth because of their cumulative advantages. Big cities develop skilled labor forces and specialized economic services. Major financial institutions concentrate in the metropolitan centers, and they tend to invest in enterprises located in their environs. Entrepreneurship, as Rivkin points out, typically comes "from the commercial and trading classes already established in the [urban] centers."[4] Cities attract producers because their populations provide accessible and concentrated markets for all sorts of goods. Elite preferences also funnel investment into urban centers, since businessmen, professionals, and government officials want to live in large cities, which offer better schools, modern health facilities, cultural activities, fine restaurants, and other amenities.

TABLE 3-2

DISTRIBUTION OF THE URBAN POPULATION BY CITY SIZE GROUPS: 1927–1980

	1927	1940	1950	1960	1970	1980
10,000–20,000	24.0	23.8	22.9	15.8	12.7	10.8
20,000–50,000	28.9	28.7	23.2	21.9	13.0	15.2
50,000–100,000	9.3	12.2	10.1	17.0	11.6	10.7
100,000 +	37.8	35.3	43.8	45.3	56.7	63.3

SOURCE: State Statistical Institute, population censuses.

Growth typically feeds on growth. Successful manufacturing and commercial enterprises generate demands for goods and services that draw additional businesses to the city. Increasing populations attract new enterprises seeking employees and customers. Economic growth spurs public investment in transportation and communications, which in turn fosters additional industrial and commercial development. The expanding city needs more lawyers and accountants, doctors and hospitals, teachers and schools, as well as restaurants and hotels, taxis and public transport, housing and utilities, theaters and museums.

In contrast with the bundle of advantages possessed by Istanbul and the other big cities, smaller cities in Turkey have had to rely heavily on public investments in industry, transportation, and other facilities to attract economic development. One analysis concludes that "the growth of intermediate-sized cities in Turkey is almost wholly dependent upon the location of publicly owned enterprises in these cities."[5]

To secure these vital public resources, however, the smaller cities must compete with Istanbul, Ankara, Izmir, and other large cities whose enterprises, officials, and local elites possess sufficient political influence to ensure that substantial public investments are made in major urban centers despite national commitments to reduce rural-urban and regional imbalances. Ankara has the added advantages of being the national capital of a highly centralized state and a city whose development was among the nation's top priorities. Rivkin emphasizes these political facts of life in discussing the receptivity of the central government to the needs of the three largest cities:

> In Ankara, those men and agencies who made development decisions at a distance from other parts of the country were confronted with problems of their own immediate environment which required some coordinated decision-making. At Istanbul and Izmir . . . voices of other powerful interest groups were raised loudly and constantly besides those of the governors to effect specific projects.[6]

TABLE 3-3
AVAILABILITY OF ELECTRICITY AND WATER BY CITY SIZE: 1973

| | *Percent of Households with* | | |
	Electricity	*Running Water*	*Toilet*
Istanbul, Ankara, Izmir	93.8	79.0	78.6
100,000–500,000	90.1	76.5	53.5
50,000–100,000	91.7	74.7	58.6
25,000–50,000	83.0	73.4	55.5
10,000–25,000	81.0	67.6	50.2

SOURCE: Unpublished data from the 1973 Hacettepe Population Survey.

Urban public investments reflect the economic and political importance of the big cities. More households in larger cities have electricity, running water, and toilets. Nine-tenths of the apartments in cities over 100,000 are connected to sewerage systems, twice the proportion in cities with fewer than 100,000 inhabitants.[7] The largest cities contain Turkey's great universities, its best hospitals, and most of its museums and theaters. Government offices are concentrated in Ankara, Istanbul, and other major urban centers.

Most loans arranged by the government's Industrial Development Bank have been in the larger cities—205 of the bank's first 401 projects were in Istanbul alone.[8] Some public investments by their nature are concentrated in the larger cities. Istanbul and Izmir are Turkey's major ports, and they are the principal beneficiaries of efforts to modernize dock and cargo facilities. Most of the subsidies for hotel construction have gone primarily to Istanbul, Ankara, and Izmir. The big cities also have gained from the massive highway program, which greatly improved their access to the hinterland's markets and labor. And one of Turkey's largest public works, the graceful bridge across the Bosphorus, linking Asia and Europe, is located in Istanbul, where it has stimulated additional development of the nation's dominant urban center.

Among cities over 100,000, the three largest have been the most successful in securing economic and political advantages. One indication is the high incomes that their residents enjoy. In 1973, incomes in Istanbul, Ankara, and Izmir were more than 40 percent greater than the average for all other cities, reflecting both higher wages in the biggest cities and the concentration of wealthier families in the major metropolitan centers. Indicative of the concentration of wealth and economic activity is the fact that almost 59 percent of the central government's total tax revenues are collected in the three largest cities, more than 37 percent in Istanbul alone.[9]

THE PRIMATE CITY

Despite the emergence of a network of major cities, Turkey's urban pattern has been indelibly designed by the predominant role of Istanbul. For centuries, Istanbul has been a primate city, disproportionately large in both size and national importance.[10] At the end of the Ottoman period, Istanbul was "the center of all Turkish affairs, economic, political and industrial as well as military."[11] In addition to the labyrinthine bureaucracy of the centralized Ottoman state, almost all Turkey's industry, commerce, universities, hospitals, and other modern facilities were located in Istanbul.

Historically, Istanbul's commanding position was based on its strategic location astride major land and sea routes. Europe and Asia are less than a mile apart where the Bosphorus meets the Sea of Marmara. Together with the Dardanelles to the west, the Bosphorus and the Sea of Marmara form the connecting link between the Black Sea and the Mediterranean. For more than two millenia, traders, caravans, pilgrims, armies, merchant ships, and navies have passed the city that straddled two continents and controlled the critical water passage, the city that began as Byzantium, became Constantinople, and is now Istanbul.

Imperial Capital

The first city built on the site of modern Istanbul was Byzantium, founded by the Greeks in 667 B.C. as a trading center. A thousand years later, in A.D. 330, Constantine the Great decided to locate the new capital of the Roman Empire at this beautiful and fateful crossroads. Built on seven hills like Rome, Constantinople was surrounded by three layers of

---

TABLE 3-4
AVERAGE FAMILY INCOME BY CITY SIZE: 1973

	Average Income	*Percent of National Average*
Istanbul	40,167	162.7
Ankara	30,489	123.5
Izmir	39,496	159.9
100,000–500,000	26,815	108.7
50,000–100,000	25,107	101.7
25,000–50,000	26,035	105.4
10,000–25,000	24,820	100.5
National	24,694	100.0

SOURCE: State Planning Organization, *Gelir Dağılımı Araştırması—1973* (Ankara, 1973).

Figure 3-1. Istanbul's Geographic Setting

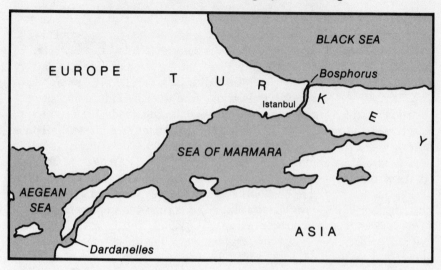

fortified walls and protected by the Sea of Marmara and the Bosphorus. With the bifurcation of the Roman Empire in the fourth century, Constantinople became the capital of the Byzantine Empire. For the next ten centuries, the city was the political, economic, religious, and cultural center of a sometimes dazzling, usually contentious, and frequently beleaguered empire. Constantinople was the largest city in medieval Europe, with a million inhabitants at Byzantium's zenith in the 10th century. Vast wealth was concentrated in the city, as were priceless artistic treasures. Among its landmarks were the church of St. Sophia, the sacred palace of the emperors, the Golden Gate, and the vast hippodrome. Aside from St. Sophia, little but the remnants of the fortified walls remain of the great Byzantine city, although the Roman walls helped shape modern Istanbul.

Over the centuries, Constantinople was besieged by Arabs from the south, Bulgarians from the north, Christians from the west, and Turks from the east. The armies of the Fourth Crusade captured and sacked the city in 1204, but were eventually expelled. Two and half centuries later, Constantinople fell for the last time, as the Byzantine Empire finally collapsed under the onslaught of Mohammed the Conqueror in 1453. The devastated and almost depopulated city became Istanbul, and was revived under Sultan Mohammed as the capital of the Ottoman Empire.

Under the Ottomans, a new golden age dawned for the city. The first order of business was repairing the walls, rebuilding the city, and revitalizing a shattered economy. As the city revived, its population grew rapidly, increasing from 50,000 in 1453 to over 500,000 a century later.[12] The reconstructed city reflected the Middle Eastern origins of its rulers and new inhabitants. Merchants and craftsmen clustered in their districts, public baths and squares were built, and central markets were established for food and raw materials. Mosques and palaces were erected, including the massive mosque of Suleiman the Magnificent and the sprawling Top-kapı palace perched above the Bosphorus, the buildings whose outlines have etched Istanbul into mankind's memory.

Under the highly centralized Ottoman system, Istanbul grew steadily as all elements of the far-flung empire were drawn into its orbit. By the end of the 18th century, its population exceeded 870,000. Concern over the rapid increase in the number of the capital's inhabitants led to imperial efforts to check the flow from the provinces of migrants who sought to improve their fortunes in the great city that now straddled both sides of the Bosphorus. European experts also were imported to prepare plans to guide the city's development. Despite the Ottoman decrees and the for-eigners' plans, Istanbul continued to expand, with the population passing one million during the first decade of the 20th century.

Increasing contact with Europe during the 19th century had enhanced Istanbul's economic dominance over its vast hinterland. Foreign capital was funneled into Ottoman Turkey through Istanbul, and European busi-nessmen and their local agents were heavily concentrated in the bustling metropolis on the Bosphorus. By the end of the century, "Istanbul had become the center for the activities of a cosmopolitan population of trad-ers, carpetbaggers, concession hunters, and administrators of foreign en-terprises."[13] Istanbul became a European outpost, the place where the imperialists controlled their growing share of the Ottoman economy.

Istanbul's development was strongly influenced by the influx of Euro-peans and their money, ideas, and life-styles. Most of the city's new facilities and services were controlled by Europeans—"from docks and quays to . . . railways, from . . . electricity, gas and water supplies to . . . tramways, all these were owned and exploited by foreigners."[14] Modern urban services were first installed at the insistence of Europeans and the westernized Turkish bourgeoisie that was beginning to emerge. European experience was borrowed in preparing building regulations, and in estab-lishing the first municipal corporation in 1854 in a section of the city with large numbers of foreign residents.

On the eve of the First World War, Istanbul was a flourishing island of modernity in a sea of peasant villages, the cosmopolitan diadem of a decaying empire. After a decade of war, occupation, and revolution, the foreigners were gone as was almost half of Istanbul's population. More important, Istanbul was no longer the capital of what was left of the Ottoman empire. The rulers of the new Turkey distrusted Istanbul, the symbol of the old regime and of colonial exploitation. Kemal Ataturk's republic would be run from Ankara in Turkey's heartland, in a planned capital dedicated to nationalism and modernization, rather than in jaded Istanbul with its cynicism and corruption.

Economic Center

Movement of the central government to Ankara meant that Istanbul could never play the role in modern Turkey that it had filled in the past. Political power no longer was concentrated in Istanbul, and much of the growth stimulated by governmental expansion would occur in Ankara rather than along the Bosphorus. But Istanbul remained the nation's industrial and business center, its greatest port, the focus of the transportation system, the center of cultural and intellectual life, and the preferred residence of Turkey's elite. If a nation of backward peasant villages was to modernize and industrialize, as Ataturk and his lieutenants so fervently desired, then Istanbul must have a major part in the unfolding drama of building a new Turkey.

So Istanbul grew once again. Between 1927 and 1950 the city's population increased by 30 percent, from 691,000 to 983,000. Drawing on its powerful economic advantages, Istanbul attracted most private industrial and commercial investment during the initial decades of the Turkish republic. And when urbanization moved into high gear after 1950, Istanbul led the way. Almost 600,000 residents were added during the 1950s, and the city's population reached 1.47 million in 1960. More than two-thirds of these new residents were migrants from smaller cities and the villages. Turkey's booming private sector was concentrated in Istanbul and its environs, and rapid economic growth continued to draw ever more people to the spreading metropolis.

Government policies reinforced Istanbul's attractions. Although the capital was in Ankara, substantial governmental activity remained in Istanbul. Many of the agencies responsible for economic development and public investment had substantial operations in Istanbul since their officials worked closely with private banks and industrialists. And a large part of their efforts was focused in Istanbul and the surrounding Marmara area. One of the central agencies located in Istanbul was the Industrial Development Bank, which made two-thirds of its initial investments in plants in Istanbul and its Marmara environs. As Rivkin notes, "concentration of IDB's resources and personnel at Istanbul with greatest accessibility to the Marmara entrepreneurs" was a critical factor in "the relatively enormous concentration in Marmara compared with other regions."[15]

Development of new industry throughout Turkey required large amounts of imported goods that inevitably flowed through Istanbul. The flood of imports necessitated public investments in the city's port facilities, which reinforced Istanbul's position as the principal funnel for commerce into Turkey. State enterprises dependent on large markets—cigarettes, glass, and textile finishing—were located in Istanbul. And Istanbul's place as the center of technical enterprises was enhanced by governmental decisions to create an Istanbul Technical University and a School of Design. For many years, "only in Istanbul was it possible for a Turk to be trained as an engineer or architect."[16]

Other public investments flowed into Istanbul, particularly during the administration of Prime Minister Adnan Menderes in the 1950s. Menderes sought to stimulate private economic development, which meant funneling more state resources into Istanbul. No longer did the nation's political leaders look on Istanbul with distrust; instead, the great city and its economic leaders were vigorously wooed by the nation's new leaders in Ankara. Public funds underwrote the construction of Turkey's first modern hotel, the Istanbul Hilton. A splendid city hall was constructed, and new boulevards installed as "Menderes (frequently photographed on a bulldozer leading the action) attacked the narrow, hilly streets of Istanbul to give the city a look of Haussmann's Paris."[17] The vast highway program increased Istanbul's accessibility, and the Bosphorus bridge directed even more commerce and goods through the great metropolis.

With growth feeding on growth, Istanbul continued to capture a disproportionate share of Turkey's expanding economy. Istanbul remains the financial, commercial, and industrial center, as well as the cultural and intellectual capital of Turkey. With less than 10 percent of the population, metropolitan Istanbul accounts for 40 percent of the nation's commerce, 34 percent of its manufacturing, and about a quarter of all transportation, communications, finance, and housing activity.[18] Well over half of all Turkish workers in petroleum, chemicals, plastics, paper, automobiles, and cement are employed in the Istanbul area.[19] Istanbul consumes 20 percent of Turkey's electricity, its streets accommodate 24 percent of the vehicles in the nation, and the city contains 44 percent of the country's hotel rooms.[20] About one-third of all publishing is done in Istanbul, and the leading Istanbul dailies account for three-quarters of newspaper sales throughout the nation.[21] Over half of Turkey's university students are in Istanbul, and nearly one-third of all health services are delivered within the metropolis.[22]

Clearly, Istanbul has remained Turkey's dominant urban center despite the loss of political primacy to Ankara. To be sure, Istanbul's dominance has been declining with the growth of Ankara and other major cities. Ankara and a number of other large cities grew more rapidly than Istanbul over the past thirty years.[23] And their share of economic activity, educational institutions, and health facilities has been increasing. Nonetheless,

Istanbul far outdistances its rivals economically and demographically. In 1980, the Istanbul metropolitan area had 4.4 million inhabitants, which was 2.5 million more than in Ankara. Close to 3.5 million people were added to Istanbul's population between 1950 and 1980, almost as many as lived in all Turkish cities in 1950. Istanbul is still the great magnet, drawing people from across the land by its economic dynamism—in 1980, more than three million of its residents were natives of other cities or villages.

The Contemporary Metropolis

Modern Istanbul has spread far beyond Constantinople's seven hills, covering 6,500 square kilometers (approximately 2,500 square miles) on both sides of the Bosphorus. About two-thirds of Istanbul's 4.4 million inhabitants live on the European side, but in recent years the Asian portion of the metropolis has been growing more rapidly. The basic settlement pattern has been linear, with development spreading from the old city north for 25 kilometers (16 miles) along the Bosphorus, west for 70 kilometers (44 miles) on the European shore of the Sea of Marmara, and east for 45 kilometers (28 miles) on the sea's Asiatic coast. Residential densities reach 300 persons per hectare (about 120 per acre) in the oldest sections at the core of the metropolis, where over 850,000 people live.

Istanbul's business center is located on the European side in the historic city and adjacent areas to the north, and contains financial, importing, corporate, retail, wholesaling, and other specialized districts. Port facilities are also concentrated in the center along the Golden Horn, the waterway that empties into the Bosphorus in the heart of Istanbul. Over half a million worked in central Istanbul in 1980, and moving them to and from their jobs sorely taxes a complex transport system composed of buses, taxis, ferries, railroads, a short transit line, and thousands of private automobiles. Modern residential development is clustered near the central business district, increasing the general congestion in the inner portions of the metropolis.

Beyond the center, Istanbul is a complex mosaic of commercial districts, industrial plants, strip development, residential areas, transportation facilities, military bases, and conservation zones that seek to preserve the beauty of the hills and forests that ring the waterways. Industrial development is more intensive on the eastern—Asiatic—side of the metropolis. Heavy industry in particular is concentrated in the east, where transportation connections with the rest of Turkey are better. Most of the industry on the European side is made up of smaller enterprises engaged in light manufacturing and related activities.[24] And clustered near industry—wherever difficult topography has discouraged conventional housing and in areas with substantial amounts of publicly owned land—

are the squatter settlements that house more than two million of Istanbul's inhabitants.

THE PLANNED CITY

Istanbul would be a much larger and even more dominant city had not the national capital been moved to Ankara at the outset of the Turkish Republic. In every sense, Ankara is a product of government. The decision to develop the city was a governmental determination, a response to political rather than market considerations. Government is Ankara's principal industry, and a highly centralized political system and an expanding role for the state ensured that government would be a robust growth industry.

Because of government, Turkey's planned national capital has experienced phenomenal growth, and the nation's urban pattern has been dramatically altered. The provincial town with 20,000 inhabitants in 1923 grew to a substantial city of 289,000 in 1950 and to a sprawling metropolis of 1.9 million in 1980, six times its planned population. Migrants streamed to this new center of opportunity in Anatolia, so many that two-thirds of its residents live in squatter housing, the highest proportion in Turkey. In effect, the development of this huge inland metropolis "has served as a dam preventing partly the flow of rural migrants to Istanbul."[25] Had government not created modern Ankara, Istanbul probably would have more than six million inhabitants, perhaps four million squatters, exerting overwhelming dominance of almost every aspect of Turkish life.

The New Capital

Ankara lies astride the caravan routes that crisscross Anatolia, and its history dates to the Hittite period, about 2000 B.C. Its strategic location led the Romans to develop the hillside town into a major provincial center, and it attracted invaders over the centuries—Persians, Arabs, Crusaders, Seljuk Turks, and Mongols. During the Ottoman period, the obscure market town was called Angora, for its major product was Angora wool. Its population, which never exceeded 30,000, was clustered around the citadel on the hill in wooden houses, two-thirds of which burned in a devastating fire in 1915. Ankara's location brought the town back into the limelight during the Turkish revolution. Its residents strongly supported Mustafa Kemal Ataturk and his nationalist movement, and the revolutionary government was established at the strategic crossroads in 1919. Four years later, Ankara was declared by the Great National Assembly to be the capital of the Republic of Turkey.

Ataturk created a new capital in Anatolia for a variety of reasons, both symbolic and practical. He wanted a dramatic symbol for the new Turkey and its principles of nationalism, republicanism, populism, secularism, etatism, and reformism. Nationalism suggested the desirability of separating the young republic from cosmopolitan Istanbul and its foreign elements. Ataturk's Turkey was to be more accessible to the people, so the capital was taken from Istanbul and moved to the neglected Anatolian heartland. Ankara, incidentally, was less accessible to Turkey's enemies than was Istanbul, which had been occupied by British, French, and Italian troops at the end of World War One. The capital would be modern, secular, and humane, with broad boulevards, attractive public buildings, beautiful parks, planned housing, and western public services. The principle of etatism meant that development of Ankara would be planned by government, not left to market forces. The central government would concentrate resources on its new capital, and in the process stimulate the development of Anatolia and weaken the stranglehold of Istanbul on the Turkish economy.

Development of the new Ankara began in 1924, when the city's first plan was devised by a German, M. Heussler. Under Heussler's scheme, the main governmental and commercial area—called Yenisehir, the "new city"—was located two kilometers south of the old town. To carry out the plan, the central government empowered the city of Ankara to expropriate four square kilometers (about 1.5 square miles) at very low prices.[26] Using this authority, Ankara's new center was quickly secured by government at bargain prices: the land now covered by Ataturk Boulevard, the main commercial street, was acquired for as little as one lira per square meter, or about two cents a square foot at 1925 prices.[27] With government securing complete control over land, Heussler's plan for Ankara's new center was fully implemented.

Yenisehir was only the first step in the development of the planned national capital. Ankara, the government decided, needed a master plan, and an international competition was held with the winning design submitted by Hermann Jansen, another German architect-planner. Jansen's plan, prepared in 1928, laid out the framework for Ankara's future growth, siting public buildings, institutions, and private development. It called for orderly growth with regulation of land speculation and timely provision of public utilities. The plan also envisaged substantial new housing construction, numerous parks, and preservation of the old citadel area. Underlying Jansen's scheme was the central government's assumption that Ankara's growth would be carefully controlled, with the planned total population of 300,000 not being reached for fifty years.

To implement the master plan, the central government created a powerful development agency, the Ankara Planning Commission. Under the direction of the Minister of Interior, the new commission was empowered to control all forms of public and private development, to expropriate land, and to regulate subdivision. One of the members of the commission was Jansen, who worked on turning his plan into reality for the next decade. Initial efforts to carry out the grand design were successful. Public funds were poured into Ankara—for its broad avenues, public buildings, parks, and the city's first hotel. Universities were built, along with theaters, museums, and hospitals. Housing for civil servants was provided by the central government, and a good deal of private housing also was constructed in accordance with the plan. All in all, "Ankara's planners could justifiably congratulate themselves on having effectively regulated both the rate and the nature of growth."[28]

Ankara's economic base was also diversified. Many private firms established in Istanbul opened offices in the new capital in order to have access to the government agencies that dealt with taxes, duties, subsidies, loans, licenses, quotas, and priorities. Industry grew, to serve both the local market and the Anatolian hinterland, whose rail and road links with Ankara were steadily improved. "Ankara, rather than Istanbul, was now the most accessible major center for entrepreneurs bent on cultivating new markets in the interior but reluctant to live outside a cosmopolitan atmosphere."[29] Growing much faster than industry, however, was services of all kinds to serve the needs of the expanding base of government employees.

Explosive Growth

By the late 1930s, Ankara was booming and feeling increasingly constrained by its master plan. The city's population more than doubled between 1927 and 1940, from 75,000 to 157,000, and was already halfway to the 1980 target of 300,000. Responding to these growth pressures, Ankara's municipal government in 1938 enlarged with central approval the development area from 20 square kilometers (8 square miles) to 160 square kilometers (62 square miles), effectively opening the entire city to new construction. In this larger area and in the face of increased pressures for development, land-use regulations were less effective. Nor were public officials able to check speculation, which increased land prices and reduced government's ability to acquire land to ensure compliance with the master plan.

With more land available for development, Ankara grew even faster in the 1940s, adding 142,000 inhabitants for a total of 289,000 in 1950. Jansen's plan had been overwhelmed—Ankara had reached its "final" population thirty years ahead of time. But the capital was yet to experience massive migration from the villages. Most of Ankara's new residents before 1950 were relatively well off—civil servants, businessmen, professionals, and skilled workers. With the help of a variety of governmental programs, housing had been provided for most newcomers.

Now a new phase of Ankara's growth began, as thousands of migrants from rural Anatolia crowded into the capital. During the 1950s, Ankara more than doubled its population, adding 361,000 for a total of 650,000 in 1960. The continuing influx from the villages boosted the city's population to 1,236,000 in 1970 and 1,878,000 in 1980. Now Ankara was a planned city only at its core—the surrounding hills were covered with the squatter settlements that housed more than 1.3 million people. Ankara's plans had not anticipated that most of its people could not afford conventional housing, or that most of its labor force would be employed in service occupations outside the public agencies and private activities that had been the basis of Jansen's design.

Despite the traumatic growth of the past three decades, modern Ankara continues to reflect Ataturk's vision. A striking national capital was designed and built, and has become a great metropolis in half a century largely because of governmental actions. Alone among Turkey's cities, Ankara was planned, and its basic urban pattern has adapted reasonably well to the sweeping changes of the past thirty years. Its location and booming expansion advanced two major national policy goals—stimulation of development in backward Anatolia and deflection of growth from Istanbul. Moreover, the spreading city, which now covers 923 square kilometers (356 square miles), proved far more accessible to the people than anyone could have imagined.

Ankara, however, is hardly a triumph for city planning. The new capital has grown faster than the other major cities and houses a higher percentage of squatters than does any Turkish urban center. Traffic congests its streets, acrid pollution fouls its air, and much of its modern residential and commercial development is indistinguishable from the helter-skelter pattern common in the newer sections of Istanbul or Izmir.

Modern Ankara also remains very much a creature of the central government. The state is by far the single largest source of jobs; those directly or indirectly employed by government account for one-third of Ankara's work force.[30] Despite a fair amount of industrial development, manufacturing and related activities are relatively small—about 11 percent of the work force in 1980 compared to 41 percent in Itanbul. Thus Ankara lacks a diversified economic base. Its work force is comprised primarily of civil servants and service workers, large numbers of whom are in the informal sector. Most of the government workers live in conventional housing located in and around the planned center, while the majority of the service workers—along with the one-sixth of the work force that is unemployed—dwell in the gecekondus that surround the national capital.

THE TURKISH METROPOLIS

Rapid growth and massive migration have turned the largest Turkish cities into sprawling metropolitan areas. Their populations are characterized by sharp differences in income, housing, access to municipal services, and general quality of life. And the most severe consequences of accelerated urbanization are concentrated in Istanbul and Ankara, as well as in Izmir, Turkey's third city.

Spreading Cities

Over the past three decades, the major Turkish cities have spread outward at increasing rates. As in all cities, most growth has occurred along the periphery. Development in the outer portions has been less intensive than in the older sections. Automotive transportation has had the same effect on the Turkish metropolis as in cities all over the world, permitting more dispersed location of jobs and residences, particularly along the main highways that radiate outward from the urban core. Rising land prices have pushed development outward in search of cheaper sites. Factories no longer cluster around port and rail facilities, and newer industries are highly decentralized in the major Turkish cities. Housing development reaches far beyond the limits of public transportation, in the form of both low-density conventional housing and squatter dwellings.[31]

As in almost all developing countries, squatter housing has been an extremely important element in the rapid spread of the Turkish metropolis. Hundreds of thousands of illegal dwelling units have been constructed in Istanbul, Ankara, and Izmir in a relatively brief period. Almost all this housing has been added at the periphery, producing over time substantial belts of squatter settlements. Although individual gecekondu dwellings typically are crowded, overall residential densities in squatter settlements are relatively low, particularly in comparison with modern conventional apartment housing. Moreover, squatter housing by its nature results in leap-frog development, as migrants move outward in search of land that they will be able to occupy illegally; in the process, the outward sprawl of the metropolis is accelerated.

Rapid outward growth has complicated the manifold problems of Turkey's cities. Development outpaces the provision of public services and bears little relationship to official plans. Local roads, water supply, waste

TABLE 3-5
CITY AND SUBURBAN GROWTH IN ISTANBUL AND IZMIR
1950–1980
(1950 population = 100)

	Istanbul		Izmir	
	City	Suburb	City	Suburb
1950	100	100	100	100
1960	149	379	159	311
1970	277	1,423	229	586
1980	282	3,393	333	1,072

SOURCE: State Statistical Institute, population censuses.

disposal and other public facilities often are nonexistent in newly settled areas. Conventional housing, squatter settlements, factories, and other activities are jumbled together as residential areas spring up around new industrial areas. With this indiscriminate mixing of functions comes increased environmental hazards for large numbers of urban dwellers on the outskirts who live around chemical works, cement factories, and other air-polluting industries.

In Istanbul and Izmir, the spreading metropolis has spilled over the core city's municipal boundaries, and the suburban areas beyond the city limits have been growing very rapidly, as shown in Table 3-5. Before 1981, there were 31 suburban municipalities in Istanbul, and Izmir had 10. Governmental capabilities in these peripheral jurisdictions are extremely limited, which complicates planning and the provision of urban services in both metropolitan areas. Lack of planning and land controls in the suburban areas encourages sprawl, as industrialists and developers move outward to escape local regulations that increase land and building costs.

Concern over metropolitan political fragmentation led the central government to incorporate 25 suburban muncipalities into Istanbul in 1981, a move that increased Istanbul's area from 290 to 1,020 square kilometers (112 to 463 square miles), and its population from 2.8 million to 4.4 million. Under its old boundaries, Istanbul, like many core cities, had run out of room for expansion and was faced with increasing costs of providing services to a metropolitan population that was residing beyond its boundaries. With consolidation, the city was able to share in more of the metropolis's growth, but also assumed the burden for providing public services over a far more extensive area, responsibilities that hardly were being carried out effectively even within its more constrained boundaries.

Ankara also has been spreading rapidly, but unlike Istanbul and Izmir, has been able to extend its boundaries in advance of new settlement. The most recent enlargement, in 1982, pushed the city limits far beyond the edge of development. Ankara's physical expansion was facilitated by the absence of other municipalities along its periphery, as well as by its special place in the Turkish system as the planned national capital. As a result of its broad territorial expanse, Ankara's officials have not been faced with the added complication of dealing with suburban governments. And since Ankara's city limits include large amounts of undeveloped land, the city has more opportunities to control urban development than has Istanbul.

Differentiated Cities

Rapid urbanization and massive migration have produced substantial socioeconomic differences in Turkey's spreading metropolitan areas. Income distribution is heavily skewed in the largest cities. The poorest fifth of Istanbul's families received only 2.4 percent of total income in 1980, while the most affluent fifth of the city's households got 69 percent.[32] Underlying these income disparities are substantial differences in the economic fortunes of educated, skilled, and established urban dwellers on the one hand, and poorly educated, unskilled newcomers on the other. Income differences grew rather than narrowed during the 1970s, as indicated in Table 3-6, as recent migrants were particularly hard hit by worsening economic conditions in the big cities.

Income differences are strongly reflected in the spatial pattern of the major metropolitan centers, largely because of the physical separation of

TABLE 3-6
INCOME DISTRIBUTION IN ISTANBUL: 1968 AND 1980
PERCENT OF TOTAL INCOME ACCRUING TO HOUSEHOLDS
BY QUINTILE

	1968	1980
Lowest 20 percent	4.7	2.4
Second Quintile	8.5	3.3
Third Quintile	12.3	4.3
Fourth Quintile	13.1	21.0
Top 20 percent	55.4	69.0

SOURCE: The 1968 data are from Istanbul Metropolitan Plan Bureau, *Income and Income Distribution: Annex to Socio-Economic Issues,* Annex 2:4 (Istanbul, 1975), the 1980 data, from Şemsettin Bağırkan, *Milliyet,* July 11, 1980.

TABLE 3-7

INCOME DISTRIBUTION BY DISTRICTS IN ISTANBUL: 1980

	Monthly Family Income	*Family Size*	*Per Capita Family Income*
Established districts:			
Etiler, Levent, Yeşilyurt	50,863 TL	2.3	22,114 TL
Suadiye, Fenerbahçe, Bakırköy	33,533 TL	2.8	11,976 TL
Gecekondu districts:			
Ümraniye, İçerenköy, Gaziosmanpaşa Zeytinburnu	7,025 TL	5.3	1,325 TL

SOURCE: Şemsettin Bağırkan, *Milliyet,* July 12, 1980.

squatter settlements from other residential development. In established districts of Istanbul, family income in 1980 was as much as seven times higher than in gecekondu areas, as shown in Table 3-7. Spatial differences in per capita income are even greater because squatter families tend to be twice the size of households in conventional neighborhoods.

A good example of the spatial differentiation of socioeconomic groups in Turkey is provided by Izmir's pattern of development, as illustrated in Figure 3-2. Families with the lowest social rank were found to be sharply separated from those of higher rank, with the lowest group concentrated in the gecekondus that surround the more affluent sections of the city and their modern apartment buildings.

Older districts at the heart of Turkey's major urban centers house far fewer lower-income families than similar areas in cities in Western Europe and North America. These areas are smaller in Istanbul and Izmir than in western cities, which developed large amounts of housing for industrial workers during the 19th century. Ankara has practically no inexpensive old housing at its core—the old quarter around the citadel encompasses less than 1 percent of the city's land and accommodates only 4 percent of its population. Moreover, most of the housing available in the older districts was priced beyond the reach of the typical migrant. Thus, availability and price pushed migrants to whatever land could be seized on the outskirts of the city. In the process, newcomers were separated from more established—and somewhat better-off—lower-income inhabitants of the major cities. Residents of older districts have higher average incomes than squatters, and a larger proportion are tradesmen and petty officials. And while squatter areas have been expanding, the

Figure 3-2. Districts of Izmir by Social Rank: 1968

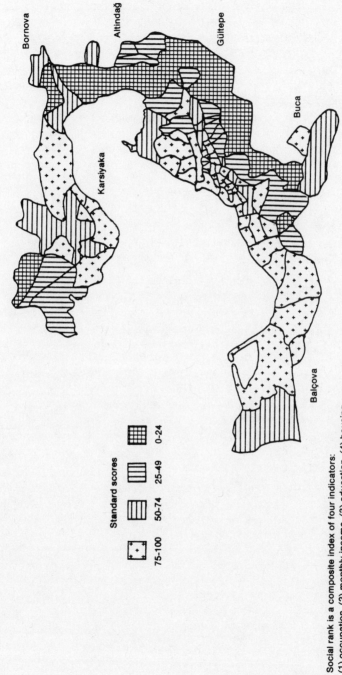

Standard scores

75-100   50-74   25-49   0-24

Social rank is a composite index of four indicators:
(1) occupation, (2) monthly income, (3) education, (4) housing.

Source: Ruşen Keleş, Izmir Mahalleleri, App. G-(2).

older sections have been losing population, as new commercial and residential development claims more and more of the central areas.

Physical isolation of the poor in squatter settlements strongly influences distribution of local services in major urban centers. Gecekondu areas begin their existence without public services, and must struggle against formidable political odds to secure basic utilities and facilities. Despite substantial victories in these battles, which are discussed in Chapter 5, wide disparities exist in access to basic public services within Turkish cities. In the world of conventional housing, the vast majority of city dwellers have running water, electricity, paved streets, and convenient local schools. In the isolated world of the gecekondus, half or more of all families lack water, electric service, decent streets, or accessible schools.

Thus, the two worlds of the Turkish metropolis live largely in separate spatial realms. The inhabitants of one of these realms have incomes, living conditions, municipal services, life-styles, value systems, and expectations that are strikingly different from those who dwell in the other realm. These differences strongly shape both the problems of the large metropolitan areas and the political objectives and resources of various elements of the urban population.

Benefits and Costs of Concentrated Development

Large cities have been the principal winners in Turkey's pell-mell rush to urbanize. They have secured most of the nation's industry and commerce, a large share of its wealth and public investments, and most of its best-educated and highly skilled people. In a land where a majority of the people live in isolated villages, Turkey's great cities boast tall buildings, sleek shops, elegant restaurants, modern hotels, and cosmopolitan populations. By almost every measure—income, skills, housing, education, health care, and access to all sorts of goods and services—residents of the metropolitan centers are better off than their country cousins.

For the most part, government has encouraged concentration of urban development in the major urban centers. Public policy has focused on the economic attractions of the metropolitan centers—their external economies, specialized labor forces, superior financial resources, and the other comparative advantages of large cities for modern industrial development. Government created Ankara and nourished its phenomenal growth with generous investments and subsidies. Istanbul and Izmir also have received substantial infusions of public funds as Turkey has sought to build a modern industrial economy based in its great cities.

At the same time, rapid urbanization has exacted its heaviest costs in the large cities. In a very real sense, the magnitude of urban problems increases geometrically as the size of urban communities expands arithmetically. With the development of huge metropolitan areas, municipal services become more complex and costly. Simple water and waste arrangements that serve smaller communities must be replaced with networks of pipes, pumping stations, and treatment plants. Lengthening travel distances and mounting traffic congestion necessitate expensive transportation investments—in expressways, traffic signals, parking facilities, buses, and rapid-transit systems. Land prices escalate more rapidly in major urban centers. Adequate housing becomes ever more difficult to provide for a growing proportion of the population, and squatting offers the only alternative for hundreds of thousands of families. Pollution is an additional hazard—it is more concentrated in massive urban areas, and thus more detrimental to health and the quality of life.

Open space, human scale, and historic areas have all suffered from the unending pressure of expansion in the major cities. Squatters have claimed large amounts of public land, reducing the prospects for recreational areas and parkland. Older housing has been torn down to make way for wider streets, new offices, and other modern facilities. Ankara's oldest sections, with clustered housing, markets, and public spaces, steadily lose their distinctiveness as change constantly remakes the city. And Istanbul's historic walls are crumbling, its elegant wooden houses falling apart, and its bazaars and courtyards occupied by squatters or small shops. "Very few parts of our architectural heritages are left," notes an Istanbul architect, "and they are living their last years."[33]

The wear and tear of life in the big cities leave their residents less satisfied with urban life than is the case with those who live in smaller urban areas. Over one-quarter of the respondents from Istanbul, Ankara, and Izmir in the 1973 Hacettepe population survey registered dissatisfaction with life in the city, compared with less than 10 percent of the residents of small cities.[34] Even more critical are urban officials, such as Istanbul's former mayor, who bluntly acknowledged that "Istanbul really is a sick city."[35] The same illness afflicts Ankara and Izmir, and has spread to other major cities such as Adana and Bursa.

Urban concentration also extracts broader costs for a nation like Turkey, which struggles to pursue a variety of developmental goals. The high costs of serving the largest cities diverts resources from other areas and needs. In particular, efforts to reduce regional inequalities are undermined if most public funds are swallowed up by the big cities. The alternative is to ignore the public investments necessitated by major urban areas. As the chapters that follow indicate, government in Turkey has vacillated when faced with the realities of the major metropolitan centers and their problems. Political leaders, not unsurprisingly, have desired the benefits of big cities without wanting to pay the costs. Political pressures have pulled government in a variety of directions. As a result, public policies have encouraged expansion of the metropolitan centers without providing adequately for their multiplying needs, and little attention has been paid to the diseconomies of scale and the adverse impact of size on the quality of urban life. To understand these often contradictory responses to the rapid growth of the major cities, we need to examine Turkey's political system in detail, turning first to governmental arrangements and then to political factors in Chapter 5.

4
CITIES AND CENTRALIZED GOVERNMENT

For government, urbanization means change—new needs, new demands, new problems, new policies, new responsibilities, new agencies. When urban growth has been as rapid as in Turkey, change easily overloads governmental arrangements. And when a governmental system is as centralized as Turkey's, the burdens of responding to the powerful forces of urbanization primarily rest with national government.

Political power in Turkey is monopolized by the center. Turkey has been called "one of the world's most centralized states" with respect to local autonomy.[1] Cities are assigned their responsibilities by the central government and are closely supervised by national officials down to the smallest detail. The center controls allocation of most public resources, with more than 90 percent of all public funds distributed through the national government's budget.

Within this highly centralized context, urbanization has proliferated the functions of local governments and multiplied demands on municipal jurisdictions without corresponding increases in power or resources for the cities. More tasks for localities means additional oversight responsibilities for national officials—and more red tape and delay for an increasingly clogged set of channels between the center and the cities. At the same time, inadequate resources and authority within cities have forced the central government to assume many urban functions. As a result, existing ministries have expanded their activities and new agencies have been created as more and more urban problems have become national burdens.

Because power and resources are so highly concentrated in Turkey, national government is the starting point for an examination of the interplay between urbanization and politics. The dominant role of central government means that the provision of public services, the pattern and pace of urbanization, and the relative growth rates of cities and regions are influenced primarily by action or inaction in the nation's capital. Despite the existence of an elaborate network of provincial, municipal, and village governments, urban public policy results primarily from central rather than local determinations. The highly centralized character of Turkish government also sustains a built-in set of influential interests—ministers and most members of Parliament, officials in the national ministries, and groups that have done well in their dealings with Ankara—which seek to sustain and expand power at the center.

THE CENTRALIZED STATE

Modern Turkey inherited its highly centralized governmental system from the Ottoman Empire. A strong center was essential for the far-flung state with its restive minorities. Local autonomy was anathema to the rulers in Istanbul, since devolving power to the non-Turkish provinces threatened the regime's very existence. Faced with growing demands for independence, the multinational empire sought to preserve itself by concentrating power at the center, an effort that ultimately failed yet strongly shaped the modern Turkish state.

In constructing their centralized system, the Ottomans borrowed heavily from Napoleon's French model. Provincial administration rested with agents of central authority rather than with locally elected councils. Centrally appointed governors, the *pashas,* were empowered to collect revenues from the local population, most of which were funnelled back to Istanbul. Local expenditures for public services were controlled by the provincial governors, who also were charged with maintaining public order. In performing their duties, the pashas were responsible solely to the center. Local residents had no formal role in the recruitment of provincial administrators and little influence on decisions affecting the allocation of public resources.[2]

Like other Middle Eastern societies, Ottoman Turkey had no tradition of independent municipalities with a heritage of local autonomy. As Weiker notes, "there was little or no concept of a city as an entity with the responsibility of providing its own governmental services."[3] Most of the administrative, service, and regulatory functions of city governments were performed by guilds *(lonca)* in the Ottoman cities.[4] Under the guilds, a system of municipal revenues, locally administered price controls, and municipal fines had developed by the second half of the 19th century.

Fire-fighting—an extremely important function in cities where most people lived in wooden houses—was in the hands of neighborhood organizations, or *mahalle*, as was local security. A third set of indigenous organizations, the foundations or *vakıf,* provided rudimentary health and social services.[5]

European models, which had supplied the framework for the centralized administrative structure, also were the basis for Turkey's initial experiments with municipal government. The new city institutions were the products of rapid urban change, particularly in Istanbul, and the concomitant inability of existing governmental arrangements to meet new needs for infrastructure and city services.[6] Paris provided the model for Turkey's first municipality, created at mid-century in Istanbul's Beyoğlu district, an area populated mostly by non-Moslems. The new government consisted of an elected council, which was assigned some functions and powers and was responsible to an appointed mayor. Another law, adopted from France in 1913, introduced provincial councils with elected members.

These changes, however, did not involve any significant devolution of authority to cities or provincial councils. The new municipal arrangements were essentially administrative devices developed by the state in an effort to provide improved local services, primarily in Istanbul's modern neighborhoods. They were completely dependent on the center for their status, power, and resources.[7] Similarly, the elected provincial councils were neither politically nor financially independent of central control, and they were primarily accountable to the governor as the representative of the centralized state. Thus, Turkey embarked on its efforts to modernize—and collaterally, to urbanize—lacking both experience with independent municipalities and a heritage of local autonomy.

The Ottoman legacy of concentrated state power was embraced by the new Turkish Republic in 1923. Kemal Ataturk and his followers sought to forge a modern nation based on secular ideals. Their instrument of change was the state, and they monopolized power in Ankara. A strong center was needed to integrate the nation, to ensure its defense, and to promote nationalism and secularism. Centralized government was essential also to husband the resources of a poor nation, as well as to develop state industries and modern transportation networks. Local autonomy could dissipate the momentum of the revolution, as well as nurture peripheral power centers in which opposition could develop.

Another factor fostering continued centralization under the Republic was the paucity of skilled personnel to carry out the ambitious plans of the new government. The available talent "had to be concentrated at the center and in easy communication with each other. Field cadres could be given only limited responsibility, reporting directly to the center, to forestall mistakes about policy implementation."[8] As government rapidly expanded, the needs of the center for skilled people were voracious, and these new officials in turn generated plans and programs that further concentrated power in Ankara.

Governmental growth and centralization were mutually reinforcing in republican Turkey. The vast expansion of government that began under Ataturk was directed from the center, and in turn greatly enlarged the central government and its responsibilities. New health and welfare programs were administered in Ankara. Extensive public works construction was directed from the capital. Public ventures proliferated; all were controlled from the center. The rapid growth of government "gave national political and bureaucratic leaders sizable resources for expanding their influence."[9]

Ataturk also maintained strict central control of Turkey's provinces and localities. The hierarchical administrative structure of the Ottomans provided the framework for center-local relations in the new republic. Provincial governors (vali) were appointed by the Minister of Interior and were the principal agents of central control outside Ankara. Provinces were further divided, and these units also were directed by officials sent out from the center. Under this system, "all major policy decisions" were made in Ankara and "then carried out in the provinces by officials directly responsible to the capital."[10]

Ankara itself was an appropriate symbol of Turkish centralization, since the city's transformation from provincial town into national capital was controlled by the national government. Compensation for the expropriated land was determined by the central government. Population projections made by central authorities were dictated to the architect who prepared the initial master plan. The national government established the Ankara Planning Commission, which was empowered to control development. It also named the commission's members, and made the planning agency responsible to the Ministry of Interior rather than to local officials.

In 1930, a system of municipal government was grafted to this hierarchical framework. Elected councils were provided, a reflection of Ataturk's desire to have "democratic local councils play an important role in modernizing cities and towns."[11] But the new arrangements did not significantly reduce central dominance. Before enactment of the Municipal Law of 1930, local government had no statutory powers. Now municipalities could be established in major cities, and they were required to carry out a number of functions. But the new local authorities had no independent sources of revenue; even property taxes were collected by the central government.[12] As a result, municipalities had to depend on national government for funds to carry out their mandated functions.

Another factor inhibiting development of more independent local authorities was the absence of opposition parties during the early decades of the Turkish Republic. Not until the Republicans permitted the establishment of more than one political party in 1945 were politicians able to make local issues subject to bargaining among rival parties, thus increasing the importance of local autonomy.

Even with the emergence of a multiparty system, city governments remained heavily dependent on Ankara. Turkey's cities are the product of a highly centralized political structure—inherited from the Ottomans, expanded by Ataturk and his followers, and maintained by its legions of officials and beneficiaries. In this context, municipalities have not developed into genuine local governments with substantial autonomy and resources. Instead, city governments in Turkey function primarily as local administrations commissioned, controlled, and financed by central government.

LOCAL GOVERNMENT

Under the Turkish Constitution, "local governments are public corporations established to meet the common local needs of the citizens of the provinces, municipal districts, and villages, whose decision-making organs are popularly elected."[13] In 1982, Turkey had 67 provinces, almost 1,600 municipalities, and approximately 36,000 villages. Provinces *(il)* are subdivided into counties *(ilce)*, and are involved in both urban and rural services since their jurisdictions typically encompass several municipalities and hundreds of villages. Municipalities—which must have populations of at least 2,000 or be seats of counties—undertake basic urban services, while villages provide essential public services in rural areas.

The number of municipalities increased almost fourfold between 1947 and 1981, not only because of population growth but also because of the attractions of assistance from the central government that was distributed exclusively to localities with the status of municipal corporations. By 1980, almost 60 percent of the population lived in municipalities. Most of these municipalities were small. As Table 4-1 indicates, over, 80 percent had populations under 10,000. In 1981, however, almost 200 municipalities were eliminated when amalgamations in Istanbul and other metropolitan areas were decreed by the central government.

Responsibilities are divided between the local administrations and the central government in a series of national laws, some of which were inherited from the Ottoman Empire. In principle, the main criterion in apportioning functions is to assign to local authorities those activities that concern everyday life, and to have the central government retain those of

TABLE 4-1

NUMBER OF MUNICIPALITIES BY SIZE: 1981

	Number	Percent of Total
Less than 2,000	189	11.9
2,000–3,000	465	29.3
3,000–5,000	374	23.6
5,000–10,000	248	15.6
10,000–20,000	147	9.3
20,000–50,000	100	6.3
50,000–100,000	34	2.1
Over 100,000	29	1.9
Total	1,586	100.0

SOURCE: Fikri Gökçeer, *Atatürk Yılında Belediyelerimiz* (Ankara: Türk Belediyecilik Derneği, 1981), p. 12.

national character. Thus, street cleaning, construction and maintenance of city roads, controlling food prices, and town planning are local functions. On the other hand, health, education, and housing are mainly the responsibility of the center. In areas like water supply, electrification, and welfare, powers have been divided among various levels of government, with local governments required to cooperate closely with central agencies.

These divisions of responsibilities have not been cast in stone. In the face of rapid urban change, reallocation of functions among governmental levels has been common. In general, local governments have lacked the resources to carry out costly new and expanded urban functions. As a result, the role of the national government has steadily widened.

Provincial Government

Provinces play dual roles in Turkey, serving both as central agents and as elements of local government. The 67 provinces are the main units of field administration for the national government, and are directed by governors *(vali)* appointed by the central government.[14] Provincial governors act on behalf of the central government, employing powers delegated by the Council of Ministers and individual ministers. They are the principal instrument of central control over localities, authorized to review budgets, regulations, and personnel actions, and empowered to remove local elected officials.

Provinces are also units of local government, with responsibilities for public works, health, welfare, and some aspects of public education. Provincial authority for these functions is divided between an elected council and a governor appointed by Ankara. As head of the provincial administration, the governor directs the province's local programs, and the council through its standing committee advises the governor on the provincial budget and related matters. As with all local governments in Turkey, provincial administrations have been completely dependent on the center for funds for their mandated responsibilities. Their freedom of action has been further constrained because the governor owes his principal loyalty to the center. As a result, provincial councils have developed little independent influence, and their weakness and lack of visibility have further reduced their political effectiveness or importance.

Symptomatic of these fiscal and political weaknesses has been the steady erosion, over the past three decades, of provincial responsibilities for local functions. In the face of rapid urbanization, the provinces have been losing many of their local functions to the central government, and to a lesser degree, to municipalities. While central agencies have flourished, the provincial share of national budgets has declined, from 18 percent of general allocations in 1929 to 0.6 percent in 1980.[15] Demands for urban services have been focused on the municipalities rather than on the less accessible and less visible provincial governments, and the central government has responded by chaneling far more resources to the cities than to the provinces. In 1976, expenditures for provincial functions were less than 10 percent of similar outlays in the municipalities.[16]

City Government

Basic authority for city governments is provided by legislation enacted in 1930 which borrowed heavily from the French system of local government. This enabling legislation, Law 1580 of 1930, established municipalities to "regulate and meet the civil and common needs of the urban population" and "to provide for their health, safety, and welfare, and to prevent the deterioration of urban order."[17]

Municipal functions are prescribed in detail by national law. All municipalities are required to protect human health, public safety, and social welfare; to control the prices of food and services; to establish public libraries, playgrounds, and public squares; and to prepare master plans.[18] Municipalities are mandated also to establish hospitals, nurseries, orphanages, slaughterhouses, wholesale markets, racetracks, and stadiums.[19] In addition, the central government permits cities to engage in a wide range of activities, including the provision of public transportation, water, gas, and electricity; development of low-cost housing; and establishment of hotels, theaters, and other commercial undertakings.[20] With

TABLE 4-2
MUNICIPAL ECONOMIC ENTERPRISES: 1980

Type of Enterprise	Total
Energy supply	450*
Water	410
Markets	360
Hotels, motels, baths, and beaches	294
Office buildings, municipal complexes, industrial estates, and rental shops	272
Freezer plants	210
Slaughterhouses	195
Garages, repair and maintenance stations	185
Theaters, conservatories, cinemas, social and cultural centers	138
Flour mills, bakeries	96
Spring water bottling installations	22
Dairies	7
Other	72
Total	2970

SOURCE: Ayşe Trak, "Belediyeler ve İşsizlik Sorunu," Union of Mediterranean Towns, Papers of the Conference, Istanbul, May 12–15, 1980.
*Transferred from municipal control to the Turkish Electricity Agency in 1982. See Chapter 6.

rapid urban growth, many of these "optional" functions have become essential municipal services and account for a substantial share of municipal activities in the larger cities.[21]

Turkish municipal governments are complex organizations. The principal components are the mayor, council, standing committee, and an array of administrative agencies. In addition, larger cities are subdivided into districts and neighborhood units. Under the 1961 Constitution mayors were elected by direct popular vote, and served four-year terms.[22] Members of the municipal council are elected on the basis of proportional representation, also for four-year terms.[23] The standing committee (Belediye Encümeni) is composed of members of the council elected by their colleagues, heads of executive departments, and other ex-officio members, and is chaired by the mayor. The administrative structure is organized around a bewildering maze of functional agencies, which perform the specific tasks assigned to municipal governments by the central government. Subdistricts (Belediye Şubesi) exist in the largest cities and are instruments of administrative decentralization, while neighborhood organizations (mahalles) are somewhat more autonomous local units.

Mayors are the most powerful and visible municipal officials in Turkey, although their ability to concentrate resources is limited by formidable internal and external constraints. The mayor is the chief executive, responsible for preparing the budget, collecting revenues, expending funds, executing contracts, carrying out municipal regulations, and managing public property. He represents the city in relations with the central government, in dealings with other municipalities, and in court. The mayor presides over meetings of the municipal council and the standing committee, and is responsible for carrying out the decisions of these bodies. All municipal agencies are under the mayor's formal control. In addition, the mayor is the representative of the central government for some functions—promulgating national laws and regulations within the city limits and performing wedding ceremonies.

All these powers, however, are constrained by other officials. Budgets are examined by the standing committee and approved by the council. A great deal of day-to-day administrative authority is shared with the standing committee. The sheer number of municipal bureaus deters effective mayoral control. Further diluting the mayor's authority is the development of functional links between municipal agencies and central ministries. Central officials oversee almost everything the mayor does. And the city's overwhelming dependence on the center for funds limits options at every turn.

Under the 1930 law, municipal policy is set by the council. It adopts the budget, sets taxes, approves ordinances and regulations, and prepares the city's works programs. In practice, however, the council has relatively little collective influence. Councils in the major cities are large and unwieldy bodies, with 100 or more members in the biggest municipalities. They meet infrequently—only three times a year for a few days at a time. The council's agenda is set by the mayor, who prepares the budget and initiates other matters that come before the municipal legislature. Rarely does the council deal in a systematic way with policy questions, or "exercise a strategic decision-making role." Instead councils "tend to be swamped with detailed matters which obscure the main issues."[24]

A good deal of the council's formal power is delegated to the standing committee, which acts for the council when the municipal legislature is not in session. The committee is empowered to make rules for the maintenance of law and order, to set transportation fares, and to fix prices for food staples. The standing committee also shares executive power with the mayor. It reviews the budget prior to submission to the council, examines monthly expense accounts, approves transfers within the budget, controls the expenditure of emergency funds, and imposes fines. Decisions on expropriations of private property by the municipal government fall within its purview.

Existence of the standing committee dilutes the authority of both the council and the mayor. Councillors who serve on the committee are out-numbered by executive officials, and "their powers to exercise checks on its decisions are very limited."[25] Mayors have no direct control over the standing committee, although they chair the body. And the mayor pre-sides over a committee controlled by "his" agency heads who constitute a majority of committee members.[26] Thus, directors of the city's principal functional agencies have an independent source of influence, particularly over fiscal management and related issues.

Administrative agencies in Turkish municipalities tend to be narrowly focused on particular governmental functions—health, public works, planning, and the like. As city responsibilities have increased, functional agencies have proliferated. Istanbul had over forty principal departments in the 1970s. In addition, municipal enterprises supply water, gas, electric-ity, and other important city services. With so many agencies, overlap-ping responsibilities for related functions are common. At the same time, municipal administration, like most Turkish bureaucracy, is organized along strict hierarchical lines with minimal communication and sharing among agencies. As a result, coordinated policy development and im-plementation are rare.

Formally, functional agencies have little autonomy in Turkish cities. Municipal departments are administratively directed and controlled by the mayor. They carry out policies established by the council or the stand-ing committee. Municipal enterprises have more independence since these public authorities are created sometimes by special laws and often are funded outside the normal municipal budget. But their prices are fixed by the city council and they are subject to other formal controls.

In practice, functional agencies enjoy considerable freedom of action. Like all specialized organizations, they derive autonomy from the nature of their tasks, from being the experts while their "controllers" are general-ists. Vertical links with national agencies performing similar tasks in-crease autonomy locally, as do special sources of funding. As already noted, the independent role of department directors who serve on the standing committee is a source of influence. And the sheer number of functional agencies in the largest cities weakens the effectiveness of may-oral control.

Mayors get some help in coping with this multiplicity of functional agencies from assistant mayors. Most assistant mayors are career officials with experience in general administration, although some engineers and architects have been appointed. Assistant mayors typically direct a set of departments for the mayor. In Ankara in the late 1970s, coordination among agencies was substantially improved by the efforts of a group of management specialists who served as assistant mayors.[27] But assistant mayors in Istanbul have had less success in bridging the bureaucratic and functional walls that separate city agencies in Turkey.

Areal subdivisions are less important in Turkish cities than are functional agencies. Subdistricts *(Belediye Şubesi)* are established if there is more than one county within the borders of a municipality.[28] Ankara has 4 subdistricts and Istanbul, 23. These subdistricts are administrative units with responsibilities for the delivery of municipal services within a particular area. Their directors are appointed by the city government; they lack any independent authority or resources, and their efforts to advance the interests of their area are usually muted.

Neighborhood or precinct organizations, the *mahalle,* are more responsive to communal interests than are the administrative subdistricts. Carried over from the Ottoman system, these organizations are created by the municipal council and are composed of an elected mahalle council and a headman, the *muhtar.* The muhtar is a representative of the state, responsible for maintaining the local registry and the voting lists, and for notarizing documents. The mahalle council has no statutory powers. Despite limited authority, the mahalles and especially the muhtar provide a grass-roots focal point where city dwellers may press demands on government, particularly in poor neighborhoods and squatter settlements. In some cities, mayors periodically assembled the muhtars to discuss local problems and concerns. The flexibility of the mahalle system permitted easy adaptation to rapid urban growth, since new settlers could apply to have their area subdivided so that a squatter area could have its own mahalle. "In addition to being a system familiar to everyone in Turkey, mahalles provide a local scale to urban government and enable the varied needs of different parts of the city to be identified."[29]

Out of this welter of officials, institutions, and responsibilities, relatively little emerges in the way of effective public services and even less in the way of coherent urban development policies. In part, the problem is endemic to city governments faced with rapid urban growth—functions proliferate, agencies develop narrow perspectives on their specialties, policymakers face incessant pressures to deal with one crisis and problem after another, and resources fall far short of needs. Complicating the situation in Turkey is the extraordinary dependence of cities on the central government for almost everything they undertake.

The Means of Central Control

As the preceding discussion illustrates, the central government completely controls the allocation of public responsibilities in Turkey. Ankara determines which functions will be performed by local governments, and which will be carried out by central agencies and provincial administrations. The national government can remove functions from local units, create new functional agencies, and redraw municipal boundaries. Most common have been national laws that have "restricted the range of municipal authority or have . . . transferred such authority *at the same time* to . . . central governmental agencies."[30] The result has been central involvement in almost every phase of urban government, with Ankara often making itself the dominant partner.

In addition to allocating governmental functions, the center controls local officials, most of whom are employees of the state. Appointments to city posts have to be approved by the Minister of Interior or his agents. Salaries for local officials are set nationally, which raises financial havoc in the large cities. In some cases, centrally mandated salary increases have prevented cities from meeting their payrolls or balancing their budgets. Although national law limits personnel expenditures to 30 percent of a city's resources, large municipalities have had to expend 70 percent or more of their revenue for salaries determined in Ankara rather than in city hall.

Administrative Tutelage

Even more pervasive are central government's direct administrative controls over local authorities, which include personnel and all other aspects of local governance. Under the system of administrative tutelage, most local actions must be approved by central officials, usually the provincial governor or appropriate national ministry. Tutelage applies to decisions, activities, organs, finance, and personnel of local governments. Using these powers, central officials may reject or amend local budgets, regulations, construction programs, bond issues, utility rates, equipment purchases, and appointment of officials. No municipality is exempt from these controls regardless of its size. Selection of assistant mayors in Istanbul and Ankara, for example, is subject to review and approval by the Minister of Interior. For most important local determinations, prior approval of central authorities is required.

Administrative tutelage is designed to ensure that local units conform to national laws, procedures, and policy objectives. Tutelage also seeks to promote cooperation and collaboration among local governments, secure minimum standards for urban services throughout the nation, and reduce disparities between regions and cities. Tutelage has steadily expanded with the growth of urban government, and the means of central control have multiplied as public responsibilities for urban Turkey become ever more complex.

In practice, tutelage ensures the dominance of the central government in Turkish urban politics. Tutelage increases bureaucratic formalities, and typically impedes city efforts to deal with local problems. Tutelage also has become entwined with the hierarchical relationships that are characteristic of Turkish bureaucracy to produce an administrative system that places local governments under very stringent control by the center.

Control of Revenues

Central government has overwhelming control over the public purse in Turkey. Allocation of revenues is a central function, and the national government has reserved most revenue sources for its own use. Despite a constitutional requirement that local authorities be provided with revenue sources in proportion to their functions, less than 10 percent of all revenues has flowed to local government. Many of the most productive taxable resources such as personal income, corporations, fuel production, and customs are reserved to the central government. Property taxes are collected by the central government in Turkey. Even the revenues derived from taxes on the incremental value of urban land and levies on real estate transactions belong to the national government. Tax rates are fixed by the central government according to its own needs, leaving cities with virtually no discretionary powers.

Under the revenue system in effect from 1948 to 1981, the central government permitted cities some local revenue sources and allocated a portion of certain national taxes to municipal and provincial governments. Direct city revenues were limited to license taxes, user fees, fines, charges for permits and income from municipal utilities, city hospitals, cemeteries, and city-owned economic enterprises. Municipal taxes, as indicated in Table 4-3, constituted a small share of total local revenues, and all local sources typically provided less than half the funds needed to underwrite municipal budgets.

Most of the property taxes collected by the central government were distributed to local governments, with 45 percent allocated to the municipalities and 35 percent to local provincial administrations. Local shares of other national taxes have been much smaller—15 percent of customs and excise duties, 8 percent of the fuel consumption tax, 5 percent of the income tax and the corporations tax, and 2 percent of the tax on state monopolies.[31] Large cities, however, received only 80 percent of the local share of these other national taxes, since the central government reserved the other 20 percent for long-term loans to cities under 50,000 for development of water supply systems, energy facilities, and sewage disposal plants, and preparation of official city maps and master plans.

Over the past three decades, this centrally controlled system provided

TABLE 4-3

MUNICIPAL REVENUES IN ANKARA: 1976

	Amount (000 TL)	Percent of Total Revenues
Municipal Taxes	101,319	13.3
Non-Tax Local Revenues	241,393	31.7
Shares of Central Taxes	266,910	35.1
Central Aid and Loans	151,225	19.9
Total Revenues	760,847	100.0

SOURCE: Ergun Türkcan, ed., *Türkiye'de Belediyeciliğin Evrimi*, Belediyecilik Araştırması Projesi 1 (Ankara: Türk İdareciler Derneği, 1978), p. 282.

local authorities with a declining share of total government revenues, despite the steady increase in the demand for local services in the wake of rapid urban growth. In 1957, municipalities received 15.9 percent of all government revenues; 15 years later their share had dropped to 8.5 percent.[32] During the 1970s, per capita municipal revenues actually declined when inflation is taken into account, dropping 17 percent between 1970 and 1974.[33] Less than half the property taxes, the bedrock of local finances almost everywhere in the world, were available to Turkish municipalities that bore the burden of providing most basic urban services. Many local taxes produced so little revenue that they were hardly worth collecting. In the scramble to increase revenues, city governments often devote more of their energy to income-producing activities—selling properties and operating public enterprises—than to providing unprofitable public services.

Under this revenue system, Turkey's major cities were inexorably pushed to the financial brink as rapid urbanization increased the scope and costs of city public services as well as the expectations of the urbanizing masses. Efforts to provide localities with more sources of income and financial flexibility were repeatedly stalled. A draft law designed to enhance local revenues was submitted to Parliament in the early 1960s, but was repeatedly withdrawn by the government for further refinements. Opposition to municipal tax reform came from those in Ankara who did not want to relinquish power, particularly to the big cities. Many national officials had serious doubts about the capabilities of municipal governments. And Parliament was reluctant to take action on municipal revenues because of the political hazards involved in supporting reforms that would impose additional tax burdens on city dwellers.

Central monopoly of revenue sources has been reinforced by the general scarcity of taxable resources in Turkey. Tax-paying capacity is extremely low for the vast majority of citizens, severely limiting the amount of resources available for all governments. Inadequate resources also result from the reluctance of elected officials to raise taxes, or to collect taxes more effectively. Property taxes, for example, amount to only 0.4 percent for homeowners, because of political pressures that keep rates low and assessments far below market value.

With needs constantly outrunning resources throughout the governmental system, the center has succumbed to the temptation to husband ever more tax revenues for its own agencies and programs. Repeatedly, the center has failed to meet its fiscal obligations to cities. Payment of local shares of national tax revenues was often postponed or canceled. Only 17 percent of the municipal shares of the major central taxes— excluding the property levy—were actually dispersed to cities between 1970 and 1978.[34] Local budgets became illusions when supposedly fixed shares of national revenues never materialized. In 1977, for example, Istanbul's budget listed its share of the national corporation tax as 60 million lira, even though the city government had not received a single lira from this revenue source for the previous six years.[35]

Lacking either adequate or predictable sources of revenue, municipal budgets bore little relation to fiscal reality, particularly in the largest cities, where pressures for local services were the greatest and unit costs the highest. City budgets typically contained fictitious revenue figures which were never realized in order to achieve the "balanced" budget required by law. Ankara, for example, secured only 76 percent of its estimated revenues in 1976, and only 51 percent the previous year.[36] During the 1970s, Istanbul was able to carry out less than a third of its budgeted investments, and by 1976 its deficit was 564 million lira, more than one-third of its expenditures.[37]

Change finally came to this ineffective financial system in 1981 when the military government pushed through a basic revision of the revenue-sharing arrangements. Under Law 2380 of 1981, 5 percent of total revenues from national taxes would be reserved for municipalities, with an additional 1 percent going to provincial local governments.[38] Cities would now receive shares of all national taxes, rather than selected national imposts as in the past. More important, the new system tripled the central revenues promised to cities, from 25 billion lira to 75 billion lira. Of these funds, 80 percent are allocated directly to municipalities according to population, with the remaining 20 percent used by the central government for projects in cities.

A companion law enacted by the military government, Law 2464 of 1981, revised municipal taxes.[39] The bewildering variety of local taxes was simplified, a number of more productive new taxes were authorized, tax rates and coverage were increased, and municipalities were given some flexibility in fixing rates between centrally established limits.[40] Munici-

TABLE 4-4
DEFICITS OF THE MUNICIPALITY OF ISTANBUL: 1968–1976

	Revenues	*Expenditures*	*Deficits*
		(thousands of lira)	
1968	407,516	425,891	18,375
1970	442,661	526,233	83,572
1972	645,781	686,020	40,239
1974	777,422	1,069,973	292,551
1976	1,061,000	1,625,000	564,000

SOURCE: For 1968 to 1974, Istanbul Metropolitan Plan Bureau, "The Provision of Local Services and the Problem of Municipal Finance," *Socio-Economic Issues,* Annex 2–6 (Istanbul, July, 1976), p. 15; for 1976, Sevim Görgün, "İstanbul Belediyesinin Finansal Durumu ve Sorunları," (İstanbul: 1977).

palities were classified according to size, with larger cities authorized to have higher tax rates than smaller ones. Cities also were permitted to collect taxes in areas beyond their boundaries when residents of those areas were receiving city services. The net result of these changes was a threefold increase for municipalities, from 10 billion lira from local taxes in 1981 to 30 billion lira. While welcoming these reforms, officials in the major cities, like Istanbul's mayor under the military government, General Abdullah Tırtıl, complained that they did not provide sufficient additional revenues to help much with the squeeze on city finances.[41]

Enactment of these substantial changes in the fiscal system was facilitated by the muting under military rule of many of the political concerns of elected governments that had formerly blocked financial reform. Though these reforms improved the cities' financial position, and though the increase in local revenues reduced municipal reliance on the center, they represented no radical change in central-local relations. The new system was promulgated by the central government, which retained the bulk of tax sources and determined local taxes. Cities remained heavily dependent on the center for the bulk of their funds through national tax shares and other central assistance and investments. Although distribution of local shares of national taxes was guaranteed by the central government, the center in the end would determine whether obligations to its fiscal wards would be honored or abrogated—as had happened so often in the past.

State Assistance and Investments

Prior to 1981, the principal response of central government to worsening financial conditions in the cities was expansion of financial assistance, primarily in the form of ad hoc reactions to particular problems and crises. Financial aid is provided through the annual state budget, by special laws, and under the discretionary powers of the central government. Assistance from the center accounted for about one-sixth of all city revenues in the 1970s, and exceeded 20 percent in the case of some larger cities. In 1974, for example, Ankara received 29.8 percent of its revenues from central aid and loans.[42]

Inevitably, financial assistance has increased central control. In the absence of adequate tax resources, central assistance is critically important to municipalities. Because of its importance, assistance is frequently used as a means of increasing the dependence of cities on the center. Local freedom of action is reduced by programs that promote reliance on central agencies for financial and technical assistance. Aid also provides Ankara with a means of differentiating among cities, particularly since so much assistance has been distributed at the discretion of central agencies.

One of the most common forms of assistance is provision of funds through ministerial budgets for particular services in selected cities. Most of these grants have gone to the biggest cities to underwrite sewage treatment facilities, housing development, and acquisition of land for public purposes. In 1967, for example, five million lira (approximately $250,000) was allocated for debts incurred by Istanbul, Ankara, and Izmir in expropriating land.[43] Cities also rely heavily on the Ministry of Reconstruction and Settlement for assistance. The Ministry provides funds for land acquisition and implementation of city plans. It also administers the National Fund for Gecekondus which provides funds for service improvements in squatter areas, land acquisition, and housing development.

A variety of credit and assistance programs is operated by the Ministry of Reconstruction and Settlement's banking agencies. The Real Estate Bank *(Emlâk Kredi Bankası)* makes mortgage loans for low-cost housing. The Bank of Local Authorities *(İller Bankası)* provides loans and technical guidance to municipalities and distributes the local shares of national taxes. In addition, the central government guarantees municipal loans from national and commercial banks, and from state economic enterprises. Without these guarantees, cities would not be able to borrow.

Another important form of assistance, and means of central control, over cities is cancellation or postponement of municipal debts. A series of laws beginning in 1965 forgave loans to the national treasury, and put off repayment of money borrowed from state economic enterprises. Five billion lira (approximately $250 million) in municipal debts were affected by moratoriums in 1965, 1971, and 1975, and another 15 billion lira (about $500 million) in 1977–1978. The major beneficiaries have been the larger cities, which have borrowed most heavily from the central agencies. These bailouts encourage unrealistic borrowing on the part of the larger

TABLE 4-5
DEBTS OF MUNICIPALITIES TO CENTRAL AGENCIES: 1978

	Debt to Agency (000,000 TL)	*Percent of Total*
Treasury	1,844	13.7
Social Security Agencies	1,927	14.3
Turkish Electricity Agency	7,100	52.8
Other State Enterprises	1,342	10.0
Out of Budget Loans	1,233	9.2

SOURCE: Talat Saral, "Türk Belediyeciliğinin Genel Görünümü," *Maliye Dergisi,* (March–April 1980), p. 59.

cities, while penalizing smaller cities, which do not borrow because of their limited repayment capacity. In addition, most of the municipalities benefiting from debt moratoriums have been located in western Turkey. For example, the share of the relatively developed regions in the 1965 moratorium was 82 percent in 1971.[44] Thus, these "benefits," like most central assistance, tend to enhance rather than reduce regional disparities in urban public services.

Ankara's urban influence is also augmented by the importance of public investment in Turkey. Nearly half of all investment is generated in the public sector. Very little of this public capital comes from the impoverished local governments. In the early 1970s, almost 90 percent of the public investment in Istanbul province was from the central government.[45] Nationally, municipal governments accounted for less than 5 percent of public capital formation in 1977.[46] As a result, national agencies underwrite most public investments in urban areas for economic infrastructure, transportation, communications, health, education, and housing. In the process, resources are distributed among regions and cities in the form of direct investments, loans, subsidies, credits, and tax advantages. Since most investment allocations are discretionary, the center's power is further bolstered.

Central monopoly of investment funds has been a major factor in Ankara's expanding role in providing education, health services, energy, and other public benefits that require large capital outlays. Capital deficiencies—along with increasing operating costs and personnel inadequacies—forced most cities and local provincial administrations to abandon their health functions to the Ministry of Health. National control of investment has led the central government to expand its responsibilities for municipal water supply.

THE STRANDS OF CENTRAL CONTROL

Centralization clearly has enormous impact on the politics of urban development in Turkey. The dominant role of the national government is the fundamental legal and political fact of life. Yet centralization does not produce monolithic control from the center, or consensus within the national government on all issues. The Turkish state consists of many component institutions. These agencies bring a variety of perspectives, interests, and constituencies to the implementation of their programs and their relations with cities. Their missions typically are narrow and their perspectives parochial, and they often compete with one another in the bureaucratic struggle to survive and grow.

A good example of conflicting perspectives at the center was the disagreement between the Ministry of Interior and the Ministry of Reconstruction and Settlement over the 20 percent of the local share of national taxes that is not distributed by formula under the 1981 law. Responding to the pressing needs of the major cities, Interior wanted the funds used mainly for services and capital improvements in the metropolitan centers. The Ministry of Reconstruction, on the other hand, successfully fought to have these funds allocated by its Bank of Local Authorities in accordance with local investment priorities developed by the Bank.[47]

In Turkey, these universal tendencies toward functional insularity are reinforced by a very hierarchical administrative tradition. As Weiker notes: "Although bureaucrats in all countries tend to protect their own 'turf,' the Turkish government appears excessively plagued by both formalism and legalism."[48] These rigid bureaucracies tend to be self-contained, with authority concentrated at the top and little internal flexibility. Most are highly legalistic in their dealings with other agencies. Narrow functional perspectives are bolstered by personnel practices that emphasize technical skills: "each administrative organization largely recruits its own officials independently . . . specialists with qualifications relating to the work of the organization mainly occupy the highest positions."[49]

Functional Instruments of Central Power

Central government in Turkey deals with local governments and urban problems primarily along functional lines. As a result central policies are developed and implemented largely in terms of the frame of reference of individual ministries and agencies rather than in the context of overall strategies of urban development or general plans for improving public services. Cities depend primarily on individual ministries for authority and assistance. The Ministry of Interior oversees local government and approves local budgets; the Ministry of Reconstruction and Settlement approves city plans and proposals for infrastructure improvements; the Ministry of Health approves the appointment of city medical directors; and the Ministry of Transportation approves public transportation fares.

Power and financial resources tend to flow along these functional channels between central agencies and local authorities. With the steady expansion of government and heavy national involvement in almost every urban activity, these functional channels have multiplied. In the process, functional alliances have proliferated between central and city officials with similar specialized interests.

Urbanization has spurred the development of new specialized activities both within existing agencies and through the creation of new organizations. An example of internal development is the expanding role of the Ministry of Interior in urban traffic, a function that grew out of its general responsibility for law enforcement. Police direct traffic, and as traffic became more of a problem in cities, the Ministry's activities expanded to include efforts to improve traffic flow. Traffic directorates were established in major cities, and a Joint Traffic Fund was created that underwrites parking, bus, and other projects designed to ease congestion.

Formation of the Ministry of Reconstruction and Settlement in 1958 resulted directly from rapid urban growth and provides an excellent example of the impact of urbanization on governmental structure and functional specialization. The new ministry was created because of the realization that "growing urban problems" required "a new and better institutional structure."[50] The goal was a more effective instrument to deal with rapid urbanization. It was given responsibility for developing urban policy, including population distribution, housing, urban infrastructure, and regional development. A number of urban functions were shifted from other ministries to the new agency—housing, building materials, planning, and technical assistance to municipalities. Some important agencies involved in urban development also were transferred to the new ministry, including the Bank of Local Authorities and the Real Estate Bank.

Although its urban mission was broadly conceived, the Ministry of Reconstruction operates primarily as a functional agency, carrying out its allotment of the central government's many urban activities. While a number of important urban responsibilities are assigned to the Ministry of Reconstruction, even more are lodged in other ministries, most of which are larger and more powerful than the Ministry of Reconstruction. And as is often the case with government organizations that encompass diverse functions, the Ministry's components enjoy considerable autonomy in carrying out their specialized duties. Responsibilities of agencies such as the Bank of Local Authorities are largely fixed by law. Regardless of its ministerial home, the Bank is responsible for distributing local shares of national taxes, guaranteeing municipal debts, channeling aid to localities, lending money and providing technical assistance for capital projects in cities, and coordinating financial relationships between the central government and local authorities.

In fact, the Bank of Local Authorities was moved from the Ministry of Reconstruction to the new Ministry of Local Affairs in 1978. The Ministry of Local Affairs was a product of the same concerns that gave birth to the Ministry of Reconstruction—urbanization was continuing to transform Turkey, and housing, transportaton, and other city problems were intensifying.[51] So a new functional agency was created, focused on the problems of city governments, rather than on housing and settlement patterns as was the Ministry of Reconstruction two decades earlier. Along with the Bank of Local Authorities from the Ministry of Reconstruction, the new ministry was given functions previously assigned to the Ministry of Interior (local government affairs) and the State Planning Office (provincial and local planning). Whatever its merits, this effort to rearrange urban responsibilities lasted little more than a year, a victim of partisan conflict that is examined in the next chapter, and after its dissolution, the defunct Ministry of Local Affairs' functional agencies were returned to their former ministries.

Orchestras without Conductors

Part of the rationale for creation of the Ministry of Reconstruction and the Ministry of Local Affairs was better coordination of urban policy development and implementation. In Turkey, as in most political systems, urbanization has spurred efforts to improve coordination while simultaneously generating demands that led to the proliferation of functional agencies. As usually happens, the development of coordinating mechanisms has not kept pace with the elaboration of functional programs, specialized agencies, and narrowly based intergovernmental relationships. As a result, functional agencies have been "allowed to establish their own systems of priorities . . . with external constraints limited largely to the total funds available in an annual budget and the requests from political leaders for specific projects."[52]

At the center, there is little effective coordination of policies of the various ministries and agencies whose activities affect either the functioning of local government or the pace of urban development. General mechanisms to orchestrate policies are weak: "Deputy Prime Ministers have usually been too busy with political matters to perform coordinative duties, . . . and the Prime Minister's office is poorly equipped with coordinators. The major potentially coordinating agencies, the Ministry of

Finance and the State Planning Organization, are frequently bypassed."[53]

On paper, the State Planning Organization has impressive powers to coordinate programs affecting the growth of cities and regions. The planning agency assists the central government in the formulation of housing, regional development, urban public services, and environmental policies. It is responsible as well for coordinating the investments of all central ministries including housing, regional development, health, education, water, energy, and transportation. In practice, however, the State Planning Organization usually has been no match for powerful ministries, and consequently has had little impact on the activities of major functional agencies.

Complicating coordination of urban programs has been the helter-skelter involvement of central agencies in cities. As Göymen points out, "this caused an overlapping of functions; duplication of effort; the emergence of uncoordinated and sometimes diametrically opposed policies in the same field; and in the less 'attractive' functional areas, failure by both levels of administration to do anything at all."[54] Overlapping responsibilities also plague agencies responsible for planning and coordination. Both the State Planning Organization and the Regional Planning Department of the Ministry of Reconstruction, for example, are empowered to prepare regional development plans and policies.

In this complicated system, new agencies frequently invade the turf of established bureaucracies. In 1979, the new Ministry of Local Affairs rushed to support the city of Ankara's development of a large-scale commercial enterprise to provide basic foodstuffs at low prices. Local Affairs' action enraged the Ministry of Commerce, which controlled TARKO, a cooperative organization with a similar mission. In the ensuing conflict, residents of Ankara went without butter over a long religious holiday, and intervention by the Prime Minister was required to resolve the dispute between the two ministers and their allies.

Even less coordination occurs outside Ankara. City governments lack the authority, resources, personnel, or political capabilities to orchestrate their multiplying relationships with the many components of the central government. Over 200 national agencies—ministerial units, independent organizations, and state economic enterprises—operate in the Istanbul metropolitan area, and none has any formal responsibility to the municipal government. Lack of information further reduces the prospects of harmonizing city efforts with national plans and programs. For the most part, "effective communication as an instrument of coordination from the central planning authorities downward, and from the local level to the center, is . . . non-existent."[55]

Provincial governors are the main instrument for coordination in the field. As agents of the center, they are supposed to direct and coordinate the work of national ministries within their provinces. Field offices of the central agencies are organized along provincial lines, and their directors report to the governor. All budget requests by individual ministries for activities within a province must be reviewed by the governor. Since 1963, provincial coordinating councils have provided the governor with an additional means of integrating the implementation of central plans and priorities.

Despite these powers, most governors lack the administrative or political resources to offer much effective areal coordination of the functional activities of powerful ministries. Resources flow in narrow functional channels; this undermines most efforts by governors to orchestrate related programs within their provinces:

> For example, the Vali may request funds for a school and a road to that school. The requests go to the Ministry of Education and Public Works respectively. He may receive the funds for the school without the funds for the road, or funds for the road but no funds for the school. . . . Each agency . . . may receive funds quite unrelated to those of any other agency, and the Vali is unaware of what his [province] will receive as a total unit until it is virtually too late to do anything about it.[56]

Coordination on the part of provincial governors has become even more difficult in the major metropolitan areas as urbanization has multiplied the activities of the central government. Governors have been hard pressed to keep track of the proliferating programs of national agencies within the most urbanized provinces. Most governors are also tightly constrained by their role and their lack of independence—they function as instruments of the center rather than as chief executives of particular territorial entities. As Rivkin points out, "these are administrators trained to carry out directives sent down from above, and they rarely act as coordinators of economic and social growth."[57] As a result, provincial government funnels rather than shapes resources and programs in metropolitan areas.

ADAPTING TO URBAN CHANGE

Rapid urbanization has severely tested Turkey's highly centralized governmental system. Ankara has sought to adapt to the needs of an urban society on its own terms. Centralization has denied cities the resources or the authority to cope effectively with accelerating demands from expanding populations. Instead of devolving authority, the center has tried to do everything, endlessly generating new programs, agencies, plans, and controls for Turkey's cities.

In responding to urban demands, the national government has scattered the metropolitan landscape with a bewildering array of governmental jurisdictions. Government in the Istanbul metropolis has understandably been called a "vast and complicated maze of central and local institutions."[58] In addition to the scores of national agencies and their regional and provincial offices, there are provincial administration, the untidy governments of the major cities, smaller suburban municipalities in some of the larger metropolitan areas, and a sprinkling of metropolitan agencies such as the Istanbul Water and Sewerage Agency and the Ankara Metropolitan Plan Bureau.

Lost Opportunities

Between 1950 and 1980, almost every effort to strengthen the capabilities of cities to deal with their problems was checked in Ankara. Proposals to reorganize local government and provincial administrations were stymied by the opposition of national political leaders fearful of losing control over local affairs.[59] Attempts to reform central-local relations in the framework of flexible intergovernmental fiscal relations also failed, as did efforts to modernize municipal administration.

Nor did the national government come to grips with the spread of urban development beyond municipal jurisdictions. Especially in Istanbul and Izmir, as indicted in the previous chapter, rapid urbanization overran existing city boundaries and steadily reduced the ability of the city governments to cope with urban growth and service needs. New municipalities were easily organized under the central government's rules in communities with 2,000 or more residents, and Istanbul and Izmir were soon ringed by suburban municipalities, many of them quite small. Most of these units provided minimal urban services and were unable to exercise control over industrial, commercial, and residential development.

Urban experts argued that metropolitan growth in Istanbul and Izmir necessitated redrawing of municipal boundaries, as well as the creation of metropolitan governmental institutions with administrative, financial, and planning powers. Under existing law, central action was required to rearrange local boundaries, establish metropolitan governments, or create area-wide agencies for water supply, public transportation, and other urban services. Turkish law did permit local governments to join together in local unions to provide services. But these cooperative efforts were voluntary; because of inadequate resources, rivalry between municipalities, and fear of the big city by small suburban units, few joint endeavors were arranged.

Metropolitan reform, as is usually the case, was strongly resisted by suburban municipalities, which sought to retain their autonomy from the city. The central government was sympathetic to those who favored the municipal status quo in metropolitan areas; it was also reluctant to establish potentially more powerful local governments. A draft law that would have permitted the central government to force municipalities to set up metropolitan governments languished in Ankara during the 1970s. Unwilling to reorganize local government in the great urban centers, the central government instead established metropolitan planning bureaus to develop master plans for Istanbul, Ankara, and Izmir and their surroundings. In typical Turkish fashion, a central response to urban needs enlarged national authority, since the new planning agencies were controlled by the Ministry of Reconstruction and Settlement.

Although responsive to the need for comprehensive urban planning, central establishment of the metropolitan planning agencies ducked the basic problems of local fragmentation. Metropolitan planning by itself provided few answers to the complex problems posed by the mélange of poorly financed local units responsible for providing basic services and controlling urban development. And the major metropolitan areas continued to lack institutions capable of undertaking area-wide development projects. Lack of such capability led the International Bank for Reconstruction and Development in 1974 to suspend its financial aid to Istanbul for the construction of a large-scale sewerage system.[60]

As urban problems intensified in the 1970s, pressures for decentralization increased. What was needed, proponents of the cities argued, was change that would preserve the benefits of centralization—the ability to redistribute national resources, to establish and enforce national priorities and standards, and to provide technical assistance to localities—while granting the cities considerable autonomy in the provision of public services. Alternate models of planning, policy-making, and resource allocation were developed and debated. But the entrenched forces in Ankara successfully defended their central bastions throughout the decade, husbanding power at the center and making as few concessions as possible to the cities.[61]

Military Government and the Cities

Three times in the past quarter-century—1960, 1971, and 1980—the military has assumed control of government in Turkey. Each of these interventions, and particularly the last, which was the longest and most pervasive, has left its mark on urban governance. Military rulers are less constrained by constituency and partisan considerations than elected leaders, and in Turkey this greater freedom of action has permitted military regimes to make changes that were politically stalemated under parliamentary government. The constitution that resulted from the 1960 military intervention contained a provision that was supposed to ensure more resources for local governments. In 1971, one of the military changes in the constitution permitted governments to indemnify the owners of expropriated property at its tax value, which was far below market value.

Far more sweeping changes in urban government occurred under the military between 1980 and 1983. Insulated from the political pressures that had checked tax and metropolitan reform for years, the ruling National Security Council acted on a number of measures that were too hot for elected governments to handle. As indicated above, new revenue-sharing and municipal tax laws were promulgated. Political fragmentation in metropolitan areas was attacked by providing for absorption of small units into central cities with populations of 300,000 or more. Through amalgamation, the central government sought "a more productive, planned, adequate, and integrated way" of providing urban services and development controls under a single local authority with area-wide jurisdiction.[62] Other innovations under the military were the establishment of a comprehensive water and sewerage agency for Istanbul, which is discussed in Chapter 6, and development of a new approach to housing in metropolitan areas, examined in Chapter 7.

None of these changes under the most recent military government, however, represented a significant dilution of central control over cities. Hierarchical by nature, militaries normally concentrate authority, and these tendencies have been reinforced for Turkey's officers by the nation's strong traditions of centralization. When the military took over in 1980, sweeping central power was immediately asserted in the cities. Elected local governments were dissolved and replaced by central appointees, on the grounds that "almost all of the locally elected bodies were so politicized as to be incapable of performing the functions conferred upon them by law . . ."[63] Existing municipal law was amended to provide for the dismissal of all elected mayors, municipal councils, and provincial elected governments.[64] New mayors for the larger cities were appointed by the Ministry of Interior, and the provincial governors appointed mayors for the smaller cities. Most of those appointed in the larger cities were provincial governors, retired army officers, or bureaucrats from the central goverment, with only four former mayors among them.[65] Functions of the municipal councils were assigned to the standing committees, which now had only appointed members—the mayor and heads of city agencies.

Elected municipal governments were reinstituted under the constitution prepared by the military government and approved by Turkey's voters in 1982. But central controls over local authorities were maintained in the 1982 Constitution. Tutelage powers are stated more explicitly than in the previous constitution, presumably to clarify central authority in light of the numerous disputes that erupted between Ankara and the big cities before 1980. Under the new provision, "the state has a right to control over the local governments within the framework defined by the law in order to provide the integrity of functions, to insure the public interest, and to meet adequately the public needs." The new constitution also permits the Minister of Interior to remove local elected officials temporarily, pending a decision by the *Danıştay,* or High Administrative Court.

Central control was also pervasive in the financial and metropolitan reforms enacted under the most recent period of military rule. As always, change came from Ankara on the central government's terms. As indicated above, the revenue-sharing and municipal tax reforms maintain tight central control over revenue sources and local tax rates. And the new procedures for consolidation in metropolitan areas are dominated by central officials. Final decisions on amalagamating local governments are made by the Council of Ministers on the basis of proposals developed by provincial governors and approved by the Minister of Interior.

5
POLITICAL INTERESTS AND URBAN DEVELOPMENT

Politics in Turkey is strongly shaped by the concentration of power and rewards at the center. All political roads lead to Ankara because of its monopoly of authority and resources. The central government is the target of most political pressures, from local as well as national interests. Influence is concentrated in the hands of actors at the center—national political leaders, top bureaucrats, and major economic interests. This national elite derives enormous advantage from centralization in the fierce competition for limited resources and has a powerful vested interest in the maintenance of the center as Turkey's political hub.

Decision-making has been highly politicized and partisan within this centralized framework. "Most Turkish governments," Weiker notes, "have not hesitated to use their patronage powers and their powers of discretion in authorizing projects to reward their clients and supporters."[1] Assistance to the cities has been heavily influenced by political considerations; and one of the primary attractions of discretionary aid programs has been the opportunities they provide for central officials to reward fellow partisans and punish party enemies in the cities. Constituencies of cabinet members, for example, have been favored beneficiaries of the National Fund for Gecekondus administered by the Minister of Reconstruction and Settlement, as have municipalities with good political connections in Ankara.

In this centralized and politicized system, cities have received attention from the center primarily on the basis of party links and political pressures. With rapid urbanization has come increased political attention to the cities by Ankara. Governmental and party leaders are sensitive to constituency concerns in a political system in which every national elected official represents a local district. More urban voters and more urbanized districts in Parliament have increased the political importance of cities and bolstered their influence in national politics. Most striking has been the responsiveness of elected officials to squatters in the wake of the explosive growth of gecekondus in the major cities.

Despite the growth of urban influence in Ankara, the ability of city governments to respond to local pressures and interests has been severely constrained by the dependence of cities on the center for authority and resources. As a result, political conflicts that arise from urban growth are difficult to resolve within Turkish cities. Lack of independence has precluded the development of autonomous local politics in cities because political participation has had higher payoffs in central than in local political arenas.

POLITICAL PARTICIPATION AND URBANIZATION

Urbanization has multiplied the opportunities for political participation in Turkey, which until recently was limited, for the vast majority of citizens, to voting. Interest groups, cooperatives, and local associations have proliferated in the cities. Neighborhood organizations have been particularly important in squatter areas, and are examined in detail later in the chapter. Because of centralization, much of this political effort has been directed toward the national government, usually through the channels of national elections and the national political parties. Participation itself became an issue in Turkish cities in the 1970s. Populist demands were common for more democracy, more participation, and more local autonomy. One response to these concerns was meetings organized by Ankara's city government in 1978 at which residents could express their views on urban problems and local issues.

Urbanization also has affected participation in elections. Turnout traditionally has been high in Turkey—89 percent of the electorate voted in the national elections of 1950 and 1954. With rapid urbanization has come some decline in participation—to 71 percent in the national election of 1965, 64 percent in 1969, and 67 percent in 1973. But in the hotly contested elections of 1977, turnout climbed to 72 percent. City dwellers are somewhat less likely to vote than are villagers—for example, 56 percent of the electorate voted in the cities in 1969 compared with 68 percent in rural areas. Özbudun suggests that higher turnout in the villages results from voting being less private and more subject to pressures by local

TABLE 5-1
VOTER TURNOUT BY AREA IN 1969 NATIONAL ELECTION

	Percent Voting
Nation as a whole	64.3
Urban	56.3
Rural	68.1
Istanbul	
City as a whole	51.7
Squatter areas	51.0
Ankara	
Squatter areas	59.7
Lower-middle-class areas	55.7
Middle-class areas	59.8
Upper-middle-class areas	60.0

SOURCE: Ergun Özbudun, *Social Change and Political Participation in Turkey* (Princeton, N.J.: Princeton University Press, 1976), pp. 201–203.

notables in small communities than is the case in cities.[2] In addition, voting is "to a greater degree the chief form of political participation" for villagers.[3]

Within cities, voter turnout in national elections is not significantly differentiated along income lines. Unlike the situation in the United States and a number of other advanced societies, the urban poor in Istanbul and Ankara vote in roughly the same proportions as do other urban dwellers, as illustrated by the data on turnout in the 1969 national election in Table 5-1. Squatters have viewed participation in elections as an important source of influence. "The right to vote," Karpat reports, "has acquired in the squatter settlement . . . both symbolic and practical meaning as an ideal avenue for transforming the communal opinion into a political will and as an instrument for participating in politics to secure some benefits."[4]

Such pragmatic considerations—of participating in politics to secure benefits—are widespread in Turkey. "Once it is shown that political participation may bring concrete results to party adherents," Weiker indicates, "the electorate can indeed be mobilized."[5] In urban politics, personal and other instrumental concerns have been far more important than ideological considerations for most participants. This has been particularly the case with squatters seeking leverage on elected officials. Two-fifths of the males in Karpat's sample of gecekondu dwellers switched parties when they voted in Istanbul. They shifted to the Justice

Party because, as the ruling party, it "had the means to grant economic advantages such as the title to the house, and to improve the quality of life in the gecekondu by installing amenities such as water and electricity in exchange for votes."[6]

More generally, the pragmatic approach of urban newcomers in Turkey manifests a significant impact of urbanization on politics. Participation in Turkey's cities is less constrained by traditional considerations than in the villages. The squatter, as Karpat points out, "was able to break away from the pressure of his elders, from traditional ties and loyalties, and to vote according to his individual preferences and interests."[7] Özbudun characterizes this transformation as one in which the "geographical and social mobility generated by urban migration tends to change the model pattern of participation from mobilized to autonomous, from deferential to instrumental participation."[8]

POLITICAL PARTIES AND THE CITIES

Political parties have provided the primary arena for this instrumentally motivated participation. From the beginnings of the multiparty system in the late 1940s, Turkey's major parties have been broad-based, competitive, and pragmatic. During the period of one-party rule, the Republican People's Party (RPP) had built a broad base of support. When additional parties were permitted, the new Democratic Party was backed by a wide range of interests, as was its successor after 1960, the Justice Party (JP).[9] To maintain their appeal to different economic, social, and sectional groups, the major parties have pursued essentially moderate courses, seeking to aggregate interest throughout Turkish society.[10]

These wide-reaching parties have relied primarily on pragmatic means to increase support and win elections. The centralized state provided bountiful political resources to the ruling party as well as great discretion in dispersing resources among programs, regions, and cities. Upon taking power, ministers packed their offices with the party faithful. Assistance and investment from the central government were funneled into cities supported by the same party. Almost every new urban program has been exploited by the party in power in Ankara. A substantial part of the National Fund for Gecekondus became a national fund for the party in power to distrubute to its constituents and clients in cities. National guarantees of municipal loans have been used extensively to bail out cities controlled by the same party as the central government. Tutelage controls over local government provide the party in power with additional opportunities to advance partisan interests, particularly by thwarting cities controlled by the opposition party.

Centralized Parties and Urban Politics

Like the government they seek to control, political parties are highly centralized in Turkey. Centralization has been mutually reinforcing for government and parties since the founding of the Turkish Republic. Kemal Ataturk created a centralized party to control the unitary Turkish state. During the one-party period, the interests of the Republican People's Party were strongly served by centralized government, which concentrated rewards at the center and reduced prospects for the emergence of an organized opposition with an autonomous local political base.

Under the multiparty system, party leaders continued to have a strong vested interest in preserving central government's dominant role. Concentration of authority and resources in Ankara provided national leaders with the means to dominate their parties by controlling the distribution of rewards. As a result, the national parties had little interest in reducing the authority of the center and their control over local affairs by supporting measures that would enhance municipal autonomy. Instead they fought hard to expand the center's urban responsibilities and to use centralized government to reward politically loyal cities and punish those controlled by the opposition.

In this system, local parties and elections are closely linked to the national parties. Local politics are "so fully integrated with national politics that national issues tend to become the chief ones in local politics."[11] Local campaigns are contested in terms of national party programs and personalities. City elections are more likely to feature slogans about joining the European Economic Community or withdrawing from the North Atlantic Treaty Organization than proposals for improving municipal services. Most voters support the same party locally as they do in national elections.

All candidates owe fealty to the national party, which provides essential resources in the campaign and afterward. Candidates for mayor in major cities have had little hope of success without backing from national party headquarters. Once elected, mayors and council members continue to be controlled by the national party. In 1977, the RPP refused to support the mayors of Ankara, Istanbul, and Izmit for reelection because the national party was dissatisfied with their handling of local affairs; and all three mayors were replaced by more pliable party candidates despite substantial personal support among voters for the incumbents in their cities.

City elections also are strongly influenced by the political advantages enjoyed by local candidates of the party that controls the central government. Voters understand that only local officials loyal to the party in power have much chance of receiving funds from the center. As a result, adherents of the dominant party in Ankara have a substantial advantage in local elections which they do not hesitate to exploit. If the incumbents in a city belong to the ruling party nationally, central funds flow into the city. On the other hand, a city administration in the hands of the opposition is harassed at every turn by the central government as the municipal election nears.

National Politics and Urban Constituencies

Centralized parties and centralized government, however, have not severed the connection between elected politicians and their constituents. Members of the Grand National Assembly are elected from territorial constituencies, with each province constituting a district, usually with more than one member. Seats are allotted to provinces on the basis of population, and candidates run at large on party lists. Candidates are nominated by provincial organizations, and local political considerations are given substantial weight.[12] The number of national legislators with local political experience increased during the 1960s and 1970s, further strengthening linkages between national politicians and their constituencies.[13]

Increasingly these national legislative constituencies are urban. The spread of urbanization has multiplied the importance of cities in more and more provinces. And with legislative seats apportioned on the basis of population, the representation of provinces containing the metropolitan centers has grown. As a result, the number of national legislators concerned with urban dwellers and their problems has steadily expanded. More involvement with cities and urban issues by national politicians tends to reinforce centralization, since the state provides the resources for national legislators to deal with their constituencies. Strengthening local autonomy would enable cities to act more independently, and thus cause politicians in Ankara to lose control over local affairs and their local constituents.

According to the Turkish constitution, members of the National Assembly are supposed to represent the entire electorate rather than their specific provincial constituency. In practice, national legislators spend much of their time seeking to bolster their local standing by securing benefits for their constituents from the central government. Deputies and senators roam the corridors of Ankara's bureaucracies in the name of their province and its cities. They bring all sorts of pressures to bear on fellow party members who are ministers and high-ranking bureaucrats in order to have their locale selected for central assistance and investments.

Concern with constituency interests involves national legislators directly in local affairs. Members of the National Assembly seek to influence a wide range of city decisions. Intervention by a powerful minister who controls central assistance of one sort or another is often irresistible. More often than not, local involvement by national politicians is highly particularistic and partisan, designed to advance the interests of particular constituents. And the ability to intervene successfully in local affairs bolsters the power of national political leaders in dealing with city politicians, officials, and groups.

The most sweeping changes in urban constituencies resulted from the dramatic growth of squatter settlements. Squatters were voters, their numbers were multiplying, and legislators from Istanbul, Ankara, and Izmir needed their votes. "The politician who sensed the vote potential of the gecekondus was quick to establish a foothold there from the very beginning. He promised titles to the land on which the squatter houses were established, city water, electricity, and transportation . . ."[14] The parties soon were competing with each other for squatter votes, organizing in gecekondus, and, in the classic instrumental fashion of urban political machines, promising to help newcomers in return for electoral support.

The constituency connection between elected officials and squatters affected both groups. As Şerif Mardin emphasizes, the sprawling shantytowns, "massive, threatening, infiltrating into city life," made "politicians think about public services, education, and welfare of a type that is increasingly directed to the large masses of the people."[15] For their part, the "political parties played a major role in increasing awareness among the lower classes about their place in society and their political rights."[16] The growing political response to gecekondu dwellers also had more direct effects. Gecekondu construction was at its peak during election years. And by assuring their squatter constituents that housing would be legalized, elected officials fostered more migration. Writing of the political fanfare accompanying title distribution in gecekondus, Metin Heper emphasizes that "these ceremonies inculcated the belief that once the squatter houses are built one would somehow obtain a title deed. Such a belief helped accelerate the migration to the urban areas. The politicians while legitimizing the completed squatter houses also encouraged new ones."[17]

The Quest for Urban Votes

During the first two decades of rapid urban growth, Turkey's conservative party was most successful in the competition for the support of newcomers in the burgeoning cities. The Democratic Party and later, the Justice Party, enjoyed a number of advantages over the Republican People's Party. The Democrats were in power at the outset of massive migration, and the new city dwellers associated the Democrats with their good fortune. As Özbudun notes, "in view of the substantial social mobility displayed by urban migrants, it is hardly surprising that they gave their support to a party which they perceived as instrumental in bringing about this change."[18]

The conservative parties were also able to capitalize on their control of the national government and the big cities. The Democrats dominated national and urban government during the 1950s, and the Justice Party won an absolute majority in the 1965 national election, while holding on to the major cities throughout the decade. Pragmatic squatters were ready to support the ruling party in return for services and legalization of their dwellings. Urban newcomers in the gecekondus also were wary of alienating the party that controlled the national and city governments. Squatters needed government even more than party leaders needed gecekondu votes. Officials had great discretion in deciding which communities were to get municipal services, or where the laws restricting squatter housing were to be enforced. And because gecekondus were illegal, the newcomers were extremely vulnerable to retaliation by public officials, who could deny them services or bulldoze their homes.[19]

In the 1965 national election, the Justice Party outpolled the RPP by margins of better than three to two in Istanbul's squatter settlements, and two to one among gecekondu dwellers in Ankara. In more conservative Izmir, the margin among squatters exceeded four to one. In building their electoral majorities in each of the major cities, the JP also ran well in lower-middle-class areas, as shown in Table 5-2. The conservatives, however, were unable to maintain their strongholds in the poorer sections of the city in the face of renewed competition from the Republican People's Party. The RPP moved to the left, emphasizing the need for greater equity and attention to the problems of the poor. Although the RPP's share of the national vote dropped in the 1969 election to an all-time low of 27.4 percent, the party made inroads on the JP's support among all classes of voters in the major cities, as shown in Table 5-3.

During the 1970s, the movement of lower-income voters toward the political left accelerated. Gecekondu votes helped the RPP win the 1973 election, votes won in part by the party's promise to legalize all squatter housing built before the end of 1973. By 1977, more than half of all voters in the largest cities were supporting the RPP in national elections, and even more in municipal contests. Republican candidates for mayor in 1973 were elected in Istanbul, Ankara, Izmir, and eleven of the other seventeen cities with 100,000 or more inhabitants. During this period, RPP votes in the squatter areas more than doubled, while the Justice Party lost half of its support, giving the RPP "clear superiority among the urban poor."[20]

Underlying the emergence of the Republican People's Party as the ma-

TABLE 5-2

**PARTY SUPPORT BY TYPE OF URBAN COMMUNITY IN THE
1965 NATIONAL ELECTION**

	Justice Party	*Republican People's Party (percent of votes cast)*	*Other Parties*
Istanbul	52.0	30.4	17.6
Gecekondus	62.4	19.1	18.5
Ankara	46.5	30.2	23.3
Gecekondus	52.5	25.8	21.7
Lower middle class	48.7	31.8	19.5
Middle class	27.4	53.1	19.5
Upper middle class	26.8	54.1	19.1
Izmir	62.1	29.8	8.0
Gecekondus	72.1	17.0	10.9
Lower middle class	73.4	17.4	9.2
Middle class	65.9	25.6	8.5
Upper middle class	54.1	36.5	9.4

SOURCE: Özbudun, *Social Change and Political Participation in Turkey*, pp. 201–203; and State Institute of Statistics.

jor political force in the large cities were a number of factors. The RPP adapted to urbanization—shifting to the left and appealing pragmatically to workers and the urban poor. In power, the Republicans nurtured their various urban constituencies with liberal gecekondu policies and increased support for large cities. Leadership played an important role, since the redirection of the RPP was largely the work of Bülent Ecevit, who sought to transform the party of Ataturk into an urban-oriented social democratic party. Ecevit was a native of Istanbul from a politically prominent family. A journalist and poet, he was elected to Parliament in 1957 at the age of thirty-two, and played a major role in the 1960s in leading the party in the direction of its new slogan—*ortanın solu*—"left of center."[21]

Political perspectives were also shifting among urban dwellers. Class interests were developing as urban newcomers were assimilated into the mainstream of city life. Initially, squatters supported those in a position to deliver immediate benefits. As these goals were satisfied with provision of basic services in squatter settlements and large-scale legalizations of gecekondus, lower-income city voters became more likely to pursue broader economic and political interests at the polls. In the words of an

TABLE 5-3
**PARTY SUPPORT BY TYPE OF URBAN COMMUNITY IN THE
1969 NATIONAL ELECTION**

	Justice Party	*Republican People's Party* *(percent of votes cast)*	*Other Parties*
Istanbul	47.8	33.8	18.4
Gecekondus	53.8	21.8	24.4
Ankara	42.4	36.0	21.0
Gecekondus	43.4	30.1	26.5
Lower middle class	47.1	32.5	20.4
Middle class	24.8	60.4	14.8
Upper middle class	25.8	60.1	14.1
Izmir	53.2	35.1	11.7
Gecekondus	60.7	22.6	16.7
Lower middle class	61.3	25.7	13.0
Middle class	58.9	32.3	8.8
Upper middle class	46.8	43.9	9.3

SOURCE: Özbudun, *Social Change and Political Participation in Turkey,* pp. 201–203; and State Institute of Statistics.

eastern migrant to Izmir who supported Ecevit and the RPP in the 1977 national election: "I believe Ecevit is able to work for the people, for the workers, more than the others."[22]

Traditional attitudes that limited general participation in politics and accepted elite domination of the political system were also under attack in the cities. An urban populism emerged that emphasized social justice, municipal autonomy, and popular participation in local affairs. These ideas were the most fully developed in Ankara under Republican Mayor Vedat Dalokay, who envisaged cities in which all strata participated in municipal governments dedicated to the equitable distribution of city services and were able to curb land speculation and claim the appreciation in land values for public purposes. Cities, it was argued, needed local government *(yerel hükümet)* rather than local administration *(yerel yönetim),* so that popularly supported local authorities could master their own resources, levy their own taxes, and make decisions independently from the center. Priority in the allocation of resources would be given to squatter settlements, and communal units would be organized to foster increased popular participation in decision making.[23] These populist strains in the cities intermingled with Ecevit's efforts to move the RPP to the left and his emphasis on more democracy and greater participation in Turkish political life.

The Party of the Cities

As its political base in the cities grew in the 1970s, the Republican People's Party became the voice of the cities in Turkish politics. And urban spokesmen, particularly the Republican mayors of the major cities, increased their influence within the party. Once the citadel of support for the centralized state, the RPP endorsed autonomy for the cities as an essential element of increasing democracy. "As the principles of democracy become operational at the local level," the RPP's 1977 program stated, "democracy becomes a reality; and as the powers of local governments are enlarged, administration becomes more efficient." But the Republicans were not ready to dismantle central controls in the name of local autonomy. Instead, "in enlarging the powers of local government, possibilities of central control in the public interest must be made more efficient."[24]

TABLE 5-4

PARTY SUPPORT BY TYPE OF URBAN COMMUNITY IN THE 1973 NATIONAL ELECTION

	Justice Party	Republican People's Party (percent of votes cast)	Other Parties
Istanbul	28.5	48.9	22.6
Gecekondus	26.7	47.5	25.8
Ankara	29.2	44.8	26.0
Gecekondus	27.7	45.9	26.4
Lower middle class	32.4	41.9	25.7
Middle class	21.8	62.6	15.6
Upper middle class	24.9	57.2	17.9
Izmir	40.9	44.6	14.5
Gecekondus	36.5	44.2	19.3
Lower middle class	41.9	44.1	14.0
Middle class	42.7	44.4	12.9
Upper middle class	37.8	50.4	11.8

SOURCE: Ergun Özbudun, "Voting Behaviour: Turkey" in Jacob M. Landau, Ergun Özbudun, and Frank Tachau, eds., *Electoral Politics in the Middle East: Issues, Voters and Elites* (London: Croom Helm, 1980), pp. 121–123; and State Institute of Statistics.

TABLE 5-5
PARTY SUPPORT IN MAJOR CITIES IN NATIONAL ELECTIONS:
1969–1977

	Justice Party	(percent of votes cast) Republican People's Party	Other Parties
Istanbul			
1969	47.8	33.8	18.4
1973	28.5	48.9	22.6
1977	28.8	58.3	12.9
Ankara			
1969	42.4	36.0	21.6
1973	29.2	44.8	26.0
1977	31.2	52.5	16.3
Izmir			
1969	53.2	35.1	11.7
1973	40.9	44.6	14.5
1977	39.7	52.7	7.6
Turkey			
1969	46.5	27.4	26.1
1973	29.8	33.3	36.9
1977	36.9	41.4	21.7

SOURCE: State Institute of Statistics.

In power, the Republicans supported increased resources and autonomy for local government, especially for major cities controlled by the
RPP. In 1978, Prime Minister Ecevit created a Ministry of Local Affairs
"to cope with administrative and financial bottlenecks of local governments, to render them more efficient, and thus strengthen democracy in
our society which is in rapid change."[25] Although the new ministry had
responsibilities for all local governments, its primary interest was larger
cities. The agency supported efforts by cities to organize into unions of
municipalities in order to exert more influence on central government.
The Ministry of Local Affairs also backed efforts by cities to expand
municipal economic activities into daily necessities, a course of action
urged by the party's vocal left wing, which was influential in a number of
major urban centers.

Under Ecevit, dealings with the cities were often highly partisan. Funds
were allocated to RPP cities and denied those controlled by the Justice
Party. Most of the unions of municipalities were created by cities with

RPP mayors, and these cities were the major beneficiaries of the funds allocated by the Ministry of Local Affairs for municipal unions. Because of the Ministry's close identification with the Republican People's Party and its big-city clientele, the new agency could not survive the loss of power by the RPP. When the JP took control of the national government in 1979 in coalition with two right-wing parties, the Ministry of Local Affairs was eliminated and more traditional channels were employed for the new government's dealings with its favored cities.

Close identification with the big cities posed problems as well as opportunities for the Republican People's Party. Many of the RPP's most vocal supporters in the urban centers were considerably to the left of the party's mainstream. One idea that generated controversy was the principle of "the producing municipality"—the city would expand its economic enterprises to include basic foodstuffs and other necessities, and thus become a primary producer for the benefit of society. As indicated above, this approach was backed by the Ministry of Local Affairs, which was very sympathetic to the ambitious goals of the RPP's radical reformers in large cities. A storm of protest came from small merchants who were well represented on RPP-controlled city councils, to the embarrassment of the party's national leadership.

Also unsettling was the radical rhetoric that emanated from a number of city halls controlled by the RPP. One mayor rejected the idea of city government as "a technical and administrative institution." Instead, he viewed the municipality as "a tool of class struggle." It should be "responsible for everything happening from one's childhood to his death." The primary task of city governments for this RPP mayor was "increasing the political consciousness of the citizens" rather than providing "roads, water, sewerage, and electricity."[26]

For the RPP's national leaders, social democracy in the cities had become too socialist and thus threatening to substantial elements of the party's electoral base. For all its endorsement of local autonomy and increased participation, the RPP remained a highly centralized political party able to deny nomination to local candidates who were out of favor at national headquarters. The Republican mayors of Ankara, Istanbul, and Izmit, all vocal advocates of more radical urban government, were defeated by more moderate candidates backed by RPP's national leaders in the party conventions that preceded the 1977 municipal elections.

Parties and City Politics

Under Turkish law, municipal governments are supposed to be apolitical. City councils are prohibited from involvement in partisan politics, nor can they express political preferences. Councils can be dissolved if they engage in political activity, and the mayor can be dismissed if he participates in political decision-making with the council.[27] In practice, however, city government in Turkey is suffused with partisanship, and the restrictions on political activity serve primarily to strengthen the hand of the central government in its dealings with cities, and particularly with cities controlled by the opposition. After all, a Minister of Interior is not likely to move to dismiss a local administration controlled by his party for partisan activity in the party's behalf.

Political considerations affect practically everything undertaken by municipal governments. Council members seek to advance party, constituency, and personal interests in their official activities and in their dealings with city agencies. Budgetary allocations for various functions and distribution of services to different sections of the city are strongly influenced by the needs and locations of party supporters. Party channels involve national legislators and party officials in city affairs. Political influence is particularly intense in zoning and land-use determinations, city-development planning, distribution of housing and gecekondu improvement funds, and municipal regulatory activity.

Party ties are also important in staffing city government. With rapid municipal expansion in the wake of urbanization came thousands of new positions to fill in the big cities, and the party faithful have had a strong claim to all kinds of jobs throughout city government. Political appointees to top posts have to be acceptable to the general headquarters of the mayor's party. Almost all assistant mayors have connections with the controlling party in a city, despite the fact that the position of assistant mayor was developed to provide increased professional assistance to the elected chief executive. And some assistant mayors have used their city position as a stepping stone to elected office.

POLITICAL DYNAMICS OF CITY-CENTER RELATIONS

Formally, city governments have no role in central determinations affecting municipalities. In the case of public services, individual ministries or the State Planning Organization decide on the priorities and technical standards for public services for every city and region. Informally, however, municipal leaders and community representatives are able to bring pressure to bear on the central government to secure a hospital, or water facilities, or a state factory for their city or neighborhood. The main channel for these pressures is the party organizations, and political considerations largely determine the receptivity of the center to pressures from the cities.

The degree to which local pressures succeed depends heavily on the number of potential votes that the party in power in Ankara expects to receive from the affected constituency. Responsiveness to demands for squatter improvements has been high because of the masses of gecekondu voters. Another major factor is the political party affiliation of the mayor and members of the council of the city in question. If they belong to the ruling party, or the party of the minister in a coalition government, their chances for success are much higher than for local officials affiliated with an opposition party.

City size also affects the success of local pressures. The central government turns away with difficulty the demands from the largest cities, whereas requests from smaller municipalities are more easily deflected. Responding to the large cities, however, is far more costly because their needs are proportionally greater than those of small communities. Most of the major urban centers are responsible for the performance of a much wider range of functions without having corresponding fiscal resources. To complete the circle, the scale of big-city needs intensifies pressures on the national government.

Complicating the political efforts of the major cities has been the lack of legal differentiation between large and small municipalities. Istanbul with its 4.4 million inhabitants and a municipality of 2,500 were subject to the same law, had identical sources of revenues, and performed similar functions. Yet many services that are not needed in smaller municipalities, or are performed by citizens through self-help schemes, require large expenditures in big cities. As a result, much of the political activity of the major urban centers has been aimed at overcoming the inequities inherent in a system that provided the same basic financial resources to all cities regardless of size.

In pressing Ankara for more resources, the large municipalities have insisted that the central government has special responsibilities for the rapidly growing metropolitan centers. Their pell-mell expansion, the cities argue, has resulted largely from central government policies affecting industrialization, settlement, and urbanization. Therefore, the mayors contend, the state had a responsibility to provide additional resources to the cities whose growth had been encouraged by national policies. In addition, the big cities pointed to the spread of urbanization beyond their boundaries, which forced them to provide urban services not only to their own inhabitants but also to the population of extensive metropolitan areas.

Growth of City Influence

Paralleling the growth of the major cities and the intensification of their needs has been the expansion of urban political capabilities in relations with the center. Although starved for resources and authority to deal with their problems, Istanbul, Ankara, and Izmir are politically important—representing sizable concentrations of voters and major aggregations of economic influence. The parties fought hard for support in the cities, promising benefits to city dwellers and paying more attention to urban leaders within their ranks. By the 1970s, as Göymen points out, "mayors of the major cities had begun to acquire considerable power and influence and were directly linked to the major political parties."[28]

As cities became more important politically, mayors intensified their demands on the central government. Municipal leaders wanted more assistance from Ankara, but they also demanded greater autonomy and resources, and, in the case of RPP mayors, wrapped their pleas for municipal independence in the rhetoric of participatory democracy and social justice. Adding to mayoral influence, particularly in Istanbul and Ankara, was the mayor's increasing visibility. Chief executives in the big cities attracted more and more attention in the national press, which was based in Istanbul and covered Ankara closely and was generally sympathetic toward the plight of the great cities. In addition, some of the mayors were good copy—Ankara's Mayor Vedat Dalokay in particular was able to dramatize his positions and his city's problems in ways that maximized press coverage. In 1975, Dalokay brought a bed to his office and went on a well-publicized three-day hunger strike to protest the failure of the central government to allocate funds to the city.

Mayors also sought to increase their influence in Ankara by organizing the cities for collective action. In 1974, the larger cities with RPP mayors broke away from the Turkish Municipal Association to form the Association of Progressive Municipalities (Devrimci Belediyeler Derneği), whose member cities encompassed 60 percent of the urban population. The new organization disbanded four years later, but in its place 11 municipal organizations were organized on a regional basis with the encouragement of Ecevit's Ministry of Local Affairs.[29] Almost 500 cities joined these unions of municipalities before they were disbanded by the military government.

City-Center Conflict

As city needs multiplied and their political influence increased, conflict between the major urban centers and the national government intensified. Under the centralized Turkish system, considerable conflict was inevitable—the central government monopolized authority and revenues, but was unable to muster the power or resources to satisfy a fraction of the cities' demands, which were articulated by mayors whose influence was growing and by national legislators whose urban constituencies were expanding. Tight central administrative and financial controls increased the likelihood of controversy, as did the steady expansion of central activities in the cities and the existence of great discretion in the distribution of central resources such as the Gecekondu Fund and the Joint Municipal Fund.

All these sources of friction were exacerbated by partisan differences. By the 1970s, constant conflict had become the normal state of affairs between the central government and cities ruled by the opposition party. With conservative coalitions in power in Ankara much of the decade, and RPP mayors in most of the major cities after the municipal elections in 1973, the stage was set for bitter struggles. Ecevit accused the Justice Party of embargoing cities that supported the RPP: "We protest against the foreign powers that put an embargo on arms sales to our country. But, now the government itself puts an embargo against the big cities. This embargo is against the Turkish nation. The Turkish people will not pardon this."[30]

Early in 1980, Ankara's Mayor Ali Dinçer delivered an impassioned indictment of the conservative government that expressed views widely held in city halls controlled by the RPP:

> We took over the administration of the municipality to be of service to the people of this city. We started very important projects like mass public transportation [and] large scale social housing. . . . What we want is to get the necessary funds to perform our services. In 1979, the people of Ankara, workers, civil servants, low income people paid taxes to the government. The city of Ankara got only 200 million lira out of it. What we want is to get back at least part of the taxes we have paid in order to provide modern services. . . . I am doing my best to render Ankara livable again; I contact the responsibles of the government every day. But I cannot get any result. It is the duty of the government not to condemn the people of Ankara to live every day in dirt, broken down sewerage canals and other unsatisfactory services and to ensure a comfortable environment. I want everyone to think about why the government does not comply with the rules of the game.[31]

From the other side, the fault lay with the cities and their irresponsible political leaders. According to a top figure in the JP, the Minister of Reconstruction and Settlement in the last government before the military intervention:

> Many municipalities, leaving aside the principal needs of the public, frequently come to Ankara to ask for funds. Cities that could not pay the salaries of their workers, attempt to open new roads and undertake big expropriations. Or you see that they build luxury gardens with pools

without meeting their water supply needs. Then, as workers begin to strike or to slow down the work . . . the State must help the cities. But the cities should give up unnecessary and expensive investments.[32]

In office, the Justice Party and its allies sought to penalize RPP cities in a variety of ways. And when the Republican People's Party was in control of the national government, it retaliated by favoring the RPP cities and punishing those ruled by the parties on the right. Under the conservatives in 1974, the Minister of Finance vetoed the applications of Istanbul, Ankara, and Izmir for financial assistance. As a result, municipal workers did not receive their wages as scheduled; and the long delays in issuing paychecks and rejection of demands for wage increases precipitated strikes in several city departments. Three years later, the RPP's Minister of Finance pardoned 15 billion lira in municipal debts, with the lion's share of the benefits going to cities under RPP control. And the RPP's new Ministry of Local Affairs proved particularly adept at allocating funds to cities with RPP administrations, neglecting those controlled by the opposition.

Perhaps the most dramatic partisan conflict was the effort in 1976 of the Minister of Interior in a conservative coalition dominated by the JP to fire Ankara's RPP mayor for alleged misuse of authority. According to the minister, the mayor made political speeches, erected a statue in a main square in defiance of the provincial governor, and incited municipal workers to strike, thus endangering public health because of the resulting piles of rubbish on the sidewalks. The minister's action, however, was nullified by the Council of State.[33]

Conflict also arises from the use of central tutelage controls to advance partisan interests. In 1975, the Minister of Energy in the conservative government refused to approve the decision of the Ankara Council increasing electricity prices. The minister claimed he did not want to see heavier burdens placed on Ankara's taxpayers; he also hoped to intensify the financial problems of Ankara's RPP administration, which would have to continue to subsidize electricity service out of its meager budget. During the same year, the Governor of Ankara, who was elected to the Senate on the JP ticket two years later, harassed the city government by turning down increases in park fees and higher rates for market stalls. Numerous other decisions of Ankara's mayor and council were opposed by the governor, leading the mayor to complain that "it is useless to have two heads for a city"—the RPP mayor and the JP's governor.[34]

Conflicts inspired by partisan differences originated in the cities as well as in the offices of the national government and its agents, and were as corrosive to intergovernmental relations as controversies that result from partisan motivations at the center. In 1976, Istanbul's RPP Mayor Ahmet

İsvan tried to prevent the connection of the new Sheraton Hotel with the municipal electric grid in order to disrupt the hotel's opening ceremony which featured the JP's leader, Prime Minister Süleyman Demirel. The year before, to the consternation of the conservative government, Mayor Dalokay of Ankara cut off municipal services to the Spanish embassy for a week in retaliation for the execution of Basque nationalists in Spain, which the mayor called a crime against humanity.[35]

The controversy over the Spanish embassy also was indicative of the structuring of city-center conflict along ideological lines in the late 1970s. Governments in the major cities were the main strongholds of the left in an increasingly polarized society, while conservatives held the central government through an alliance with right-wing extremists. Some city streets and parks were renamed for the left's martyrs in the terrorist violence that finally culminated in the military intervention of 1980. Like so many other aspects of Turkish political life, city-center relations eventually were paralyzed by partisan conflict that was unable to curb violent confrontation between the extremists of the right and left, confrontation which is examined in the concluding section of this chapter.

POLITICAL INTERESTS IN TURKISH CITIES

A wide variety of groups attempt to influence governmental policies that affect urban areas in Turkey. Because of the key role of political parties in the Turkish political system, much of this group activity is directed through party channels. Group influence is enhanced because party organizations provide access to elected officials and governmental agencies. Cultivating major groups by advancing their interests, in turn, provides the parties with opportunities to win support with substantial blocs of voters. To protect their interests, of course, groups have had to adjust their party connections in the face of shifting partisan fortunes, particularly the displacement of the Justice Party by the Republican People's Party in most of the larger cities. In this respect, urban groups have proved to be as pragmatic as most other participants in Turkish politics, and typically have pursued collective interests across party lines.

Merchants Associations

Associations or guilds of small merchants and craftsmen *(esnaf)* are perhaps the most influential interests in municipalities, and, not coincidentally, have had the closest party ties. These organizations are established under national law, which requires that all members of a particular trade or craft belong to the appropriate association. Nationally the various merchants associations have over two million members, and in the cities most of them are in the middle- and lower-middle-income groups. In the Ankara area, there were 60 associations in 1981 with almost 140,000 members, the largest being the Drivers Association with over 40,000 members.[36]

Merchants associations have three primary political goals—to limit competition, minimize government fees on their activities, and keep prices as high as possible. To advance these objectives, all of which are affected by municipal regulations, the associations have been extremely active in city politics.[37] Close links have been forged with local party organizations and city governments. Merchants associations usually are well represented in the highest local organs of the parties. At the same time, leaders of the associations depend on party support to maintain their positions, since without party backing an association cannot produce favorable governmental action for its members.

Among the political parties, the associations traditionally have had close relations with the Justice Party. Practical considerations dictated this alliance, since the JP was in power in most of the larger cities for many years. The conservative JP was also more in tune with the political and economic views of most small businessmen. But the pragmatic merchants associations were able to adjust to the resurgence of the Republican People's Party in the cities in the 1970s. As Weiker notes, the "instrumental rather than ideological character of this aspect of *esnaf* activity is reflected in the fact that as many local associations can sometimes be found affiliated with the RPP as with the right-wing parties."[38]

As a result of the intimate links between the merchants associations and the parties, these groups supply a substantial number of candidates for local office. One study indicated that half of the members of the municipal councils in Ankara, Izmit, Antalya, and Zonguldak were small businessmen and craftsmen.[39] From these strong bases in the council, small merchants usually are well represented on the Standing Committee and other municipal committees that deal with matters of vital concern to tradesmen. In Ankara, the chairman of the city council's Tariff and Regulation Committee in the 1970s was the vice-president of the marketplace workers' association, and he later became deputy mayor responsible for markets.

Through their ties with party organizations and representation on municipal councils, small business organizations have been extremely influential in ensuring that city fees and municipally fixed prices for various goods are acceptable to their members. For years, marketplace workers in Ankara and their well-placed leader were successful in blocking an increase in the rent charged by the city for space in the markets. As a result, rents were kept ridiculously low—.4 lira per square meter in 1980, or less than one cent for ten square feet. Only after the military intervention, and the subsequent dissolution of municipal councils, were the fees increased to a more reasonable 25 lira per square meter.

In seeking to advance their economic interests through the use of political influence, small merchants become involved in urban development issues. Associations have fought hard for public development of small industry zones to provide modern facilities for craftsmen, auto repair, and other trades. The largest of these small business groups, the Federation of the Drivers and Automobile Operators of Turkey, has a substantial impact on urban transportation policies. One of the drivers' component units, the Association of Taxi and Minibus Drivers, protects the interests of group taxi *(dolmuş)* operators and has opposed efforts to construct mass transportation systems in Ankara and Istanbul.

The drivers defend their interests vehemently and have backed up their demands with drastic actions. When the Interior Ministry decided to end special licensing for group taxis, thus reducing the value of the licenses purchased by dolmuş operators, the taxi and minibus drivers association successfully opposed the government's action. The drivers insisted "that not even the Prime Minister could effectuate" the new licensing policy, and that they "would not recognize the 'inconsiderate administration' in this respect."[40] In addition to the normal means of using political parties and government to advance their interests—the president of the national federation was twice elected to the National Assembly on the Justice Party ticket—the drivers have been willing to flex their economic muscles to advance their political interests. In 1970, all Turkey was tied up for two days by the drivers in a work stoppage in protest against proposed tax increases in draft municipal revenue legislation, and in 1975 all transportation was halted for one day.[41]

Other Economic Interests

Other economic interests are less directly involved with municipal governments than are the small merchants, but they are concerned with issues of urban growth, city services, and taxes. Major economic interests in the cities benefit from the centralized political system, since they "are able to demand the attention of a centralized government."[42] Business associations and organized landowners generally have opposed governmental intervention in urban housing and land markets. These interests also have pressed Parliament to squelch attempts to increase property taxes. Influential landowners have enjoyed great success in securing favorable actions from local councils and from the central government. Landowners won a major victory in 1963 when their efforts resulted in the Constitutional Court's invalidating the provision of the City Development

Law that permitted municipalities to take 25 percent of the land in the city without indemnity.[43] Pressures from landowners were instrumental in the enactment of legislation in 1954 that permitted ownership of individual apartments, and in 1965 that authorized condominiums. In each instance, more intensive residential development was made possible, thus increasing the value of urban land holdings. Low property tax rates and self-assessment procedures also reflect the political influence of landowners.

Business interests in particular cities are brought together in chambers of commerce and industry. All commercial and industrial employers with 10 or more employees must belong to these semiofficial bodies, which are joined into the national Union of Chambers of Commerce and Industry and Commodity Exchanges.[44] Chambers have been involved in planning industrial parks, and usually have enthusiastically supported more development. In the Istanbul area, however, chambers of commerce have opposed further growth because overcrowding makes the operation of industrial enterprises more costly, more difficult, and less productive. As a result, industrial interests backed the deconcentration of population within the Marmara region, and cooperated in the 1960s with the Istanbul Metropolitan Planning Bureau in the preparation of a plan designed to curb future migration to the area.

Labor Unions

Aside from municipal employees, labor has not played a major role in urban politics in Turkey. Unions have been strongest among more skilled workers in large factories; as a result, they primarily have defended the interests of the better-paid members of the working class and been little concerned with the urban poor, who rarely belong to trade unions. Perhaps the main urban priority of the unions has been housing policy. Unions generally have supported central intervention in local housing and land markets to increase the supply of housing for workers. They have sought to expand the limited housing programs initiated by the government and to increase interest in worker housing on the part of city government. The unions also have pressed the central government to overhaul cumbersome lending procedures in housing programs and increase the amount of funding allocated per worker. And without much effect, they have complained about the deleterious impact of land speculation and inflated construction costs on the production of worker housing under government programs.

Defense of the interests of their members also has led unions to oppose some housing and land programs developed by the central government. In 1963, unions protested against limitations on the maximum floor space for social housing, which was designed to increase the number of units constructed with the same amount of investment. A few years later, unions refused to pay their share of the national fund to improve squatter settlements on the ground that union members should not shoulder this burden because they did not live in gecekondus. The union effort to avoid contributing to the squatters fund was successful, and the contested provision of the gecekondu law was eventually annulled by the Constitutional Court.

Labor unions became increasingly active in city politics in the 1970s, as some union leaders saw local influence as a means of increasing labor's power at the national level. Political and economic demands were mixed in wage negotiations, demonstrations, job actions, and strikes. Unions joined RPP officials in efforts to expand the role of city governments in the production of basic goods and services. In Ankara, unions played a leading role in the creation of Kent-Koop, a housing cooperative that worked closely with the municipal administration in developing a new town for 300,000 people.

Municipal Employees

Rapid urbanization steadily enlarged the municipal work force in Turkey; in the process city employees became increasingly influential participants in urban politics, able to claim a steadily growing share of city revenues and to disrupt the operations of municipal government through strikes and slowdowns. Between 1950 and 1980, municipal employment increased almost sevenfold, from 18,000 to 120,000. About one-sixth of the municipal employees in 1980 were civil servants, whose salaries were set by national law; the remaining 100,000 were workers whose wages were determined by collective bargaining.

Urban growth increased municipal employment in two ways. First, the tasks and size of city government were expanded. Second, rapid urbanization generated large amounts of surplus labor in the cities, creating strong pressures on municipalities to expand employment. More municipal jobs were attractive to the major political parties—as a means of attracting votes, rewarding supporters, and reducing the appeal of radical political movements that sought to capitalize on urban unemployment. Especially after 1974, when the Turkish economy began to experience increasing problems, municipal employment increased greatly, more than doubling during the 1970s, as indicated in Table 5-6.

The pell-mell expansion of municipal work forces far exceeded the cities' financial capacity, which added to their money woes, intensified urban demands for more funds from the central government, and led to increasingly disruptive labor actions by municipal employees. Complicating the problem for the cities was the growing power of labor unions,

TABLE 5-6

MUNICIPAL EMPLOYMENT: 1950-1980

	Civil Servants	Workers	Total
1950	5,977	11,983	17,960
1959	9,199	27,794	36,993
1965	11,364	31,822	43,186
1970	14,093	39,025	53,118
1980	20,000	100,000	120,000

SOURCE: Fehmi Yavuz, *Türk Mahallî İdarelerinin Yeniden Düzenlenmesi Üzerinde Bir Araştırma* (Ankara: Türkiye ve Orta Doğu Amme İdaresi Enstitüsü, 1966), p. 117; and Ergun Türkcan, ed., *Belediye İşlevlerine Nicel bir Yaklaşım* (Ankara: Türk İdareciler Derneği, 1981), p. 115.

which organized municipal workers, whose efforts won substantial wage increases every two years. As personnel expenditures consumed more and more of municipal budgets, cities were unable to meet their payrolls. In 1975, Istanbul's total revenues were 844 million lira, while its personnel costs were 944 million lira. Unpaid workers protested through job actions and strikes. By the late 1970s, labor conditions in Turkey's cities were chaotic and municipal government was often at a standstill. Between 1977 and 1980, there were 62 strikes of city workers, compared with only 27 in the previous decade.[45]

Worsening municipal labor problems were quickly caught up in the bitter partisan conflict between RPP-controlled cities and conservative governments in Ankara. Mayors blamed the national government for failing to provide the resources needed to pay city workers. Eager to retain the political support of city employees and their unions, mayors openly endorsed the strikes against their cities. Diyarbakır's mayor publicly supported "the just struggle of the workers," while the mayor of Izmir declared that "I cannot defend any practice that would break the strikes of my workers even though it is against me."[46] For Ankara's mayor, the struggle was not between the city and its employees, but between the city and the central government. "Workers slowing down the work are not against the mayor, but they are against the government that insists in penalizing the RPP municipalities."[47]

In the end, there were no winners in the municipal labor struggles spawned by rapid urbanization, expanding city employment, empty exchequers, and the unremitting search for partisan advantage. Municipal services, inadequate at best, were constantly interrupted by labor disputes that left trash uncollected and buses not operating. City-center conflict was intensified and further politicized. For every urban claim that

conservative central officials were responsible for municipal labor problems, the Justice Party and its allies accused RPP mayors of hiring
superfluous employees and of using municipal jobs to reward loyal party
members. Municipal workers exercised increasing influence in the cities,
but at the cost of alienating other interests because of their disruptive
tactics and their identification with highly partisan politics and radical
trade unionists.

The Middle Class

Outside the sprawling squatter settlements, urban dwellers in Turkey
rarely are organized along communal or other lines to advance their political interests. In one sense, the urban middle class has not needed to
organize to secure benefits. Until recently, government identified closely
with middle-class values and needs, and most urban public resources
were devoted to providing services to middle-class neighborhoods. Before 1950, the middle class clearly was dominant in Turkish cities, and
well into the period of rapid urbanization, middle-class ideals and
priorities strongly influenced governmental actions, which were carried
out by officials who themselves were stalwarts of the urban middle class.

But the position of the middle class has been steadily eroded by the
massive influx of migrants. For established city dwellers, the newcomers
were a blight that undermined the quality of life in *their* cities. They
regarded migration as "a peasant invasion . . . complaining about the
disappearance of city manners and of privacy."[48] Migrants were blamed
for crowded public facilities, traffic congestion, and urban blight; the
newcomers were readily associated with crime, prostitution, and drugs.
The spreading gecekondus were widely seen as a menace—ugly, threatening to public health, contemptuous of private property and the law, and a
breeding ground for violence and revolution. Conflict was intensified as
middle-class families moved outward in the spreading metropolis where
new conventional housing often adjoined squatter settlements. Many in
the middle class supported stern measures to check migration, prevent
the establishment of gecekondus, tear down existing squatter settlements,
and return squatters to their villages.

During the early years of the massive migration, government was responsive to middle-class grumblings about the newcomers. Efforts were
made to deter migrants, demolish gecekondus, and relocate squatters who
had settled in the path of middle-class housing. These attempts, however,
were largely ineffective, overwhelmed by the sheer numbers of migrants
and their growing political and economic influence. Numbers count, especially in a democracy with highly competitive political parties, and the
middle class lost the numbers game in Turkey's urban centers. Both major

parties competed energetically for support from the urban newcomers, which foreclosed the emergence of either a middle-class party in the cities or partisan cleavage along established resident-newcomer lines.

By the 1970s, middle-class urban dwellers had become a diminishing minority in Ankara and Istanbul. Elected officials depended less and less on middle-class support. Government priorities shifted to improving services in squatter settlements, regardless of the mayor's political party. Public rhetoric was even more skewed toward the needs of the poor, and became increasingly radical and inflammatory as the cities moved sharply to the left. At the end of the decade, it had become politically and ideologically impossible to express public discontent about migrants and gecekondus. Resentment smoldered in the established neighborhoods, but the middle class remained politically passive, with no politicians eager to champion the interests of a group with a declining share of the vote, and whose members remained much better off than the urban masses.[49]

Despite their general lack of political articulation, middle-class city dwellers have organized when they have perceived specific needs, as in the case of rent control. Rising housing costs have prompted the organization of tenants' associations in the major cities, which have pressed for the revival of rent control. Rents were controlled between 1939 and 1963, a reflection of the responsiveness of the political system to the urban middle class in the pre-squatter period. Recent efforts to restore rent controls have been successfully opposed by landlords, who wield more political clout than their tenants.

Squatters

Unlike the middle class, squatters have organized effectively for political action. Government has been much more important to squatters than to established city dwellers. Public officials held the keys to survival of squatter communities, to title to gecekondu dwellings, and to desperately needed municipal services. Karpat's survey of residents of the Hisarüstü, Baltalımanı, and Celâlettin Paşa squatter settlements in Istanbul indicated that "politics occupied a central place in all facets of gecekondu life. The migration from the village, the establishment of the settlement, employment problems, the use of city amenities, such as electricity, water and transportation, and a variety of other problems were all related to and solved through politics."[50] To advance their political interests, squatters created neighborhood associations, traded community support at the polls for benefits, joined political parties and worked in campaigns, elected their own kind to local office as their numbers increased, and otherwise sought to capitalize on the political potential represented by masses of voters concentrated in gecekondus.

Group solidarity tends to be high in gecekondu areas, with large numbers of people having shared political objectives, which facilitates collective action despite the meager resources of most squatters. Family and village ties were strong, as relatives and friends clustered together for mutual assistance and protection. Survival of the settlement was the common goal, and survival "depended above all on the inhabitants' solidarity, organizational skill, and concerted action."[51] Relatives, friends, and neighbors worked together building one another's houses, and developing primitive public facilities. Solidarity was reinforced by the hostility of officials and established city dwellers, particularly during the initial stages of gecekondu development when squatters counted for little politically.

Neighborhood associations, organized under the same national law as merchants associations, provided an important instrument for political action in gecekondus. Ostensibly created to improve the physical appearance of the settlement and serving as social and community centers for their members, these societies for settlement improvement (*Gecekonduyu Güzelleştirme Derneği,* literally, gecekondu beautification associations) became vital links between gecekondu dwellers and the political parties, local authorities, and central government. Their political objectives were governmental recognition of their communities, provision of public services, and legalization of individual dwellings through the granting of a land deed, or *tapu.* In addition, the gecekondu associations provided opportunities for indigenous leaders to emerge from the squatter community, "a new type of leadership . . . based not on the previous religious, tribal or communal authority held in the village of origin, but chiefly on organizational skill and ability to present and defend the interests of the settlement in political and administrative circles."[52]

The principal political resource of the gecekondu associations was the votes of their members. But for this resource to be effective, gecekondu leaders had to be able to deliver blocs of votes behind the favored party or candidate. "The problem of voting in a united front was relatively more important in local than national elections: water, electricity, sewage, and other amenities needed by the *gecekondus* could only be provided by the local government."[53] Building on group solidarity and common interests, as well as the deference that most squatters paid their leaders, gecekondu associations forged blocs of voters—in pursuit of goals both for a particular settlement and for more general objectives shared by members across the city or nation—that impressed elected politicians. As migrants continued to pour into the cities, the squatter vote steadily grew, further increasing the influence of the gecekondu organizations. From this enlarging political base, gecekondu leaders bargained with municipal leaders for public utilities, street improvements, bus service, schools, and other community facilities. And the increasingly impressive political clout of squatters brought from the central government increased funding for gecekondus, and, more important, legalization of the homesites of hundreds of thousands of squatters.

A key pressure point for improving local services was the elected *muhtar,* the head of the official neighborhood or precinct organization, the *mahalle,* and the main channel between communities and city hall and the provincial administration. Because of the limited size of the mahalles and the geographic concentration of squatters, gecekondu dwellers quickly constituted substantial or controlling blocs of voters. Muhtars and candidates in mahalle elections in squatter areas were responsive to this new political force in their midst, or were retired from political life.

Inevitably, as their numbers grew, politically cohesive squatters took control of mahalles away from more established settlers, and were able to serve gecekondu interests more directly. Karpat describes the poignant outcome of one such transition in an Istanbul mahalle, and underscores the role of political skill in advancing squatters into the mainstream of Turkish urban life:

> The seat of the *muhtarlık,* a one-room office, was located now in the squatter settlement. As though paying homage to the victor, the established residents of the old district of Rumelihisar grudgingly climbed the hill to see the new *muhtar* in the *gecekondu.* . . . There was no doubt that power in Rumelihisar was in the hands of the *gecekondu* dwellers. They had come a long way. Though ignored and despised by the old Rumelihisar residents, they established a firm foothold in the area; and then gradually manipulating the political apparatus, they captured the chief political office in the district. They called themselves now not *gecekondu* dwellers, but residents of Rumelihisar in Istanbul.[54]

Despite their impressive solidarity and political gains, squatters did not constitute a monolithic force in urban politics. Substantial numbers of newcomers did not follow the majority in supporting the Democrats and then the Justice Party during the first two decades of accelerated urban growth, and the RPP in the 1970s. Many squatters had little to do with gecekondu associations or other political activities. In one Istanbul gecekondu,

> an Association for Settlement Improvement . . . was first established in 1964 but did not continue for very long. It started again in 1973. Its professed purpose is to act as a pressure group to protect the property, develop the community, and to secure the basic urban facilities. The residents do not know or understand what the Association is trying to do. They feel the Association has done no harm, but has not shown any great activity to further their well-being either.[55]

Nor was the political mobilization of squatter interests without its seamier side. Those with political connections in gecekondus often used their influence for personal gain. Land was grabbed from other settlers with the blessing of local officials. Public services were secured for plots that could be rented or sold at considerable profit. And squatters who did not buy land from these influential profiteers ran the risk of having their homes demolished by the city. Squatters also found that political promises frequently were not kept, and that bribes were necessary to keep police and other local officials at bay. In Istanbul's Rumelihisarüstü gecekondu, squatters "were given false hopes and information. Especially for political benefits, they were given promises but did not have them fulfilled. Also, on several occasions the squatters had to pay bribes to the minicipal agents and police officials."[56]

THE CHANGING URBAN ORDER

Rapid urbanization, as the preceding pages emphasize, has had far-reaching implications for political life in Turkey. Parties and elected politicians have become increasingly oriented toward cities and their voters. Mayors developed substantial political influence as cities grew, as did the multiplying ranks of city merchants, municipal employees, and squatters. Urban growth added new lines of cleavage to Turkish politics—between cities and the central government, between Republican mayors and conservative governments, and between established city dwellers and the hordes of urban newcomers.

Sweeping urban change, however, has not been for the most part accompanied by intense social and political conflict in Turkey. Massive migration to the cities did not create a large *lumpenproletariat* alienated from the rest of society, easily radicalized, and prone to disruptive political behavior, as anticipated by many observers during the 1960s. In Ankara's gecekondus, Malcolm Rivkin saw a "concentrated urban mass . . . physically close to the center of national power [becoming] a tinderbox."[57] Lucien Pye argued that discontented and unemployed migrants in rapidly urbanizing nations had "become in a sense loaded revolvers pointed at the responsible government and on the verge of being triggered off at the slightest provocation."[58] After closely examining gecekondu development, Granville Sewell concluded in 1966 that "a crisis seems inevitable as frustrations, hostility, and proximity heighten. The existing socio-political framework can be maintained only until resources and tempers reach a critical state, then there will be a change, perhaps accompanied by a radical shift to the political left or right."[59] Turkish officials and commentators were particularly fearful that the gecekondus would be breeding grounds for the radical left.

These apocalyptic visions have not materialized in Turkey, in the sense of widespread class warfare in the cities. To be sure, violent clashes have periodically erupted in gecekondus. One of the most severe occurred in 1974, when "the municipal authorities in Istanbul sent out destruction teams, provoking a violent demonstration of residents armed with crude weapons." The confrontation "awoke memories of the bloody insurrec-tions which had marked the close of the Ottoman empire and the estab-lishment of Kemalist authority. But more frightening was the potential association of this . . . rebellion with the communist movement."[60] In Istanbul and elsewhere, however, squatters were seeking acceptance of their settlements, not revolutionary change or the overthrow of the gov-ernment.

Turkey's experience supports the generalization that no automatic link exists between massive influxes of poor migrants into cities and political destabilization.[61] For two decades, sweeping urban change produced a pragmatic politics of assimilation. In the 1970s, however, politics became increasingly polarized in Turkish cities. Conflicts intensified, radical groups on the left and the right attracted substantial followings, and vio-lence wreaked havoc with urban life. Although cleavage did not occur primarily along the have–have not lines foreseen by some, discontent among the urban poor played a part in the politics of disorder that charac-terized Turkish cities in the years preceding the military intervention of 1980.

The Politics of Assimilation

Most of the villagers who flocked to Turkish cities after 1950 were not attracted to radical politics because they were able to extract substantial benefits from the existing political and economic system. Traditional ma-chine politics—organizing blocs of voters for collective benefits—was a more realistic approach to their immediate needs than riots and class warfare. The migrants were pragmatic and upwardly mobile rather than desperate revolutionaries—they came to the city to share its economic, social, and political benefits, not overthrow the regime. They wanted to improve and own their homes, and prudently avoided disruptive political activity that might jeopardize their hard-earned gecekondu investment. Moreover, government, the state, the *devlet baba,* was their benefactor, not their enemy. They were far more likely to repeat the saying *Allah devlete zeval vermesin*—"may God preserve the state" than shout revolu-tionary slogans.[62]

Far from constituting the rootless and atomized mass, as pictured in some visions of the urban *lumpenproletariat* in developing countries, migrants to Turkish cities established a variety of connections. As pointed out above, family, village, and friendship ties were strong among urban newcomers. Squatters joined political parties and worked in campaigns. Gecekondu associations served as an important focal point of social and political life, and their development, as Özbudun points out, "undercut the assumptions of anomie and social disorganization among urban migrants and indicate a relatively successful adaptation to the urban setting."[63]

Politics itself was an integrating force. Democracy not only provided the swelling ranks of urban newcomers with a means to extract benefits from government, but also made the migrants participants in the political system, and as their influence grew so did their vested interests in the existing arrangements. As a result, politics "played a major role in speeding the squatters' integration into the city by sharpening their consciousness of self, place and role in society. It also increased their communication with city and national party leaders."[64]

A critical element of this politics of assimilation, as pointed out in Chapter 2, was economic expansion in the cities. Rapid economic growth absorbed most of the migrants, even though many were employed in marginal service occupations. An expanding urban economy also provided the political system with resources to respond to the demands of squatters for improved services and public facilities. And by generating opportunities for the newcomers in the mushrooming cities, the broadening economic base deflected demands for radical change.

Assimilation, of course, is a process of change, and the assimilated are changed by the experience. As migrants were integrated into urban society, their political perspectives and objectives broadened. "With further modernization," as Özbudun emphasizes, "the urban poor become more responsive to sector inducements and more inclined to engage in class-based political participation."[65] One result, as noted earlier, was the shift of migrants away from the Justice Party toward the Republic People's Party, a shift from instrumental voting designed to secure immediate benefits from the party in power to support for the party that promised more substantial change in Turkish society.

Escalating demands were increasingly difficult to satisfy by doling out street improvements and connections to city water lines, particularly as the numbers of squatters mounted faster than city economies could grow. Newer migrants were less easily incorporated into the urban political economy than earlier arrivals. At the same time, a new generation was coming of age in the gecekondus—second-generation urban dwellers who were better educated and less passive politically than their elders. As the Turkish economy faltered in the 1970s, the politics of assimilation was severely strained, particularly for the impatient younger gecekondu dwellers and for the newest arrivals who found footholds harder to secure in the city.

The Politics of Disorder

Deteriorating prospects for urban newcomers was only one element in a complex set of changes that were at work in Turkey and its cities in the 1970s. "Increasing politicization and participation, coupled with more egalitarian policies and a falling rate of economic development," observes Özbudun, led "to increasing polarization, social strife, and political violence."[66] Urban violence initially erupted in the late 1960s, but the combatants were mostly left-wing students and their adversaries on the radical right rather than gecekondu dwellers. Armed conflict in the cities between groups such as the Turkish People's Liberation Army and the Grey Wolf commandos on the far right, along with intensifying economic problems, precipitated the military intervention of 1971.

As the 1970s unrolled, politics became increasingly polarized, especially in the cities, and extremist violence caught more and more urban Turks in its deadly crossfire. As indicated above, most of the major cities came under control of the Republican People's Party, which intensified city-center conflict when the right controlled the national government, as it did during much of the decade. The Justice Party was forced to the right by the need to forge coalitions with the religious National Salvation Party and the fascist National Action Party. Conflict escalated and violence spread, as central officials looked the other way when urban commandos affiliated with the National Action Party attacked radicals on the left.

By the late 1970s, Turkish cities were being racked by increasingly violent confrontations between the extreme left and the far right. For the most part, these clashes were rooted in political and ideological conflict between the left and the right, conflict that was exacerbated by worsening economic woes and the social strains occasioned by rapid urbanization. By and large, violence did not originate in squatter areas, but spread to the gecekondus, fueled by discontent with rising unemployment and unsatisfactory living conditions. Squatters were caught up in the increasingly deadly conflicts, which claimed over 3,600 lives between 1978 and 1980, but so were almost all other strata of society—politicians, public employees, workers, students, university professors. In the increasingly polarized cities, lower-level police officers, many of whom lived in gecekondus, joined right- and left-wing police associations that afforded protection to like-minded groups, contributing to the breakdown of law and order.

Conflict between extremists on the left and right spilled into squatter

TABLE 5-7
VIOLENCE AND SOCIOECONOMIC CHANGE: 1974–1980

	1974	1975	1976	1977	1978	1979	1980
Persons killed	27	37	108	319	1,095	1,362	2,206
Economic growth rate	7.4	8.0	7.7	4.0	3.6	1.5	−0.6
Exchange rate in US dollars	14	15	17	19	25	47	87
Wholesale price index	100	34	52	81	176	214	359
Unemployment index	100	114	142	141	167	174	186

SOURCE: Ruşen Keleş and Artun Ünsal, *Kent ve Siyasal Şiddet* (Ankara: Siyasal Bilgiler Fakültesi, 1982), p. 22.

settlements in all the major cities in the late 1970s. Gecekondus were divided between armed leftist and rightist bands, and were known as "liberated quarters." Squatter areas caught up in this deadly conflict usually were newer and self-contained districts where unemployment was high and public services meager. As the Governor of Istanbul emphasized, "There is an authority gap in newly formed gecekondu areas, since it takes quite a long time to establish local governments there."[67] Conflict also was exacerbated by the proximity of different income groups. Almost 60 percent of the violent actions in Istanbul between 1975 and 1979 were in gecekondu districts adjacent to middle- and upper-class housing development.[68]

Rapidly escalating internal war brought down democratic government in Turkey in 1980, as the military intervened to restore order, particularly in the violence-racked cities. Turkey's political parties were swept away, along with elected officials at all levels of government. Democratic politics were suspended, but most of the political conflicts that have come with rapid urbanization were bound to reemerge in the 1980s.

6
PROVIDING URBAN SERVICES

In rapidly urbanizing societies, provision of public services is largely reactive. Migrants crowd into the city, urbanization spreads outward, shops and factories cluster in various patterns, and government struggles to supply essential services. Provision of water and roads in response to growth triggers further expansion in adjacent areas, generating demands for extending water lines farther, or improving roads to housing or factories. Squatters complicate the problem, since they locate in areas often difficult to service because of terrain and drainage problems. Moreover, squatters by definition are not constrained by development controls which can be used to ensure that new settlement will be adequately serviced.

Turkey provides a classic case of the impact of rapid urbanization on public services. Three decades of accelerated city growth overwhelmed the urban public sector in Turkey. No major public service has kept pace with the enormous increase in urban population or the territorial expansion of cities. Water supply, sewage disposal, drainage, electrical power, streets, public transport, health facilities, and schools are seriously deficient in every city. Pollutants foul the air and water of most Turkish cities. Ankara has one of the worst air pollution problems in the world—"pollution exceeds U.S. standards for a safe concentration 75 percent of the time."[1] The coastal waters around Istanbul are increasingly polluted by industrial wastes and inadequately treated sewage. To the east of Istanbul, more than 120 industrial plants in and around the rapidly growing city

133

of Izmit dump their wastes into the Sea of Marmara, producing pollution of "alarming proportions."[2]

For more than thirty years, Turkey has been displacing and deferring the public costs of urban development—in effect, urbanizing beyond its means in an effort to reap the benefits of modernization. The cost has been high—in terms of unfulfilled basic needs, poisoned air and water, and lost opportunities to shape the future through the development of city infrastructure in advance of development.

To be sure, government in Turkey has recognized the potential in using water and sewer lines, transport investment, and construction of schools and other facilities as a means of controlling urban development. The Third Five-Year Plan, which covered the period 1973–1977, sought to use "infrastructure investments . . . as a means of stimulating and directing . . . city expansion areas."[3] But shaping settlement patterns with public services requires considerable skill at concentrating resources. In Turkey, government generally has been unable to muster the resources, free itself from constituency pressures, control land effectively, or enforce its plans. As a result, public services rarely have been provided in advance of development. Nor has the absence of public services had much impact on settlement patterns, since the construction of illegal housing has spread urbanization without regard to the availability of water lines, sewers, roads, or schools.

By and large, then, city services have followed urbanization, usually inadequately provided and heavily skewed in favor of higher-income areas. Exceptions exist—instances where public services or facilities have influenced settlement. One striking example is the great bridge across the Bosphorus in Istanbul. Another is the role of public service provision in speeding the integration of gecekondus into the city, thus reducing their isolation and enhancing their attractions. Inadequate public services also stimulate nongovernmental activities that can influence urbanization. Communal development of public facilities and services in squatter settlements is one such response. Group taxi service falls into the same category—in this case reflecting the failure of regular public transportation to meet the needs of burgeoning urban populations, large numbers of whom were low-income squatters living in isolated locations.

Efforts to provide urban services in Turkey have been shaped by the governmental system and political factors that have been examined in the past two chapters. Highly centralized government denies cities the power, resources, and flexibility to meet their legal obligations to provide public services. Inadequate resources handicap efforts by governments at all levels to supply urban services and make the tasks of the larger cities impossible. Central agencies have assumed a variety of urban service responsibilities, and in the process further complicated the governmental mosaic in metropolitan areas. Political considerations strongly influence the distribution of central resources among cities and their allocation among functions. Often intense pressures from elected officials, economic interests, municipal employees, and squatters affect decisions concerning service extensions and improvements, the location of facilities, rates for public services, and regulations affecting private providers of essential city services.

Urbanization not only increases needs for public services, but also amplifies demands for improvements. After making the transition from village to city and establishing themselves in squatter settlements, urban newcomers have been unwilling to settle for rudimentary municipal services. Life in the city with its mobility and mass communications heightens awareness of the unequitable distribution of public goods and services among different income groups. With raised consciousness comes more assertiveness. The urban newcomer, as Ankara's Mayor Vedat Dalokay emphasized in 1977, "sees it is his right to demand something from the state, and he is using that right."[4] More migrants meant more votes, which put more political muscle behind increasingly insistent demands for schools, better health care, regular municipal services, and more convenient transportation. In essence, the political changes produced by rapid urbanization steadily undermined Turkey's ability to defer the public costs of urban development, but these political changes did not result in a corresponding increase in governmental capacity to provide public services.

ADEQUACY OF CITY SERVICES

By almost any measure, basic urban services fall short of minimal needs in all Turkey's major cities. In 1975, 52 percent of all urban households lacked running water, and 43 percent were without electricity.[5] Ankara, the planned national capital, is able to provide regular water service to only 70 percent of its population, and roughly the same proportion of households is served in Istanbul, Izmir, and Bursa.[6] In Ankara and Istanbul, as well as in other major cities, water frequently is not available around the clock. In 1977, 38 percent of all public water systems were rated unsatisfactory in terms of bacterial contamination, and 12 percent in terms of chemical contaminants.[7] Only 20 percent of the urban population was connected to sewers in 1977, and most wastes were not adequately treated before being dumped into rivers or the sea. Little space has been acquired in most cities for parks and recreational areas, schools and health facilities are overcrowded, roads and highways are badly congested, and public transportation is woefully inadequate.

At the heart of most of these problems is lack of resources in the face of rapid population growth. Consider the interplay of expanding needs and limited resources in the case of garbage collection in the major cities:

> As a result of . . . increased housing and population density . . . keeping cities clean became an independent organizational problem. The number of large municipalities that are able to provide garbage collection services is practically zero in Turkey. . . . Trash is collected in open bags and left in open places, often on the streets where children play. . . . Especially in gecekondu areas remote from city centers, the residents' health is vulnerable to this hazard because garbage is so rarely collected.[8]

In 1976, Ankara could muster only 400 lira per capita for urban services, barely half the 750 lira per person that the city government estimated was needed.[9] Cities have been particularly squeezed for capital investments in expanding and rehabilitating infrastructure. Public investments in water supply and electrification, almost all of which came from the central government, accounted for 7.4 percent of all public investments in 1975; by 1980 they had dropped to 3.3 percent.[10] As the State Planning Organization noted in 1981: "Since the limited financial resources allocated to these costly capital investments are far from being sufficient enough, the infrastructure deficit tends to grow at increasing rates every year."[11] A study of Istanbul's capabilities concluded in 1978 that the municipality would be "hard pressed . . . to effect much if any investment spending at all, even by way of rehabilitation of existing roads, sewers, and so on."[12]

Service provision is also hindered because trained personnel are in short supply throughout urban Turkey. At all levels of government, personnel "are either insufficient in number or inadequately trained. Most of the large cities lack qualified personnel trained in technical fields and urban management."[13] Cities have difficulty attracting talented and technically qualified individuals because of low salaries and rigid promotion policies, both of which are established for all cities by the central government. Istanbul's municipal government, notes one report, is "severely handicapped . . . by the level of rewards in the official pay scales, which have fallen well behind that of comparable groups [and] by the inflexibility of the official staff structure, which puts severe hindrances in the way of equating rewards to responsibilities and effecting adjustments in establishments to meet changing needs."[14] Partisan considerations in staffing city government further reduce the number of able managers and specialists in city government. And the political power of municipal employees reduces the efficient utilization of personnel in the provision of services.

DISTRIBUTION OF URBAN SERVICES

Aggregate data on city services conceal the wide gap in the services available to the components of Turkey's dual urban society. In all the major cities, public services are concentrated in established areas, the neighborhoods with conventional housing and higher-income residents. Clark distinguishes between what he calls the "planned" and "unplanned" areas of Ankara:

> In planned areas streets are laid out in a regular pattern and are designed to carry motor transport; housing is of modern construction . . . ; and these areas always have city water, sewage and electricity. Unplanned areas, in contrast, are those containing squatter settlements . . . or old traditional style housing. . . . Streets are often just irregular lanes between the houses, and city services are introduced only after considerable settlement has taken place.[15]

Lack of Services in Squatter Settlements

Squatter settlements begin their existence with a weak claim on public services. They are created illegally on land belonging to someone else or to the state. At the outset of rapid urban growth, city governments were under no obligation to provide services to gecekondus, and remained reluctant to divert scarce resources until forced to respond by the squatters' growing political influence. More established urban dwellers resisted the extension of local services to gecekondus, strongly preferring to have limited public resources invested in their own districts.

In addition to these legal, financial, and political constraints, development of public services in squatter settlements was inhibited by topographical and jurisdictional considerations, as well as by the sheer scale of the squatter population and its needs. Gecekondus often were located on very marginal sites—hillsides, gullies, and areas subject to flooding—all conditions that made road building, drainage, and installation of utility lines difficult and expensive, especially after housing was illegally constructed with little thought to provision of utilities. Extension of municipal services also was inhibited by location of gecekondus on the city's periphery or beyond municipal boundaries. Distant locations are expensive to serve with water, sewers, and electrical lines. And the establishment of settlements outside city limits often placed squatters in local jurisdictions that were unable to provide municipal services.

Most important of all was the sheer scale of the squatter population and its needs. Between 1945 and 1980, an average of almost 27,000 gecekondus were built annually, housing 135,000 people. Thus, a city the size of Venice or Little Rock was being added each year, a city of overcrowded jerry-built houses on marginal sites with no thought given to public service provision in its development—and a city full of poor people who could not begin to generate tax revenues to cover the cost of needed public services. Regardless of the other complications, meeting the basic service needs of this unending flow of newcomers was beyond the capability of the Turkish political system. Even though political pressures from organized squatters soon led to service improvements in gecekondus, striking disparities continued to exist in access to basic urban services in all Turkey's major cities.

Two decades into the great exodus to the cities, the Ministry of Reconstruction estimated that 49 percent of all squatter housing lacked running water, 52 percent were without electricity, and 60 percent had no sewage disposal.[16] Poor sanitation and inadequate public health efforts resulted in higher disease rates in squatter areas than in better-off districts. In 1966, infectious diseases were more than twice as common in a typical gecekondu in Istanbul than in the city as a whole, and 60 squatters died of cholera in Istanbul's Sağmalcılar gecekondu in 1970.

Other facilities and services were woefully inadequate in most squatter areas. Streets were ungraded rutted paths of packed earth, easily eroded and often impassable after rain, and at night, unlit and dangerous. Gecekondus did not receive regular police protection. Only 49 primary schools were available to serve Ankara's vast gecekondu population in 1966, less than one-fifth of the estimated need.[17] Because schools were often far from squatter neighborhoods and across busy thoroughfares, travel for school children was frequently unsafe. Bus service rarely met the needs of gecekondu dwellers, forcing them into more expensive group taxis and increasing their isolation from the rest of the city. Parks and recreational facilities were nonexistent, as were community centers and welfare services.

The contrasts in city services between established neighborhoods and gecekondus were painfully apparent to squatters as they crisscrossed the metropolis on their way to jobs, schools, and shops. Many had to look no farther than out their windows to see how the other half lived. "It is difficult to understand how the squatters could have tolerated their misery when just across the street there was both water and electricity," writes Karpat of an Istanbul gecekondu. "It is even harder to understand how the 'proper' residents of Rumelihisar . . . could have tolerated the squalor across the street."[18]

Political Pressures and Municipal Services

From the start of rapid urbanization, improvement of city services has been a prime concern for most squatters. Over 80 percent of the respondents in a study of gecekondus in thirteen cities in 1967 cited the need for municipal services as the most serious problem faced by their community.[19] In a more recent survey in Ankara, 83 percent of the squatters complained about lack of recreational facilities, and 80 percent about inadequate sanitation and refuse collection.[20] Despite their poverty, squatters were prepared to pay for desperately needed roads, utilities, schools, and other services. Residents of an Ankara gecekondu were "willing to help the municipality in every way we can. If they say find 20,000 liras ($2,000) and we will build a school for you, then we will find the 20,000 liras for them . . . we ask people to give contributions, each according to his ability."[21]

Another indication of the intensity of squatter concern about inadequate services was the residents' willingness to devote their spare time to improving community facilities. In Ankara's gecekondus during the 1960s, "residents participated actively in the provision of public utilities. Most settlers were happy to follow rural practice and help dig trenches for water and sewerage mains and to improve local roads."[22] Settlers in Rumelihisarüstü, an Istanbul gecekondu, paved dirt roads, installed local sewers, and built a police station and post office for their community.[23]

Squatters also helped themselves to public services. Rumelihisarüstü's self-help sewers were illegally connected to the Istanbul sewer system. Water and electric lines also were tapped by gecekondu dwellers without official permission. As squatters become more numerous and influential, officials often were "tolerant of illegal activity as long as the squatters do not ask for services which would cost time, personnel and money for the municipality."[24]

Reflecting these concerns, improved services have been a strong motivating factor in bringing squatters together for collective political action. Gecekondu dwellers pointed to their pressing needs, contended that the city government did not treat them equitably, and backed up their arguments with growing political clout. Since services were useful only if the public authorities accepted the illegal communities—and since some services could not be provided to householders who lacked title to their plot—campaigns to secure water, electricity, schools, and other services were closely entwined with efforts to secure governmental recognition of the squatters' homesites.

In response to persistent political efforts by organized squatters, whose ranks were steadily enlarging, municipal governments extended electricity and water, improved drainage and waste disposal, built roads and schools, and extended public transportation routes to gecekondu areas. In the major cities were created special units, such as Ankara's Housing and Squatting Division, to develop comprehensive approaches for gecekondu improvements. Political responsiveness also increased central funds for service improvements, particularly after the enactment of the Gecekondu Improvement Act of 1966, which underwrote road, water supply, and electrification projects.

By the 1970s, there was widespread acceptance on the part of political leaders in the cities and the central government, of the validity of squatter claims for public services. Municipalities also were devoting an increasing share of their limited resources to serving squatter areas, as was the central government with its urban funds. Public services played a critical role in transforming older gecekondus into stable settlements, with paved roads, city water and electricity, bus service, schools and police stations, commercial districts, and traffic jams—communities that are often hard to distinguish from legally settled areas into which they blend.

Despite these substantial efforts and accomplishments, few gecekondus, particularly the newer areas, approached parity in public services with conventional city neighborhoods. Resources were limited, and, as indicated above, the scale of the enterprise was enormous as migrants continued to flood to the cities. Local officials rarely were eager to serve gecekondus, which they saw as blights on their city, in addition to being "the most difficult places to take public services."[25]

Political considerations were often paramount in distributing service improvements and new public facilities, as might be expected in programs that were rooted in political pressures from the urban poor. Squatter areas that voted "right" did much better than those that backed losers in municipal elections. Established gecekondu leaders developed the best relations with local and central politicians, and captured the lion's share of the benefits for their communities. Moreover, priorities in service programs often resulted from their political visibility rather than their contribution to systematic efforts at community development. And the release of funds for gecekondu improvements tended "to be confined to vote-catching sprees at election time."[26]

In addition to responding to political pressures to favor this or that settlement, city officials were influenced in other ways to provide services to particular squatter areas. Bribery sometimes produced action from venal municipal officials in bureaucracies where payments under the table were common for services rendered. Self-interest on the part of city employees was also a significant factor in the provision of services to squatter settlements. Substantial numbers of lower-ranked city employees soon were living in gecekondus, and many used their inside position to secure priority treatment for their communities in the provision of water, electricity, schools, road improvements, sewers, police protection, and other public services.

Efforts to distribute public services more equitably were also seriously handicapped by the reactive nature of squatter improvements. City services followed development, and thus usually had to accept as given the gecekondu's location, terrain, and settlement pattern. "It is extremely costly," as one urban planner emphasizes, "to provide infrastructure and services to these areas after this irregular and unplanned growth has occurred."[27] The limited resources available purchased far fewer improvements than would have been the case if roads and public utilities had been provided in advance of development.

In addition, provision of city services to gecekondus usually was poorly coordinated. As Heper points out, "Schools are built but there are no passable roads to those schools. The municipality extends municipal services with one hand and threatens to tear down the houses with the other."[28] Responses to emergencies or political pressures resulted in initial installations of water lines or roads that were quickly outmoded, or failed to meet national standards for gecekondu improvement areas. Services also were strained by improvements and additions to squatter homes, resulting in higher residential densities, more use of water and electricity, and pressures on roads, schools, and other facilities. Repaving streets, expanding schools, and increasing water and power capacity all increased the costs of providing services to squatter settlements and reduced the resources available to do the job properly in newly developing gecekondu areas.

If employed in timely fashion, resources for public services could have provided opportunities to shape the pattern of squatter settlement by offering urban newcomers sites with basic services in suitable locations approved by local authorities. Instead, strategic use of infrastructure was largely precluded by the scale of the problem, insistent constituency demands from existing gecekondus, and inadequate resources. As Sevim Aksoy has pointed out, "services . . . provided only after development has taken place . . . reduce the power of the physical planner to control and direct urban development, as one of his assets (public finance) is spent on development that has already occurred."[29]

ORGANIZING PUBLIC SERVICES

Responsibilities for urban public services typically are affected by a number of organizational dimensions, including the nature of the task, division between public and private agencies, number of local political jurisdictions, and the pattern of allocation between national and subnational units. Functional considerations tend to create public service agencies organized around particular tasks or groups of tasks. In Turkey, as indi-

TABLE 6-1
MUNICIPAL SERVICE AGENCIES IN ISTANBUL

Board of Economic Inspection	Markets
Building Control	Municipal Theaters
Cemeteries	Parks and Gardens
Cleansing Services	Planning
Electricity, Tramway & Tunnel Authority	Real Estate and Expropriation
Fire	Sewerage
Gas Undertaking	Technical Works
Health Services	Tourist Services
Housing and Gecekondu	Warden Force
Industrial Personnel and Social Services	Water Undertaking
Library and Museums	Welfare Home
Maps and Land Survey	

cated in Chapter 4, functions tend to be defined narrowly rather than broadly, with the result that responsibilities for public services are distributed among numerous agencies in major cities, as illustrated by the listing of public service organizations in Istanbul in Table 6-1.

Most of these specialized tasks are performed by public rather than private agencies in urban Turkey. The public sector has steadily expanded in the wake of rapid urbanization, which has greatly increased the number of unprofitable public services—and the amount of service—that must be provided. Private suppliers of public services are most important in transportation, and their role is examined in the final section of this chapter.

Political fragmentation within metropolitan areas divides responsibilities for basic municipal services among local jurisdictions, often resulting in substantial variations in the nature and quality of services in different localities. In the Istanbul and Izmir metropolitan areas, where suburban jurisdictions have surrounded the central city, outlying municipalities generally have provided fewer and lower-quality services than has the core city. Political fragmentation also complicates the provision of facilities and services that flow over municipal boundaries, especially water supply, sewage, highways, mass transportation, and control of air and water pollution. Often, functional agencies with area-wide jurisdictions are organized for these tasks, but this has not been the usual practice in urban Turkey because of political and financial constraints on local joint ventures, and because of the preemptive role of central government in the provision of many major urban services.

As the previous two chapters indicate, centralization has an over-

Central Istanbul
—Michael N. Danielson

The face of urban Turkey—a melange of modern buildings, older housing, and sprawling
squatter settlements in Ankara
—Ministry of Reconstruction and Settlement

Plans . . .: Jansen's sketch for a Roman bath amid dramatic vistas of Ankara's hillsides.
—Ankara Metropolitan Plan Bureau

. . . *and Reality:* Jansen's plan never contemplated the possibility of squatters staking their claims to the city's hills and ravines.
—Ministry of Reconstruction and Settlement

Illegally constructed apartment buildings crowd their sites in Ankara
—Michael N. Danielson

Social housing constructed adjacent to an Ankara gecekondu.
—Ministry of Reconstruction and Settlement

Gecekondus cling to an Ankara hillside
—Michael N. Danielson

New housing under construction in Ankara
—Michael N. Danielson

Apartment and office buildings in one of Ankara's most attractive areas
—Michael N. Danielson

Migrants and their housing in Ankara
—Ministry of Reconstruction and Settlement

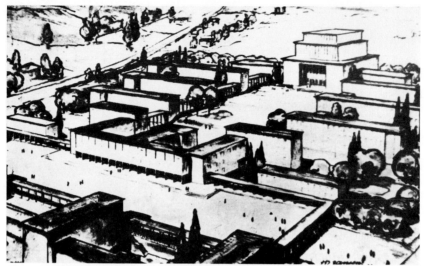
Hermann Jansen's sketch for the central governmental complex in Ankara
—Ankara Metropolitan Planning Bureau

Ankara's old quarter—an Anatolian hill town
surrounded by a sprawling modern metropolis.
—Michael N. Danielson

Modern Ankara, with commercial and public buildings lining the broad avenues laid out by the capital's master planners.
—Michael N. Danielson

Government-financed housing for well-off families in Istanbul
—Ministry of Reconstruction and Settlement

An example of the wooden housing
that once predominated in Istanbul.
—Michael N. Danielson

A gecekondu in transition in Istanbul, as improvements
and additions are made to the basic structures.
—Michael N. Danielson

Dolmuş taxis lead the crowded way
up from the Golden Horn in Istanbul.
—Michael N. Danielson

powering impact on the organization of municipal services in Turkey. Ankara decides which services cities can provide, determines how many resources will be available to underwrite city services, sets standards for most municipal undertakings, and oversees local administration. National politicians influence city decisions affecting the nature, location, and quality of local services and facilities. With the growth of cities, central agencies have steadily expanded their urban responsibilities, often at the expense of municipal governments. The result is a complex web of central involvement in urban services with the main legal, financial, and political strands woven primarily by the national government. (See Table 6-2.)

Urban Services and the İller Bankası

As indicated in Chapter 4, responsibilities for urban public services are distributed among a large number of central agencies, most of which have fairly narrow functional perspectives. The most important central agency in the provision of urban services is the İller Bankası, the Bank of Local Authorities. Created in 1945 and lodged after 1957 in the Ministry of Reconstruction and Settlement, except for a brief sojourn in the ill-fated Ministry of Local Affairs, the İller Bankası succeeded the Bank of Municipalities (Belediyeler Bankası), which was established in 1933 to help cities provide services. The İller Bankası plays a major role in the development and financing of municipal facilities. Its primary concerns have been water supply and electricity. The Bank provides loans for capital construction, and assumes responsibility for technical supervision and control over construction financed by its loans.[30]

The İller Bankası, however, does not have exclusive responsibility for urban water supply, electric power, and waste disposal. The Bank is primarily concerned with municipalities with populations between 3,000 and 100,000, and its staff and resources reflect this limited urban mission. The large cities, which presumably need less technical assistance, are supposed to deal directly with the central agencies that provide the function, such as the State Hydraulic Works and the Turkish Electricity Agency. In practice, however, the İller Bankası has been more responsive to urban needs than have central functional agencies, and the Bank has underwritten projects in major cities. In Istanbul, for example, the Bank developed an area-wide scheme for dealing with waste water.

By the end of 1975, the İller Bankası had undertaken basic service installations in almost every municipality, investing in the process over nine billion lira in urban services. These outlays, however, represent only a fraction of the pressing local needs for municipal infrastructure. Faced with more demands than possibly can be satisfied with its limited resources, the Bank has had to cope with severe political pressures from its local clients, and from national politicians eager to bolster their position with city voters. The Bank's sensitivity to political considerations is evident in the yearly pattern of its investments, with the largest allocations being made in the years preceding national or local elections.

In responding to these pressures, the Bank has engaged in substantial deficit operations. Between 1947 and 1960, during the initial spurt in urban growth, the Bank allocated 518 million lira although its revenues were only 297 million lira, with the deficit being met by the central treasury.

TABLE 6-2
RESPONSIBILITIES FOR PUBLIC SERVICES IN URBAN AREAS

	Investment	*Maintenance*	*Operations*
Infrastructure			
Roads, squares	M C	M	—
Sewerage	M C	M	—
Parks, cemeteries	M	M	M
Water	M C E	M C E	M E
Electricity	C	C	M
Gas	M E	M E	M E
Telephone	C E	C E	C E
Urban Services			
Garbage collection	M	M	M
Street cleaning	M	M	M
Fire fighting	M	M	M
Police	—	—	C M
Traffic control	M C	M C	M C
Public transportation	M E	M E	M E
Social and Cultural Functions			
Education	C M	C M	C M
Health services	C M	C M	C M
Old age homes, orphanages	M C	M C	—
Low cost housing	M C	M C	—
Religious services	C M	C M	C M
Historical preservation	C M	C M	C M
Libraries and cultural centers	M C	M C	M C
Playgrounds and stadiums	M C	M C	

SOURCE: State Planning Organization, *Yerleşme, Bölgesel Gelişme, Kentleşme ve Konut,* IV. Beş Yıllık Kalkınma Planı Özel İhtisas Komisyonu Raporu (Ankara, February 1977), pp. 161–163.
Key: M—Municipal government
    C—Central government
    E—Economic enterprise, public or private

TABLE 6-3
INVESTMENTS IN MUNICIPAL SERVICES BY THE İLLER BANKASI:
1946–1976

	Investment (000 TL)	Percent of Total
Electric power	3,833,623	41.4
Water supply	3,803,482	41.1
Other services	1,319,985	14.3
Planning	296,453	3.2
Total	9,253,985	100.0

SOURCE: İller Bankası.

TABLE 6-4
SHARE OF INVESTMENTS OF THE İLLER BANKASI FINANCED
THROUGH THE CENTRAL BUDGET: 1972–1976

	Total Investments (000 TL)	Central Budget Funds (000 TL)	Central Funds as Percent of Total
1972	502,114	138,900	27.7
1973	814,675	442,675	54.3
1974	1,412,814	912,000	64.6
1975	2,192,230	1,400,000	63.9
1976	3,593,000	2,522,000	70.2

SOURCE: İller Bankası Dergisi, no. 5 (May 1976), p. 151.

With the continued onslaught of rapid urbanization and the concomitant rise in municipal needs for infrastructure investments, the central government has responded by providing an increasing share of the Bank's capital from the central budget. By 1976, the state was underwriting 70 percent of the İller Bankası's urban investments, as shown in Table 6-4.

Centralizing Major Urban Services

For many public services, especially those that require large capital outlays and highly qualified personnel, the simplest course of action for central government has been to assume direct control. Almost complete responsibility for education and health care gradually passed to national ministries. Water supply, which was a well-developed municipal function, is now largely in the hands of central agencies. A law enacted in 1968 made the State Hydraulic Works of the Ministry of Energy and Natural Resources responsible for preparing and implementing water projects for cities with 100,000 or more inhabitants.

A good example of the steady expansion of central authority for urban infrastructure is provided by electric power. Municipalities developed their own power systems, with assistance from the İller Bankası and, in the case of larger cities, from the Turkish Electricity Agency, which is part of the Ministry of Energy and Natural Resources. In the early 1970s, the national government centralized energy production, creating an interconnected power grid fed by several hydroelectric installations in Anatolia. The Turkish Electricity Agency was given a monopoly in the production, operation, distribution, and sale of energy. Municipalities no longer could produce electricity, and their generating facilities were taken over by the central agency.

Cities, at least for a while, were permitted to retain their distribution networks, and to distribute power within their boundaries. But central officials were eager to eliminate the cities' remaining role. In 1975, the Minister of Energy and Natural Resources attempted to annex the Ankara Electricity and Gas Establishment. The municipal government fought the takeover attempt, filing a suit against the minister's decision in the Council of State, which took the case to the Constitutional Court, which sided with the city on the grounds that a municipality had the right to run its own electricity agency.

National energy officials, however, triumphed a few years later when the centralizing process was completed under the military government. With the city's political voices stilled, and high priority being given to "rational" organization of governmental activities, a law enacted in 1982 brought all power operations under the Turkish Electricity Agency. The central government took over the cities' distribution facilities, and all municipal power agencies were transferred to the Turkish Electricity Agency. Istanbul claimed the takeover would deprive the city of 20 billion lira in revenues, and General Abdullah Tırtıl, Istanbul's mayor under the military government, asked the central government for 30 billion lira to cover the loss.[31]

The potent influence of central government on provision of major urban services is also illustrated by creation of the Istanbul Water and Sewerage Agency. The agency was established in 1981 under a special law enacted by the National Security Council. The new agency was empowered to provide water and sewerage service within the municipality of Istanbul, to take over existing municipal facilities, and with the consent of the central government to enlarge the scope of its service area to include urbanized areas beyond Istanbul's boundaries. It was given a monopoly over supply and distribution of drinking and industrial water, collecting and processing of sewerage, and prevention of all kinds of water pollution.

Organization of the Istanbul Water and Sewerage Agency was a natural response to complex technological and financial problems. Istanbul's serious water, waste, and pollution problems required comprehensive treatment and an area-wide approach. Moreover, funds from the World Bank for the Greater Istanbul sewerage project would not have been forthcoming in the absence of an effective means of implementing the project. The new agency was given substantial sources of funds—user fees and contributions from beneficiaries of water and sewer installations, a share of municipal revenues, and central assistance. And immediately after the agency's creation, the World Bank came through with a credit of $88 million for the sewerage project.

In providing these substantial capabilities for improved infrastructure on an area-wide basis, the central government also substantially eliminated city government from a role in water and sewers, traditionally municipal functions. The new agency replaced Istanbul's Water Supply Administration, which was a unit of the city government. The Istanbul Water and Sewerage Agency was placed under the firm control of the central government—its general director was named by the Minister of Interior. Moreover, this centrally controlled agency was assigned 10 percent of Istanbul's share of revenues from the central government, a substantial bite from the hard-pressed city treasury. Other municipalities in the metropolitan area also were assessed 10 percent of their central revenues for the Istanbul Water and Sewerage Agency, even though they were not guaranteed that their contributions would result in any direct water or sewer service from the agency.

Istanbul was represented on the agency's general council, which was responsible for overall policy-making, by the mayor of Istanbul, eight other municipal officials, and the Istanbul Chamber of Commerce. But these municipal delegates were outnumbered by central government's representatives—from the Ministries of Agriculture, Defense, Health, Industry, Interior, Public Works, Reconstruction and Settlement, Rural Affairs, Tourism, as well as the İller Bankası, State Water Works, and the Under Secretariat of Environment in the Prime Minister's office. Clearly, whatever benefits would flow from the new agency, national officials rather than city government were now calling the shots on water and sewer problems in Istanbul.

COMPLEX PROBLEMS—THE CASE OF TRANSPORTATION

Of all the urban services, transportation probably offers the most opportunities to shape settlement patterns. Transportation corridors, junctions, and terminals attract development—witness the higher residential densities along rapid transit lines, the location of industrial and commercial establishments at strategic intersections of modern expressways, and the

concentration of offices around rail, bus, and ferry terminals. Road builders, transit officials, and urban planners consciously seek to use transportation investments to influence urban development, and settlement
patterns in many metropolitan areas testify to the success of some of
these efforts—for example, the bridges, tunnels, and highways of New
York's Robert Moses and its Port Authority, the stimulation of high density commercial and residential development by Toronto's subway system, and the use of rapid transit to link planned new towns with
downtown in Stockholm.[32]

Urban transportation is a complex undertaking involving a variety of
functional actors, both public and private actors and a variety of functional agencies—road building, traffic control, parking, trucking, buses,
taxis, automobile operators, conventional railroads, transit lines, and,
where water must be crossed, bridge and tunnel agencies as well as ferries. Rarely are the activities of this multitude of interested parties effectively orchestrated by public agencies with broad functional or areal
power. Further complicating the politics of urban transportation is the
magnitude of the capital investments required to develop, expand, and
modernize urban roads, transit systems, parking facilities, and traffic-
control networks. In addition to being capital-intensive, most elements of
urban transport are also labor-intensive—operators for public transportation, drivers for taxis, trucks, and private vehicles—which multiplies the
number of individuals with a direct stake in public determinations.

Efforts to meet transportation needs in Turkey's major cities have been
strongly influenced by inadequate resources, the dominant role of the
central government, functional fragmentation, and the absence of area-
wide institutions with authority to deal with transportation comprehen-
sively. Rapid urbanization has greatly increased demand for
transportation, at the same time spreading development far beyond the
reach of established services and facilities. An added complication was
the haphazard development of squatter housing, which generated demand
for transport services in areas difficult to serve under the best of circumstances. As a result of these developments, escalating urban growth overwhelmed conventional public transportation services, leading to the
widespread provision of informal services by group taxi operators. At the
same time, the public sector has been unable to expand highways, traffic-
control systems, and parking facilities fast enough to keep up with spiral-
ing automobile usage. In the face of these monumental challenges,
governmental transport efforts have mostly reacted to urbanization with
too little too late.

The Congested City

The vast majority of travel in Turkey's urban centers is along city streets
and highways—in private automobiles, buses, trolleys, taxis, and trucks.

Only in Istanbul do other modes of transport carry a significant proportion of travelers; and even in the great metropolis with its extensive rail system and numerous water crossings, the nonautomotive share of ridership is small, with railroads accounting for 8.3 percent of trips by public transportation, and boats another 13 percent. In Ankara, only 2.6 percent of journeys on public transport are by railroad.[33]

With high rates of urban growth, travel on streets and highways—by both public and private means—has expanded far more rapidly than has the capacity of the transportation system. Ankara's population, as shown in Table 6-5, grew almost five times faster than the number of buses in the city between 1935 and 1978. Lack of resources prevented Istanbul from making any significant additions to its bus fleet after 1973, despite an estimated need of 120 new buses a year just to maintain existing levels of service for a rapidly increasing population. With its aging buses and trolleys providing increasingly less adequate service, riders on the municipal system dropped from 746,000 in 1970 to 630,000 in 1976.[34]

Inadequate public transportation has attracted large numbers of private operators, most of them operating minibuses or group taxis—*dolmuş*. Almost half of all trips by public conveyances in Istanbul in 1970, as shown in Table 6-6, were made by minibuses and group taxis. In Ankara, minibuses and group taxis hauled 26 percent of total trips in 1979, including those by private cars, as indicated in Table 6-7. The close relationship between dolmuş-minibus ridership and the availability of regular public transportation is illustrated by declining dolmuş-minibus usage after 1978 as Ankara undertook a vigorous expansion of municipal bus services. Dolmuş literally means "full up," with the driver waiting until his vehicle is filled with passengers traveling to the specified destination or intermediate points along the route. Minibuses carried 9 to 14 passengers, while group taxis hauled 5 to 7 riders in a dazzling variety of vehicles— vintage Citroens, DeSotos and Edsels from the 1950s, new Mercedeses, and Anadols manufactured in Turkey.

As noted in Chapter 2, dolmuş-minibus service is the transportation counterpart of the gecekondu, what Ibrahim Şanlı terms "a people's solution to the unserved transportation needs of people . . . providing effective service throughout the metropolitan area at reasonably low fares and with no direct demands from the public purse."[35] Expansion of this informal transport system was closely linked to migration and squatting. Regular public transportation has been least effective in gecekondu areas, with cities extending service to squatter areas only in response to pressures, and then limited by inadequate resources and equipment. As transport demand increased with migration and the spread of squatter settlements, dolmuş-minibus services appeared spontaneously and expanded rapidly. But the convenience and flexibility of these relatively inexpensive services, as well as the inadequacies of conventional public transportation,

TABLE 6-5
INCREASES IN BUSES AND POPULATION IN ANKARA: 1935–1978

	Buses		Population	
	Number	Index	Number	Index
1935	80	100	123,000	100
1955	107	134	451,000	368
1965	142	178	906,000	738
1975	228	285	1,701,000	1,386
1978	280	350	2,060,000	1,678

SOURCE: Ankara Belediyesi, *Ankara Kent İçi Ulaşım Etüdü Ulaşim Modeli* (Ankara, 1979), p. 5.

TABLE 6-6
TRIPS BY MODE OF PUBLIC TRANSPORTATION IN ISTANBUL: 1970

Mode	Number of Trips	Percent of Trips
Municipal buses and trolleys	745,600	26.9
Minibuses	685,600	24.8
Dolmuş	650,450	23.6
Passenger boats	337,400	12.2
Railroads	231,150	8.3
Private bus companies	82,700	3.0
Dolmuş boats	32,800	1.2

SOURCE: H. İbrahim Şanlı, *Dolmuş-Minibus System in Istanbul: A Case Study in Low-Cost Transportation* (İstanbul: İstanbul Teknik Üniversitesi Matbaası—Gümüssüyü, 1981), p. 24.

TABLE 6-7
TRIPS BY MODE IN ANKARA: 1979

Mode	Number of Trips	Percent of Trips
Bus	733,000	28.0
Private automobile	680,000	26.0
Minibus	497,000	19.0
Taxicab	262,000	10.0
Dolmus	183,000	7.0
Other	262,000	10.0

SOURCE: Ankara Belediyesi, *Ankara Kent İçi Ulaşım Etüdü Ulaşım Modeli* (Ankara, 1979), p. 12.

attracted many dolmuş riders who were neither poor nor residents of gecekondus.

With the rapid expansion of dolmuş-minibus services came increased traffic and congestion. Load factors were low, particularly for group taxis with their five to seven passengers, so large numbers of vehicles were needed to carry the thousands of dolmuş and minibus riders in Ankara and Istanbul. By 1976, 3,300 minibuses and 16,000 group taxis were operating long hours on Istanbul's overloaded streets. Paralleling the increase in these for-hire vehicles was explosive growth of private car ownership, a reflection of economic prosperity, an expanding middle class, and Turkey's substantial investment in automobile production.[36] More and more private cars crowded onto outmoded road systems. During the 1970s, 150 additional private cars were squeezed onto Istanbul's streets and highways every day, and by 1982 223,000 private vehicles were registered in the metropolitan area.

Vehicles multiplied far more rapidly than road capacity, producing steadily worsening traffic congestion. Traffic jams got bigger and lasted longer, delays increased, tempers grew shorter, air and noise pollution intensified, and traffic accidents mounted—creating in Istanbul and Ankara what came to be called "traffic anarchy." For many people, the most troubling element was the rapid rise in vehicular accidents. Traffic accidents increased over sevenfold between 1955 and 1977, with cities accounting for three-fourths of the 56,765 accidents in 1977, a year in which almost 3,300 people were killed by vehicles in the cities.[37]

Much of the blame for deteriorating conditions on city streets was heaped on the minibuses and group taxis, the most visible and controversial component of the urban transport system. As Şanlı notes, the dolmuş-minibus system was "blamed for the 'anarchic' urban transport situation in Istanbul by planners, academicians, the officials, the policy makers and even the public that is served by the system."[38] Dolmuş and minibus drivers were often reckless on the road, rude to other motorists and their passengers, and unscrupulous in their dealings with customers. Many operators ignored traffic regulations and had problems with the police, and their vehicles frequently were overcrowded and involved in accidents. The dolmuş and minibus operators also were easy to blame because they were numerous, vocal, and well-organized politically.

In reality, private cars were a far more significant factor than minibuses and group taxis in the hobbling of Istanbul, Ankara, and other major cities. Almost all the increase in vehicles in the 1970s came from private automobiles, since the number of minibuses and taxis was limited by government. In Istanbul, there was no increase in dolmuş vehicles after 1966 and minibuses after 1967. Moreover, private car owners were just as ready as taxi and minibus drivers to ignore traffic signals and parking regulations. Traffic anarchy reflected the breakdown of a complex and poorly coordinated transportation system, not merely the surly behavior of its most outspoken component—the rough-and-ready dolmuş and minibus drivers.

Agencies in Search of Policy

Prior to the 1970s, urban transportation attracted relatively little attention in systematic terms. Other concerns that piled on Turkish cities in the wake of rapid urbanization received higher priority—basic public utilities, expanding schools and health facilities, and dealing with the critical housing problems of gecekondu dwellers. Transportation responsibilities were divided among a variety of agencies—road building, traffic control, municipal buses, commuter railroads. Each struggled within its sphere of operations to meet mounting demands while suffering from severely limited resources. Neither the central government, nor governors in metropolitan provinces, nor city governments gave much thought to overall transportation development until growing public concern over "traffic anarchy," carnage on the roads, and woeful public transport focused attention on the system as a whole.

Responsibilities for urban transportation are highly centralized in Turkey, with local governments having little authority over many of the component elements. Most of the system is controlled by central agencies with national functional perspectives rather than urban concerns. Major roads in metropolitan areas, including the Bosphorus Bridge and the peripheral highway that circles Istanbul, are built and maintained as part of the intercity road network by the General Directorate of Highways in the Ministry of Public Works. Commuter railroads are operated by the State Railways as part of the national rail system, and Istanbul's ferry services are provided by the Turkish Maritime Bank, which, like the State Railways, is a component of the Ministry of Transportation and Communications.

The central government also plays a dominant role in traffic control, which has received strong emphasis in Turkish urban transportation policy. General responsibility for highway traffic, vehicle and driver registration, and traffic safety is lodged in the Traffic Directorate of the General Directorate of Security within the Ministry of Interior. Provincial traffic units carry out central policies and regulations, and general policy oversight is provided by the Central Traffic Committee in the Ministry of Interior.

Within urban areas, the most important transportation agency is the Provincial Traffic Committee. This body deals with traffic regulations, highway safety, and licensing and operating procedures for buses, minibuses, and taxis—including fares, routes, and limitations on the number of minibuses and group taxis. The Provincial Traffic Committee is an instrument of the central government in each province. All its actions must be approved by the Traffic Directorate in the Ministry of Interior. Agents of the center predominate on the committee, which is headed by the provincial governor and includes officials from the military, the Traffic Directorate, the Highway Directorate, and the Ministries of Reconstruction, Education, and Agriculture. Local interests have fewer members on the Committee—represented in Istanbul are the city government, the Istanbul Taxi and Dolmuş Drivers' Association, and the Istanbul Bus Owners Association.[39]

In a pattern common to other major urban services, local responsibilities for transportation have diminished in the wake of rapid urbanization. Before 1953, most of the functions exercised by Provincial Traffic Committees belonged to cities which, under the Municipal Law of 1930, were authorized to regulate traffic and public transportation. These powers were reclaimed by the central government in the Highway Traffic Law of 1953, and assigned to central and provincial agencies as indicated above. Municipalities were left with some operating responsibilities—for traffic signals and signs, street repair, and public transportation service—but almost no authority to make policies to deal with their traffic and public problems.

Traffic and transportation issues, however, are too important—and too volatile politically—for city governments to ignore. Istanbul, for example, "has preferred to remain active in traffic and transportation improvements, claiming . . . that it should be given powers to deal effectively with the problem of urban transportation in Istanbul."[40] Istanbul took the initiative in regulating dolmuş and minibus service, setting routes and fares in 1958, subject, however, to the approval of the Istanbul Provincial Traffic Committee. The city "retained its own advisors to recommend improvement projects and take actions to implement these projects."[41] Istanbul also used municipal police to help the understaffed traffic police cope with the city's monumental traffic problems, despite the fact that the municipal officers are not authorized to enforce the traffic code.

In Ankara, the city government under Mayor Ali Dinçer developed a comprehensive program to shift riders from private automobiles and groups taxis to municipal public transportation. Over 200 buses were purchased, and the central government was persuaded to transfer buses operated by various ministries for their personnel to the city. Reserved bus lanes were developed in central Ankara to speed service to the major employment centers. Three months after the construction of the special bus route, ridership on the municipal lines had increased 70 percent.[42] Most controversial was the city's decision in 1979 to phase out dolmuş service. Dolmuş operations in central Ankara were successfully terminated in 1983, providing another example of the ability of military government to take actions in the cities that would have been fraught with peril for elected officials.

Under Mayor Dinçer, Ankara also sought to develop a rapid-transit system after plans that had been developed by the central government failed to produce any concrete results. The city's scheme called for a 25-kilometer system, with costs kept down by having only 10 percent of the line underground, using cars manufactured by the Turkish Railways Agency, and having the city government undertake electrification. The plan was caught up in the partisan conflict that poisoned relations between the large cities and the central government in the late 1970s. When the central government failed to respond, Ankara sought to begin construction of the metro line on its own. But these efforts were blocked by central officials in 1980 and later abandoned when Dinçer and the city council were removed by the military government.[43]

Transportation planning responsibilities also are fragmented in the major urban centers. City governments prepare local master plans that include transport facilities, but the city government has no control over most of the agencies that develop and control transportation. Area-wide transportation planning has been undertaken since the early 1970s by metropolitan planning bureaus in Ankara, Istanbul, and Izmir. But these planning offices, which are units of the Ministry of Reconstruction and Settlement, also lack authority over the many public entities with transport responsibilities including the city governments. In Istanbul, for example, cooperation between the city government and the Greater Istanbul Master Plan Bureau has been rather ineffective—as reflected "in the independent actions of the Municipality to improve traffic flow and general transport situation in the city."[44]

Within this complex system, individual agencies tend to pursue relatively narrow functional goals. At the same time, overlapping responsibilities, the existence of three layers of government, and pervasive central control and oversight, necessitate cumbersome procedures and endless red tape. Consider, for example, the Electricity, Tramway, and Tunnel Authority of Istanbul, which operates the municipal public transport lines. Operational responsibility for the authority "is divided among the Governor, the Mayor, the Provincial Traffic Committee, the Ministries of Interior, Energy, Finance, Public Works, Reconstruction, and Customs." To establish a new bus route, the authority "has to get permission of the Provincial Traffic Committee which 'has the powers to prevent this if they consider that priority is to be given on that route for another class of vehicle.'" To increase bus fares, the authority "applies to the mayor of Istanbul for changes. He decides and submits it to the

Municipal Executive Committee for its approval. The last step is the ratification of the Ministry of Energy and Natural Resources."[45]

The Failure to Concentrate Resources

By and large, this complex set of arrangements has reacted to the transportation needs generated by urbanization rather than attempting to shape the urban pattern through strategic investments in transport facilities and services. Resources rarely have been concentrated on comprehensive transportation objectives. Instead, the multitude of agencies has struggled with limited resources to catch up with the demands unleashed by rapid urbanization.

Most transport investment has gone into highways, and primarily into trunk roads built and maintained by the national government, a reflection of both the center's superior resources and the priority given to modernizing the intercity road system. Despite substantial construction, none of the major cities has a highway network that adequately handles steadily increasing traffic volumes. Istanbul's major new highways, the limited access peripheral road, the Bosphorus Bridge, and the new bridge over the Golden Horn in central Istanbul were congested soon after they were opened; and both bridges were exceeding their daily capacity of 100,000 vehicles in 1977, eight years earlier than planned.

Much less attention has been paid to intraurban arterials and city streets. Istanbul's traffic problems are complicated by miles of narrow streets in the older sections. Roads are wider and boulevards broad in the newer parts of Istanbul and in much of Ankara outside gecekondu areas. But indiscriminate apartment-house construction, rapidly rising automobile ownership, and a pervasive lack of parking space overload most of these streets. In Istanbul, as Ahmet Keskin points out, "in the existing built-up areas, by increasing the building heights, under various kinds of pressures, undesirable density levels have been reached to such an extent that the roads have already been choked up."[46]

Inadequate resources plague urban transportation at every turn. Impoverished city governments have not been able to muster the resources to replace worn-out buses or expand their fleets at anywhere near the rate of population growth. The Galata and Ataturk bridges in central Istanbul badly need repair if they are to continue to serve the heavy traffic that surges across the Golden Horn almost continuously. And without major investments by the central government, there is no way to turn into reality the ambitious plans for rail transit systems in Istanbul and Ankara. An estimated 120 billion lira ($600 million) is needed to construct the first stage of Istanbul's metro, which if built would carry 30,000 passengers an hour between Yenikapı and Ayazağa in the congested core.[47]

Instead of concentating resources, the existing arrangements usually work at cross-purposes. Despite overlapping responsibilities and central oversight, there is little effective coordination across agency lines of urban transport services and facilities. Istanbul, for example, has a transportation non-system. Buses, commuter trains, ferries, minibus and dolmuş vehicles all go their separate ways, as do the road-building and traffic-control agencies. Far better for the three million travelers who struggle around Istanbul each day would be an integrated system, such as that recommended by the Greater Istanbul Master Plan Bureau, composed of buses with preferential rights of way, closely linked to improved rail and ferry services including a rail tube under the Bosphorus, and fed by minibus and dolmuş connections with areas beyond the bus system.[48] But such coordination appears beyond the reach of Istanbul's functionally fragmented transport agencies, despite the obvious potential for integration in a highly centralized governmental system.

Despite these weaknesses, government has influenced settlement patterns in Turkey's major cities through transportation investments. Highways have been the most influential—because most urban transport in Turkey is vehicular and because no major investments have been made in other modes, such as rail transit, which could affect the locations of residences and jobs. Istanbul's peripheral highway and the Bosphorus Bridge have attracted development, which has helped overload these arteries more quickly than anticipated by their builders. And construction of a second bridge across the Bosphorus along with 42 kilometers of connecting roads to alleviate this congestion, at an estimated cost of 38 billion lira ($190 million), will stimulate development in the less intensively settled northern portion of the Istanbul region.

But even the new roads have not had a dramatic effect on the pattern of development in Istanbul and Ankara, in the manner of Stockholm's subway or Los Angeles's expressways. In part this reflects limited fiscal resources, which have not permitted public agencies to concentrate resources in advance of development—even the Bosphorus Bridge was primarily a reaction, both to surging auto and truck traffic in the Istanbul metropolitan area and to mounting intercontinental vehicular travel through Istanbul. The impact of transportation has also been limited by the rapidity of growth, which has constantly outstripped infrastructure provision, and, in the case of squatter settlements, by new housing for millions of people—housing that has ignored the availability of public services.

7
GOVERNMENT AND HOUSING

The Turkish Constitution promises that "the State shall take measures to meet the housing needs of the poor and of low-income families in accordance with their health requirements."[1] For the vast majority of villagers who flocked to the cities after World War II, this commitment was not met. Government has supplied precious little housing for the poor—the public sector accounts for less than 10 percent of total investment in housing, and most of these funds have benefited middle-class urban dwellers. Nor has government been able to control the massive development of squatter housing. As a result, large amounts of urban housing are overcrowded and unhealthy, constructed illegally without reference to building codes or other public standards.

Goverment's housing efforts in Turkey have been indelibly shaped by the frantic pace of urbanization. Rapid urban growth created needs for housing that could not be met by the public or private sector. Increased demand drove up prices for housing and land in the cities at the same time that hundreds of thousands of poor migrants were crowding into the metropolitan centers. "Almost from the early stages of urbanization," note planners Ali Türel and Özcan Altaban, "cities have not been able to absorb newcomers through the provision of low-cost rental housing or with the processes of subdivision of existing housing stock. Since the rate of growth was so rapid the costs of land and housing [have] risen steeply and the migrants have never been able to afford accommodation in central locations."[2]

Mounting demands for housing in the wake of accelerating urbanization were not matched by increased governmental efforts to provide shelter. Quite the opposite was the case. Housing was given low priority by the central government throughout the decades of rapid urban growth, as the central government concentrated investments on industrial development. During the 1950s, the ruling Democratic Party's strong support of the private sector helped fuel a boom in apartment-house building, but directed very few resources into lower-cost housing. Turkey's First Five-Year Development Plan, covering the years 1963 to 1967, considered housing investments unproductive, and the plan successfully sought to reduce public and private outlays for housing; investment in housing dropped from 24 percent of total investment in 1963 to 19 percent in 1967. Subsequent national plans pursued the same general strategy of discouraging capital outlays for housing, and in 1981 housing investment accounted for only 18 percent of total investment.[3]

Housing's low priority was also reflected in limited public outlays for shelter. Direct governmental expenditure accounts for less than 5 percent of total housing investment. Indirect involvement through housing credit programs operated by the central government's Real Estate Bank (*Emlâk Kredi Bankası*) and the Social Insurance Agency (*Sosyal Sigortalar Kurumu*) increased the public share somewhat. During the second plan period (1968–1972), government investment reached 9.3 percent of the total for housing, but by 1981 public outlays had dropped to 6.7 percent.[4]

Limited public investment has reduced the ability of government in Turkey to use housing as a means of shaping urban development. Large housing programs controlled by government have substantial potential for influencing settlement patterns, as indicated in cities as diverse as Stockholm and Singapore.[5] Planned development in Ankara's early years was fostered by public housing investment. Since 1950, however, the combination of low public priority for housing and rapid urban growth has precluded any sustained effort to use public housing to guide development along desired paths.

Reliance on the private sector for housing does not automatically eliminate governmental prospects for influencing urban development. Land-use and building controls can be used to restrict and channel private development, as has been the case in many suburbs in the United States.[6] In Turkey, however, local building controls have had little impact on private construction. Public regulation has been weak in conventionally developed areas, resulting in a private marketplace that has built—and frequently overbuilt—with minimal reference to governmental plans and priorities. Government has had even less direct influence on the location of squatter housing, since gecekondu development essentially ignores public regulations and plans.

Provision of private housing can also be shaped by national credit, tax, and regulatory policy. Such efforts have had a mixed effect in Turkey. As noted above, central efforts to reduce housing investment were successful. But little headway was made on the related objective of shifting private investment from luxury dwellings to smaller and less expensive units that would better serve housing needs in the cities. The First Five-Year Plan advanced "the principle that the housing sector should not be a profit-making field, but instead, housing investments should be accepted as a social service."[7] Social housing standards were established and limits placed on luxury housing. These policies, however, were ineffective, and housing production continued to fall far short of the central government's estimates of needs. Private builders were not ready to forego profits, and government was unwilling to make the investments needed to establish housing as a social service. The state could not force the private sector to undertake unprofitable activities. The result, as conceded by the State Planning Organization in 1981, was that "government control and programming over housing production has been quite weak . . ."[8]

Despite these problems, governmental housing policies have had a substantial impact on the pattern of development in Turkey's major cities. Most significant has been acceptance of squatter settlements as the only realistic way to urbanize rapidly, an acceptance prompted by limited resources, a responsive political system, and the mutual needs of squatters and elected politicians. Permissive squatter policies accelerated migration, and in so doing further increased the political influence of the urban poor as their numbers grew. Acceptance of gecekondus took the pressure off government to invest more in housing, thus increasing reliance on the private sector for both conventional and indigenous housing. Only in the 1980s was a serious attempt made to break out of this circle with new policies designed to enlarge substantially government's role in the provision of urban shelter.

HOUSING IN URBAN TURKEY

In 1975, the average city dwelling in Turkey housed 5.5 people in 2.6 rooms. Slightly over half of all urban housing units did not have running water and 41 percent lacked electricity. Substantially higher proportions of households are served with basic utilities in the three largest cities, with 78 percent having water and 94 percent electricity. Most homes are owner-occupied—64 percent for all urban housing. The proportion of rental units tends to increase with the size of the city—40 percent of Ankara's households reside in rented property, and, in Istanbul, 47 percent.[9]

Aggregate data, of course, lump together conventional housing and

TABLE 7-1

HOUSING CONSTRUCTION COSTS: 1963–1980

	Cost per Dwelling Unit in TL	Index 1963 = 100	Wholesale Price Index
1963	26,676	100	100
1966	27,362	103	112
1969	36,240	136	132
1972	43,201	162	199
1975	98,076	368	343
1978	326,846	1,225	751
1980	964,178	3,614	2,551

SOURCE: Ali Türel and Özcan Altaban, "Urban Growth and the Role of the State in the Provision of Housing in Turkey," paper presented to the 18th Congress of the International Society of City and Regional Planners, Istanbul, September 1–9, 1982, p. 14.

NOTE: Construction costs do not include land.

squatter dwellings. Almost all conventional housing built in recent years has water and electric service, and three quarters of the formal units are connected to municipal sewer systems. Conventional units are built primarily by private builders for middle- and upper-income families. Most of these dwellings are large—the average floor area of conventional housing constructed since 1960 has been 100 square meters (or over 1,000 square feet). The average cost of conventional housing kept pace with inflation between 1963 and 1975, rising from about $3,000 in 1963 to $8,000 in 1975. After 1975, as indicated in Table 7-1, housing prices began to increase much more rapidly than prices in general, and the average unit built in 1980 cost more than $19,000.

Production of conventional housing steadily increased throughout the decades of rapid urban growth, slowing only in the wake of Turkey's general economic problems in the late 1970s. Demand was strong for middle-class housing in the expanding cities, and a prolonged boom in private-housing construction began in the early 1950s. Substantial fortunes were made, since "the intensity of demand for housing from middle income groups insured high levels of return . . . within short periods and enabled large profits for contractors mostly engaged in parcel based housing."[10] As the pace of private housing quickened in the large cities, land prices rose rapidly and land speculation became increasingly attractive, all of which accelerated housing costs. Karpat reports that "some lots around Ankara and Istanbul that sold for 50 liras in 1949 went up to 50,000 liras in 1965 and permitted a rapidly growing class of urban entrepreneurs to accumulate capital." Many of the newly rich land speculators moved into housing development, building "luxurious dwellings in order to assure themselves a steady income and safeguard the value of their money."[11]

Government encouraged the boom in private housing, in response both to pressures from the housing industry and to the political attractions of providing benefits to the urban middle class. The central government's mortgage-credit programs, which are examined later in the chapter, enlarged the ranks of city families that could afford new housing in the private sector. Construction of condominium apartments was facilitated by laws permitting partial ownership of a building. And new social housing was exempted from taxes for five years under legislation enacted in 1970.

Government was less successful in controlling conventional housing development. Much of the new housing was in apartment units, which had not been common previously in Turkish cities. Buildings were crammed into areas where land was available, with little regard to crowding or amenities, often on sites previously occupied by single-family dwellings. Residential densities rose rapidly in many sections of Istanbul and Ankara, producing overloaded public facilities, mounting traffic congestion, and anarchic parking. Construction methods and materials were often shoddy, as builders cut corners in the face of rising prices. In the rush to build and avoid costly delays, building codes and other public regulations often were ignored, resulting in substantial numbers of conventional buildings that were constructed illegally.

Private housing construction began to falter in the late 1970s. Rising construction costs priced more and more urban dwellers out of the market for conventional housing. Sharp hikes in interest rates in 1980 further reduced the demand for new housing. Falling production in the 1980s intensified housing needs that had continually outpaced housing production during the earlier boom years. As indicated in Table 7-2, licensed housing production continually fell short of government estimates of need, with an average annual shortfall of 20 percent. Because of the breathless pace of urbanization, housing production was on a treadmill. Even though construction more than doubled between 1965 and 1975, the number of new housing units fell from 2.6 for each 1,000 city residents to 1.2 per 1,000 during the decade.

Families that flooded into the cities from the villages, as well as lower-income city dwellers, were squeezed by growing housing shortages and rising rents for existing housing. "Between 1955 and 1965 rents in the three major cities of Istanbul, Ankara and Izmir increased by two and a half. Consequently low income groups had to spend close to one third of their income for rent."[12] One way to overcome the lack of adequate housing within their means was to do what the urban poor always have done—

TABLE 7-2
LICENSED HOUSING PRODUCTION IN TERMS OF HOUSING NEED:
1963–1977

	Licensed Construction	Need	Deficit in Units	Deficit percent
1963	57,300	100,600	43,300	44
1965	80,500	110,500	30,000	27
1967	99,400	121,300	21,900	18
1969	132,100	174,000	42,000	24
1971	153,000	194,600	41,600	19
1973	194,900	213,200	18,200	9
1975	192,200	242,200	50,000	21
1977	235,500	273,200	37,700	14

SOURCE: Ministry of Reconstruction and Settlement, "Low Standard Housing with Special Reference to Squatter-Housing Problem in Turkey." Report to Committee on Housing, Building and Planning, Economic Commission for Europe.

crowd into areas that quickly became slums. Existing dwellings were subdivided, "particularly large, old houses in central areas, as migrants move in with relations or friends."[13] As many as seven or eight people were jammed into a single room. Crowding into older buildings was more common in Istanbul with its fairly large stock of aging housing than was the case in Ankara, whose old quarter encompassed less than 1 percent of the city's area.

For most newcomers who could not afford adequate housing, squatting was a more attractive alternative than the limited accommodations available in slums. For all the difficulties involved in establishing a family in a gecekondu, squatter housing typically was cheaper and more spacious than whatever older housing was available. Gecekondus also had locational advantages for lower-income city dwellers, since many squatter settlements grew up close to new industrial developments. And, of paramount importance, squatting held out the possibility of owning one's home for a modest investment. So the gecekondus flourished, attracting not only migrants but also poor city dwellers who were priced out of the normal housing market.

SQUATTER HOUSING

"We had many difficulties when building this house. Policemen came and took away the shovels and other tools. They also took me to the police station where I told them the truth. I said, 'I cannot afford to rent an apartment. I have my job in Ankara, so I have to live here. I must build a gecekondu.' "[14] This simple tale was repeated thousands and thousands of times, occasionally with more problems with the authorities, frequently with less trouble. The first gecekondus appeared at the end of World War II on the outskirts of Ankara and Istanbul. Growth was rapid as the urban economy revived after the privations of the war and a steady stream of villagers arrived in the cities in search of work. In Istanbul, settlers erected the first gecekondu in Zeytinburnu in 1947; six years later the settlement housed close to 50,000 people.[15]

Squatters moved onto both private and public land. For those who

FIGURE 7-1

SQUATTER SETTLEMENTS IN ISTANBUL: 1980

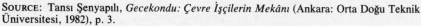

SOURCE: Tansı Şenyapılı, *Gecekondu: Çevre İşçilerin Mekânı* (Ankara: Orta Doğu Teknik Üniversitesi, 1982), p. 3.

Figure 7-2. Squatter settlements in Ankara : 1980

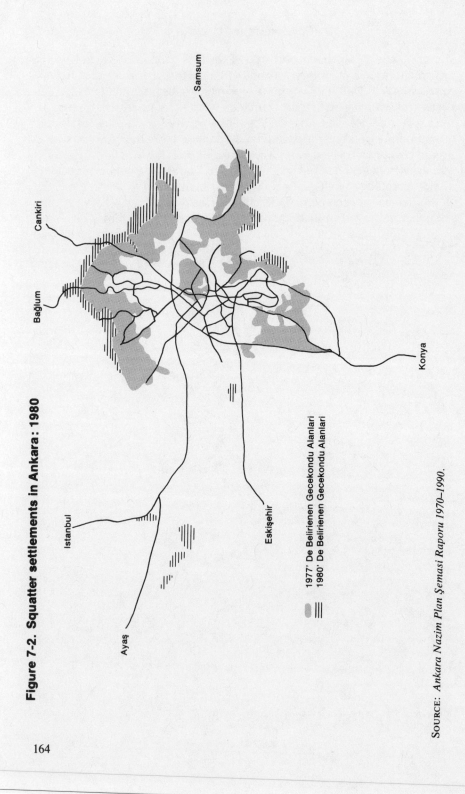

1977' De Belirienen Gecekondu Alanlari
1980' De Belirienen Gecekondu Alanlari

SOURCE: *Ankara Nazim Plan Şemasi Raporu 1970–1990.*

could afford to purchase a plot, private land offered more security, since the buyer would own the land even though the dwelling was being illegally constructed. Private owners often sold at depressed prices land that had been invaded by squatters, or that was adjacent to gecekondu housing. A gecekondu in Istanbul, originally established in 1958 on municipal land, expanded six years later "onto privately owned land. The individual who had a valid legal title agreed to sell the land to the invaders at 12 liras per square meter, which was a very low price, merely to avoid conflict with the squatters."[16]

Most squatters, however, were unable to purchase private land. Instead, they occupied private property or, more commonly, built on public land. Two-thirds of all gecekondus have been erected on government land, which was plentiful in and around the major cities, particularly in Ankara where the state had acquired vast tracts in the process of developing the planned national capital. Claiming unused public land was a common practice in rural Turkey, where "land ownership could be established by use. . . . By village standards the expanses of unused land around Turkish cities were unclaimed land."[17] Each year, more unused land was claimed as new gecekondus sprang up and existing settlements expanded, with marginal public land the most fertile soil in which to plant new settlements.

By 1980, 4.75 million squatters were living in 950,000 gecekondu units. Officially, gecekondus are defined as "dwellings erected, on land and lots which do not belong to the builder, without the consent of the owner, and without observing the laws and regulations concerning construction and building."[18] Thus, gecekondus include housing constructed without a building permit on land owned by the builder, as well as dwellings illegally built on land owned by someone else or by the state. Gecekondus housed in 1980 more than 23 percent of the urban population and made up 21 percent of the urban housing stock. Almost two-thirds of all squatter housing was built in and around Istanbul, Ankara, and Izmir. Three out of every ten squatters in 1980 lived in Ankara, where they accounted for 72.4 percent of the capital's population.

Houses "Which Land in the Night"

Officials and city dwellers reacted to the pioneer squatter settlements with hostility. Police were ordered to demolish the illegal dwellings, and many early settlers had to rebuild their homes or abandon their plot in the face of vigorous law-enforcement efforts. Seemingly in a hopeless legal position, building without permits on land that did not belong to them, squatters were given a reprieve by the law. Under Turkish law, inhabited dwellings could not be demolished without a court order. Thus, the

TABLE 7-3

SQUATTER HOUSING IN ANKARA: 1950–1980

	Number of Squatter Houses	Number of People Living in Squatter Housing	Percent of Urban Population Living in Squatter Housing
1950	12,000	62,400	21.8
1960	70,000	364,000	56.0
1970	144,000	748,000	60.6
1980	275,000	1,450,000	72.4

SOURCE: KENT-KOOP.

gecekondu, the houses "which land in the night," the basic structure erected in haste and stealth, in a single night if possible, so that the dwelling could be "inhabited" the next day, and thus not be torn down unless city officials secured a court order.

Early gecekondus reflected this precarious legal situation. Houses were hastily built, usually with low quality materials, and they were grouped together for security from a hostile outside world. Spatial organization in the gecekondus was strongly influenced by village settlement patterns.

> Houses were tightly packed and followed the traditional courtyard plan. Communal open space was restricted to the narrow streets and paths which wound up the slopes and the feeling predominated of an urban village in which strangers could easily be spotted. This sense of group identity was an essential basis of gecekondu life. It was impossible to finance or actually build a house quickly without considerable local support and so migrants tended to settle in areas of the city where they knew someone from their village.[19]

Nestled together for protection, hurriedly built to foil the authorities, and the only viable form of housing for most urban newcomers, gecekondus spread across the urban landsape. Development of new squatter areas often was organized, with the occupation of the land carefully planned in advance and building materials cached in readiness for the frenzied initial construction.

> The organizers of the invasion are usually a small group of people, often with previous experience, who engage in the act either in response to pressure from relatives and fellow villagers or simply for profit. The participants in the invasion are usually related and known to each other; moreover, in order to strengthen their ranks, new people and acquaintances, including relatives and friends from the village, may be invited to

participate. The larger the number of participants and the bigger the settlement, the more difficult it becomes to demolish it, if indeed, the authorities and the police care to do so.[20]

Gecekondu development quickly spawned a variety of entrepreneurs. Developers specialized in forming new settlements and often reaped substantial profits. Gecekondu landlords acquired numerous dwellings, which they rented or sold to less enterprising squatters. Merchants opened building materials yards near areas being occupied by squatters, supplying lumber, concrete blocks, roof tile, windows, and doors. Carpenters and masons were available to perform the more difficult aspects of construction. And to plan and direct the operation, an experienced craftsman-contractor *(kalfa)* could be hired, who would lay out the site, determine the materials needed, arrange for purchase and transport of supplies, and get the house built if possible before the authorities arrived.

From a distance, the settlements produced by this process are picturesque—little white buildings with red tile roofs clinging to the steep hills and sharp ravines of Ankara and Istanbul. And the names the squatters have chosen for their settlements would put a suburban developer in the United States to shame—Golden Mountain *(Altındağ)*, White Brook *(Akdere)*, and Great Mountain *(Uludağ)*.[21] Up close, reality was a good deal harsher, especially in the early years when few public improvements had been made.

> Dust is toe deep in summer and mud is ankle deep in winter—except when frigid winds lock the quagmire in ice. There are few roads; these are usually mere tracks, not paved roads. Outhouses have adjoining cesspools and open drains running down the hills. Long lines of women [are] seen forming before dawn to catch the brief trickle of water that will flow from an occasional fountain. Yet, electric wires frequently traverse the neighborhoods, and the houses are taxed as residences.[22]

Nature of Gecekondu Housing

Squatter housing in Turkey tends to be a good deal more substantial than the flimsy shanties found in many Asian and Latin-American cities. Despite the necessity for haste and the possibility of demolition, brick construction has been common. Gecekondus built around 1960 involved an average investment of 9,000 lira, or about $1,000. Fifteen years later, the outlay was around 24,000 lira, or $2,000, and represented four to six months' wages for the typical squatter.

Governmental policy influenced the quality of gecekondu housing. As the threat of demolition faded, and as government came to accept squatting as inevitable, gecekondu housing was built less rapidly and to higher standards with better materials. Larger units were constructed on bigger plots, with a nine-meter-by-nine-meter plan common, resulting in 900 square feet of living space. With fewer concerns about security, houses were less likely to be clustered, and were now built facing outward.[23] Most dwellings were expanded and improved once the threat of displacement had passed. "When the home owner is reasonably assured of the survival of the home," writes Metin Heper of the residents of an Istanbul gecekondu, "a considerable part of the family income is spent on home improvement." From one or two rooms, the house "grows without pattern into more rooms, kitchen(s) and toilet(s) as the family size increases due to births, relatives and friends arriving from the villages."[24] Over time, with improvements, provision of public services, and development of shops and other amenities, established gecekondus were increasingly difficult to distinguish from other lower-income urban neighborhoods.

Despite relatively high standards compared to squatter housing in many developing nations, most gecekondu dwellings have serious deficiencies. Overcrowding is common, with families often doubled up in a single dwelling. Gecekondus average 2.6 people per room, compared with 2.1 for all urban housing. Large amounts of squatter housing are located on sites that were never suitable for residential development, leading to severe drainage, sewage, and access problems. Because of poor drainage, squatter housing is often damp and musty, while raw sewage creates more serious problems in some units. Ventilation and light frequently are inadequate. Even with higher quality materials and substantial improvements, many units are structurally unsound, with 70 percent estimated to need repairs.

The Quest for Home Ownership

From the beginning, one of the strongest attractions of squatter settlements was the desire of migrants and other low-income city dwellers to own their homes. This goal has been achieved by about 60 percent of all gecekondu dwellers. The desire to own one's land was deeply rooted in the peasants who flocked to the cities, many of whom had owned land in their villages. Land was security in a nation with primitive social services—"the squatter perceives his squatter house not just as shelter but as his insurance for the future."[25]

Possession of a land deed, or *tapu,* freed the gecekondu dweller from the fear of eviction or demolition by local officials. Without deeds, squatters were not eligible to participate in official gecekondu improvement programs. Ownership also spurred home improvements, in sharp contrast to the deterioration of most rental properties occupied by low-income urban dwellers. Last, but hardly least, were the potential financial benefits that resulted from owning their homes. Squatters were well aware that "once they acquired the *tapus*, the market value of their shacks would skyrocket, especially if the looks of the *gecekondu* improved, as invariably it did."[26]

Government was the critical factor in the legalization of squatter housing. Market forces may have pushed the urban poor into squatter settlements, but politics legalized the process, and in so doing amplified both gecekondu development and the migration that fueled squatting. Beginning in the 1950s, when the ruling Democratic Party sought to win favor among squatters by granting land deeds, all the major political parties promised gecekondu dwellers titles in return for votes. For their part, as pointed out in Chapter 5, squatters have tried to extract pledges on titles from the parties in return for electoral support. As more and more gecekondu dwellers secured land deeds, squatting became less risky, and more migrants were drawn to the city. Government in effect enlarged the pot of gold at the end of the rainbow for migrants to Turkish cities.

Gecekondus in Transition

Whatever the broader costs, squatter housing has offered lower-income urban households substantial benefits. Squatters were able "to obtain a plot of land free or at modest cost levels near centers of employment and to control the extent and phasing of their expenditure on housing."[27] Beyond the direct housing benefits, squatter settlements also played a critical role in easing the assimilation of migrants into the city. Gecekondus provided a foothold in the city for urban newcomers, offering community solidarity and mutual assistance in the struggle to survive in a hostile environment. Migrants from the same family, village, and region tend to cluster together in squatter settlements. Solidarity was reinforced by communal efforts to establish a gecekondu, secure deeds, and obtain public services.

With the passage of time, gecekondus changed. Established squatter areas and their inhabitants were slowly assimilated into the city. As squatters secured public services, titles to their homes, and more general acceptance, communal ties became less important. Gecekondus also were becoming more heterogeneous. Some settlers moved up the economic ladder, but preferred not to leave familiar surroundings. And lower-middle-class families were drawn to gecekondus as squatter housing became more secure, more attractive, and more appealing financially in comparison with conventional shelter. As one observer notes, "rents in Istanbul are very high and the residents of gecekondus in fact include white collar workers, municipal officials and others whom most Istanbullers probably would not consider typical gecekondu dwellers."[28]

At the same time, gecekondu development was becoming more expensive and more commercialized. Land for squatter housing grew increasingly scarce as more and more migrants piled into the major cities. In the face of these shortages, land speculators became more active in the 1970s, and prices for gecekondu plots began to rise sharply. Even plots lacking clear title commanded high prices. In place of informal squatter development involving relatives, friends, and fellow villagers, organized real estate markets emerged. Larger-scale gecekondu development "resulted in a form of land subdivision in which plots are arranged as in a commercial housing estate."[29] As a result of these changes, "instead of obtaining a cheap plot near friends or relatives, new settlers . . . had to move well out of the city, pay large sums for a plot on exposed hillsides which were difficult to develop and then live surrounded by strangers."[30] And the houses were more likely to be built by commercial builders, which further increased costs and reduced communal efforts.

Rising land costs and growth pressures also have transformed some squatter areas into apartment districts. As the large cities expanded, apartment developers were increasingly hard pressed to find suitable sites for new buildings. Some of the most attractive locations were occupied by gecekondus, and what had been unused land claimed by squatters was now valuable urban real estate. Quickly, apartments replaced squatter houses in the favored locations since "few gecekondu occupants could afford to resist the opportunity of realizing large profits and becoming owners of one or more apartments by selling the 'use-rights' they had to their plot."[31] Thus, with a critical assist from government which had given the squatter something to sell by legalizing what had been illegally acquired, some gecekondu dwellers moved in one generation from impoverished squatters to owners of substantial city properties.

COPING WITH SQUATTER HOUSING

The rapid spread of squatter settlements in Turkey's major cities confronted government with particularly difficult choices. The nation clearly lacked the resources to provide adequate housing for most of the poor migrants who flocked to the cities. Government also could not easily prevent the establishment of gecekondus, despite the strong opposition of landowners, established city dwellers, and local governments. Moreover, migrants were essential if Turkey was to urbanize and industrialize. Further complicating the problem was mounting political pressures from the growing mass of squatters who sought governmental recognition of their communities and property rights.

Faced with these constraints and pressures, governmental policies have pursued a variety of objectives, which "have often been ambivalent and conflicting."[32] Contradictions have resulted from efforts to satisfy incompatible goals. Prohibition and demolition of illegal housing were the initial cornerstones of Turkish squatter policy. But these negative policies increased the housing shortage that caused squatting. As squatters continued to pour into the cities, politicians added to the confusion by legitimizing housing that was supposed to be demolished. Efforts to encourage low-cost housing increased the contradictions—"while the laws [were] demanding a forceful means of destroying gecekondu, at the same time, the law [was] permissive in giving governmental aid to the people."[33] New policies constantly were added, but old ones rarely were abandoned. As a result, gecekondu objectives and responsibilities multiplied far faster than resources or results.

The Failure of Prohibition

Government's initial response to gecekondus was to prevent the establishment of squatter settlements and thus protect private property and public lands from illegal occupation. Illegal housing was to be torn down by city governments in accordance with a 1924 law that authorized municipalities to demolish dwellings built on unowned land.[34] Additional legislation enacted in 1949 bolstered local authority to get rid of squatter housing.[35] Reflecting widespread concerns of property owners in the major cities, the law dealt severely with squatters who occupied private property. Gecekondus built on private land were subject to immediate demolition, and squatters on private property could be sent to prison. Provision also was made for local officials to secure assistance from the central police if squatters resisted municipal law-enforcement officers.[36]

Despite these and subsequent laws that promised harsh treatment to illegal housing, demolition proved an ineffective policy. Part of the difficulty was inherent in the 1924 law, which required local authorities to secure a court order before tearing down an inhabited dwelling. As seen earlier, gecekondus literally were built overnight to ensure that the house was occupied before it was spotted by the police. Once official notice was taken of the illegal dwelling, the squatter was informed that the house would be torn down on a certain date. "On receipt of a demolition order, the settler simply applied to the courts stating that the building was inhabited."[37] Only rarely were city officials able to secure the necessary court order to demolish the contested dwelling. Courts were overwhelmed by squatters' applications for relief, and titles to the land in question often were unclear.

Nor were the squatters without friends in court. Court officials and judges were often sympathetic, and procedural delays favored the squatter who was living in his house while the case was creeping through the court system. Granville Sewell has described the situation in Ankara's courts during the initial efforts to check gecekondu construction:

> Papers are "lost" or interminably "processed." Every apparatus of delay and subterfuge is employed to aid the builder for the simple reason that virtually all the lower echelons of the government offices will be living in the gecekondu themselves or will have close relatives there. Even if the case ever comes up before the overburdened court, it is usually thrown out on a technicality. After all, the judges may reason, one-third of Ankara's population—and similar proportions in other cities—are said to be living in gecekondu. If the case does go against the builder, the judgment can be appealed for a pittance, and the cycle is repeated.[38]

Besides the formidable legal obstacles, local officials faced other barriers in seeking to demolish squatter housing. Police were persuaded to ignore illegal buildings, sometimes with the help of bribes. Complicating law enforcement was the fact that poorly paid municipal police officers were also moving into gecekondus. Their sympathies clearly were with their neighbors rather than with city hall. More generally, the police were being asked to enforce unpopular laws—never an easy task. Poorly trained and lacking weapons, the city police faced settlers who often resisted demolition. The prospects of using force on women was another deterrent to police action:

> Police hesitated to move against women occupants because of fear of incurring assault charges. Nor could they turn half-dressed women out of their houses. Another frequent means of avoiding house destruction was for the woman to claim herself a widow, severe calamity in an underdeveloped country where charity is not a state institution. When women were more seriously threatened, there were cases of them standing on the roofs of their houses, threatening to throw their babies to the ground or jump themselves if molested.[39]

Demolition was also deterred by the sheer numbers involved, which magnified the problems involved in securing court orders and ensuring that police enforced the law. Moreover, even demolition did not faze many squatters, who returned to rebuild and thus rechallenge local authorities. In the face of these formidable constraints, city governments were unable in any systematic fashion to enforce the laws prohibiting squatting. Instead, selective enforcement was common, with the worst housing singled out for demolition. Of course, this policy "acted as a good incentive to build a house well and maintain it in good condition!"[40]

Growing numbers of gecekondu dwellers also increased the political deterrents to demolition. Elected politicians often came to the aid of gecekondu constituents threatened by local officials. Some came directly to the aid of squatters, joining them in opposition to police action. More often, strings were pulled to deter or undercut municipal law enforcement. Sewell recounts one example of political intervention in an Ankara gecekondu:

> The first gecekondu . . . were destroyed by police. But they were rebuilt, then joined by additional houses. After about ten were built, the local housing control officer decided to shift tactics. Police began to destroy all water containers in the new community. Each day, water cans were upset and jugs broken. The populace appeared discouraged, so that police considered victory only a matter of time. Then one day when the police patrol climbed the hill to search for water, a fire department water tank was found stationed at the top. Upon inquiry, the local control officer discovered that it was there at the request of the local Democratic assemblyman. The war was over.[41]

More generally, prohibitory policies were undermined by political acceptance of squatters and their settlements. While city officials were expected to get rid of illegal dwellings, national and political leaders were promising squatters title and other benefits. In the end, political considerations determined public policy—squatters had votes, squatters were increasing in numbers, and there were no viable alternatives. Reinforcing these calculations was the fact that squatter housing benefited powerful political interests. Industrialists and other influential employers were bound to see advantages in an inexpensive housing system that helped keep wages down.[42]

Prohibition continued as an official policy as successive gecekondu laws provided for the demolition of squatter dwellings erected after the enactment of the legislation. Just as regularly, however, existing illegal housing was legitimized by the very law that was reiterating the prohibition on new gecekondus. Each step in the process undermined the previous one, further reducing the credibility of demolition as a deterrent to new gecekondu construction.

Officials have continued to tear down squatter houses in Turkish cities, but only sporadically and in response to specific pressures or political considerations. Complaints from landowners whose property has been invaded can bring govenmental intervention, particularly if the individual is well connected politically. Periods of tough enforcement have sometimes followed political change. After the military interventions of 1960 and 1980, there were interludes of fairly vigorous enforcement of the prohibition on new settlements. But political realities eroded enforcement after the restoration of elected governments in 1961, and most cities curbed the bulldozer as the 1963 municipal elections approached. Demolition also was used to punish squatter settlements that had been infiltrated by student radicals in the 1970s. In one such "liberated quarter," Ümraniye gecekondu in Istanbul, many people were wounded in 1977 when settlers clashed with police who had been ordered to tear down illegal dwellings.

The Hope of Alternative Housing

Prohibition failed because restrictive policies did not address the housing needs of migrants and other poor urban dwellers. From the beginning of squatting, there was recognition that prevention of gecekondus would require positive as well as negative measures. Without some means of providing acceptable housing for migrants, prohibition was a political and practical impossibility. Where were poor people to live, asked police officers, judges, and other officials charged with enforcing the law, as well as businesses that hired the newcomers. How could politicians support the eviction of their constituents if government was unable to provide housing alternatives? The bottom line was clear—"the shortage of low-cost housing [was] increased each time that a unit [was] demolished."[43]

As early as 1948, an effort was made to answer these questions by providing alternatives to squatter housing. Two laws were enacted: One authorized municipal government to improve gecekondu areas and sell publicly owned land to settlers at nominal prices; the other facilitated the development of inexpensive housing by cooperatives through easy credit and tax exemptions.[44] Neither of these laws, however, had much impact on gecekondu dwellers. Only those who had lived in the city for a year were eligible to purchase municipal land, which excluded substantial numbers of potential squatters. And individual participants in these programs needed capital, so that most of the beneficiaries were not penniless squatters, but middle-class families who could afford regular housing.

These housing programs were expanded in 1953 and again in 1959. State lands were transferred to municipalities under more favorable terms in an effort to spur city programs.[45] But the programs remained both too restrictive and too expensive for the vast majority of gecekondu dwellers. Moreover, the major burdens for gecekondu improvement were assigned to underfinanced city governments already overwhelmed by rapid urbanization. Despite good intentions, viable alternatives to squatting had not been developed during the years between 1948 and 1960. Demolition was fading as a threat despite harsh provisions in the 1953 legislation, and gecekondu development was accelerating, spurred by parallel governmental actions that provided public services and land titles.

The Gecekondu Law of 1966

As the 1960s began to unroll, governmental policy sought to come to terms with the reality of massive squatting. Increasingly, squatter settlements were seen as the inevitable consequence of rapid urbanization and Turkey's level of economic development. The negative emphasis on prohibition and demolition gave way to a more positive approach that identified gecekondus with urbanization, industrialization, and modernization. "Urbanization and its accompanying 'gecekondus' are not considered today an undesirable phenomenon in Turkey," the government contended in a request to the United Nations for help in rehabilitating squatter housing. "Instead, the rapid growth of cities and the existence of gecekondu areas—planned or unplanned—are considered positive factors in national development, for, from them are to come the workers for the proposed massive industrialization programme of the decade of the 1970s."[46]

The new approach was articulated in Turkey's First Five-Year Plan for national development, prepared in 1963. Improvement rather than demolition was now the keystone of squatter policy. Public utilities were to be provided, along with technical assistance and credits for home improvements. Priority also was given to resolving land ownership in squatter areas, so that settlers could secure title to their property. Only those squatter dwellings that could not be improved were to be torn down, and demolition was conditioned on the provision of shelter for those who would lose their homes.[47]

In effect, the plan sought to control squatter settlements, and thus influence the pattern of urban development, by focusing demand. The worst housing in the poorest locations would be torn down. New low-cost housing would be located by government rather than by squatters, and provided with public services in advance of settlement. And to ensure that resources were concentrated on these policy goals, basic responsibility for squatter housing was to be shifted from municipal administrations to the central government.

From these general policies emerged the Gecekondu Law of 1966, Turkey's most comprehensive attempt to deal with squatter housing.[48] The legislation proposed a multifaceted approach to squatter settlements involving elements both new and old—legalization, improvement of existing housing, clearance of unacceptable gecekondus, site preparation, development of low-cost housing, and prohibition of new squatter settlements. The ambitious program was under the general direction of the Ministry of Reconstruction and Settlement, which was empowered to establish priorities among and within cities for the areas that were to be improved, cleared, and resettled. Specific plans and programs were developed by city governments in accordance with central guidelines, and had to be approved by the Ministry of Reconstruction, which in practice closely controlled local implementation.

Under the law, municipalities were empowered to grant land deeds for houses that had been erected on public land but that met minimal standards. Possession of a land deed entitled the squatter to public services. Only those settlers who secured titles to their land were eligible for home improvements. Lacking valid deeds squatters could not obtain local permits to rebuild or enlarge their homes, nor were they eligible for the government's credits and technical assistance made available by the Gecekondu Law of 1966.

Improvement was the second major element of the 1966 program, and involved both public services and renovation of housing. Gecekondu improvement areas were delimited by city governments, subject to approval by the Ministry of Reconstruction. Within these areas, structurally sound gecekondus were eligible for public services and government assistance with renovations. For each area, improvement plans were prepared by the city government. Infrastructure investments were financed by central and city funds, and by the squatters who benefited from extensions of water, electricity, and other municipal services.

One of the central objectives of the 1966 law was to differentiate between gecekondu housing that was worth preserving and that which had to be removed. About one-third of all gecekondus were placed in the latter category, including housing that was blocking high-priority public projects, that surrounded historic buildings and buildings, that was endangered by floods and landslides, and, most important, that was sufficiently dilapidated to pose a substantial threat to public health and safety. Clearance could not proceed until government had provided relocation housing for those losing their homes.

Those displaced by clearance were to be resettled in gecekondu prevention areas, which were also to be open to other low-income families. City governments would acquire land for these areas. After the installation of public services, housing would be developed on the plots—through sale of the improved land to individuals and cooperatives, erection of core houses by the government with the buyer completing construction, or construction of low-cost apartments. In addition, government provided technical assistance to home builders and long-term low-interest loans. In return for this public assistance, participants were not allowed to sell their subsidized dwellings.

To finance this ambitious undertaking, the Gecekondu Law of 1966 established two funds, one for municipalities and the other under the direct control of the Ministry of Reconstruction. Cities were obligated to contribute at least 1 percent of their annual revenues to the municipal fund. Financial resources also were available to cities for squatter improvements from the national government, from interest on loans made from the fund, and from contributions from squatters who benefited from public service improvements. The National Fund for Gecekondus was underwritten primarily by appropriations in the national budget. Additionally, a number of central credit institutions were required to contribute a portion of their annual profits to the squatter fund.

Successes and Failures

Enactment of the Gecekondu Law of 1966 was heralded as the beginning of a speedy and final solution of the squatter problem. Good gecekondus would be improved, bad ones eliminated, and new housing provided. And since the problem was being solved, squatting would no longer be necessary—so the law forbade new settlements, providing for the swift demolition of all gecekondus constructed after the law went into effect. Obviously, these expectations were wildly optimistic in light of the previous two decades' experience and the limited resources that would be available to implement the new legislation. As Sevim Aksoy has noted, "the law was unrealistic in simply stating that from that time onward, no further *gecekondu* areas were to be established, since there was at that time . . . no reason to assume that the existing institutions and laws were sufficiently strong and purposeful to restrain this form of development."[49]

And they were not—the provisions for demolition of new housing were as ineffective as past prohibitions. Deadlines were continually extended to exempt newly constructed gecekondus, as elected officials responded to their growing squatter constituencies. Symbolic of the failure of effort to halt new settlements was the Gecekondu Law of 1976. Enacted before a national election, the new legislation legalized all squatter housing built on public lands after the enactment of the 1966 law.

While prohibition was a predictable failure, the ownership and improvement elements of the 1966 program were, on balance, successful. Substantial numbers of gecekondu dwellers obtained title to their land. Legalization spurred the development and improvement of housing that people could afford, ensured the permanence of homeownership, increased the value of squatter housing, and provided strong incentives for the improvement of dwellings and communities. Granting titles to squatters also was redistributive—in effect, property rights to valuable public land were transferred to low-income city dwellers.

Clarifying and granting titles, however, was time consuming, often holding up the improvement phase of the program, which could not proceed until settlers had land deeds. In addition, the benefits of ownership were not shared by all squatters. Renters in gecekondus gained nothing, while some gecekondu landlords received disproportionately large benefits. Legalization also encouraged squatting on public lands, thus reducing its availability for other public purposes. And the dwindling supply of public land further reduced government's opportunities to use its land to influence urban development.

Gecekondu improvements also distributed substantial benefits to squatters. Public services and home improvements were made available at prices that most low-income families could afford. One assessment of the impact of the 1966 law concludes that "by the late 1960s housing conditions for many gecekondu residents were agreeably better than for many middle income households living in expensive apartments within polluted and overcrowded central locations."[50]

Implementation of gecekondu improvements often required surmounting formidable obstacles within city government. The 1966 law devolved complex responsibilities on city governments that lacked both the financial and the administrative resources to act effectively. A variety of city agencies were involved, and coordination was usually lacking among the functionally isolated bureaucracies of municipal government. Lack of personnel and funds often delayed the preparation of gecekondu improvement plans. For example, maps showing boundaries and land ownership had to be prepared, which "required a crew of men for surveying and measuring on the site. It was also necessary to develop accurate maps fully integrated with the coordinates of Istanbul. The Municipality did not have enough personnel to carry out these tasks quickly."[51]

More generally, the gecekondu-improvement program suffered from the general inadequacy of the resources made available by the 1966 law. Neither fund was sufficient given the magnitude of the problems of existing gecekondu housing, to say nothing of the amounts needed to mount a vigorous program of clearance, relocation, and new housing development. Resource problems were intensified by highly partisan allocations of the National Fund for Gecekondus. As indicated in Chapter 5, assistance usually was distributed to maximize political returns rather than focus resources where needed most for squatter improvements.

Meager resources were an even greater problem with the clearance and squatter-prevention programs, neither of which had much impact on urban housing conditions. Lack of funds to provide shelter for those dislocated precluded much clearance. Only 32,500 units had been marked for removal and relocation of inhabitants through 1982. Land acquisition for squatter prevention areas also proceeded very slowly, with only 40,000 plots allocated by 1982. Available resources also were spread too thinly across the nation to have much impact on the problem in the biggest cities, with over 600 squatter prevention zones designated in 360-odd municipalities.[52] In Istanbul, only 3 of 12 prevention areas were developed, and the 4,000 units of housing constructed were negligible in light of housing needs in the huge metropolis.[53]

Problems were also encountered in allocating land available for the construction of housing in prevention areas. The number of families seeking homesites far exceeded the land available under the program. Priorities for the allocation of land were set by the Ministry of Reconstruction, and were designed to ensure that those most in need receive housing plots. To be eligible, families were not supposed to own a house, flat, or land suitable for building a home. Municipal governments, however, were unable to enforce these provisions because of administrative weaknesses and political pressures. Nor was the objective of distributing land exclusively to the poor maintained. A regulation enacted in 1976 defined lower-income families eligible for the program as those with yearly incomes of 38,000 lira for a couple, with an additional 4,000 lira for each child, which was higher than the average urban family income. As a result, middle-income families were the principal beneficiaries of the housing projects constructed under the 1966 Gecekondu Law.

But most important was the failure of gecekondu-prevention areas to attract squatters, who preferred to help themselves to land rather than participate in the government's self-help program. As İbrahim Şanlı points out, "squatters found it much easier to simply erect a *gecekondu* than to build a proper dwelling and be indebted to financing agencies of the central government."[54] Ankara used the Gecekondu Law of 1966 to develop sites with public services for squatters, but the program "never attracted popular interest, probaby because costs were higher and controls greater than in informal settlements. Delays in developing sites and allocating to potential applicants, also contributed to their failure and so these projects remained essentially as a slogan."[55]

The Gecekondu Law of 1966 was most successful when government ratified demand for squatter housing by granting titles and providing improvements. Efforts to focus and modify demand through clearance, site development, and prohibition had considerably less impact. Legalization and improvement, however, involved some governmental focusing of demand, since granting of titles, provision of public services, and renovations increased the attractions of some settlements compared with others. Perhaps the most important lesson learned from the 1966 programs was that far more resources would have to be concentrated on housing and community development to modify significantly the economic and political demands that produced gecekondus.

Slowly but surely the conclusion emerged that effective squatter policy required a major commitment to low-cost social housing. The Third Five-Year Development Plan (1973–1977) emphasized the need for large-scale production of social housing by the government, as well as more effective sites and services programs.[56] These priorities were reiterated in the Fourth Five-Year Plan (1978–1982), which called for the use of public land and expanded public credits for low-income housing and the creation by city governments of cooperatives to build social housing.[57] The question was whether resources could be mustered for massive investments in low-cost housing, and whether the new housing programs would benefit gecekondu dwellers or middle-income families as in the past.

INCREASING THE HOUSING SUPPLY

As indicated at the outset of this chapter, government in Turkey has played a minor role in the provision of conventional housing in the cities. Government has built little housing directly, relying instead on various credit programs to lower financing costs. And these governmental efforts to increase the housing supply have primarily benefited middle- and upper-income urban families, while providing practically no new housing for poor city dwellers.

Housing for the Middle Class

Turkey's initial efforts to increase the supply of housing in cities was centered in Ankara. During the new capital's first decades, adequate housing was in short supply for the rapidly growing corps of civil servants. In response to these needs, the central government built public housing for government employees, provided incentives for the formation of housing cooperatives, and granted individual subsidies to some public officials.[58] In this instance, government was taking care of its own, almost all of whom had middle-class or better incomes.

After World War II, housing policy sought to stimulate home ownership and private housing construction through mortgage programs. In 1946, the Real Estate Bank *(Emlâk ve Kredi Bankası)* was created as the central government's principal source of housing credit. The Bank was authorized to provide long-term, low-interest mortgages to middle- and lower-income families for up to 90 percent of the cost of a house. Initially, mortgages were available only for individual houses, and most of the Real Estate Bank's housing credits financed housing for civil servants in Ankara.

During the 1950s, housing-finance programs expanded, as a result of both the growing significance of urban voters and pressures from private housing interests. With the emergence of a two-party system, "easy home financing became one of the Democrats' appeals to the city dwellers.

Zafer, the official party paper, adopted . . . a slogan that every Turk should become a homeowner."[59] New housing credit programs were established for government employees, military personnel, and state enterprises. Housing construction also was stimulated by tax exemptions for new housing.

Additional demand for private housing was unleashed in 1954, when the central government enacted legislation permitting the ownership of individual apartments and concomitantly expanded the mortgage programs to include apartments.[60] The liberalized policies on apartments resulted from pressures from landowners for higher densities and larger profits, as well as from the obvious need for apartment construction in the inner sections of the major cities and the inability of middle-class city dwellers to afford single-family housing in the face of rising land costs. In 1965, landowners secured a new law on condominiums that facilitated more intensive apartment development.[61] The lure of higher profits led to "technically young buildings [being] replaced with higher buildings," and what the Ministry of Reconstruction and Settlement terms, "sort of an urban renewal process" was "completed in larger cities in the second half of the 1970s."[62]

Between 1946 and 1982, the Real Estate Bank financed 350,000 housing units, the vast majority of which went to middle- and upper-income urban dwellers. Although the mortgage program was supposed to serve lower-income families, upper limits on loans meant that subsidized mortgages were "never sufficient to buy a good house, and in the large cities most of the borrowers [were] forced to look for additional funds from other sources to buy an apartment."[63] Few lower-income families among potential borrowers could muster the extra credit, and thus were unable to participate. Even more slanted toward the well off was the Real Estate Bank's housing-construction program, which produced some attractive and well-planned housing, but these expensive homes have been far beyond the means of most urban dwellers.

Government also has fostered the development and financing of housing cooperatives, which produced about 7 percent of the total conventional housing between 1950 and 1980. The major sponsor of cooperative housing has been the central government's Social Insurance Agency, created in 1946, which provides long-term low-cost mortgages for workers' cooperatives. Despite the enormous housing needs of workers, and insistent pressures from labor unions for an expansion of the workers' cooperative program, the Social Insurance Agency financed only 170,000 units between 1946 and 1982, an annual average of under 5,000 units. Only 3 percent of all members of the Social Insurance Agency have received housing assistance. A major impediment to worker participation is the requirement for a 10-percent down payment. And among those eligible, white-collar workers have been far more aware of the agency's program and procedures than have lower-income factory and manual workers, and have been far more likely to secure subsidized housing.

As indicated earlier, housing programs were developed as early as 1948 to provide alternatives to squatter settlements. But these measures, like other government housing efforts, rarely reached the urban poor. The initial program, established by the Building Encouragement Law of 1948, provided land at cost, credits from the State Housing Bank, and tax exemptions that would lower costs.[64] But loans covered only 75 percent of the cost, so that capital was required to participate, and the resulting housing was too expensive for squatters. As a result, middle-income residents wound up in projects such as Yenimahalle, which was developed under the Building Encouragement Law by Ankara's city government. With its winding streets and attractive low-rise dwellings, Yenimahalle is one of Turkey's most successful middle-class housing developments; by the early 1980s the area had developed into a satellite city with over 350,000 residents.

For those who could afford subsidized housing, the benefits were substantial, given the rising cost of housing and the pervasive shortage of adequate shelter. For many, the temptation to cash in on the increasing value of their subsidized housing was irresistible, and houses and apartments were sold or rented at considerable profit. After renting or selling their government-financed home, beneficiaries of the housing financing programs often moved to gecekondus, and revenues from this real estate were the principal source of income for some. Such moves were legal since restrictions were not imposed on the sale or rental of housing acquired with government mortgages.

These housing-finance programs tended to amplify housing demand, and, in the process, influenced development patterns in the major cities. As in the United States, where government policies stimulated the demand for suburban housing and thus accelerated the decentralization fo the metropolis, Turkish housing-finance policies encouraged the development of middle- and upper-income housing. Apartment-house construction was spurred in Istanbul, Ankara, and Izmir, and it led to substantial increases in residential densities in the inner sections of all three cities. By encouraging the flow of scarce resources into private housing for the better off, government policy reduced the resources available for improving housing for lower-income families, and thus reduced public capabilities to provide alternatives to squatter settlements.

Government housing policies also reinforced the role of the private sector. Housing purchased with public credits was constructed by private contractors, usually on privately held land. Private housing interests sought to enlarge government's role, while maintaining their own dominant position in supplying land and building homes. They argued for a higher priority for housing in national economic plans and vigorously supported new legislation to enlarge government credit and cooperative programs.

Because the housing programs relied on private entrepreneurs for implementation, little attention was given to land use and environmental considerations. The finance agencies did not "require that a building be located in an area and constructed at a density that is in accordance with some form of planning instrument or appropriate environmental standard." As a result, in the wake of the 1965 condominium law, high-rise apartments replaced smaller buildings "on precisely the same lots, with precisely the same road system that once served low-density areas."[65]

The Housing Law of 1981

As housing problems worsened during the 1970s, pressures began to build for substantial policy changes. Private housing production was in the throes of a prolonged slump because of high interest rates and inflated costs. Existing housing programs reached only a small proportion of the population, most of whom were relatively well off. Almost no alternative housing had been provided for squatters, whose numbers continued to increase rapidly. The Third and Fourth Five-Year Plans called for the mass production of social housing, but plans without resources produced no concrete results. Annual housing needs for the early 1980s were estimated at 330,000 units, of which over 90,000 dwellings a year would have to be produced by the public sector, necessitating a threefold increase in subsidized housing.[66]

As policies were debated, proposals considered, and laws drafted, considerable attention was given to the question of the role of the private and public sectors, as well as to the closely related issue of which group would benefit from enlarging governmental involvement in housing. Many officials and planners sought to emphasize the public sector in order to increase the production of social housing. The Fourth Five-Year Development Plan emphasized the need to shift from small-scale private producers to large-scale mass production of social housing with substantial government involvement. Builders and landowners stressed the need for stimulation of private housing construction, a perspective that was shared by the Ministry of Reconstruction and Settlement, which had close ties to the housing industry. One side argued that private builders cared only about profits and could not play a constructive role in the development of social housing; the other contended that private builders had the know-how to get housing built.

The dispute over the shape of a new housing policy was caught up in the pervasive conflict between the Republican People's Party and the conservative coalition led by the Justice Party. The RPP favored a stronger governmental role and in 1979 established a New Settlements Fund for use in acquiring and preparing sites in the major cities for the development of new communities. Back in office the following year, the JP set forth a National Housing Policy that placed greater emphasis on the private sector.

These various threads of policy finally were woven into major new housing legislation in 1981 under the direction of the military government, as well as in the Constitution adopted in 1982.[67] Law 2487 of 1981, the Law on Collective Housing, dramatically increased Turkey's commitment to housing. No longer was housing investment to be the stepchild of national development policy. A Public Housing Fund was created to be underwritten by 5 percent of the national budget—which would provide 100 billion lira ($1 billion) at the outset if the promised financing materialized. Efforts were made to reduce the costs of housing. Urban land could be expropriated for housing construction at its tax value rather than market value, which, given the notorious underassessment of property, promised to reduce significantly land costs for social housing. Mass production was to be emphasized, as was the construction of smaller houses in large projects in order to lower unit costs and increase the number of dwellings constructed. Projects were to have a minimum of 750 units in newly developed sites.

The law represented a victory for those who favored public over private approaches to increasing housing production. Initial drafts of the new legislation prepared by the Ministry of Reconstruction would have funneled state housing funds directly to private builders. But critics of the housing industry prevailed, and the legislation approved by the National Security Council assigned responsibility for implementing the program to public social security agencies and cooperatives. Underlying this setback for private housing interests was the widespread conviction that reliance on the private sector was part of the housing problem, not part of the solution. Builders and landowners also were less able to protect their interests with the military government than was the case with elected politicians, although after the Law was enacted they continued to press vigorously for favorable amendments. Within the private sector, property owners were bigger losers than construction interests. Landowners and speculators were faced with real losses if their properties were expropriated at costs far below market prices. Builders, on the other hand, would secure contracts to construct much of the housing for cooperatives and social security agencies, which were not able to erect homes on their own. And the promised rise in public investment in housing would, if fulfilled, substantially increase the total amount of construction undertaken by private contractors.

Like other urban reforms adopted by the military government, the new housing program was highly centralized. Control over the new programs was firmly lodged in the Ministry of Reconstruction, which was responsible for selecting sites and contracting for construction. City governments, which had been actively developing large-scale projects, particularly in Ankara and Istanbul, had less freedom of action under the 1981 Law. Funds were available from the central government only if cities organized housing cooperatives.

Large cities were also given lower priority than smaller cities in the allocation of housing credits by the central government. One reason for favoring smaller cities was the desire to lower unit costs, since land and construction costs were substantially higher in the metropolitan centers. Preferential treatment for smaller municipalities also was supposed to influence the urban development pattern by deflecting growth away from the major cities. Further complicating the problems of big cities under the 1981 Law were the priorities adopted by the Ministry of Reconstruction and Settlement, which targeted housing subsidies on development areas identified by the State Planning Organization, and thus away from major urban centers. How much impact these measures would have on the fortunes of the larger cities was unclear, especially once elected governments were restored. Housing problems were too serious in the urban centers to deny big cities their share of central housing funds, and elected national officials were bound to be responsive to Turkey's largest concentrations of people and voters.

Even more problematic was whether sufficient resources would be made available to finance the ambitious collective housing program. The 1981 Law promised to increase government investment in housing fourfold, from 6.7 percent of total expenditures in 1981 to 28.4 percent in 1982.[68] In fact, only one-fifth of the anticipated government funding of 109 billion lira was realized, resulting in no real increase in government investment in housing during the new program's initial year. Ostensibly, limited funds were provided in 1982 because not enough cooperatives had been organized. But at the root of the failure to muster the promised financial resources lay economic constraints and budgetary pressures likely to limit severely Turkey's ability to meet its new housing commitments in future budgets. In 1983, again, only one-fifth of the promised amount was made available, and the Ministry of Finance indicated grave doubts about the wisdom of fixed national commitments to housing and other functions, terming the collective housing legislation "a bad law. If you write down all such laws and add together the appropriations they provide, there will be no budget at all. . . . We do not have such a large budget to distribute to every one."[69]

Even if the promised resources materialized in the future, the collective housing program was unlikely to realize its goal of providing housing for families that were not reached by previous governmental efforts. Social housing was supposed to be built for lower-income families, with projects built near industrial zones for workers and in areas "where unhealthy urbanization and squatter housing reach high proportions."[70] But, like earlier programs, collective housing was based on home ownership. Substantial down payments were required—20 to 25 percent, depending on the size of the unit—to secure mortgages from the Public Housing Fund. And the required capital had to be accumulated within three years in a housing savings account. As in the past, capital requirements automatically excluded most lower-income families. In fact, the recommended monthly income for participation—59,000 lira in 1981 (about $600) exceeded the top salary of civil servants, thus constituting a substantial financial strain for many middle-class families, to say nothing of gecekondu dwellers.

That the collective Housing Law resulted from a desire to broaden social housing opportunities is clear. Government was given a more powerful role than in the past, subsidies were increased, housing savings made more attractive, and a variety of cost-cutting avenues explored. Yet as Ali Türel and Özcan Altaban emphasize, "the new Housing Law is unlikely to make substantial changes in the composition of the supplied housing types in the short run, since housing credits are not expected to reach most of the low income families."[71] Underlying this outcome was the cost of supplying new housing, particularly through subsidized mortgages rather than subsidized rents. And in choosing to continue an emphasis on ownership rather than rental programs, politics was as important as economics. Home ownership is highly valued in Turkey—by those who live in squatter as well as conventional housing, and politicians have responded with home ownership for those who can afford conventional housing and land titles for those who live in gecekondus. In so doing, the political system largely foreclosed other housing options, producing in 1981 an expansion of past programs aimed at the middle class rather than a new direction that might have offered more direct benefits to those with the most serious housing problems.

City Initiatives in Housing

During the long gestation process of the 1981 Housing Law, efforts to shape settlement patterns through large-scale housing projects were under development in the major cities. Ankara was the pioneer with plans for a new town for 300,000 on the city's outskirts. By 1981, the first of 60,000 homes were under construction in Turkey's largest planned community, with health, welfare, education, transport, and shopping facilities on the drawing boards for the 1,034 hectare site (about four square miles). The city's plans also included industrial development adjacent to the new town to create at least 50,000 jobs. Istanbul had begun planning a 44,000-unit community for 220,000 future residents in Halkalı, and smaller new settlements were being developed in Izmir, Anatalya, and Eskişehir.

Ankara's new town was conceived in 1973 during the administration of Mayor Vedat Dalokay as a means of helping solve the city's housing problems and of influencing urban development. The capital's master plan called for channeling future growth in the western corridor along the Ankara-Istanbul highway, which would situate new development upwind from Ankara's choking air pollution. The new town was located nine miles to the west of central Ankara and was called Batıkent, literally West Town. Batıkent was seen as the blueprint for a better urban future—providing housing for migrants, preventing squatter settlements, focusing growth, and providing a model that could be replicated. As one of Batıkent's planners later explained:

> Through this project [it] is hoped to absorb a high percentage of the newcomers to Ankara, meet their housing needs in Batıkent, and initially limit and later on completely channel the coming flood of people to new growth areas like Batıkent. Thus this project is basically a "gecekondu" prevention scheme. Towards this aim Batıkent area, by itself, is not sufficient, so the project is meant to reproduce itself by diverting funds to the expropriation of new suitable areas to create new Batıkents.[72]

In the centralized Turkish system, Ankara could not proceed with the new town without approval and cooperation from a variety of national agencies. Little progress was made in winning support for Batıkent from the central government during Mayor Dalokay's administration. Relations between RPP-controlled cities and the conservative government were generally bad in the mid-1970s, and particularly acrimonious in the case of Ankara's controversial mayor. In 1977, however, the cast of characters changed, as Dalokay was replaced by Ali Dinçer and the RPP took control of the central government. Dinçer persuaded the Ministry of Reconstruction to help the city expropriate land for the project. Assistance also was forthcoming from the Ministry of Finance and the new Ministry of Local Affairs. Close collaboration between Ankara's experts and officials in the ministries helped secure central approval for Batıkent's plans with minimal delays.

The plans that emerged from these negotiations still sought to shape development by dealing systematically with the housing problems caused by rapid urbanization. "This new city is being built primarily for confronting the vast housing demands of the newcomers in Ankara. . . . People who are living in squatter settlements will have the chance to live with the minimum necessary standards."[73] In Dalokay's initial scheme, most of the housing would be inexpensive rental units. But the blueprint developed by municipal and central officials shifted the emphasis to home ownership, with only 4,500 rental units out of the projected 60,000 dwellings. Financial necessity dictated that homes for purchase prevail, since mortgage subsidies were not available for rental units. However lofty Batıkent's objectives, with 92.5 percent of the units for sale, most of the beneficiaries were bound to be middle-income families who could afford to purchase homes. Batıkent's designers hoped to keep prices within reach of lower-middle-income families and factory workers through expropriation (which lowers land costs) and emphasis on industrialized housing construction to reduce building costs. As in other housing programs, the rhetoric of providing alternatives for squatters faded before economic and political realities.

Once approval was secured, an instrument had to be created to carry out the complex task of developing the new community. What was needed was a means of concentrating resources on a particular development objective, an assignment that could not easily be filled by either city or central agencies. The instrumentality needed broad political support in an increasingly polarized city, as well as a variety of skills—in planning, organizing, training, construction, management, and negotiating with city and central agencies. To fill this bill, a nonprofit agency, the Union of Housing Cooperatives in Batıkent, or Kent-Koop (city co-op), was organized in 1979 by the city of Ankara. Mayor Dinçer skillfully brought together unions, labor federations, and merchants associations of different political perspectives, thus insulating Batıkent from ideological and partisan conflict. "We want," the mayor insisted, "Batıkent to be a roof under which all workers and other people can come together and use their weight in economics and politics."[74]

Kent-Koop was a new departure for Turkey: In a nation where the state typically created governmental instruments to carry out public tasks, a nongovernmental organization was charged with undertaking a massive public project. Kent-Koop described its role as "the coordinator between the various bodies local and national, private and state owned which are providing the funds and making the construction."[75] The city government had supplied land and basic infrastructure, and intended to keep a close watch on Batıkent's development, to make sure that the city's interests were protected; good relations were essential with central agencies to secure housing credits and other investments; and the efforts of the private contractors who would build the new community had to be orchestrated. In addition, Kent-Koop had to stimulate interest in the project from prospective residents, organize cooperatives, complete the detailed planning of Batıkent, train personnel, and build public and political support more generally.

In most respects, Kent-Koop successfully concentrated resources on its development objectives during its initial years. The new organization proved far more flexible and less constrained by political considerations than most government agencies. An attractive new community was designed with considerable open space, staged provision of infrastructure, controlled development of housing and commercial facilities, local bus service, and a planned rail link to central Ankara. Neighborhoods with 5,000 residents were combined into larger communities, with appropriate schools, recreational facilities, health services, and shopping facilities. A variety of housing types and densities were to be constructed, with two-thirds of all dwelling units in high-rise structures. After four years of work, the main road network at Batıkent was completed and basic public services were installed for the first 8,200 homes under construction. And 1,000 units of the adjacent industrial site were already in business—mostly small electronics, printing, engineering, and auto shops. Furthermore, Batıkent was influencing development more generally in Ankara, as larger firms built offices, factories, and distribution centers in an industrial zone next to the new community.

Despite these accomplishments, Kent-Koop faced formidable problems in realizing its ambitious plans. New towns are inherently complex endeavors, requiring great political skill in securing funds from a variety of sources for all the different components: land, basic services, roads, housing, schools, health facilities, and the rest. Functional agencies control most of these resources—and in Turkey, most are central functional agencies—and their priorities do not necessarily coincide with those of the developers of a new town. Ten different national ministries had to be persuaded to commit resources for facilities at Batıkent, as did a number of agencies within Ankara's financially hard-pressed municipal government. Even more critical is capital to develop housing, since without units to place on the market the new town organization cannot generate the revenues needed to continue development.

In the case of Batıkent, housing funds were always the most problematic element. Land and basic infrastructure had been provided by Ankara, and $66 million in long-term credits from the European Resettlement Fund underwrote the initial phase of construction. Kent-Koop's ability to move to large-scale housing development depended heavily on housing credits from the central government. Given this dependence, Ankara and Kent-Koop strongly favored more government investment in housing. The 1981 Collective Housing Law, however, was a mixed blessing for Batıkent. One problem was the financing arrangements, which promised to exclude lower-middle-class families from participation, thus further skewing the eventual population of Batıkent from that envisaged at the outset by Mayor Dalokay. More troublesome was Kent-Koop's inability to secure funds under the new law, initially because of the complex eligibility requirements in the collective housing program, and then as a result of allocation policies developed by the Ministry of Reconstruction and Settlement which favored smaller municipalities. Ironically, at the same time that Kent-Koop was unsuccessfully seeking credits from the new Public Housing Fund, the head of the military government was promising support for Batıkent.

As in the past, words and actions have often moved at cross-purposes in the case of urban housing in Turkey. Kent-Koop may well overcome its problems with the key central agencies. Repeatedly, Kent-Koop demonstrated ability to dramatize its problems, as well as mobilize influential members among its 75,000 constituents in the member cooperatives—including journalists, performing artists, professors, military and high-ranking police officers—in efforts to secure favorable decisions from government officials. And if Kent-Koop continues to secure resources, Batıkent seems likely to have a substantial impact on Ankara's future development along predetermined lines. As in the initial implementation of the original plan for the national capital, government concentrated resources in the case of Batıkent, and the impact on settlement patterns may well be substantial. But in this case, as in all the other conventional housing programs, government was unable to concentrate resources on the development of alternative housing for squatters, who undoubtedly will surround Batıkent and its adjacent industries in the not-too-distant future.

8
SHAPING URBAN DEVELOPMENT

Public utilities, transportation, and housing all provide significant opportunities for government to shape urban settlement patterns, opportunities that by and large have not been seized in Turkey. In the case of
public services and housing, however, influencing urban growth is a de-
rivative objective, growing out of the primary goal of meeting public
needs for water, electricity, access, and shelter. These governmental activities may be differentiated from those whose primary purpose is control
of urban development—land-use standards, building regulation, urban
planning, and national strategies for urbanization and regional development.

In Turkey, the ability of government to use development controls and
planning to influence urbanization has been severely constrained. Most
land is privately owned, and private property rights are strongly protected
by law. Similarly, most building is undertaken by private parties. Efforts
to regulate private land use and building have been hobbled by inadequate
resources, lack of trained personnel, political pressures, and corruption.
Moreover, urbanization has been so rapid that growth often has overwhelmed the limited capabilities that are available to control urbanization. As a result, land-use and building controls have been weak, and local
plans have not affected most locational decisions. The most striking evidence of the failure of land, building, and planning controls are the hundreds of thousands of squatter houses that surround the metropolitan
centers, but just as telling are the substantial numbers of conventional
apartments and factories that have been constructed illegally or erected

191

with scant regard for infrastructure, environmental, or aesthetic considerations.

Government efforts to shape urbanization through development controls and planning reflect both the fragmentation and the centralization of the Turkish political system. Numerous municipal, provincial, and central agencies control urban settlement and investment, deriving their authority from a jumble of legal sources. Over "two hundred laws and regulations bear directly upon Istanbul's physical development. Many of them are out-dated, and they reflect no consistent and systematic set of policies on urbanization and land use."[1] Activities of functional agencies are poorly coordinated with development controls and planning. The central government is heavily involved in municipal land, building, and planning activities. Provincial and national agencies share responsibilities for regional development. National planning by its nature is a central function, but many interests have a hand in formulating overall strategies that are supposed to guide urban and regional development.

As the pages that follow indicate, Turkey has employed a variety of means in an effort to control urban development. Rare, however, has been an effective concentration of resources on development objectives. Public controls have had minimal impact on the pattern of land use. Urban plans have made few impressions on sprawling growth in the major cities. And national plans and regional development efforts have had modest success at best in deflecting urban growth away from the major urban centers.

GOVERNMENT AND URBAN LAND

Land is an invaluable resource for shaping urban development. Urbanization inevitably involves changes in land use, and government has the most potential for determining development when it controls land. Governmental prospects for guiding urbanization are greater when land is publicly owned than where it is privately held. Government typically has more freedom of action with public land than with private property. Private land generates more political interests and influence and is more expensive to acquire and use for public purposes. Public ownership, however, does not guarantee anything with respect to shaping urban development. Controls over land—whether publicly or privately held, have to be related to development objectives. Resources must be concentrated and activities of various public agencies and private parties orchestrated.

In Turkey, public capabilities for effectively controlling land have been declining for more than a century. Government's vast land holdings have contracted, as public lands have passed into private hands. On the eve of rapid urban growth, "much of the land outside city boundaries was both undeveloped and unclaimed. As such it was officially state property and could be acquired by government departments."[2] But this opportunity to use public lands to guide development was swept away by the flood of squatters who occupied a great deal of this vacant public land. Meanwhile, land prices climbed sharply in and around the cities, fueled by accelerating urbanization and widespread speculation. Government was unable to impose effective controls on the private land market. Soaring land prices crippled public efforts predicated on government acquisition of land, and private development often has been oblivious to city regulations and plans.

Until the middle of the 19th century, almost all land in Ottoman Turkey belonged to the state or to religious foundations (vakıf), and control over most urban land was in the hands of government officials.[3] Private property was recognized by the Land Law of 1858, which permitted those who had leased state lands—usually administrators who had taken advantage of their official positions to secure large tracts—to secure ownership rights. Powerful landlords now owned substantial amounts of land in the cities, and by the end of the century these private holdings had caused "a collapse of the traditional Ottoman pattern of urban development, and subsequent growth became haphazard and difficult to control."[4]

Private property was recognized by the Turkish Republic, with the Constitution protecting individual ownership, provided that private rights did not conflict with the public interest. In reality, public purposes have often been sidetracked by the rights of property owners, rights which have been bolstered by substantial political influence. Private property has been expensive to acquire for public purposes because government has been obligated to compensate owners at market value for expropriated land.[5] In 1971, the provision of the Constitution dealing with expropriation was changed to provide for compensation at tax value rather than market value, a measure which would have greatly reduced the cost of acquiring private property given the gross undervaluation of property in Turkey. This change was bitterly opposed by property owners, and eventually was overturned by the Constitutional Court. After 1980, another effort was made, by the military government this time, to base the price of expropriated land on tax value, but these new measures have not been tested in court.[6]

Soaring Land Costs

Rapid urbanization intensified demand for land, resulting in sharp increases in land prices. Between 1953 and 1969, the value of land within Ankara's boundaries grew from 2.4 billion lira to 45.9 billion lira, a nineteenfold increase that was six times the inflation rate during these years.[7] Land that sold for 10 lira or less a square meter in the 1950s was bringing upward of 450 lira per square meter two decades later.[8] In 1979, land in central Istanbul was selling for 200,000 lira ($5,000) per square meter; at the same time, serviced land for conventional housing was priced between 30,000 and 70,000 lira ($750 or $1,750) per square meter, and property in squatter areas cost anywhere from 3,000 to 20,000 lira ($75 to $500) per square meter.[9]

Accompanying the rapid rise in land prices, and accelerating the process, was rampant land speculation. Large tracts of land in and around the cities were subdivided and sold for substantial profits. In the process, "the value of urban land was rapidly and artificially inflated" and "many of the prospective buyers were cheated as to the qualities and locations of these subdivisions."[10] Speculation was encouraged by the low tax rates and the undervaluation of taxable property, as well as by permissive governmental policies toward conventional development and squatter settlements. Metin Heper describes how speculators use government to drive up land prices in gecekondu areas:

> In the cities there is a need for "Implementation Plans" on top of the Reconstruction Plans for the owners of land to be able to "use" their property. Where the municipalities have not developed implementation plans, the owners induce the municipality to develop partial implementation plans, and then sell their land at exorbitant prices. . . . Where Reconstruction Plans have not been yet developed, the houses are built and the settlement completed without the necessary permits. Then political pressure is exerted upon the municipality to extend municipal services to these areas. The land is divided into minute parcels and sold. . . . Sometimes that land outside of the urban areas is presented as belonging to the public, and people are encouraged to establish their squatter houses. Once such squatter areas develop and become an urban area, the original owners of the land sell their land to the squatters at very high prices.[11]

Inflated prices for land have affected a variety of government programs. Urban land speculation has been widely viewed as contributing to the expansion of "all of the large urban centers . . . in a chaotic fashion, without a comprehensive plan of development."[12] Increased land prices raised the cost of housing for urban dwellers, and had particularly adverse effects on moderate- and low-income families who were supposed to benefit from public housing programs. As indicated above, owners whose property was expropriated had to be compensated at market prices, a requirement that escalated program costs as land prices rose rapidly. Cities lacked the resources to buy land at the periphery for resale to lower-income families at nominal prices, thus undermining the sites and services aspects of the gecekondu-prevention efforts.

Rising land costs, along with limited resources, also prevented many cities from implementing the provisions of the Municipal Law of 1930 designed to advance planned development and prevent speculation through land purchases. Cities were authorized to acquire land, prepare it for development in accordance with municipal plans, and resell the land at reasonable prices, but little was done to realize this opportunity to guide settlement. Moreover, when cities have acquired land, they usually have been unable to use public land effectively to influence urban development. Lack of funds to develop and implement programs, inadequate staff, and pressures from private development interests have all constrained city use of public land. In addition, cities have sold significant amounts of their land in order to raise money to repay debts and meet current expenditures, despite an oft-stated national policy of increasing public land holdings in the cities.

An unsuccessful effort was made to curb land prices in 1969 with the creation of the National Land Office under the Ministry of Reconstruction and Settlement. The new agency was empowered to acquire and stock land for low-cost housing, industrial development, and tourism. Plans and infrastructure would be developed where needed, and improved land sold or leased for public or private development. Through purchases and sales of land, the new agency was supposed to stabilize prices, thus discouraging speculators. The Land Office also was responsible for coordinating control of public lands.

In a pattern common to Turkish efforts to cope with urbanization, goals and expectations far outran resources in the effort to dampen prices and facilitate land acquisition for planned development. Only 250 million lira ($25 million in 1969) was made available in a revolving fund, an amount that steadily bought less as land prices skyrocketed. Some land was purchased which facilitated housing and industrial development in Istanbul, Ankara, and other cities. But the overall impact of the Land Office on development was negligible—in 1977, the agency's total holdings in fifteen large cities were less than 1,400 hectares (about 550 acres).[13] Insufficient resources also prevented the Land Office from having an appreciable impact on land prices or land speculation. As one government official ruefully notes, "We could not stop speculation and we could not plan enough land and provide this land with basic utilities. Especially in big cities the fringes are occupied with housing first and now, we are trying to integrate these areas with urban centers, which is much more costly and not rational in many ways than . . . vice versa."[14]

Building and Zoning Controls

Modern Turkey inherited a piecemeal set of building and land regulations developed in Ottoman cities during the 19th century. Ottoman officials tended "to deal with development problems in an ad hoc fashion, rather than treating cities as organic entities that required comprehensive planning. Regulations were made to control building density, building heights and street widths, but no comprehensive planning concepts were developed."[15] Government regulations were prompted by land-tenure considerations, water shortages, fire prevention, and protection of historic sites, mosques, and public buildings. Fire was the greatest concern in cities and towns crammed with wooden houses. Between 1853 and 1906, over 200 major fires raged in Istanbul, consuming 36,000 dwellings.[16] Efforts were made to widen streets and require the use of masonry in areas rebuilt after fires. But Ottoman building standards often were honored in the breach, particularly in Istanbul where growth continually overwhelmed efforts to build and use land with more concern for the common good.

The Turkish Republic's initial land-use measure was Law 486 of 1924, which allowed cities to demolish buildings erected on land that the occupant did not own.[17] Potentially a powerful instrument to prevent illegal construction and squatting, the 1924 Law was rendered largely ineffective, as seen in the last chapter, by the need for municipal officials to secure a court order before inhabited dwellings could be demolished.

Authority for cities to regulate land use was provided in 1930 with enactment of the Public Hygiene Law.[18] Public health rather than planning or controlling urban settlement patterns was the prime concern of the 1930 legislation. Municipalities were empowered to distinguish between residential and industrial zones in order to protect residential areas from noise, noxious fumes, and other hazards. Not until the passage of the Town Planning Law of 1957 were cities assigned more general authority for zoning land, limiting building heights and residential densities, and controlling subdivisions.[19] The 1957 Law also required cities to ensure that proposed development conformed to municipal plans and building regulations before issuing construction permits.

These laws provide Turkey's cities with a limited set of instruments to control urban development. In effect, as Istanbul's former Mayor, Ahmet İsvan, has emphasized, "the city's only planning tool is the power to withhold building permits."[20] Regulating development through building permits is constrained by inadequate resources, lack of trained staff, governmental complexity, and corruption. Without funds and personnel, most cities were unable to prepare the official maps and zoning plans that were supposed to guide issuance of construction permits. Instead of regulating construction to advance city development goals, "municipalities contented themselves with issuing construction permits only. In doing so, they were interested solely in the technical standards of the construction."[21]

Inspection was haphazard, with too few trained inspectors and frequent corruption of poorly paid inspectors. Those who ignored building regulations rarely were punished, and it was cheaper to pay off officials than comply with municipal development controls. As a result, as Istanbul's mayor has admitted, "people either build without a permit or bribe local officials to provide one."[22] Corruption reached beyond inspectors, staining not only those involved in preparing regulations and plans, but also highly placed bureaucrats and elected officials. Rare was the local politician who did not take a lively interest in development controls, and political intervention commonly led to circumvention of city standards. As the Minister of Reconstruction and Settlement pointed out in 1982:

> We constantly encounter appeals and sometimes even strong pressure from citizens for exceptions to be made. A person considers the zoning plan a very good one if it allows his lot to increase in value and bad if it does not. Therefore he resorts to all possible means to have it changed to suit his interests."[23]

Overlapping responsibilities between municipal agencies complicated the regulatory process, leading to delays that increased the temptation for builders and landowners to bypass normal procedures. Delays also resulted from close central oversight of municipal land-use and building regulation. For example, subdivision plans prepared under the 1957 Town Planning Law had to be approved by the Ministry of Reconstruction and Settlement. Under the cumbersome procedures, "delays were considerable and speculators or other interested parties were able . . . to ignore the regulations."[24] In the view of the Istanbul Chamber of Industry, bureaucratic tangles were a primary cause of uncontrolled industrial development. To secure approval from the city government and the Ministry of Reconstruction took "at least six months. No industrialist can wait such a long time, and if he does wait there is no guarantee that the decision will be in his favor. Therefore the best way for him is to build illegally the factory without getting the necessary permit from the government."[25]

Building and land-use regulation was even less effective in suburban municipalities than in central cities. These small local governments rarely had qualified personnel to prepare regulations, carry out inspections, and otherwise enforce standards on landowners and builders. In dealing with urban development, they did "not apply the existing rules and regulations in the same pattern. Each has its own interpretation of the existing legislation. Personality factors and local politics as well as lack of qualified technical personnel are responsible for the different modes of implementation."[26]

The result, as in Ottoman Turkey's efforts to set land and building standards, was a regulatory system that could not cope with rapid urbanization and its concomitant development pressures, influential private landowners, and multiplying opportunities for profit. A report on Istanbul nicely captures the reality of land and buildings controls in modern urban Turkey: "Many buildings are erected without the builder seeking permission. . . . Buildings which have been permitted are not built in accordance with permission. . . . Few permissions for change of use are sought compared with the number of changes which actually occur."[27] Some of the most spectacular results of this process are found in Ankara, where a forest of illegal high-rise apartment buildings were constructed in the 1970s at Karşıyaka next to the planned community of Yenimahalle.

A final factor encouraging construction of conventional buildings outside the law was the periodic legalizations of gecekondus and other nonconforming buildings. Thus, the apartments at Karşıyaka—built on top of one another and lacking adequate water pressure, parking, and other public facilities—and similar residential complexes elsewhere in Ankara and in other cities were covered by the gecekondu legalization law enacted by the military government in 1983.

URBAN PLANNING

City planning came to Turkey as part of the influx of Western ideas and economic interests in the 19th century. Most early planning was undertaken by Europeans. Istanbul's first general plan was prepared by a German architect, Wilhelm von Moltke, during the 1880s. Europeans also played central roles in city planning in the years following the Turkish Revolution. As indicated in Chapter 3, Ankara was designed in the 1920s by two Germans, Heussler, who prepared the plan for the core of the city, and Jansen, who was responsible for the master plan. In Istanbul, plans were drafted by urban designers from Germany and France, Herman Elgotz in 1933 and Henri Prost in 1936.[28]

These early imported efforts set the style of Turkish urban planning for decades. City plans were monumental and static, emphasizing physical form and beautification rather than urban function and growth dynamics. Turkish planners were preoccupied with "the appearance and arrangement of individual buildings rather than their use or location within the city."[29] Urban planners have been criticized by the State Planning Organization for preparing city plans that "are inelastic, blueprints without alternatives" that are "too static to adapt themselves to rapidly changing economic and social conditions."[30]

Municipal Planning

Among its many provisions, the Municipal Law of 1930 required all municipalities to prepare plans.[31] Three years later, all municipalities were required to prepare plans to guide development over the next half-century. Planning under this legislation, the Municipal Roads and Buildings Act of 1933, dealt primarily with street and block size, as well as building density and heights, rather than general urban growth and settlement patterns.[32] City-planning powers and responsibilities were elaborated in the Town Planning Law of 1957, which required all cities with populations over 5,000 to prepare master plans with two components: development plans specifying land-use zones and growth strategies; and implementation plans for turning designs into reality.[33]

Municipal planning under these laws was closely controlled by the central government. Under the Municipal Roads and Buildings Act of 1933, all cities were subject to the same detailed central standards for planning and construction regardless of their size or distinctive characteristics. Master plans prepared under the 1957 legislation have to be approved by the Ministry of Reconstruction and Settlement, which can refer the plan back for specified amendments or make changes unilaterally. Cities have to get the Ministry's approval to appoint the director of the planning department. Central officials also strongly influence municipal planning because they supply much of the data used by cities. The Ministry is empowered to prepare plans for municipalities without their consent in the event of natural disasters, or to secure compliance with the Gecekondu Law of 1966, or to ensure coordinated development planning among local governments in metropolitan areas. Plans also are prepared for municipalities by the Bank of Local Authorities, either within the Bank or through planning consultants.

In sharp contrast to the pervasive, and usually dominant, role of the central government in municipal planning has been the absence of citizen participation or political debate. Planning has been viewed as a technical enterprise requiring specialized training and expertise, rather than a dialogue involving the public about which values should be advanced in city development. "No public discussion was permitted during the plan preparation period nor were people invited to express opinions on the proposals." Only after the plan was approved by the Ministry of Reconstruction was it "made public for thirty days before being put into effect to enable interested parties to appeal to the Council of State, Turkey's administrative court of appeal."[34]

What is most striking about all these required activities is how little impact municipal planning has had on development in Turkey's major cities. Effective planning in advance of development is rare, as is enforcement of official plans. City plans have not provided realistic blueprints for controlling urbanization. Nor have they been able to "identify either future needs for investment in public works or the most economical and efficient forms of investment."[35]

Aside from the initial designs for Ankara, city plans have been irrelevant to the raging forces of urban growth that have transformed Istanbul, Ankara, Izmir, and other urban centers. Nowhere has municipal planning adequately anticipated growth, with the result that master plans quickly are rendered meaningless by population increases far beyond those projected by the planners. Outdated plans were replaced with new plans, which acknowledged unexpected growth but did not come to grips with the dynamics of rapid urbanization. By the mid-1950s, Ankara's original planned population of 300,000 was already exceeded, and this prompted preparation of a new plan. The new scheme ignored mushrooming growth along Ankara's periphery, blithely assuming a maximum population of one million. "As it happened, the projected total population was reached within eight years of the plan's acceptance, making it redundant before it could be put into practice."[36] And because the planners' efforts were quickly negated by unanticipated growth, municipal plans were unable to guide building regulation as provided in the 1957 Town Planning Law.

Municipal planning has also suffered from its isolation, both from general policy-making and from the activities of functional agencies that commit public resources for public utilities, transportation, housing, education, health, and other activities. With sparse resources and meager political influence, city planners were unable to orchestrate the development activities of powerful public agencies, especially those operated by the central government. Nor did municipal plans have much influence on functional investments, which tend to be made by individual public agencies on an ad hoc basis in response to specific priorities and pressures for the particular service or facility. Most striking has been the lack of effective coordination between city planning and housing, which have been "pursued independently of each other, and at times even in a contradictory manner."[37]

Nor has municipal planning been able to find a comfortable place in the urban political world. For a long time, city planning in Turkey, as in other societies, strove to be above politics. But isolation was impractical in the highly politicized world of the Turkish city, especially when plans jeopardized the profitable schemes of landowners and builders. Development interests, backed by their political supporters, pressed for favorable planning changes. Special-interest politics flourished in the closed world of urban planning, where the public was excluded and decisions made in secret. Development interests were "extremely successful in modifying plans and it became relatively common, for example, for landowners to effects a change in land use zoning regulations where they found them restrictive. Thus land officially designated for recreational open space would suddenly appear coloured as suitable for high rise residential development on official plans."[38]

Metropolitan Planning

As urban development spread beyond city boundaries, efforts were made to extend planning to encompass all the urbanizing area. The first area-wide planning agency was created in Istanbul in 1960, with the establishment of the Marmara Regional Planning Organization under the Ministry of Reconstruction and Settlement. Impressed with the need to consider the city's future in an area-wide context, Istanbul officials were instrumental in setting up the Regional Planning Organization, and worked closely with the new agency and its foreign consultants. A regional plan for Eastern Marmara was prepared that emphasized Istanbul's importance to the national economy, stressed the need to attract more industry to Marmara, and urged higher-density development in order to provide basic services and infrastructure more economically.[39]

A few years later, the central government established metropolitan planning bureaus for Istanbul, Ankara, and Izmir.[40] Like the Marmara Regional Planning Organization, the new planning agencies were units of the Ministry of Reconstruction. Initially, the metropolitan planning bureaus concentrated on research. Planning was viewed primarily in technical terms, with a heavy emphasis on social-science expertise and methodology. Demographic, socioeconomic, and land-use data were collected and analyzed. Projections of future patterns of urbanization were made, and growth alternatives developed. The agencies were staffed by professional planners and social scientists. Specialists named by the Ministry of Reconstruction predominated on the metropolitan planning board, and municipalities were represented on the boards by their planning directors.

The metropolitan planners strongly preferred "better" urban development. For example, the master plan for metropolitan Istanbul sought to ensure that new development would be healthful and planned, that new industrial development would not generate pollution, that transportation would be efficient and equitable, that more recreational areas and open spaces would be provided, that energy would be utilized optimally, and that housing needs would be met. These and other objectives would be sought within the framework of increasing "the international importance of Istanbul . . . without jeopardizing its natural and historical values" while creating "necessary functions and services for its further growth and development in accordance with the national development" goals.[41]

The question, of course, was how to translate general goals into specific plans that would influence decisions affecting urban development. The answer for the planners, not surprisingly, was preparation of physical plans that dealt with the location of housing and industry, with the provision of transportation and utilities and needs for other public services. Preparation of these plans, however, was time-consuming. While the planners toiled, urbanization continued apace in Istanbul, Ankara, and Izmir, with all sorts of development decisions being taken on an ad hoc basis by scores of public agencies as well as vast numbers of private actors.

One way to influence development was to attempt to inform some of these ongoing determinations that were not going to wait for the completion of the master plan. Thus were the metropolitan planning bureaus drawn into the development process. Involvement was informal because there were "no firm arrangements for the use of [the draft plan] for immediate decisions pending the publication and approval of the plan."[42] Nonetheless, these interventions provided a technical and metropolitan perspective which otherwise would not have been considered in a number of important determinations affecting urban development.

The metropolitan planning bureaus also influenced municipal planning and development policy. Formally, the metropolitan agencies were serving the cities, which were responsible for approving and implementing the area-wide plan. In practice, city planners relied on the metropolitan bureaus for data and technical assistance. In addition, development of city plans was closely coordinated with metropolitan planning, since the Ministry of Reconstruction and Settlement used the work of the metropolitan bureaus as the basis for evaluating municipal plans.

Metropolitan planning has been more sophisticated than municipal planning, showing more appreciation for the dynamics of urban growth and less preoccupation with formal urban design. But metropolitan planning has not been plugged into an effective means of implementation. The planning bureaus only recommend, with action coming from the municipalities and central agencies. Formal approval of metropolitan plans comes from the city governments and the Ministry of Reconstruction. Cities were supposed to implement, along with central agencies whose programs would be guided by the metropolitan development plans. City governments, however, were just as constrained in carrying out metropolitan as municipal plans. The blueprint for the Istanbul area, approved in 1980, relied heavily on municipal land and building regulation, a process that had demonstrated almost no capability to constrain private development.

Implementing master plans requires a means of concentrating resources on development goals. Even if effectively administered, land and building controls are essentially reactive, and "incapable by themselves of coping with the development pressures generated by the private sector."[43] Land-use controls need to be combined with positive governmental action that focuses public resources on the plan's objective. The Greater Istanbul Master Plan Bureau proposed the development of a growth center 20 kilometers to the west of the city, to house two million people and relieve congestion at the core. Clearly, implementation of this recommendation required far more than improved land and building regulation. Land would have to be acquired, roads and utilities installed, housing investments committed to the area, and the activities of scores of public agencies made to conform to the plan. Progress toward realizing the goal of Ankara's metropolitan plan of shifting development to the west came less through regulation than from the attempt to concentrate resources on the new town of Batıkent.

Bringing diverse resources to bear in accordance with plans is devilishly difficult when the resources are controlled by agencies different from those that have prepared the plan. Functional agencies prefer to carry out their own plans—for metropolitan transportation, or area-wide utility service, or city schools, or regional health care. Implementation of metropolitan plans is particularly hobbled when the planning process stands alone, as has been the case in Turkey. Almost all the agencies whose efforts must be harmonized have different constituencies, and no mayor exists with a metropolitan constituency. Further handicapping efforts to focus resources in accordance with metropolitan plans is the reinforcement of functional autonomy by centralization. As pointed out in Chapter 4, the central units that make most public investments in urban areas have successfully resisted efforts to coordinate their activities by the State Planning Organization, the Ministry of Reconstruction, provincial governors, and mayors; all of these have a good deal more political clout than metropolitan planners.

The national government sought to facilitate implementation of metropolitan plans in typical fashion—by creating complex coordinating mechanisms that barely functioned. Overall orchestration of metropolitan planning was lodged in an Inter-Ministerial Coordination Council for Development in Metropolitan Areas. Established in 1972, the Council also was supposed to pave the way for development of metropolitan institutions to carry out area-wide plans. Within metropolitan areas, planning councils were set up to coordinate development planning and implementation. The councils were dominated by central officials—the Planning Council for Greater Istanbul had representatives from nine central agencies and only one local elected official, Istanbul's mayor. These diverse groups neither coordinated nor implemented very much nationally or in metropolitan areas, and, in fact, rarely even met.

With little means of implementation, metropolitan planning, like municipal planning, tends to be largely irrelevant to the surging forces of urbanization that constantly alter the landscape in and around the major cities. Even the more sophisticated efforts of metropolitan planners are quickly made obsolete by rapid growth. The Istanbul plans, for example, designated a number of areas on the Asia side of the metropolis for planned expansion as metropolitan sub-centers with populations between 100,000 and 200,000. But by the time the plan had been formally approved in 1980, these areas had "grown to reach and possibly exceed the proposed sizes; and spontaneously, rather than in accordance with the specific policies of the plan."[44]

DEVELOPMENT STRATEGIES AND URBANIZATION

Land-use controls and urban planning attempt to shape urbanization primarily through influencing decisions that affect physical development. Although the scope of these activities may be fairly broad, including entire urban regions, implementation in a mixed political economy such as Turkey's depends largely on individual determinations by public and private actors. Physical controls on development thus deal primarily with decisions made within metropolitan areas that affect particular parcels of land, most of which are fairly small in comparison with the metropolis as a whole.

In addition to seeking to influence settlement patterns by means of small-scale physical plans and standards, government can seek to shape urbanization through broad-gauge development controls. Government can attempt to regulate migration, and thus limit the size of the urban population and the amount of investment in city housing and infrastructure. More common are efforts to guide settlement by means of public investment. Government capital can be used to stimulate development of smaller cities in an effort to limit the growth of the largest cities. Funds can be channeled to less-developed areas in order to reduce regional and rural-urban disparities that stimulate migration to cities.

In Turkey, as pointed out in Chapter 2, government has made little effort to control migration directly. While constraints on mobility have attracted some support, particularly from established city dwellers incensed by the flood of migrants, most national leaders have been unwilling to risk the adverse political consequences of attempting to restrain the movement of millions of voters. In essence, the responsiveness of the Turkish political system to the mass of voters has precluded government from using direct broad-based controls as a means of influencing urban development.

National investments, on the other hand, have been employed from the earliest years of the Turkish Republic to stimulate and guide development. As emphasized in Chapter 1, modernization was Ataturk's overriding goal, and public resources were channeled into the effort to build a modern industrial nation. Development in the new Turkey also was to be widely distributed so that the Anatolian hinterland shared in the benefits of modernization. Over the decades, the central government has attempted to influence the location of jobs and people through a variety of investments plans, priorities, and programs. In 1960, national planning was formalized with the creation of the State Planning Organization to prepare national development plans.

Modernization and Urbanization

In Turkey's pell-mell rush to modernize, urbanization has been more a result than an objective. Modernization meant creation of a secular state, social reform, public improvements, and, above all, industrialization. Relatively little systematic thought was given to the growth of cities, although urban growth was a natural concomitant of industrial development, a liberalized society, and public improvements, since all these policies distributed more benefits in the cities than to other areas. New factories, schools, health facilities, transportation terminals, and modern public utilities were far more likely to be located in cities and towns than in the countryside. More generally, cities were seen as the pinnacle of modern society, with Ataturk himself indicating that even the most remote parts of Anatolia should enjoy the benefits of urban services and culture.

Turkey's only explicit urban development goal during the first post-revolutionary decades was the creation of a new national capital. But even the building of Ankara, as indicated in Chapter 3, was motivated primarily by nonurban considerations. Ankara was part of Ataturk's effort to break the links with the past by creating a bold new center for modern Turkey. The planned capital in Anatolia also symbolized the new regime's commitment to regional development.

Aside from the substantial investments in the development of Ankara, Turkey's plans and priorities have consistently favored industrial development over urban facilities, services, and housing. From the beginning of the republic, economic growth was the primary goal, with public investment focused on industrial plants and supporting infrastructure. Industrial investment was accepted as the most appropriate means of developing a self-sufficient economy and reducing dependence upon foreign manufactured goods. Industrialists, financial interests, and beneficiaries in commerce and construction provided powerful support for policies that favored industrial development.

Turkey's economic planners, like their counterparts in most urbanizing nations, have viewed public expenditures for city services and facilities as less productive than industrial development. Urban conditions, it was assumed, would improve as industry grew. In fact, as seen in Chapter 2, industrialization so stimulated urbanization that city growth quickly outpaced the expansion of industry. For planners, the answer to overurbanization was to accelerate industrial development in order to provide jobs for the migrants crowding into the major cities. And so the national development plans pumped more investment into industry during the 1960s and 1970s. Whatever their impact on the national economy, continued priorities for industrial development exacerbated the turmoil inherent in rapid urban growth. Most central resources were earmarked for industrial projects, while housing, utilities, and other urban needs were starved for funds. The impact of the national emphasis on industrial investment was magnified by a highly centralized political system in which the center's priorities became those of cities heavily dependent on the central government for their powers and financial resources.

Low priority for municipal services and facilities, however, did not lead the central government to seek to restrict urban development. Quite the contrary; national plans encouraged urbanization, which has been seen as essential to continued industrial development. In effect, Turkey's overall strategy has been to spur rapid urbanization by concentrating public resources on industrial development, but not to face squarely the consequences of these policies for the cities and their inhabitants. The Second Five-Year Plan called for increasing "the rate of social urbanization to the maximum, while ensuring the efforts to achieve this goal be kept to the minimum."[45] Within this general context, national planners have groped without much success for some means of controlling the raging forces of urban growth and change.

The First Five-Year Plan, covering 1963 to 1967, acknowledged the importance of urbanization in Turkey's social and economic development. But the national planners were troubled by the rate of urban growth and the diseconomies of scale in metropolitan areas. The plan called for more balanced urbanization, with city growth geared to job creation, and development of new urban centers to deflect growth from major cities. Also emphasized was the connection between conditions in villages and migration to cities. "Inadequate employment opportunities in agriculture encouraged urbanization," and the answer to restraining urban growth lay in "programs that will encourage people to stay in rural areas."[46]

Five years later, the planners switched gears, now extolling the benefits of rapid urban growth and the particular attractions of big cities for economic development. "The population in large cities presents characteristics not found in small urban centers," the second plan concluded, and "these characteristics accelerate economic and social development."[47] Instead of limiting expansion of metropolitan centers through dispersion of urban development, the second national plan welcomed growth in urban areas large and small, emphasizing that "the growth of large cities will not be prevented but will be supported."[48]

Now the emphasis clearly was on encouraging urbanization rather than attempting to restrain growth in the burgeoning cities. Unable to restrain the forces of urban growth and change, Turkey decided to go with the flow. Migration and rapid urbanization were accepted as inevitable, as was urban growth in advance of industrialization. So, the second plan announced, "urbanization will be supported and use will be made of urbanization as a tool for development."[49] Economic expansion would be led by the major cities, whose growth would spill over to stimulate development in surrounding areas, generating "new forms of employment, absorbing new migrants to the city, and transforming Turkey into a nation of thriving, industrialized urban settlements."[50]

In choosing to emphasize the positive in this conceptualization of urbanization as an independent variable in the development process, the planners were able to downplay the implications of rapid urbanization for the quality of life, housing, and other basic needs. They also were conceding what was obvious: the urban tide could not be stemmed, and Turkey was sorely pressed to provide even minimal services to those flooding into the big cities. Subsequent plans muddied these waters further. The Third Five-Year Plan, for example, echoed the first plan in seeking to prevent people from moving to big cities in the absence of adequate employment. But the third plan's overriding concern was to accelerate industrialization, which implied even more rapid growth of the major industrial cities.

What has been missing in all these efforts to influence urban development through national planning is effective links between general plans and specific policies. By and large, the plans have stated general goals—as in the fourth plan, which called for increasing the supply of urban land, curbing speculation, and using urban land as a means of guiding urbanization—without providing the means to achieve these objectives. National plans tend to ignore past experience and underestimate the resources needed to implement ambitious plans. Even if more resources were available, concentration would be difficult because so many policy goals are set forth in the plans, without any clear sense of which are more important. Is, for example, encouraging growth in the largest cities a higher priority than stimulating urban growth centers or improving village conditions? The planners' answer, reflecting the complex political and organizational stakes in such questions, is "do everything." And a little bit of everything has been done, and urban development has been influenced to some degree in the process. But hard choices have not been made in the national planning process, resources have not been concentrated on priority urban goals, and firm links have not been forged between policy goals and the myriad activities of governmental agencies that affect settlement patterns.

Nor has national development planning been connected with physical planning in the metropolitan areas. Central planning has focused on investment decisions rather than spatial patterns, whereas urban planning has grappled with settlement primarily in terms of land use. Spatial planning does not fall within the purview of the State Planning Organization, which concentrates on strategies for sectoral development. Physical planning is a separate realm under the direction of the Ministry of Reconstruction. Links between investment and urban planning are weak, and almost no effort has been made to devise urban strategies that blend broad-scale public investment policy with more specific development objectives in particular metropolitan settings. As a report on planning in Istanbul points out, "a marriage between sectoral and spatial planning at the national level has proved difficult to arrange; at the metropolitan level of Greater Istanbul it has been conspicuously absent."[51]

Regional Development and Urban Concentration

Every government since the proclamation of the Republic has sought to reduce inequalities among Turkey's diverse regions. Ataturk saw regional development as a means of integrating the nation by distributing benefits through the new state that was emerging from the shattered Ottoman Empire. Modernizing influences would be brought to the backward hinterland as part of the effort "to introduce the education and value patterns of a modern economic state."[52] Regional development also provided a rationale for creating a new capital at Ankara and for channeling government resources into Anatolia, which was Ataturk's principal source of support during the turbulent years when the new regime was forged.

Turkey's initial efforts to reduce spatial inequality used urbanization as a means of stimulating regional development. Creation of a new capital in Ankara gave Anatolia a major urban center and reduced Istanbul's dominance. Growth outside Istanbul and Izmir also was encouraged by industrial and infrastructure investments in key provincial towns. New rail lines linked these towns with Ankara and the seaports, while development of state industries modernized their economies. The result of these governmental efforts was the "transformation of many provincial towns into modern cities by making them centers for their respective hinterlands and by initiating extensive municipal construction projects."[53]

With the quickening of the pace of urbanization following World War II, attention turned to the connection between regional disparities and urban development. By stimulating poor areas, officials hoped to slow migration and ease the burdens of mushrooming growth in the major urban centers. Conscious efforts were made to use state industrial investments to head off the flow to the major cities by providing work opportunities in provincial centers close to areas of emigration."[54] During the 1950s, "over forty state factories were built in almost as many locations. Only one was in Istanbul, three in Ankara, and all but twelve were located outside the Marmara and Aegean regions."[55]

While these policies did not greatly reduce migration to Istanbul, Ankara, and Izmir, government was able to stimulate the development of a number of secondary cities. "Seven cities slightly under 50,000 had doubled or more in size during the decade (Erzincan, Denizli, Kütahya, Isparta, Kırıkkale, Karabük, and Osmaniye). All had both highway and rail access, and the first six possessed state industries which underwent expansion or were newly constructed after 1950."[56] Without question, government rather than the private sector was the key to the development of these cities. Government used public funds to shape and stimulate urban development in smaller cities in poorer regions. Without these public investments, these cities would have developed more slowly with less industry, and even more people and jobs would have been attracted to the major cities.

While government policies through the 1950s played a significant role in spreading urbanization and industrialization, these efforts had relatively little impact on the eastern and southeastern regions, which continued to lag far behind the urbanized western provinces in industrialization, income, and public services. Ataturk's ambitious plan for the establishment of regional universities as nuclei for future growth centers was not realized for decades. Regional development plans prepared in the late 1940s for the backward east were never implemented. The poorest areas were largely ignored in the dispersing of industry and urban development, and the fledgling cities of eastern Turkey were the weakest competitors for new investment with Istanbul and other established urban centers.

Not until the 1960s were systematic efforts undertaken to deal with regional inequalities. Turkey's national planners proposed to redirect public investments in order to reduce income and service disparities among regions, and in so doing to foster a less disruptive pattern of urbanization. Lack of development in the poor regions fueled migration to the cities. At the same time, rapid urbanization threatened to widen regional disparities. Large cities accounted for a steadily increasing share of the urban population, and, with their high unit service costs, claimed a growing share of the limited resources available for urban infrastructure. Moreover, the planners saw residents and enterprises in the burgeoning major cities benefiting from an easing of growth that was adversely affecting both the quality of life for most and the ability of government to meet essential service needs.

The First Five-Year Plan (1963–1967) gave priority to underdeveloped regions in the distribution of public investments, and measures were formulated to encourage the private sector to direct their investments to such regions. Emphasis in the Second Five-Year Plan (1968–1972) shifted to a growth poles strategy, designed to stimulate development in the poorer regions around selected urban centers. Instead of the dispersed pattern of investments set forth in the First Plan, growth centers would be encouraged in Anatolia, which would provide alternatives to the sprawling metropolises of western Turkey. This strategy was consistent with the second plan's theme of using urbanization to trigger development. Investments would be concentrated in the most promising cities in the backward regions, and thus produce more balanced urbanization. By focusing investment in new centers, the planners hoped to spur regional development without sacrificing their primary objective of industrial growth.

As in the case of urban policy in the national plans, formulation of regional development strategies has proved far easier than implementation. Decentralizing development is inherently difficult. Large established urban centers, as pointed out in Chapter 3, have enormous economic and political advantages over smaller less-developed cities. Growth feeds on growth, increasing investment opportunities, markets, services, and amenities. Higher incomes and wider opportunities attract the most ambitious and able from poorer regions. Investors and entrepreneurs are reluctant to commit themselves to areas whose prospects depend primarily on government. Growth also generates political influence, and increasing populations and economic resources steadily enhanced the political ability of the major cities to secure resources from the central government. Pressures from the prosperous regions, reinforced by the influence of national political figures from these areas, ensured a substantial flow of public resources to Istanbul, Ankara, and other major urban areas and their environs. Resources were never concentrated on growth poles because "investment in industry continued to flow into large urban agglomerations, and the investors could not be induced to shift their regional preferences."[57]

Implementation of regional development plans was also undercut by conflicting priorities. Industrialization remained the prime development goal, and dispersing investment to enhance territorial social justice has not been viewed by most economic planners as an efficient way to industrialize. Economic inefficiency was accepted in the early years of the Turkish Republic because of the pressing need for national unity. "Without such an overwhelming concern," Hasan Gençağa contends, "it is highly doubtful that the Government would have made the sacrifices in economic efficiency that were required by the Turkish territorial development policy."[58] Conflict between regional development objectives and industrialization goals was posed most explicitly in the Third Five-Year Plan (1973–1977), with the central government emphatically choosing industrialization over regional equity. "Implementation of the principle of a more balanced development," argued the planners, "should not be allowed to impede the observance of national economic [growth] criteria in making national investments."[59] The planners blithely assumed that the problem of less-developed regions would be spontaneously resolved as the rate of economic growth increased.

Fundamental conflict also exists between Turkey's urban and regional development policies. Unrestricted urban growth focused in the largest centers is not compatible with efforts to reduce regional inequalities and promote territorial social justice. And to complete the circle of contradictions, failure to reduce regional differences—and rural-urban disparities—results in faster rates of growth for major cities. Larger cities mean higher unit costs and more pressing needs for a bigger share of national resources at the inevitable expense of poorer regions and their cities.

Whatever resources are available for regional development are not easily concentrated on particular areas. Instead, there are bound to be many claimants, particularly in a nation with many poor areas whose demands are pressed by their representatives at the national capital. Only in the case of Ankara were central resources effectively focused in a single area, and development of a new national capital was obviously a special case. Elsewhere, "political objectives determined dispersion of the remaining effort as widely as possible. . . . Government gave small doses of attention to a large number of towns and cities."[60] Because of the successful efforts of political parties in power to reward their supporters, the number of provinces designated for priority development rose from 23 in 1968 to 40 in 1977.[61] These political pressures increased the beneficiaries of tax advantages and credit assistance provided by the central government in priority development areas, but in so doing spread more thinly the limited resources available for regional development, thus decreasing the impact in any particular region or growth center.

Regional development has been handicapped further by the absence of planning and other government agencies organized on a regional basis. Provinces rather than regions are the major subdivision of the Turkish state, and none of the provinces is large enough to encompass an entire region. About half the major central agencies have regional organizations, but these regions are defined to meet the needs of particular functional agencies with each agency defining its regions differently. Turkey's post-war constitutions have permitted the establishment of institutions comprising more than one province for regional development purposes, but the creation of a new layer of government has been resisted by those who benefit from the existing system.[62] As a result, "regional planning and administration, in the sense of a systematic, integrated, cross-sectoral approach to a geographic area, either gets done at the provincial level . . . or at the center. The provinces are poor, understaffed and geographically too small for sensible planning of some functions, while the Central Government is distant and remote from the problem."[63]

In the absence of regional governmental units, regional development plans have been prepared in Ankara by the State Planning Organization and the Ministry of Reconstruction, both of which are authorized to devise regional growth strategies. Conflicts and delays resulted from this overlapping authority, and from the different perspectives of the agencies, with the State Planning Organization interested in sectoral planning and the Ministry of Reconstruction concerned with physical development. Ad hoc agreements eventually divided regional planning tasks among the two agencies, with the Ministry of Reconstruction responsible for data gathering, research, analysis and plan making, and the State Planning Organization for approving and directing the allocation of resources and for setting up the incentives and priorities for development of regions. Under these arrangements, regional development schemes were prepared for Marmara, Çukurova, Keban, Antalya, and Zonguldak.

Despite the active role of central agencies in preparing regional plans, as well as the emphasis on regional development in national plans, the key central units have no effective means of ensuring compliance by functional agencies. In connection with the designation of growth centers by the Ministry of Reconstruction, a World Bank report notes that "the Ministry's identification of growth centers may have had some intangible effect on other ministries' choice of investments, but there was no formal compulsion."[64] Regional plans have no legal authority, and no very active constituency pressing for their execution. Even the State Planning Organization, the most important central agency for regional development, has been unwilling to "use its discretionary power in favour of the investment proposals made by the regional plans."[65]

Rural Development and Urban Growth

Like most rapidly urbanizing nations, Turkey has considered rural improvement as well as regional development in the search for ways of slowing migration to the cities. Improved conditions in the villages presumably would keep more people in the countryside. Rural development also promised to check the vicious circle of migration, in which the ablest leave for the cities, further reducing the viability of village life, and thus pushing more people off the land. Those who leave are younger, "more liberal, more open-minded, and more ambitious . . . than those with a more traditional world view who elect to stay behind. . . . Thus a brain drain occurs, with large cities attracting the very people" that a rural area "requires to further its own prosperity and development."[66]

Although despair over the unending flood of migrants from the villages periodically stirs interest in revitalizing the countryside, systematic efforts to improve rural conditions face even more formidable obstacles than does regional development. The needs of Turkey's 36,000 villages are enormous. Resources are limited and not easily concentrated on the most promising locales. National priorities emphasizing industrialization are even less well served by rural improvement schemes than by regional development. Rural areas are weak political competitors for scarce resources. For all these reasons, rural Turkey has been systematically shortchanged for decades in the distribution of public goods, services, and investments.

Moreover, agricultural modernization and improvements in transportation, the major governmental programs in the countryside, accelerated migration to the cities. During the 1950s, a major push was made to improve rural conditions using Marshall Plan assistance from the United States to build roads and provide tractors. But these "government programs enacted to keep peasants gainfully employed on the land . . . backfired by expediting the farm-to-city movement. Passage from rural areas throughout the nation to the three centers of Ankara, Istanbul, and Izmir soon became a relatively simple matter."[67] Government also encouraged more specialized agriculture emphasizing cash crops, a transformation that added more displaced farmers to the pool of potential migrants to the city.

More recently, rural development has stressed improved education, health, and housing. But the sheer number of villages overwhelms available resources. Most villages are too small—with 500 or fewer inhabitants—to provide an adequate base for modern education, training, and health services, or to develop a self-sufficient economic base. To overcome the problems of numbers and scale, Turkey's national planners have advocated bringing the city to the countryside. Government would stimulate new urban centers in rural areas by giving selected areas priority in public services and offering incentives to private investors. Thus, rural improvement has come to resemble regional development, and has faced the same constraints of limited resources, conflicting priorities, inability to concentrate resources on development objectives, and the superior political influence of the cities. An added constraint is the resistance of powerful rural interests to changes that threaten their economic and political dominance.

Development Planning in Perspective

Highly centralized political systems have inherent advantages over decentralized governmental arrangements in directing the flow of national resources in accordance with general plans for development. Centralized polities control most public resources, a situation which provides substantial potential for concentrating resources on development objectives. But centralization, as the Turkish experience with national planning and urbanization indicates, does not guarantee success. Authority at the center in Turkey, as in most political systems, is dispersed rather than concentrated. Planning and coordinating agencies tend to be weaker than functional agencies, whose activities are not easily meshed with the objectives of the grand plan. Nor in a democracy like Turkey are territorial interests easily ignored, since the representatives of industrialized and undeveloped areas constantly influence the allocations of the centralized state.

Under Turkey's centralized governmental and planning arrangements, clear-cut policies for regional development, rural improvements, and urban growth have not been established and maintained over time. After two decades of national development planning, Turkey had yet to develop a coherent national urban policy that seeks to direct the pace and pattern of urbanization, and which is closely orchestrated with other development policies and with urban planning. Instead, objectives and priorities have shifted from plan to plan, which has prevented the central government from focusing resources effectively. Vacillation reflects the lack of consensus on basic development objectives, as well as inadequate means of achieving any systematic set of urban policy goals.

Regional and rural development efforts in Turkey have fallen far short of their ambitious goals of reducing spatial inequalities and slowing the march to the cities. Efforts to stimulate the development of secondary centers have spurred growth in many locales, but have not eased significantly the pressures on the largest cities. Substantial regional and rural-urban disparities persist and continue to fuel massive migration to the major cities. By some measures, differences between the richest and poorer areas have grown. Marmara's share of bank deposits increased from 40 percent in 1963 to 45 percent in 1980.[68] The national share of value added in manufacturing in the 40 provinces designated as priority regions for development dropped from 13.3 percent in 1963 to 7.3 percent in 1974. "Similarly," notes the State Planning Organization, "the share of 18 provinces that are in Eastern and Southeastern Anatolia decreased from 7.8 percent in 1963 to 4.0 percent in 1974."[69]

Yet, without these governmental efforts, regional differences undoubtedly would be greater, and the large cities would have captured even more growth. Government's regional development policies were most influential in the early years, which illustrates the importance of timing in influencing development. During this period, as Lloyd Rodwin emphasizes, Turkey "opened up its interior and changed the rate and location of urban development in different regions by means of powerful, but crude, instruments: the shifting of a capital, the development of a basic transportation system, and the manipulation of infrastructure investments."[70]

Decentralization of state industries both increased the number of regional urban centers and accelerated their growth. In the process the amount of industrial activity concentrated in the largest cities was reduced, as was their overall share of urban development. Government initiated development that otherwise was unlikely, thus influencing the urban pattern. In the absence of this governmental intervention, urbanization would have been different, since private investors would have concentrated most of these activities in the major cities, especially Istanbul.

The most striking success of Turkish development policy was the creation of a new national capital at Ankara. Government initiated development, controlled the land, concentrated financial and organizational resources, and was not subject to diverse constituency demands. Ankara exists because the national government devoted "an enormous amount of energies and investment to building up the capital and its assets. This was a multi-faceted effort, involving many discrete yet related sectors of activity, and sustained over a thirty-year period."[71] But Ankara also underscores the difficulties of shaping urban development in a complex polity. Within the city, growth generated pressures that overwhelmed both master plans and public development controls. And in the rest of Turkey, Ankara did not provide an easily replicated model for stimulating urban growth centers, since "the transfer of national decision-making power to this spot, which acted as the basis of Ankara's transformation, could not be duplicated elsewhere as a development tool."[72]

9
GOVERNMENT AND THE METROPOLIS

Turkey's cities bear striking witness to the powerful, complex, and contradictory changes wrought by rapid urbanization. In one of the world's most dramatic urban settings, modern Istanbul relentlessly pushes outward from its ancient origins. Near the center are glittering shops, luxury hotels, office towers, and phalanxes of new apartments, the realm of an affluent and cosmopolitan elite. Bisecting and binding the metropolis are expressways and the soaring bridge across the Bosphorus; they funnel thousands of vehicles into the congested streets and stalled traffic of central Istanbul. Farther out are the spreading industries that are the pride of modern Turkey, but which cannot generate enough jobs for the flood of urban newcomers. Filling the spaces between industry, commerce, conventional housing, and public facilities are the endless gecekondus, climbing the hillsides and dotting the ravines.

Ankara is perhaps the most fitting metaphor for Turkey's urban experience. The planned national capital, with its broad boulevards, massive government buildings, and national monuments, speaks volumes about Turkey's urban aspirations—its association of modernization with the city, its desire to have a city symbolize the new nation. And the sprawling squatter settlements, jerry-built speculative apartments, haphazard public services, and endless revisions of city plans as growth constantly exceeds expectations—these are the essence of urban reality in contemporary Turkey.

Urbanization has been both a success and a failure in Turkey. For millions, the march to the cities has been a success story. Jobs are more plentiful and incomes higher than in the villages. Hard work and political action have secured inexpensive housing for most migrants and home ownership for a majority of gecekondu dwellers. Although city services leave much to be desired, they are almost always superior to what is available in the villages.

Success has been societal as well as individual. Urbanization has brought economic growth and development, higher incomes, a more skilled work force, and a healthier and better-educated population. For the most part, this massive transformation of Turkish society has been peaceful, with relatively little of the disruption that can accompany sweeping social change. Assimilation of migrants has been eased by the substantial homogeneity of modern Turkey. Conflict also was moderated by economic growth, which enabled millions of newcomers to secure a foothold while reducing the intensity of competition with more established groups.

Politics played a critical role in accommodating urban change. A democratic political system with highly competitive parties provided the means of response to the pragmatic desires of urban newcomers for housing, jobs, and public services. By responding to these needs, politicans gave new city dwellers a vested interest in the existing political system. A representative political system also augmented the influence of urban interests as cities grew and slowly but surely altered the plans, priorities, policies, and practices of a complex array of governmental institutions.

These successes, however, have been bought at heavy cost. Entwined with individual and societal success have been much personal hardship and collective failure. Rapid urbanization has overwhelmed Turkey's cities. Population growth has consistently outpaced industrial expansion, resulting in widespread unemployment. Large numbers of migrants have marginal jobs and low incomes. Urban Turkey has been plagued by acute housing shortages, with hundreds of thousands of city dwellers living in substandard gecekondus that lack essential public services. Uncontrolled growth has polluted air and water, clogged streets and highways, and undermined most efforts to design more effective cities. Wealth and income remain heavily skewed in Turkey's cities; so is the distribution of public goods as a consequence of governmental housing, transport, and service policies that favor affluent urban dwellers.

Both success and failure reflect Turkey's attempt to reap the benefits of urbanization without paying the price. Rapid economic growth has been the primary national goal, with migration and accelerating urbanization welcomed as essential concomitants of modernization and economic development. Turkey's leaders, however, have not matched their enthusiasm for urban development with effective action to meet the inevitable costs of rapid urbanization. Public investment has been funneled into industrial development rather than into housing, municipal infrastructure, and social services.

The headlong pursuit of industrialization at almost any cost has concentrated urban development in the largest cities, which have had irresistible economic, political, and social attractions for public and private investment. Turkey eagerly sought to skim the benefits from the big cities without facing up to the costs. As a result, the major cities have expanded far beyond the ability of their public services, infrastructure, and economic base to handle the changes. Pell-mell growth has loaded monumental burdens on transportation, water, police, education, and other services. Accompanying the phenomenal growth of Istanbul, Ankara, and other metropolitan centers have been deadly levels of pollution, soaring land prices, rampant speculation in real estate, endemic housing shortages, and fearsome development pressures that often sweep away governmental efforts to control urbanization and exacerbate the human turmoil and dislocation that accompany unending growth and change.

Neglect of the costs of urbanization, however, became increasingly difficult as cities continued to grow. As people crowded into cities, demands mounted for adequate municipal services, more schools, better housing, and convenient transportation. Particularly insistent were the urban poor, who sought to use their growing numbers to narrow the sizable gap that separated better-off city dwellers and the masses of squatters. With increased political influence and sophistication came demands for social justice and fundamental political change.

At the same time that urban pressures were escalating, Turkey's ability to respond was being eroded by mounting economic difficulties. Hard times fueled ideological conflict and political polarization, which in turn fed on the growing discontent in the cities and erupted in terror in Istanbul, Ankara, and other urban centers. In 1980, the parliamentary system collapsed, torn apart by a crippled economy and anarchy on the streets. A heavy price was paid by the rapidly urbanizing nation for living beyond its means both internationally and internally. Despite all the individual successes and collective benefits, the first three decades of massive urbanization ended with the Turkish political system losing most of the battles against the raging forces of urban growth and change.

URBANIZATION AND THE POLITICAL SYSTEM

Turkey's experience underscores the complexity of the interplay between urban and political development. Clearly, rapid urbanization has had sweeping impact on government and politics. Public tasks have multiplied, bureaucracies expanded, with central-local relations overloaded, and financial resources depleted. Unremitting urban growth has dramatically enlarged the public agenda in Turkey, compelling the undertaking of new tasks and complicating the performance of existing functions. Rarely is governmental expansion very orderly in rapidly urbanizing societies. Instead, government responds in piecemeal fashion, producing a bewildering array of laws, programs, agencies, and governmental relationships.

Most of the demands generated by urbanization are translated into specific needs—for increased water supply and sewage treatment, more schools and health facilities, professional police and fire protection, better highways and public transport, and more effective planning and development controls. Most of these activities are the province of specialized agencies, whose expansion is one of the principal consequences of urbanization. Turkey provided fertile ground for the growth of functional agencies to perform urban tasks. Governmental organizations in Turkey are self-contained and hierarchical, with a bureaucratic tradition that discourages coordination across functional lines. So new wine has been put into old bottles, with urbanization enlarging and enhancing the influence of functional bureaucracies, particularly the central agencies that came to control most urban programs.

Urbanization also generated new conflicts and intensified existing cleavages. Urban growth means more rewards, more demands, and more interests. Massive squatting, for example, made urban land a hotly contested issue, widened socioeconomic conflict in the cities, and spurred the emergence of the urban poor as a potent force in Turkish politics. In the wake of urban change, some interests have gained influence, including squatters, municipal employees, functional bureaucrats, merchants, and entrepreneurs whose fortunes have risen with rapid urbanization. Among these last are gecekondu developers, dolmuş operators, land speculators, and apartment builders. Others have lost ground, most notably the urban middle class, whose interests no longer automatically prevail in Turkey's cities.

More sophisticated political participation has been another consequence of urbanization. Voting turnout has been lower than in the villages, but urban newcomers have used the ballot pragmatically to advance their interests. And city dwellers have engaged in a wider range of political activities than have villagers, using neighborhood associations, labor unions, and party organizations to press their demands on government. Participation itself became an important issue in the cities in the 1970s with the rise of an urban populism that linked citizen involvement, responsive government, and social justice.

Interests also evolved as the dynamics of urbanization unfolded. Witness, for example, the shifting political perspectives of migrants, who moved from pragmatic concerns about government services and land title to broader issues based on class and ideology. Using politics first to secure a foothold in urban society, and then to win a more assured place in the city, gecekondu dwellers began to demand more equitable treatment from governments that continued to skew the distribution of most public goods and services in favor of more affluent city dwellers in established neighborhoods.

As more and more people crowded into the cities, political parties and elected officials responded to the growing power of urban voters. Urbanization multiplied the interests that had to be catered to in order to win national elections, while sharply increasing the number of national legislators with urban constituencies. The major parties scrambled to win support in the booming cities—central funds poured into the metropolitan centers under the Democrats in the 1950s, squatters were pragmatically wooed by the Justice Party in the 1960s, and local autonomy and urban social justice became rallying cries of the Republican People's Party in the 1970s. Within cities, the power of numbers inexorably increased the political weight of lower-income city dwellers, although politicians tended to respond more with rhetoric than with resources to this new political reality.

Urbanization also tended to concentrate political influence in the major cities that contained the largest blocs of votes and much of the nation's political and economic elite. Istanbul, Ankara, and other metropolitan centers were able to capture the lion's share of public investments for services, economic development, public facilities, housing construction, and gecekondu improvements. Successful use by big cities of political and economic muscle fostered their continued rapid growth, and thus reinforced their political and economic advantanges over less favored cities and regions in the competition for scarce resources.

Despite the sweeping impact of rapid urban growth on the Turkish political system, the relationship between urbanization and politics is not a simple demand-response mechanism. Social, demographic, technological, and economic changes usually pose general challenges for politics rather than specific imperatives. Political and governmental responses— or nonresponses—to demands generated by socioeconomic change tend to be strongly affected by the nature of the political system. Thus, the relationship between politics and urbanization generally is interactive. The political system is affected by urbanization but within distinctive parameters which, in turn, have an impact on urbanization.

The interplay between urbanization and politics in Turkey underscores the importance of political variables. Consider, for example, central-local relations; they are always strained by urbanization. The growth of cities increases local needs, the influence of local elites, and local desire for autonomy. But urbanization also compels more central involvement in cities—in the form of resources, rules, skills, and responses to political demands. In Turkey, urban growth generated these pressures in the context of a highly centralized governmental and political system, whose responses to urbanization reinforced centralization and reduced the autonomy of cities. This outcome was not preordained by urbanization, which dictates neither highly centralized nor widely decentralized responses, but by the nature of Turkish politics. Patterns of central-local interaction are deeply embedded in most political systems, and they rarely are swept away by urban change. Instead, urbanization influences the preexisting context, but it is powerfully influenced by this framework.

In Turkey, central government dominated the process of governmental expansion in response to urbanization, preventing the substantial increases in local capabilities that usually accompany urban growth. Underlying this response was the concentration of most of the nation's governmental and political resources at the center prior to the advent of rapid urbanization, and the existence of a wide range of interests served by a highly centralized political system.

The overpowering dominance of national government in Turkey has exaggerated the centralizing trends inherent in urbanization. The central government has claimed more and more urban responsibilities, with its resources spread thinly over an ever-increasing set of urban needs, and its control over local governments strained by the top-heavy bureaucratic and political controls imposed by the center on the cities. Instead of sharing resources with cities, the center monopolizes public funds, using its superior financial position to extend control. Highly centralized political parties have reinforced concentration, foreclosing the development of autonomous politics in the cities and fostering the distribution of resources through the central government in order to bolster the influence of national political leaders. As a result, almost everything involving cities is determined in national political arenas rather than in local ones, which in turn draws all participants in urban politics to the center. And with action concentrated at the center, the answer to urban problems almost automatically has been an increase of national control—over transport, health, water and sewers, energy, and housing.

Democracy also illustrates the interaction between urbanization and political variables. Competition for elected offices shapes the manner in which demands arising from urbanization are processed by the political system. Democracy sharpens the representation of interests, intensifying pressures on government. Turkey's politicians could not easily ignore the expanding cities, or their multiplying voters, or their powerful economic interests. Rapid urban growth spurred the parties to compete for support in the cities. In particular, democracy enhanced the influence of large organized interests in the cities—merchants, public employees, and, most dramatically, urban newcomers. Open and competitive politics provided squatters with substantial leverage on elected officials, the use of which significantly influenced Turkey's pattern of urbanization. Responsiveness to the political influence of gecekondu dwellers produced permissive policies that encouraged squatting and migration, thus intensifying the rate of urban growth, augmenting the ranks of the urban poor, and further increasing the political weight of the settlers.

By sharpening the representation of political interests, and increasing the pressures on government, democracy also greatly complicates the tasks of government in the wake of urbanization. Democratic politics in Turkey intensified conflict over urban issues among political parties, social and economic groups, and the central government and cities. The result often was stalemate on fundamental issues such as financing urban government, reorganizing government in metropolitan areas, and providing housing for lower-income city dwellers.

Only when direct representation of diverse interests had been suspended during periods of military government was decisive action possible on a number of key urban issues. Thus, after the 1980 military intervention, the financial system was reformed to provide more resources to the cities, local governments were amalgamated in Istanbul and Izmir, an area-wide water and sewer agency was created in Istanbul, major new housing legislation enacted, the groundwork laid for the establishment of metropolitan governments, and dolmuş operations banned in Ankara.

At the same time, experience during the most recent period of military government underscores the vitality and persistence of urban interests. Landowners and builders pressed vigorously for a central role in the 1981 collective housing legislation, and when they were unsuccessful, launched a persuasive campaign to amend the law. Enforcement of prohibition against new gecekondu construction was balanced with legalization in 1983 of all squatter and other nonconforming housing built since the previous granting of titles in 1976. And while the military government ended years of bickering between local governments and central agencies by adopting the Istanbul metropolitan plan, it also amended the plan "to accommodate industrialists' demands—in one case, a green area plucked out to be replaced with a tanning factory."[1]

Another example of the interaction between urbanization and politics is provided by Turkey's political parties. Government in Turkey is highly partisan, with determinations of all sorts politicized. Urbanization increased the rewards and claimants—growing cities and expanding government in urban areas meant more prizes and more participants. Party programs and personnel were strongly affected by rapid urban growth.

But the highly politicized setting also shaped both the presentation of demands and government's responses. The party system structured the mobilization of demands arising from urbanization. Parties were the prime channel for urban interests, and cities and their residents had no hesitation about using partisan politics to further their interests. Nor did the party in power have any qualms about rewarding supporters and punishing opponents in the distribution of government investments and programs in the cities. Few participants in Turkish politics expect that government will be neutral or nonpartisan, and they behave accordingly, pressing for political advantage at every turn. In this kind of political system, urbanization reinforced politicization, especially when the major cities were controlled by the party in opposition nationally. At the same time, urbanization was influenced by the highly partisan responses of government to the needs and demands of an increasingly urban society.

Pragmatic parties encouraged transactional politics in the cities. As in the United States during the heyday of political machines, urban newcomers traded electoral support for government help with their pressing needs. More established groups used the highly politicized system to advance their interests—in zoning changes, housing subsidies, low rents in public markets, and nonenforcement of land and building regulations. The almost limitless permeability of the political system by well-connected interests constantly undercut efforts to regulate urban development, thus fueling the uncontrolled settlement of vast amounts of the Turkish metropolis.

INFLUENCING URBAN DEVELOPMENT

As in most societies, urbanization's impact on the Turkish political system is more apparent than governmental influence on settlement patterns. Government in Turkey often has failed to define clear strategies to guide urban development, and more frequently has been unable to carry out its plans. Every major Turkish city is surrounded by hundreds of thousands of illegally built squatter dwellings. Large amounts of conventional housing and industry are constructed in violation of land and building regulations. City and metropolitan plans have had little impact on the location of most development in urban Turkey. Housing programs have produced little housing, most of which has not gone to the intended beneficiaries among city dwellers. Rampant speculation and wild building sprees amplify development pressures unleashed by rapid urbanization. Opportunities to shape development have been squandered by the inability of government to control even its own land, much of which has been seized by squatters or sold to help reduce municipal deficits.

In light of what has happened, the common conclusion that government in Turkey has failed to influence the forces of urban growth and change is understandable. Writing about Turkey's largest urban concentration, Sevim Aksoy finds that "the metropolitan area of Istanbul has grown haphazardly, without an appropriate structure or any coordination of the forces of growth."[2] We would not insist that government has had great success in controlling urbanization over the past third of a century in Turkey—certainly not in the face of the evidence presented in the preceding chapters. But we would emphasize two elements that often are slighted: first, the difficulties that control of urban development poses for any political system, and particularly for one with Turkey's characteristics; and second, the substantial impact that governmental actions have had on urban development in Turkey despite numerous obstacles and failures.

Under the best of circumstances, governments do not easily control urban development. Resources must be concentrated on clearly defined objectives in a timely fashion, in the face of pressures unleashed by urbanization, pressures that tend to disperse resources, multiply public objectives, and outpace governmental efforts to guide growth. Rapid and massive urbanization of the kind experienced by Turkey greatly complicates all these problems. Everything seems to happen at once—so much is needed by so many so quickly and pressures are so insistent that the imperatives of rapid growth overwhelm government. Accelerating urbanization can outpace provision of public services in advance of development, and this means of control soon was irrelevant in most of urban Turkey. Instead, government devoted much of its urban resources to responding to what had happened rather than to influencing future development. When rapid urbanization involves squatting, government's task is even tougher, since normal land and service controls rarely affect squatters.

When rapid urbanization and squatting combine with severely constrained resources, government's task becomes far more arduous. Turkey has not lacked urban development objectives, nor occasionally farsighted plans such as the initial efforts to develop low-cost alternative housing for squatters. But urban plans and promises consistently outrun resources, especially in a relatively poor nation. Housing policy illustrates the formidable obstacles erected by inadequate resources. During the early years of the Turkish Republic, the potential of housing investment to shape development was demonstrated in Ankara. But little use was made of this lesson in later years because public capital could not be spared for shelter. Recent efforts to guide growth through large-scale housing projects in planned communities, most notably at Batıkent on the western outskirts of Ankara, can succeed only to the degree that public funds are made available and concentrated on the development objectives that Batı-kent was designed to serve.

The difficulties inherent in public efforts to guide urban development are magnified in a mixed political economy such as Turkey's, where most land is privately owned and most locational decisions are made by private parties. Market forces exert powerful pressures that frequently run counter to government's development objectives, as in the case of land prices in Turkey's cities. Private locational decisions are more difficult for government to influence than are those of public agencies, since the decisions of private groups require the application of complex land and building regulations that in Turkey have been difficult to administer and easily subverted by political pressures or illegal actions. Public control of development in Ankara was most effective when much of the city's land was owned by the state.

Democracy also affects the ability of government to influence urban settlement. Throughout most of the period of rapid growth, Turkey had a responsive political system that was sensitive to an expanding set of urban constituencies. Inevitably, the political system responded to many of the same preferences that were driving the private sector—the desire for improved housing, the opportunities for profit in the booming cities, and the attractions of open land on the metropolitan fringe. Few politicians were prepared to alienate powerful industrialists, influential home builders and landowners, or the burgeoning squatter vote, regardless of what city, metropolitan and national plans proposed about industrial locations, apartment building, or gecekondu housing.

Democracy also complicates defining objectives and setting priorities, essential elements of any successful strategy for influencing urban development. Never are these tasks easy because the parameters are complex and the choices hard. In Turkey, urban policy cuts across such major questions as migration, squatting, industrial development, housing production, infrastructure provision, rural overpopulation, agricultural modernization, and regional development. Should urban strategy favor large or smaller cities, serve industrial or regional development, foster growth or equity? In grappling with these thorny questions, Turkey's leaders were pushed and pulled by the multiplicity of interests that were able to voice their preferences in a representative polity. The tendency in Turkey, as in most plural political systems, was to state broad goals and attempt a bit of everything in order to satisfy the many claimants, rather than concentrate scarce resources on clearly defined development objectives.

Despite these realities, government in Turkey has had a substantial impact on urbanization. Migration, settlement patterns, location of jobs, and provision of housing have been affected by governmental actions and inactions. Gecekondu policies have had perhaps the widest impact on urban development. Legalization and improvement programs amplified demand for gecekondu housing by increasing the attractions of squatting. Government's permissive policies also encouraged migration, as more people were drawn to the cities by the promise of inexpensive housing. By stimulating gecekondu development and migration, government also accelerated the outward spread of the metropolis as squatters claimed increasing amounts of marginal land along the urban periphery.

Squatter housing illustrates how government can influence urban development in ways that are neither planned nor anticipated. Gecekondu policies were not designed to amplify migration or accelerate urban sprawl. Instead, legalization, provision of public services, and improvement programs were ad hoc responses to political realities and the perceived lack of viable alternatives. Nonetheless, these policies had a powerful impact on the rate and pattern of urban development in the major cities.

Government policies have also influenced city development by focusing demand. Public investment policies that favored industrialization concentrated new factories and major infrastructure in the major cities and their surroundings. Highway construction in the metropolitan centers strongly influenced the location of new industries, spurred the decentralization of jobs, and stimulated residential and commercial building along the new transport corridors. Government housing policies increased demand for apartments, resulting in the construction of more units than would otherwise have been built, in the process increasing residential densities in the major cities.

Most significant have been explicit governmental efforts to stimulate and initiate urban development. State industrial investments were critical in accelerating the growth of a number of secondary cities. As was the objective, these efforts helped spread the benefits of urbanization to less-developed regions and deflected migrants from the largest cities. Without a deliberate policy of fostering urbanization outside the major cities there would be fewer urban centers in Turkey, and even more growth would have been concentrated in Istanbul, Ankara, Izmir, Bursa, and Adana.

Ankara provides a classic case of government initiating development with profound consequences for subsequent urbanization. Government decided to move the capital to Ankara, planned a modern city, and concentrated resources on these development goals. Not until Ankara was well established did market forces and private decisions begin to play a significant role in the city's development. The public commitment to Ankara altered Turkey's urban pattern, deflecting growth from Istanbul and Izmir and stimulating the modernization of Anatolia.

During the past decade, government again initiated development in Ankara, in the Batıkent project on the city's western fringe. Public action planned and produced something quite different from what would have resulted from the working of the private land and housing markets, or the free flow of squatters in search of vacant land. Infrastructure was installed in advance of development, housing clustered into neighborhoods, and community facilities sited in accordance with a comprehensive development plan. More generally, public development of Batıkent has pulled urban settlement westward in accordance with the master plan for the metropolitan area.

Turkey's experience indicates that government can influence urban development, but that resources are not easily concentrated on development objectives over time, particularly in a relatively poor society with intensely partisan democratic politics. Far more often than not, opportunities to shape urban settlement have been missed because of inadequate resources, crosscutting constituency pressures, failure to coordinate the complex array of government agencies with urban responsibilities, weak land and building controls, irrelevant planning, and a general lack of effective public instruments with sufficient areal and functional scope to shape the future.

GOVERNMENT AND THE FUTURE METROPOLIS

That Turkey will have more urban dwellers and larger cities in the future is not in doubt. The State Planning Office estimates that by 1995 40 million people—or two-thirds of the nation's anticipated population—will be living in cities.[3] Fastest growing will be cities with populations between 100,000 and a million, causing a continued decline in the overall share of Istanbul, Ankara, and Izmir. Nonetheless, the three metropolitan centers will continue to expand in absolute terms. Istanbul is expected to have 9 million inhabitants by the turn of the century, while Ankara will reach 5.4 million and Izmir 4.5 million. Growth will continue to spill over the boundaries of the large cities into surrounding areas, fueling the expansion of "complex concentrations in the industrial regions of Marmara, Aegean, and Çukurova where large cities are flanked by other cities of lower sizes."[4]

As in the past, urban growth will generate fearsome pressures for development, for housing, and for public services. One official estimates that eight million new urban housing units will be required by the end of the century.[5] And failure to produce needed housing will add more people to the ever-spreading gecekondus that ring the cities. Urban water needs will double, and "problems of drinking water and sewerage will require an investment of 660 billion lira" ($3.3 billion) in the coming decade alone.[6]

Whatever the exact dimensions of future urban growth, government in

Turkey will continue to struggle with complex urban issues in the context of cities crowded with poor migrants. Resources will remain scarce, with intense competition for them among a variety of interests. Asking whether government will solve Turkey's urban problems is unrealistic. The relevant question is whether urbanization can be made less costly and more equitable in broad societal terms. The answer lies largely in the hands of government, which holds the key to more balanced development, more effective control over land use, and greater public investment in urban infrastructure, city services, and social housing.

More effective control of urban development in the future will depend on Turkey's ability to muster and concentrate resources on defined objectives. Of critical importance is the provision of more resources for urban development. Without more funds for urban infrastructure and housing, government's ability to influence settlement will be severely handicapped. A key element in government's success in controlling Ankara's growth during the early years was the availability of substantial resources. By contrast, inadequate funding doomed governmental efforts to shape urban settlement in the gecekondu programs. Resources were meager in the light of needs for clearance and provision of alternative housing, and resources were spread too thin in response to political pressures to have much influence on housing patterns. The promise of the 1981 housing law and imaginative development schemes such as Batıkent will remain unfulfilled unless the central government honors its commitment to earmark 5 percent of the national budget for housing.

Dramatic increases in funding for housing and urban infrastructure, however, will be difficult to achieve. One of the reasons that Turkey has slighted the cities is lack of resources, and the nation's recent economic difficulties have further constrained its ability to underwrite ambitious development programs in the cities. Other national priorities continue to compete with urban needs for scarce resources—defense, agriculture, regional development, ,and, most important, industrial development. More funds for urban programs probably mean less for industrialization, a trade-off that has not been attractive to Turkey's leaders. Cities have far outpaced the growth of their industrial bases, which for many officials emphasizes the need for continued priority for industrial development to provide jobs for existing and anticipated urban dwellers.

Turkey also needs clearer urban development objectives: resources have to be concentrated on definable goals. Like most complex and dynamic societies, Turkey has pursued a multitude of objectives. Urbanization has been encouraged and discouraged; big cities stimulated and restrained; housing emphasized and deemphasized; regional development promoted and ignored. The quest has been elusive for a national urbanization policy that clarifies these objectives and which is orchestrated with other development policies. Of the policy alternatives available, perhaps the most promising is the concept of growth poles recommended by the first two development plans. Concentration of investment and population in a few major urban centers in the less-developed regions would spread economic opportunity and improved public services to underprivileged segments of society without losing the advantages of urban scale. Residents and enterprises in the burgeoning major cities would benefit from an easing of growth; too-rapid growth adversely affects the quality of life for all.

The problem with clear-cut urban development objectives, of course, is that they involve winners and losers and thus are difficult to impose, particularly in a responsive political system. Concentration of political and economic influence has shielded the metropolitan centers from policies that would divert already inadequate resources to lesser cities. Attempts to satisfy the multitude of claims from poorer areas has spread regional development funds thinly across the nation, precluding much concentration of effort in growth centers.

Perhaps the answer lies in formulating more modest development objectives in particular metropolitan areas rather than attempting to devise a national urbanization policy that seeks to direct the pace and pattern of urbanization. The initial development of Ankara—with central resources heavily concentrated on a particular city—is one model that could be used for growth centers, although the political rationale for focused investment in the national capital is likely to be more persuasive than for a secondary city. Batıkent offers another model for an urban strategy based on comprehensive local development schemes—in this case a new town designed to advance the overall plan for the growth of the metropolitan area. The face of urban Turkey would have been a good deal different if resources had been focused over the past two decades on a few Batıkents in Istanbul, Ankara, and Izmir.

Government's ability to influence urban development also rests heavily on its capacity to implement plans, policies, and programs. Turkey's experience underscores the importance of governmental capability. Its early success in locating, planning, and developing Ankara resulted from Ataturk's strong political leadership. A decisive government committed resources and used its power to implement an imaginative plan. More recently, government has not even been able to enforce the law in the face of the intense pressures unleashed by rapid and unremitting urbanization. Squatters illegally occupied large amounts of vacant land, apartments and industrial complexes were erected in defiance of zoning and building regulations, and city plans were routinely ignored by private developers and public agencies.

Urban planning has been particularly ineffective in Turkey. After the early success in Ankara, planners have had little influence on development in any of the major cities. Plans have failed to anticipate the velocity of growth, the need for inexpensive housing, and the pressures that these developments would generate on land. Planning has been separated from implementation, particularly from the development decisions of the central agencies whose investments help shape the metropolis. The potential of planning linked to implementation is demonstrated in Ankara's past and present, in the use of the formidable political and governmental resources of the center to build central Ankara as planned, and in the development of Batıkent.

Efforts to make urban government more effective in Turkey must begin at the center, given the virtual monopoly of power and resources by national officials and agencies. Changes in the governmental system come from Ankara, as illustrated by the flurry of reforms after 1980 that revamped city revenues, governmental structure in metropolitan areas, responsibilities for urban housing development, and provision of water and waste treatment in greater Istanbul. Much of the expertise in dealing with urbanization is lodged in the Ministry of Reconstruction and Settlement, the İller Bankası, and other central agencies. Centralization is also deeply imbedded in the Turkish political system, with parties, interest groups, business firms, and labor unions all strongly oriented toward the center.

Highly centralized systems clearly have significant potential for more effective controls on urban development. Strong central governments can establish national priorities, enforce national standards, and redistribute national resources. Efforts to alter the urban pattern—for example, by moderating the growth of metropolitan centers and accelerating development in smaller cities—must come from the center. National agencies also have obvious advantages in dealing with many of the complex problems of modern urban society that require sophisticated expertise, particularly in a nation like Turkey with relatively limited technical resources.

But Turkey's experience suggests that centralization does not necessarily lead to effective concentration of resources in urban areas. Central government in Turkey has attempted to do too much, intervening in everything rather than strategically, and in the process usually failing to concentrate its resources effectively. Multiplying urban responsibilities have overwhelmed the central government, reducing rather than enhancing its ability to shape the urban future. In a governmental system dominated by strong functional agencies, the center is unable to coordinate the myriad activities of specialized national units that affect urban development. Central plans—whether for all cities or particular metropolitan areas—rarely have much influence on the programs of central agencies. And because the center does everything, Ankara is the focus for all the political pressures generated by a rapidly urbanizing society, pressures that overloaded the national political system and contributed to the paralysis that led to military intervention in 1980.

Centralization has also denied cities much capability to influence urban development. Cities are weak and impoverished wards of the central government; their governments lack sufficient resources and power to deal effectively with urban problems. Tight central control stifles local initiative and drains away political energies in often bizarre conflicts between mayors and agents of the central government. Only rarely have cities taken the lead in efforts to influence settlement patterns, as in the case of the development of Batıkent. Ankara's mayors pushed this proposal, and the political skill of Mayor Dinçer turned the plan into reality. But Batıkent moved ahead only after central approval was secured, and its future depends heavily on the availability of housing funds from the national government.

For Turkey, the challenge of effective urban government is to find a way to use the inherent advantages of a centralized political system to focus resources in ways that encourage local initiative, leadership, and adaptation. Cities need more autonomy and resources so that land and building can be controlled, so that compliance with urban plans can be secured from private parties and public agencies, and so that more of the conflicts that inevitably arise from urbanization can be resolved locally.

More effective urban government also requires substantial restructuring of public responsibilities in metropolitan areas beyond the recent amalgamation of local governments in Istanbul and Izmir. Amalgamation addresses the problem of inadequate areal jurisdiction, but does not provide smaller-scale governments responsive to the needs of particular communities within the metropolis. The next logical step for Turkey would be two-tier government for the major metropolitan areas. This was under active consideration by the central government in 1983. The area-wide level would be responsible for regional functions such as transportation, water, sewerage, regional parks, and housing, and the district level would undertake street cleaning, garbage collection, and other local functions. Its implementation would increase the overall capabilities of urban government to provide services and manage growth, while increasing the accessibility of government to city dwellers through relatively small elected councils.

Turkey also needs to facilitate the creation of development agencies that can concentrate resources on specific objectives. One model is provided by the Istanbul Water and Sewerage Agency, Turkey's first metropolitan special district. Another approach is exemplified by Kent-Koop, the agency created to plan and develop Batıkent. The Istanbul agency has broad areal scope, which is essential for control of development through provision of basic infrastructure. Kent-Koop, on the other hand, offers wide functional scope within a defined area and has facilitated coordinated development of infrastructure, housing, and other development according to a detailed plan. The trick, of course, is to realize the advantages of these comprehensive instrumentalities while maintaining policy control in the hands of multipurpose government. This is probably best accomplished by tying special districts and development agencies to areawide government.

Our purpose in these last paragraphs has been to explore the implications of change in the light of what has happened, rather than to detail blueprints for governmental reform. Urban development and political change are dynamic processes, constantly interacting. The challenge for Turkey is less one of specific reforms than of the general problem of husbanding and concentrating resources on objectives that command wide support. For the past three decades, support has been mobilized through a highly competitive and politicized party system that often magnified conflict and immobilized government. Strenuous efforts were made in 1983 by the military government to create new parties. How much the new parties differ from the old remains to be seen. What is clear is that any party seeking broad support must be responsive to the complex needs and demands of Turkey's urban dwellers, and any party that hopes to rule a rapidly changing urban nation needs to concentrate resources more effectively than was the case during much of the past quarter century.

To have more influence on urban development, Turkey must be willing to pay the costs of urbanization as they are incurred, rather than defer them to an even more costly future. Failure to face up to urban needs has exacted the heaviest costs from the hundreds of thousands of newcomers who cling to the margins of city life. They and all the other city dwellers caught up in the great transformation of Turkish society will continue to expect much from government, both demanding effective action and disagreeing over what is needed. That government can make a difference is clear. Whether it will depends on the interplay of the many factors that have shaped the politics of urban development in Turkey. Istanbul and Ankara, after all, are vibrant testaments to the vision of inspired political leaders, to the intimate links betwen city and state, and to the enduring kinship of city, citizen, and civilization.

NOTES

Chapter 1

1. Lucien W. Pye, "The Political Implications of Urbanization and the Development Process," in *Social Problems of Development and Urbanization*, vol. 7 of Science, Technology and Development, United States papers prepared for the United Nations Conference on the Application of Science and Technology for the Benefit of the Less Developed Areas (Washington, D.C.: U.S. Government Printing Office, 1963), p. 84; reprinted in Gerald Breese, ed., *The City in Newly Developing Countries: Readings on Urbanism and Urbanization* (Englewood Cliffs, N.J.: Prentice-Hall, 1969), p. 401.

2. The discussion in this and the following paragraph is adapted from material originally presented in Henry S. Bienen and Michael N. Danielson, "Urban Political Development," *World Politics*, vol. 30, no. 2 (January 1978), pp. 264–265.

3. Among the many studies of urbanization in Turkey that concentrate on squatter settlements are İbrahim Öğretmen, *Ankara'da 158 Gecekondu* (Ankara: Siyasal Bilgiler Fakültesi Yayınları, 1957); Gönül Tankut, "Ankara'da Gecekondu Problemi," *Mimarlık ve Sanat*, no. 7–8 (1963); Granville H. Sewell, "Squatter Settlements in Turkey: Analysis of a Social, Political and Economic Problem," Ph.D. thesis, Massachusetts Institute of Technology (Cambridge, Mass., 1966); İbrahim Yasa, *Ankara'da Gecekondu Aileleri* (Ankara: Sağlık ve Sosyal Yardım Bakanlığı, Soysal Hizmetler Genel Müdürlüğü, 1966); Emre Kongar, "Altındağ Gecekondu Bölgesi ve Altındağ'da Kentle Bütünleşme," *Amme İdaresi Dergisi*, vol. 6, no. 3–4 (1973); Charles W. M. Hart, *Zeytinburnu Gecekondu Bölgesi* (İstanbul: İstanbul Ticaret Odası Yayınları, 1969); Kemal H. Karpat, *The Gecekondu: Rural Migration and Urbanization* (Cambridge: Cambridge University Press, 1976); Geoffrey K. Payne, "Ankara: Housing and Planning in an Ex-

panding City," a research report submitted to the Social Science Research Council, 1977; Kemal Kartal, *Kentleşme ve İnsan* (Ankara: Türkiye ve Orta Doğu Amme İdaresi Enstitüsü, 1978); Tansı Şenyapılı, *Bütünleşmemiş Kentli Nüfus Sorunu* (Ankara: Orta Doğu Teknik Üniversitesi, 1978); and Tansı Şenyapılı, *Gecekondu: Çevre İşçilerin Mekânı* (Ankara: Orta Doğu Teknik Universitesi, 1982).

4. The material in this and the following paragraph is adapted from Bienen and Danielson, "Urban Political Development," pp. 265–266.

5. For an excellent approach to comparative urban political analysis that begins with the common features of urbanization in developing nations, see Joan Nelson, *Access to Power* (Princeton, N.J.: Princeton University Press, 1979).

6. For a lively discussion of the differences in the timing of urbanization, industrialization, and population growth, see Barbara J. Ward, *The Home of Man* (New York: Norton, 1976).

7. Bienen and Danielson, "Urban Political Development," p. 266.

8. These data are based on classifying as urban the population of cities with 10,000 or more inhabitants. This definition is discussed in Chapter 2.

9. Walter F. Weiker, *The Modernization of Turkey: From Ataturk to the Present Day* (New York: Holmes & Meier, 1981), p. xv.

10. Ergun Özbudun and Aydın Ulusan, "Overview," in Ergun Özbudun and Aydın Ulusan, eds., *The Political Economy of Income Distribution in Turkey* (New York: Holmes & Meier, 1980), p. 3.

11. Karpat, *The Gecekondu,* p. 202.

12. Ibid.

13. Weiker, *The Modernization of Turkey,* p. xvi.

14. Michael N. Danielson and Jameson W. Doig, *New York: The Politics of Urban Regional Development* (Berkeley, Cal.: University of California Press, 1982), p. 2. Much of the discussion in this section is adapted from the first chapter of the Danielson-Doig study.

15. Considerable overlap exists in the Marxist and dependency approaches to urbanization; see Manuel Castells, *The Urban Question: A Marxist Approach* (Cambridge, Mass.: Massachusetts Institute of Technology Press, 1977); David Harvey, *Social Justice and the City* (Baltimore, Md.: Johns Hopkins Press, 1973); John Walton, *Eliţes and Economic Development: Comparative Studies of the Political Economy of Latin American Cities* (Austin, Tex.: University of Texas Press, 1976); and Bryan Roberts, *Cities of Peasants: The Political Economy of Urbanization in the Third World* (Beverly Hills, Cal.: Sage Publications, 1979).

16. The most detailed development of this theme is presented in Robert C. Wood, with Vladimir V. Almendinger, *1400 Governments: The Political Economy of the New York Region* (Cambridge, Mass.: Harvard University Press, 1961). See also Raymond Vernon, *Metropolis 1985* (Cambridge, Mass.: Harvard University Press, 1960); York Willbern, *The Withering Away of the City* (University, Ala.: University of Alabama Press, 1964); and Edward C. Banfield, *The Unheavenly City Revisited* (Boston: Little, Brown, 1974).

17. See Mübeccel Kıray, *İzmir: Örgütleşemeyen Kent* (Ankara: Sosyal Bilimler Derneği, 1972) and İlhan Tekeli, *Bağımlı Kentleşme: Kırda ve Kentte Dönüşüm Süreci* (Ankara: Mimarlar Odası, 1977).

18. Danielson and Doig, *New York,* p. 9.

19. Ibid., p. 10.

20. Şerif Mardin, "Turkey: The Transformation of an Economic Code," in Ergun Özbudun and Aydın Ulusan, eds., *The Political Economy of Income Distribution in Turkey* (New York: Holmes & Meier, 1980), p. 24.

21. Kutlu Güzelsu, "Metropolitan Istanbul 1982," paper presented to the 18th Congress of the International Society of City and Regional Planners, Istanbul, September 1–9, 1982, p. 9.

22. The discussion in the remainder of this section is based on Danielson and Doig, *New York,* pp. 23–32.

23. Ibid., p. 25.

24. Ibid.

25. Ibid., pp. 26–27.

26. Ibid., p. 28.

27. Ibid., p. 30.

28. F. Stuart Chapin, Jr., "Foundations of Urban Planning," in Werner A. Hirsch, ed., *Urban Life and Form* (New York: Holt, Rinehart and Winston, 1963), p. 218; and F. Stuart Chapin, Jr., *Urban Land Use Planning,* 2nd ed. (Urbana, Ill.: University of Illinois Press, 1965), p. vi.

Chapter 2

1. Officially, Turkey defines as "urban" all localities that are given, by law, an administrative status as the seats of a province *(il)* or a county *(ilce).* By this criterion, 67 provinces and 549 counties were classified as urban in 1981, and Turkey was 43.9 percent urban in 1980. A more useful definition regards as "urban" localities of 10,000 or more inhabitants, an approach widely used by nations and international agencies. This definition avoids including small rural towns in the urban category simply because of their administrative status. Of course, population size can be a misleading criterion because it does not take into account the socioeconomic characteristics of particular units. Systematic data of the sort needed for a more sophisticated socioeconomic definition of urban settlements, however, are not available for Turkey. Therefore, the 10,000-inhabitant definition is increasingly employed by the State Planning Organization and by most scholars, and is used throughout this volume. There were 320 localities with populations of more than 10,000 in 1980, compared with 66 in 1927. In 1982, the State Planning Organization began to use 20,000 residents as the standard for urban communities.

2. Baran Tuncer estimated that crude birthrates per 1,000 in the late 1960s were 43.9 for villages and 31.4 for cities; see "A Study of the Socio-Economic Determinants of Fertility in Turkey," discussion paper no. 121, Economic Growth Center, Yale University (New Haven: 1971). See also Serim Timur, "Socio-Economic Determinants of Differential Fertility in Turkey," paper presented at the Second European Population Conference, Council of Europe, Strasbourg, August 31–September 7, 1971.

3. Evidence of the role of step migration is provided by studies of the Turkish Demographic Survey, which indicate that more migrants come to the cities from

other cities than from rural areas. See *Türkiye Nüfus Araştırmaşında Elde Edilen Hayati İstatistikler,* 1966–1967 (Ankara: Hacettepe Basımevi, 1970), pp. 161–164; and the discussion in Ergun Özbudun, *Social Change and Political Participation in Turkey* (Princeton, N.J.: Princeton University Press, 1976), pp. 188–190.

4. A survey by the State Planning Office in 1971 found that 43 percent of the respondents had lived in rural areas before migrating abroad; see Suzanne Paine, *Exporting Workers: The Turkish Case* (Cambridge: Cambridge University Press, 1975), p. 188. Another survey indicated that 37 percent had left for Europe from villages under 5,000 and 15 percent more from towns with populations between 5,000 and 20,000; see Ahmet Aker, *İşçi Göçü* (İstanbul: Sander Yay, 1972).

5. See Nermin Abadan-Unat *et al., Migration and Development* (Ankara: Ajans-Türk Press, 1976), p 267; and Ruşen Keleş, "The Effects of External Migration on Regional Development in Turkey," paper presented to the Conference on National and Regional Development in the Mediterranean Basin, St. Aidan's College, University of Durham, April 13–17, 1982, pp. 12–13.

6. The 1.6 million Turkish workers and their families in Western Europe in 1978 represented .35 percent of the national population, but their numbers equaled 5 percent of Turkey's total employment and 40 percent of domestic industrial employment. With the decline in employment opportunities in Europe, increasing numbers of Turkish workers have migrated within the Middle East in recent years; in 1980–1981, 120,000 were employed in the oil-producing states, primarily Libya.

7. Request by the Turkish Government in 1970 in accordance with ECOSOC Resolution 1224 (XLII Session), Ankara, 1971, quoted in Kemal H. Karpat, *The Gecekondu: Rural Migration and Urbanization* (Cambridge: Cambridge University Press, 1976), p. 65.

8. According to Article 18 of the 1961 Constitution, "every individual shall be entitled to travel freely; this freedom can be restricted only by law for the purposes of maintaining national security or for preventing epidemics. Every individual shall be entitled to reside wherever he chooses. The freedom can be limited only by laws when necessary to maintain national security, to prevent epidemics, to protect public property, and to achieve social, economic and agricultural development." Under Article 23 of the 1982 Constitution, "Everyone has the right to freedom of residence and movement. Freedom of residence may be restricted by law for the purpose of preventing offences, promoting social and economic development, ensuring sound and orderly urban growth, and protecting public property."

9. The exchange rate for the Turkish lira in 1973 was approximately 10 to a dollar. Inflation reduced the lira to 12 to a dollar by 1975, 50 per dollar in 1980, and 205 per dollar in 1983.

10. These data are derived from a large-scale survey rather than census data: see Tuncer Bulutay, Serim Timur, and Hasan Ersel, *Türkiye'de Gelir Dağılımı: 1968* (Ankara: Siyasal Bilgiler Fakültesi Yayınları, 1971); and State Planning Organization, *Gelir Dağılımı Araştırması—1973* (Ankara, 1976). For a discussion of the problems inherent in the use of the income data in the 1968 and 1973 surveys, see Kemal Derviş and Sherman Robinson, "The Structure of Income Inequality in Turkey: 1950–1973," in Ergun Özbudun and Aydın Ulusan, eds., *The Political*

Economy of Income Distribution in Turkey (New York: Holmes & Meier, 1980), p. 85.

11. According to the 1970 census, 77 percent of all urban households had electricity, and 66 percent had running water; 13 percent of the rural households were served with electricity, and 14 percent with water; see State Statistical Institute, Census of Population, *Social and Economic Characteristics of Population* (Ankara, 1975), pp. 220–221.

12. İller Bankası, *Atatürk'ün Doğumunun 100 Yılı* (Ankara, 1982), p. 89.

13. Ibid., p. 154.

14. In 1975, 51 percent of the population in villages of less than 2,000 was literate, compared with 83 percent in Istanbul, 78 percent in Ankara, and 77 percent in Izmir.

15. In 1975, there were 168 deaths per 1,000 births in villages compared with 113 per 1,000 in cities.

16. See Karpat, *The Gecekondu,* pp. 73–74; and Oğuz Arı, "Ankara'da Yetenekli Devamlı Endüstri İşcileri Sorununun İncelenmesi," *Boğaziçi Üniversitesi Dergisi—Sosyal Bilimler,* vol. 1 (1973), p. 18.

17. İbrahim Şanlı, "Internal Migration in Turkey," in İbrahim Şanlı, Yücel Ünal, and İsmet Kılınçaslan, *Internal Migration and Metropolitan Development in Turkey* (Istanbul: Reyo, 1976), p. 82.

18. Bayındırlık Bakanlığı, Karayolları Genel Müdürlüğü, *Cumhuriyetin 50 Yılında Karayolları,* Publication no. 213 (Ankara, 1973), pp. 89, 101.

19. See Malcolm D. Rivkin, *Area Development for National Growth: The Turkish Precedent* (New York: Praeger, 1965), pp. 104–105.

20. For general analyses of regional differences in Turkey, see Melvin Albaum and Christopher S. Davies, "The Spatial Structure of Socio-Economic Attributes of Turkish Provinces," *International Journal of Middle East Studies,* vol. 4, no. 3 (July, 1973), pp. 288–310; Ruşen Keleş, "Regional Disparities in Turkey," in Turkish Society for Housing and Planning, *Türkiye'de Bölge Planlaması Alanındaki Gelişmeler,* Publication no. 2 (Ankara, 1964), pp. 101–135; and K. S. Srikantan, "Regional and Rural-Urban Socio-Demographic Differences in Turkey," *Middle East Journal* vol. 27, no. 3 (Summer 1973), pp. 275–300.

21. In this discussion, as well as in Figure 2–2 and Table 2–5, Turkey's provinces are grouped into seven regions, as follows: Marmara—Balıkesir, Bilecik, Bursa, Çanakkale, Edirne, İstanbul, Kırklareli, Kocaeli, Sakarya, Tekirdağ; Aegean—İzmir, Aydın, Denizli, Manisa, Muğla; Black Sea—Samsun, Trabzon, Zonguldak, Ordu, Amasya, Giresun, Rize, Kastamonu, Sinop, Artvin, Gümüşhane, Çorum, Bolu, Tokat, Cankırı; Central Anatolia—Afyon, Ankara, Eskişehir, Kayseri, Kırşehir, Konya, Kütahya, Nevşehir, Niğde, Sivas, Yozgat, Isparta, Burdur, Uşak; Southern Anatolia—Adana, Antalya, İçel, Gaziantep, Maraş, Hatay; Eastern—Ağrı, Bingöl, Bitlis, Elazığ, Erzincan, Erzurum, Kars, Muş, Tunceli, Van, Malatya; southeastern—Diyarbakır, Urfa, Mardin, Siirt, Hakkâri, Adıyaman.

22. See Erol Tümertekin, *Türkiye'de Şehirleşme ve Şehirsel Fonksiyonlar* (Istanbul: Publications of Istanbul University, Faculty of Letters Press, Institute of Geography, 1973).

23. State Planning Organization, *Gelir Dağılımı Araştırması—1973.*

240   The Politics of Rapid Urbanization

24. See Michael N. Danielson and Ruşen Keleş, "Urbanization and Income Distribution in Turkey," in Ergun Özbudun and Aydın Ulusan, eds., *The Political Economy of Income Distribution in Turkey* (New York: Holmes & Meier, 1980), pp. 287–288.

25. Differences in the distribution of public credits are even more striking on a per capita basis, with the western regions receiving 2,843 lira compared to 4.1 lira in the east; data provided by the Turkish Union of Banks.

26. State Statistical Institute, *Statistical Yearbook of Turkey 1981*.

27. Rivkin, *Area Development for National Growth*, pp. 1–2.

28. World Bank, *Turkey: Prospects and Problems of an Expanding Economy*. A World Bank Country Report (Washington, 1975), p. 175.

29. Ali Türel and Özcan Altaban, "Urban Growth and the Role of the State in the Provision of Housing in Turkey," paper presented to the 18th Congress of the International Society of City and Regional Planners, Istanbul, September 1–9, 1982, p. 4.

30. Turhan Yörükan, *Gecekondular ve Gecekondu Bölgelerinin Sosyo-Kültürel Özellikleri, İmar ve İskân Bakanlığı* (Ankara: Ministry of Reconstruction and Settlement, 1968), pp. 22–26.

31. Organization for Economic Cooperation and Development, *Economic Surveys, Turkey,* November 1978, p. 31.

32. State Planning Organization, *Dördüncü Beş Yıllık Kalkınma Planı: 1979–1983* (Ankara, 1978), p. 300.

33. For a detailed discussion of the second world of the Turkish city, see İlhan Tekeli, Yiğit Gülöksüz, and Tarık Okyay, *Gecekondulu, Dolmuşlu, İşportalı Şehir* (İstanbul: Cem Yayınevi, 1976).

34. See Karpat, *The Gecekondu,* p. 2.

35. For a discussion of this point, see Timur Kuran, "Internal Migration: The Unorganized Urban Sector and Income Distribution in Turkey, 1963–1973," in Ergun Özbudun and Aydın Ulusan, eds., *The Political Economy of Income Distribution in Turkey* (New York: Holmes & Meier, 1980), p. 359.

36. City earnings were more than expectations for 75.6 percent of the respondents, as much as expectations for 12.1 percent, less than expectations for 9.7 percent, and 2.7 percent were uncertain; unpublished data from the 1973 Hacettepe University Population Survey.

37. The full range of answers was: Life in the city is better, 82.7 percent; the same, 1.7 percent; worse, 7.5 percent; and uncertain, 8.2 percent; unpublished data from the 1973 Hacettepe University Population Survey.

38. Tansı Şenyapılı, *Gecekondu: Çevre İşçilerin Mekânı* (Ankara: Orta Doğu Teknik Üniversitesi, 1982), p. 235.

39. Karpat, *The Gecekondu,* p. 140.

40. Ibid., p. 35.

41. Şanlı, "Internal Migration in Turkey," p. 80.

42. See Charles W. M. Hart, *Zeytinburnu Gecekondu Bölgesi* (İstanbul: İstanbul Ticaret Odası Yayınları, 1969), pp. 83, 240–243; and İbrahim Yasa, *Ankara'da Gecekondu Aileleri* (Ankara: Sağlık ve Sosyal Yardım Bakanlığı, Sosyal Hizmetler Genel Müdürlüğü, 1966), p. 85.

43. See Hart, *Zeytinburnu Gecekondu Bölgesi,* pp. 96, 264–266; Yasa, *Ank-*

ara'da Gecekondu Aileleri, pp. 78–83; and Ruşen Keleş and Orhan Türkay, *Köylü Gözü ile Türkiye Köylerinde İktisadi ve Toplumsal Değişme,* Türk İktisadi Gelişmesi Araştırma Projesi no. 13 (Ankara: Siyasal Bilgiler Fakültesi, Maliye Enstitüsü, 1962), p. 59.

44. Özbudun, *Social Change and Political Participation in Turkey,* p. 195.

45. The full range of answers was: Migrants' life in the cities is better than in the village, 79.1 percent; the same as in the village, 3.9 percent; worse than in the village, 2.2 percent; some better and some worse, 8.4 percent; depends on specific conditions, 0.8 percent; and didn't know, 5.6 percent; unpublished data from the 1973 Hacettepe University Population Survey.

46. Kemal H. Karpat, "The Politics of Transition: Political Attitudes and Party Affiliation in the Turkish Gecekondu," in Engin D. Akarlı and Gabriel Ben-Dor, eds., *Political Participation in Turkey* (Istanbul: Boğaziçi University Publications, 1975), p. 91.

47. See "Istanbul'da 1970 ile 1980 Arasinda Ortalama Fiyat Artışları," *Milliyet,* November 16, 1980.

48. See Ruşen Keleş and Artun Ünsal, *Kent ve Siyasal Şiddet* (Ankara: Siyasal Bilgiler Fakültesi, 1982), pp. 52–53.

Chapter 3

1. State Planning Organization, *Urban Public Finance Policies,* Country Report II, SPO Pub. no. 1760, Social Planning Department Pub. no. 333 (Ankara, April 1981), p. 40.

2. Only two cities had more than 100,000 residents in 1927—Istanbul and Izmir; by 1940, there were three, as Ankara grew rapidly; Adana and Bursa were added in 1950; and four more cities expanded past 100,000 by 1960.

3. State Planning Organization, *Dördüncü Beş Yıllık Kalkınma Planı: 1978–1983* (Ankara, 1978), p. 228.

4. Malcolm D. Rivkin, *Area Development for National Growth: The Turkish Precedent* (New York: Praeger, 1965), p. 6.

5. Hasan Gencağa, "Growth Determinants of Urban Centers of Different Sizes" (Ph.D. thesis, Columbia University, 1976), p. 199.

6. Rivkin, *Area Development for National Growth,* pp. 137–138.

7. See Ruşen Keleş, "Urbanization in Turkey," an International Urbanization Survey Report to the Ford Foundation, (New York, 1972), p. 77.

8. See Rivkin, *Area Development for National Growth,* p. 111.

9. *Günaydın,* August 29, 1982.

10. For a discussion of the concept of the primate city see Mark Jefferson, "The Law of the Primate City," *Geographical Review* 29 (April 1939), pp. 226–232.

11. Alan Moorehead, *Gallipoli* (New York: Harper & Row, 1956), p. 41.

12. These population estimates and those in the next paragraph are from Ayten Çetiner, "On Population, Growth, and Development of Istanbul," Special Report 1 in H. İbrahim Şanlı, *Dolmuş-Minibus System in Istanbul: A Case Study in Low-Cost Transportation* (İstanbul: İstanbul Teknik Üniversitesi Matbaası—Gümüşsuyu, 1981), p. 197.

13. Şerif Mardin, "Turkey: The Transformation of an Economic Code," in Er-

242   The Politics of Rapid Urbanization

gun Özbudun and Aydın Ulusan, eds., *The Political Economy of Income Distribution in Turkey* (New York: Holmes & Meier, 1980), p. 35.

14. Yahya Sezai Tezel, "Turkish Economic Development, 1923–1950: Policy and Achievements" (Ph.D. thesis, Cambridge University, 1975), p. 59.

15. Rivkin, *Area Development for National Growth,* p. 115.

16. Ibid., p. 75.

17. Ibid., p. 118.

18. These estimates are based on Istanbul's share of Turkey's gross national product in 1978 for manufacturing (33.5 percent), commerce (39.6 percent), housing construction (26.1 percent), transportation and communication (24.9 percent), and finance (24.4 percent); see Erdoğan Özötün, *Türkiye Gayri Safi Yurt İçi Hasılası,* (Ankara: State Institute of Statistics, 1980), pp. 51, 65.

19. These data are for 1979; see İstanbul Sanayi Odası, *İstanbul Metropolitan Alanında Sanayi Yerleşim Planlaması* (İstanbul, 1982), p. 15.

20. Çetiner, "On Population, Growth, and Development of Istanbul," p. 202.

21. Walter F. Weiker, *The Modernization of Turkey: From Ataturk to the Present Day* (New York: Holmes & Meier, 1981), p. 165.

22. Çetiner, "On Population, Growth, and Development of Istanbul," p. 202.

23. In recent years, the distribution of population among Turkey's three largest cities has conformed quite closely to the rank-size rule, which states that the population of any given city tends to equal that of the primate city divided by the rank of the particular city. In 1980, the actual and predicted populations under the rank-size rule (based on dividing Istanbul's population by the city's rank) for the largest cities were:

Rank and City	1980 Population	Predicted Population
1. Istanbul	4,433,000	—
2. Ankara	1,878,000	2,217,000
3. Izmir	1,097,000	1,478,000
4. Adana	575,000	1,108,000
5. Bursa	445,113	887,000

For a discussion of the rank-size rule, see George K. Zipf, *Human Behavior and the Principle of the Least Effort* (Cambridge, Mass.: Addison-Wesley, 1949).

24. Approximately 60 percent of the 2,160 hectares (5,335 acres) of industrial development in the metropolitan area is on the eastern or Anatolian side; see Çetiner, "On Population, Growth, and Development of Istanbul," p. 204.

25. Ruşen Keleş, "Regional Disparities in Turkey," in Turkish Society for Housing and Planning, *Türkiye'de Bölge Planlaması Alanındaki Gelişmeler,* Publication no. 2 (Ankara, 1964), p. 119.

26. See Law 583 of 1925, Law Concerning the Expropriation of Land Required for the Construction of a New Quarter in Ankara and of Marshy Lands.

27. See Ruşen Keleş and Geoffrey K. Payne, "Town and Country Planning in Turkey," in Martyn Wynn, ed., *Planning and Urban Growth in Southern Europe* (London: Mansell, in press).

28. Ibid.

29. Rivkin, *Area Development for National Growth,* p. 56.

30. Tuğrul Akçura, *Ankara: Türkiye Cumhuriyetinin Başkenti Hakkında*

Monografik Bir Araştırma (Ankara: Orta Doğu Teknik Üniversitesi, 1971), p. 37.

31. See Rauf Beyru, *İzmir Şehri Üzerinde Bir İnceleme* (Ankara: Orta Doğu Teknik Üniversitesi, 1969); Akçura, *Ankara: Türkiye Cumhuriyetinin Başkenti Hakkında Monografik Bir Araştirma;* and Istanbul Metropolitan Plan Bureau, *Büyük İstanbul Nazım Plan Raporu* (İstanbul, November 1970).

32. Şemsettin Bağırkan, *Milliyet,* July 11, 1980. See also Süleyman Özmucur, "Distribution of Income in Istanbul," Istanbul Metropolitan Planning Bureau, Technical Memorandum no. 117 (İstanbul, January 1975), p. 8.

33. Turgut Cansever, quoted in Steven V. Roberts, "Migration a Problem in Istanbul," *New York Times,* February 29, 1976.

34. Respondents were asked whether they were satisfied with urban life; those answering positively, classified by city size, were as follows:

Istanbul, Ankara, Izmir	74 percent
100,000 to 500,000	87 percent
50,000 to 100,000	83 percent
25,000 to 50,000	86 percent
10,000 to 25,000	92 percent

Calculated from unpublished data from the 1973 Hacettepe Population Survey.

35. Mayor Ahmet İsvan, quoted in Roberts, "Migration a Problem in Istanbul."

Chapter 4

1. Walter F. Weiker, *The Modernization of Turkey: From Ataturk to the Present Day* (New York: Holmes & Meier, 1981), p. 228.

2. See Osman Nuri Ergin, *Türk Sehirciliğinin Tarihi İnkişafı* (İstanbul: Cumhuriyet Gazetesi ve Matbaası, 1944).

3. Weiker, *The Modernization of Turkey,* p. 228.

4. See Gabriel Baer, "The Administrative, Economic and Social Functions of Turkish Guilds," *International Journal of Middle East Studies,* vol. 1, no. 1 (1970), pp. 28–50.

5. See Korel Göymen, "The Restructuring of Local Administration in Turkey," in Korel Göymen, Hans F. Illy, and Winfried Veit, eds., *Local Administration: Democracy versus Efficiency?* Analysen no. 103/104 (Bonn: Friedrich Ebert Stiftung, 1982), p. 138.

6. See İlhan Tekeli, "Can Municipalities in Turkey Be Considered as Institutions of a Civic Society with a Broad Social Base?" in Korel Göymen, Hans F. Illy, and Winfried Veit, eds., *Local Administration: Democracy versus Efficiency?* Analysen no. 103/104 (Bonn: Friedrich Ebert Stiftung, 1982), pp. 69–73.

7. See Morroe Berger, *The Arab World Today* (New York: Doubleday, 1964), p. 75.

8. Malcolm D. Rivkin, *Area Development for National Growth: The Turkish Precedent* (New York: Praeger, 1965), p. 51.

9. Weiker, *The Modernization of Turkey,* p. 228.

10. Rivkin, *Area Development for National Growth,* p. 51.

11. Ruşen Keleş, "Decentralization: Experience and Prerequisites," in Korel Göymen, Hans F. Illy, and Winfried Veit, eds., *Local Administration: Democracy*

versus Efficiency? Analysen no. 103/104 (Bonn: Friedrich Ebert Stiftung, 1982), p. 119.

12. Law 1580 of 1930, Municipal Law of 1930.

13. Article 127, Constitution of 1982; the language is almost identical with Article 116 of the Constitution of 1961.

14. Each province is further subdivided into counties or subprovinces *(ilçe)*, and districts *(bucak)*. Like the provincial governor, the directors of subprovinces and the districts are agents of the central government, appointed by the Minister of Interior.

15. See Korel Göymen, "The Restructuring of Local Administration in Turkey," framework paper submitted to the Friedrich Ebert Stiftung for the meeting on Turkish Local Administration, Bonn, July 5–6, 1982, p. 21.

16. See Weiker, *The Modernization of Turkey,* p. 228.

17. Law 1580 of 1930.

18. Preparation of master plans was required in the Municipal Law of 1930, but was modified by subsequent legislation in 1953, 1957, and 1971, and is discussed further in Chapter 8.

19. Under the 1930 law, performance of these additional functions is required for only those municipalities whose revenues exceeded certain limits (slaughterhouses and wholesale markets for those with revenues of 50,000 lira or more; hospitals, nurseries, and orphanages for those with revenues in excess of 200,000 lira; racetracks and stadiums for those whose revenues topped 500,000 lira). These standards, however, became meaningless because of the decrease in the value of the Turkish lira in the half-century following the enactment of basic enabling legislation for municipalities.

20. Other optional functions include museums and zoos and operating savings, mortgage, and charity institutions.

21. Under the law, municipalities are not permitted to appropriate funds for optional functions until all mandatory activites are properly performed. This requirement, however, has little impact on the actual provision of local services in the major cities.

22. Before 1963, mayors were elected by municipal councils, either from among the members of the council or from outside.

23. As pointed out below, all mayors were fired and local councils dissolved after the military intervention in 1980. The 1982 Constitution provided for local elections every five years instead of four-year intervals, as had been the previous practice.

24. Institute of Local Government Studies, University of Birmingham, "Istanbul Municipality: Developing Capacity for Municipal Management," Consultant's Report, Co-operative Action Programme, Turkey—Project (78)37, CT/5018, Technical Co-operation Service Organization for Economic Co-operation and Development (Paris: September 6, 1978), p. 7. The report deals with Istanbul, but its conclusions apply to municipal councils in the other large cities.

25. Ibid., p. 41.

26. Membership on the standing committee is prescribed in the Municipal Law of 1930.

27. For the work of this group of experts, see Korel Göymen, ed., *Bir Yerel*

Yönetin Öyküsü: 1977–80 Ankara Belediyesi Deneyimi (Ankara: Özgün Matbaacılık Sanayii, 1983).

28. The process of creating subdistricts is complex, requiring application of more than half of the voters of an eligible area or of the municipal council to the provincial administration, popular approval in the affected area, review by the High Administrative Court *(Danıştay)*, and approval by the Council of Ministers, and final approval by the President.

29. Ruşen Keleş and Geoffrey K. Payne, "Town and Country Planning in Turkey," in Martyn Wynn, ed., *Planning and Urban Growth in Southern Europe* (London: Mansell, in press).

30. Göymen, "The Restructuring of Local Administration in Turkey," p. 140.

31. Municipalities received 45 percent of the property taxes collected by the central government within their boundaries. Other national taxes were allocated primarily on the basis of population, but with a minimum per capita share for each municipality. In 1975, the minimum allocation was approximately 100 lira (about $5) per capita, which added up to 200,000 lira, a sizable sum for a poor village. These grants were the reason so many rural communities sought to obtain municipal status.

32. İsmet Kılınçaslan, *Büyük İstanbul Şehrinde Hizmetler ve Belediye Giderleri Analizi Üzerine Bir Deneme* (İstanbul: İstanbul Teknik Üniversitesi, 1974), p. 58.

33. Ergun Türkcan, ed., *Yeni Bir Belediyeciliğe Doğru,* Belediyecilik Araştırması III (Ankara: Türk İdareciler Derneği, 1982), p. 100.

34. Talat Saral, "Türk Belediyeciliğinin Genel Görünümü," *Maliye Dergisi,* (March–April 1980), p. 57.

35. See Institute of Local Government Studies, University of Birmingham, "Istanbul Municipality: Developing Capacity for Municipal Management," p. 111.

36. Ankara Belediye Başkanlığı, *1976 Mali Yılı Çalışma Raporu* (Ankara, June 1977), p. 35.

37. See Istanbul Metropolitan Plan Bureau, "The Provision of Local Services and the Problem of Municipal Finance," *Socio-Economic Issues,* Annex 2–6 (Ankara, July 1976), p. 3.

38. Law 2380 of 1981, Law Concerning Giving Shares to Municipalities and Provincial Local Administrations Out of the General Tax Revenues.

39. Law 2464 of 1981, Municipal Revenues Law.

40. Under the new municipal tax law, the principal local taxes were an occupation tax, advertisement tax, entertainment tax, fire insurance tax, levies on fuel consumption, gas and electricity consumption tax, and use of telephone, post, and telegraph.

41. At a press conference, General Tırtıl indicated that Istanbul would realize only one billion lira in additional revenues under the new law; see *Milliyet,* November 12, 1982.

42. See Ergun Türkcan, ed., *Türkiye'de Belediyeciliğin Evrimi,* Belediyecilik Araştırması Projesi 1 (Ankara: Türk İdareciler Derneği, 1978), p. 282.

43. See Fehmi Yavuz, Ruşen Keleş, and Cevat Geray, *Şehircilik* 2d ed. (Ankara: Siyasal Bilgiler Fakültesi, 1978).

44. See Ruşen Keleş, "Belediye Gelirleri ve Mali Denkleşme," *Amme İdaresi Dergisi* vol. 5 (March 1972), pp. 72–74.

45. In 1972–1973, investments in Istanbul province by central agencies totaled 1.368 billion lira compared with 150 million lira in investments by all local governments.

46. See Association of Turkish Industrialists and Businessmen, *1977 Yılı Programı ve 1977 Yılı Bütçesi Üzerine Görüşler, Öneriler* (İstanbul, 1977), pp. 15–16.

47. Before the enactment of the 1981 revenue-sharing measure, the Banks of Local Authorities through its Joint Municipal Fund administered the 20 percent of the local share of national taxes that was withheld for discretionary grants.

48. Weiker, *The Modernization of Turkey*, p. 226.

49. Clement H. Dodd, *Democracy and Development in Turkey* (North Humberside: Eothen Press, 1979), p. 32.

50. Selman Ergüden, "An Overview of the Housing Sector in Turkey," paper presented to the 18th Congress of the International Society of City and Regional Planners, Istanbul, September 1–9, 1982.

51. Another important consideration in the creation of the Ministry of Local Affairs was the desire of the Republican People's Party to increase local autonomy and resources, and is discussed in Chapter 5. A third element was the increasing preoccupation in the late 1970s of the Ministry of Interior with its security functions as violence and terrorism mounted, which limited the ministry's ability to deal with its local government responsibilities.

52. Rivkin, *Area Development for National Growth*, p. 136.

53. Weiker, *The Modernization of Turkey*, p. 226.

54. Göymen, "The Restructuring of Local Administration in Turkey," p. 140.

55. Ruşen Keleş, "Urbanization in Turkey," an International Urbanization Survey Report to the Ford Foundation (New York, 1972), p. 153.

56. Albert Gorvine, *An Outline of Turkish Provincial and Local Government* (Ankara: Faculty of Political Sciences, 1956), p. 13.

57. Rivkin, *Area Development for National Growth*, p. 137.

58. Istanbul Urban Development Project, General Urban Planning Study, "Draft Interim Report," Phase I (Istanbul, 1975), p. 1.

59. See Arif T. Payashoğlu, *Merkezi İdarenin Taşra Teskilatı Üzerinde bir İnceleme* (Ankara: Türkıye ve Orta Doğu Amme İdaresi Enstitüsü, 1965); and Fehmi Yavuz, *Türk Mahalli İdarelerinin Yeniden Düzenlenmesi Üzerinde bir Araştırma* (Ankara: Türkiye ve Orta Doğu Amme Idaresi Enstitüsü, 1966).

60. Aid was resumed after the creation of the Istanbul Water and Sewerage Agency under the military government in 1981, with $88.1 million being provided in 1982.

61. As pointed out in the next chapter, demands for local autonomy and defense of centralization became entangled in partisan conflict in the 1970s, with the Republican People's Party advancing the interests of city government and the Justice Party defending centralization.

62. Law 2561 of 1981, Law on the Amalgamation of Small Localities Surrounding Larger Cities with These Larger Cities.

63. Keleş, "Decentralization: Experience and Prerequisites," p. 123.

64. In fact, these changes amended the Constitution of 1961 whose Article 116 allowed dissolution of an elected organ only by the decision of the High Adminis-

trative Court. But under the Law on Constitutional Order promulgated by the military, any law enacted by the National Security Council automatically amended the Constitution of 1961 if there was a contradiction between the law and the constitution.

65. In the 67 municipalities that are provincial capitals, which accounts for almost all Turkey's larger cities, the occupations of appointed mayors in 1981 were as follows:

Governors and vice governors	24
Retired army officers	19
Central government officials	13
Professionals	5
Former mayors	4
Municipal officials	2

See Türkcan, *Yeni Bir Belediyeciliğe Doğru*, pp. 281–282.

Chapter 5

1. Walter F. Weiker, *The Modernization of Turkey: From Ataturk to the Present Day* (New York: Holmes & Meier, 1981), p. 226.

2. Ergun Özbudun, *Social Change and Political Participation in Turkey* (Princeton, N.J.: Princeton University Press, 1976), p. 133; and Ergun Özbudun, "Voting Behaviour: Turkey," in Jacob M. Landau, Ergun Özbudun, and Frank Tachau, eds., *Electoral Politics in the Middle East: Issues, Voters and Elites* (London: Croom Helm, 1980), pp. 107–143.

3. Weiker, *The Modernization of Turkey*, p. 143.

4. Kemal H. Karpat, "The Politics of Transition: Political Attitudes and Party Affiliation in the Turkish Gecekondu," in Engin D. Akarlı and Gabriel Ben-Dor, eds., *Political Participation in Turkey* (Istanbul: Boğaziçi University Publications, 1975), p. 91.

5. Weiker, *The Modernization of Turkey*, p. 143.

6. Karpat, "The Politics of Transition," p. 116.

7. Ibid.

8. Özbudun, *Social Change and Political Participation in Turkey*, p. 210.

9. The Democratic Party ceased to exist after the military intervention of 1960. Most of the party's top rank were brought to trial and convicted, and former Prime Minister Adnan Menderes and two other party leaders were executed. The Justice Party was organized in 1961 and inherited most of the Democrat's electoral base.

10. See Weiker, *The Modernization of Turkey*, p. 121.

11. Özbudun, *Social Change and Political Participation in Turkey*, p. 149.

12. See Suna Kili, *1960–1975 Döneminde Cumhuriyet Halk Partisinde Gelişmeler* (İstanbul: Boğaziçi Üniversitesi Yayınları, 1976), p. 369.

13. See Weiker, *The Modernization of Turkey*, p. 26; and Kili, *1960–1975 Döneminde Cumhuriyet Halk Partisinde Gelismeler*, p. 225.

14. Kemal H. Karpat, *The Gecekondu: Rural Migration and Urbanization* (Cambridge: Cambridge University Press, 1976), p. 64.

15. Şerif Mardin, "Turkey: The Transformation of an Economic Code," in Ergun Özbudun and Aydın Ulusan, eds., *The Political Economy of Income Distribution in Turkey* (New York: Holmes & Meier, 1980), p. 44.

16. Karpat, "The Politics of Transition," p. 108.

17. Metin Heper, *Gecekondu Policy in Turkey: An Evaluation with a Case Study of Rumelihisarüstü Squatter Area in Istanbul,* assisted by Mark H. Butler and Nedret T. Butler, Boğaziçi University Publications no. 146 (Istanbul: Boğaziçi University Press, 1978), p. 41.

18. Ergun Özbudun, "Income Distribution as an Issue in Turkish Politics," in Ergun Özbudun and Aydın Ulusan, eds., *The Political Economy of Income Distribution in Turkey* (New York: Holmes & Meier, 1980), p. 76.

19. See Özbudun, *Social Change and Political Participation in Turkey,* pp. 210–212.

20. Özbudun, "Income Distribution as an Issue in Turkish Politics," p. 76.

21. See Weiker, *The Modernization of Turkey,* pp. 123, 267.

22. See Steven V. Roberts, "Turks Are Moving Toward the Left as New Jobs in Industry Lure Them from the Land," *New York Times,* May 31, 1977.

23. Ankara Belediyesi Başkanlık Uzmanları, *Toplumcu Belediye* (Ankara, 1977), pp. 9–13. For the views of the former RPP mayor of Istanbul, see Ahmet İsvan, "Halkın Belediyesi Olmak," *Mimarlık* (1977).

24. See CHP, *Parti İçi Eğitim Calışmaları El Kitabı, Program ve Seçimlerin Teknik Hazırlıkları ile İlgili Bilgiler* (Ankara, 1977), pp. 223–235, 251–256.

25. *Hükümet Programı* (1978), p. 1.

26. Mayor Aydın Erten of Gültepe, quoted in Demirtaş Ceyhun, *Bir Yeni Dev* (Istanbul: Tekin Yayınevi, 1977), pp. 171–177.

27. Dissolution of a municipal council or dismissal of a mayor is initiated by the provincial governor, reviewed by the minister of interior, and decided by the High Administrative Court in a judicial proceeding.

28. Korel Göymen, "The Restructuring of Local Administration in Turkey," in Korel Göymen, Hans F. Illy, and Winfried Veit, eds., *Local Administration: Democracy versus Efficiency?* Analysen no. 103/104 (Bonn: Friedrich Ebert Stiftung, 1982), p. 139.

29. See Ruşen Keles and Fehmi Yavuz, *Yerel Yönetimler* (Ankara: Turhan Kitabevi, 1983), pp. 244–245.

30. Quoted in *Milliyet,* August 1, 1975.

31. Quoted in *Milliyet,* February 12, 1980.

32. Quoted in *Milliyet,* May 5, 1980.

33. See Ruşen Keleş, "Yerel Yönetimlerde Güncel Oluşumlar," *Tütengil'e Saygı* (İstanbul: İstanbul Matbaası, 1981), p. 158.

34. Mayor Vedat Dalokay, quoted in *Cumhuriyet,* May 24, 1977.

35. The affair was brought before the High Administrative Court for a determination of whether the action by the mayor was political, and thus prohibited under the law. The court ruled in favor of the mayor because the cutting of service was not a partisan political act of the kind covered by the law. See Keleş and Yavuz, *Yerel Yönetim,* pp. 161–162.

36. See Doğan Pazarcılı, Necat Aksu, and Güngör Tuna, "Esnaf ve Beldiye," graduate seminar, Faculty of Political Science, Ankara University, 1981.

37. Municipal licensing of trades and crafts is severely constrained by the political success of the merchants associations in securing from the central government the means to restrict entry into a trade. Under the basic law governing associations, Law 507, drivers associations, for example, supervise the licensing of taxi drivers, while merchants associations can limit the number of bakeries or coffee houses in a particular area.

38. Weiker, *The Modernization of Turkey*, p. 94.

39. Ankara Belediye Başkanlık Uzmanları, *Toplumcu Belediye*, pp. 50–51.

40. See H. İbrahim Şanlı, *Dolmuş-Minibus Service in Istanbul: A Case Study in Low-Cost Transportation* (İstanbul: İstanbul Teknik Üniversitesi Matbaası—Gümüşsuyu, 1981), p. 145.

41. A threatened national work stoppage by the drivers in 1979 was prevented by military officials.

42. Andrew Finkel, "Community Power in Turkish Cities," in Korel Göymen, Hans F. Illy, and Winfried Veit, eds., *Local Administration: Democracy versus Efficiency?* Analysen no. 103/104 (Bonn: Friedrich Ebert Stiftung, 1982), p. 93.

43. The landowners persuaded their allies in the Justice Party to bring the case, since under the 1961 Constitution only political parties had recourse to the Constitutional Court.

44. In 1977, there were over 240 local chambers; see Ayşe Öncü, "Chambers of Industry in Turkey: An Inquiry into State-Industry Relations as a Distributive Domain," in Ergun Özbudun and Aydın Ulusan, eds., *The Political Economy of Income Distribution in Turkey* (New York: Holmes & Meier, 1980), pp. 455–480.

45. See Yıldırım Koç, "1974–1980 Döneminde Belediyelerde İşçi-İşveren İlişkileri," *Toplum ve Bilim*, no. 17 (Spring 1982), pp. 108–114.

46. Quoted in *Milliyet*, August 9, 1979.

47. Press conference, Mayor Ali Dinçer, June 1980.

48. Karpat, *The Gecekondu*, p. 62.

49. Weiker views the political prospects of the urban middle class less pessimistically. "Pressures," he writes, "may well mount to assure that the needs of the middle-class neighborhoods are met first, and while persons from these neighborhoods still occupy positions of local power. Such tensions may increase rapidly if there is continuance of a tendency shown strongly by most governments since the start of the multiparty period to grant *gecekondu* areas funds out of proportion to other felt needs"; *The Modernization of Turkey*, p. 231.

50. Karpat, "The Politics of Transition," p. 92.

51. Karpat, *The Gecekondu*, p. 81.

52. Karpat, "The Politics of Transition," p. 92.

53. Karpat, *The Gecekondu*, p. 225.

54. Ibid., pp. 229–230.

55. Heper, *Gecekondu Policy in Turkey*, p. 50.

56. Ibid., pp. 52–53. Heper notes that the Assistant Director of the Housing and Squatter Department of the city of Istanbul was caught in 1977 taking bribes of 40,000 lira (about $2,100).

57. Malcolm D. Rivkin, *Area Development for National Growth: The Turkish Precedent* (New York: Praeger, 1965) p. 11.

58. Lucien W. Pye, "The Political Implications of Urbanization in the De-

velopment Process," in *Social Problems of Development and Urbanization,* vol. 7 of Science, Technology and Development, United States papers prepared for the United Nations Conference on the Application of Science and Technology for the Benefit of the Less Developed Areas (Washington, D.C.: U.S. Government Printing Office, 1963), p. 87; reprinted in Gerald Breese, ed., *The City in Newly Developing Countries: Readings on Urbanism and Urbanization* (Englewood Cliffs, N.J.: Prentice-Hall, 1969), p. 404. See also Samuel P. Huntington, *Political Order in Changing Societies* (New Haven, Conn.: Yale University Press, 1968), and the excellent review of this literature in Özbudun, *Social Change and Political Participation in Turkey,* pp. 183–186.

59. Granville H. Sewell, "Squatter Settlements In Turkey: Analysis of a Social, Political and Economic Problem," Ph.D. thesis, Massachusetts Institute of Technology (Cambridge, Mass., 1966), p. 209.

60. Ibid., p. 55.

61. See Joan Nelson, *Access to Power* (Princeton, N.J.: Princeton University Press, 1979), and Wayne A. Cornelius, "Urbanization and Political Demand-Making: Political Participation Among the Urban Poor in Latin American Cities," *American Political Science Review,* vol. 68, no. 3 (September 1974), pp. 1125–1146.

62. See Karpat, "The Politics of Transition," p. 93.

63. Özbudun, *Social Change and Political Participation in Turkey,* p. 196.

64. Karpat, "The Politics of Transition," p. 117.

65. Özbudun, *Social Change and Political Participation in Turkey,* p. 213.

66. Özbudun, "Income Distribution as an Issue in Turkish Politics," p. 79.

67. Governor Nevzat Ayaz, quoted in *İstanbul Bayram Gazetesi,* August 13, 1980.

68. The districts were Eminönü, Fatih, Kadiköy, and Şişli; see Ruşen Keleş and Artun Ünsal, *Kent ve Siyasal Şiddet* (Ankara: Siyasal Bilgiler Fakültesi, 1982), p. 68.

Chapter 6

1. World Bank, *Turkey: Prospects and Problems of an Expanding Economy.* A World Bank Country Report (Washington, 1975), p. 175.

2. Environmental Problems Foundation of Turkey, *Environmental Profile of Turkey* (Ankara, 1981), p. 74.

3. İsmet Kılınçaslan, "Governmental Programs Affecting Internal Migration in Turkey," in İbrahim Şanlı, Yücel Ünal, and İsmet Kılınçaslan, *Internal Migration and Metropolitan Development in Turkey* (Istanbul: Reyo, 1976), pp. 176–177.

4. Quoted in Steven V. Roberts, "Modernization Leaves Turkey's Culture in Disorder and Its People Seeking an Identity," *New York Times,* May 23, 1977.

5. See Cevat Geray, "Konut Gereksinmesi ve Karşılanması," *Amme İdaresi Dergisi,* vol. 14, no. 2 (June 1981), p. 42.

6. See United Nations Development Programme, Project of the Government of Turkey, Project Document, "International Drinking Water Supply and Sanitation Decade Technical (TST) Support," TUR/81/012/A/01/14, in *Resmi Gazete,* no. 17813 (September 15, 1982), p. 16. In all Turkey, only 341 of 1,024 com-

munities with more than 3,000 population had adequate water supply, 621 had inadequate systems, and 62 were without a public water system.

7. Ibid., p. 15. The diseases associated with bacterial contamination were hepatitis, typhoid, paratyphoid, dysentery, and brucellosis, with hepatitis by far the most common.

8. Ruşen Keleş, "Urbanization, Population and the Environment," in Environmental Problems Foundation of Turkey, *Population and Environment Conference* (Ankara, December 1982), p. 200.

9. Ankara Belediyesi Başkanlığı, *1976 Mali Yılı Çalışma Raporu* (Ankara, June 1977), p. 36.

10. State Planning Organization, *Urban Public Finance Policies,* Country Report II, SPO Pub. no. 1760, Social Planning Department Pub. no. 333 (Ankara, April 1981), p. 36.

11. Ibid., p. 35.

12. Institute of Local Government Studies, University of Birmingham, "Istanbul Municipality: Developing Capacity for Municipal Management," Consultant's Report, Co-operative Action Programme, Turkey—Project (78)37, CT/5018, Technical Co-operation Service, Organization for Economic Co-operation and Development (Paris, September 6, 1978), p. 115.

13. Ruşen Keleş, "Urbanization in Turkey," an International Urbanization Survey Report to the Ford Foundation (New York, 1972), p. 77.

14. Institute of Local Government Studies, University of Birmingham, "Istanbul Municipality: Developing Capacity for Municipal Management," p. 68.

15. John Clark, "The Growth of Ankara, 1961–1969," *Review of the Geographical Institute of the University of Istanbul,* International Edition, no. 13, (1970–1971), p. 121.

16. See İmar ve İskan Bakanlığı, *13 Büyük Şehirde Gecekondu,* Ministry of Reconstruction and Resettlement (Ankara, 1968).

17. See İbrahim Yasa, *Ankara'da Gecekondu Aileleri* (Ankara: Sağlık ve Sosyal Yardım Bakanlığı, Sosyal Hizmetler Genel Müdürlüğü, 1966).

18. Kemal Karpat, *The Gecekondu: Rural Migration and Urbanization* (Cambridge: Cambridge University Press, 1976), p. 94.

19. See İmar ve İskan Bakanlığı, *13 Büyük Şehirde Gecekondu.*

20. See Ankara Metropolitan Area Master Plan Bureau, "Summary: Environmental and Urban Service Standards in Ankara," Publication no: 3 (Ankara, 1970), p. 2.

21. See Granville H. Sewell, "Squatter Settlements in Turkey: Analysis of a Social, Political and Economic Problem," Ph.D. thesis, Massachusetts Institute of Technology (Cambridge, Mass., 1966), p. 97.

22. Geoffrey K. Payne, "The Gecekondus of Ankara," *Process Architecture,* no. 15 (May 1980), p. 78.

23. See Metin Heper, *Gecekondu Policy in Turkey: An Evaluation with a Case Study of Rumelihisarüstü Squatter Area in Istanbul.* Assisted by Mark H. Butler and Nedret T. Butler, Boğaziçi University Publications no. 146 (Istanbul: Boğaziçi University Press, 1978), pp. 48, 54.

24. Ibid., p. 53.

25. Ibid., p. 40.

26. David H. Drakakis-Smith, "Slums and Squatters in Ankara," *Town Planning Review*, vol. 47, no. 3 (July 1976), p. 228.

27. Suavi Akansel, "Habitat for All: What Is the Solution," paper presented to the 18th Congress of the International Society of City and Regional Planners, Istanbul, September 1–9, 1982.

28. Heper, *Gecekondu Policy in Turkey*, p. 38.

29. Sevim Aksoy, "The Housing Problems of Istanbul and the Gecekondu Phenomenon," *Planning and Administration*, no. 1 (1980), p. 47.

30. The İller Bankası also assists municipalities with the preparation of official base maps, planning surveys, and master plans, activities examined in Chapter 8.

31. See *Milliyet*, November 12, 1982.

32. For a discussion of the impact of urban transportation policies on development in the New York metropolitan areas, see Michael N. Danielson and Jameson W. Doig, *New York: The Politics of Urban Regional Development* (Berkeley, Cal.: University of California Press, 1982) and Robert A. Caro, *The Power Broker: Robert Moses and the Fall of New York* (New York: Alfred A. Knopf, 1974); in Toronto, see Harold Kaplan, *Urban Political Systems: A Functional Analysis of Metro Toronto* (New York: Columbia University Press, 1969) and Albert Rose, *Governing Metropolitan Toronto: A Social and Political Analysis, 1953–1971* (Berkeley, Cal.: University of California Press, 1972); and in Stockholm, see Thomas J. Anton, *Governing Greater Stockholm: A Study of Policy Development* (Berkeley, Cal.: University of California Press, 1975).

33. These data are for 1970: for Istanbul, see H. İbrahim Şanlı, *Dolmuş-Minibus System in Istanbul: A Case Study in Low-Cost Transportation* (İstanbul: İstanbul Teknik Üniversitesi Matbaası—Gümüşsuyu, 1981), p. 24; for Ankara, see Ankara Belediyesi, *Ankara Kent İçi Ulaşım Etüdü Ulaşım Modeli* (Ankara, 1979), p. 5.

34. See Şanlı, *Dolmuş-Minibus System in Istanbul*, pp. 3, 25–26.

35. Ibid., p. 34.

36. Anadols (Ford), Murats (Fiat), and Renaults are assembled in Turkey, with annual production reaching 38,000 vehicles in 1983.

37. *Environmental Profile of Turkey*, pp. 212–215.

38. Şanlı, *Dolmuş-Minibus System in Istanbul*, p. 2.

39. Other members of the Provincial Traffic Committee in Istanbul are representatives of the Society for the Prevention of Traffic Accidents and the Technical University of Istanbul; see Ahmet Keskin, "Urban Transportation in Istanbul: An Overview," Special Report 2 in H. İbrahim Şanlı, *Dolmuş-Minibus System in Istanbul: A Case Study in Low-Cost Transportation* (İstanbul: İstanbul Teknik Üniversitesi Matbaası—Gümüşsuyu, 1981), p. 229.

40. Şanli, *Dolmuş-Minibus System in Istanbul*, p. 31.

41. Ibid.

42. See Korel Göymen, ed., *Bir Yerel Yönetim Öyküsü: 1977–1980 Ankara Belediyesi Deneyimi* (Ankara: Özgün Matbaacılık Sanayii, 1983), p. 164.

43. See Ankara Belediyesi, *Birinci Toplutaşım Kongresi (Bildiriler)* (Ankara, 1978); and Ankara Belediyesi, *İkinci Toplutaşım Kongresi (Bildiriler)* (Ankara, 1979).

44. Şanlı, *Dolmuş-Minibus System in Istanbul*, p. 31.

45. Yücel Ünal, "Legal and Administrative Aspects of Transportation and the Dolmuş-Minibus System in Istanbul," Special Report 3 in H. İbrahim Şanlı, *Dolmuş-Minibus System in Istanbul: A Case Study in Low-Cost Transportation* (İstanbul: İstanbul Teknik Üniversitesi Matbaası—Gümüşsuyu, 1981), p. 234.

46. Keskin, "Urban Transportation in Istanbul: An Overview," p. 215.

47. See *Milliyet,* January 26, 1983.

48. See Şanlı, *Dolmuş-Minibus System in Istanbul,* p. 29.

Chapter 7

1. Article 49 of the Constitution of 1961. The Constitution adopted in 1982 provided in Article 57 that "the State shall take measures to meet the needs for housing with the framework of a plan which takes into account the characteristics of cities and environmental conditions and supports community housing projects."

2. Ali Türel and Özcan Altaban, "Urban Growth and the Role of the State in the Provision of Housing in Turkey," paper presented to the 18th Congress of the International Society of City and Regional Planners, Istanbul, September 1–9, 1982, p. 5.

3. See Selman Ergüden, "An Overview of the Housing Sector in Turkey," paper presented to the 18th Congress of the International Society of City and Regional Planners, Istanbul, September 1–9, 1982, pp. 2–5.

4. Ibid.

5. See Thomas J. Anton, *Governing Greater Stockholm: A Study of Policy Development* (Berkeley, Cal.: University of California Press, 1975).

6. See Michael N. Danielson, *The Politics of Exclusion* (New York: Columbia University Press, 1976); and Michael N. Danielson and Jameson W. Doig, *New York: The Politics of Urban Regional Development* (Berkeley, Cal.; University of California Press, 1982), especially Chapter 3.

7. Ergüden, "An Overview of the Housing Sector in Turkey," p. 4.

8. State Planning Organization, *Urban Public Finance Policies,* Country Report II, SPO Pub. no. 1760, Social Planning Department Pub. no. 333 (Ankara, April 1981), p. 37.

9. See Ergüden, "An Overview of the Housing Sector in Turkey," p. 2; and State Institute of Statistics, *Household Income and Consumption Expenditures Survey Results: 1978–1979* (Ankara, 1982).

10. Türel and Altaban, "Urban Growth and the Role of the State in the Provision of Housing in Turkey," p. 6.

11. Kemal H. Karpat, *The Gecekondu: Rural Migration and Urbanization* (Cambridge: Cambridge University Press, 1976), p. 57.

12. Metin Heper, *Gecekondu Policy in Turkey: An Evaluation with a Case Study of Rumelihisarustu Squatter Area in Istanbul,* assisted by Mark H. Butler and Nedret T. Butler, Boğaziçi University Publications no. 146 (Istanbul: Boğaziçi University Press, 1978), p. 13.

13. David W. Drakakis-Smith, "Slums and Squatters in Ankara," *Town Planning Review,* vol. 47, no. 3 (July 1976), p. 227.

14. Quoted in Granville H. Sewell, "Squatter Settlements in Turkey: Analysis

of a Social, Political and Economic Problem," Ph.D. thesis, Massachusetts Institute of Technology (Cambridge, Mass.: 1966), p. 266.

15. See ibid., p. 186.

16. Heper, *Gecekondu Policy in Turkey,* p. 44.

17. Ibid., p. 46.

18. Law 775 of 1966, Gecekondu Law.

19. Geoffrey Payne, "The Gecekondus of Ankara," *Process Architecture,* no. 15 (May 1980), p. 78.

20. Karpat, *The Gecekondu,* p. 78.

21. See Sewell, "Squatter Settlements in Turkey," pp. 44–45.

22. Ibid., p. 44.

23. See Payne, "The Gecekondus of Ankara," pp. 78–79.

24. Heper, *Gecekondu Policy in Turkey,* p. 46.

25. Ibid., p. 56.

26. Karpat, *The Gecekondu,* p. 89.

27. Ruşen Keleş and Geoffrey K. Payne, "Town and Country Planning in Turkey," in Martyn Wynn, ed., *Planning and Urban Growth in Southern Europe* (London: Mansell in press).

28. Sevim Aksoy, "The Housing Problems of Istanbul and the Gecekondu Phenomenon," *Planning and Administration,* no. 1 (1980), p. 42.

29. Payne, "The Gecekondus of Ankara," p. 82.

30. Keleş and Payne, "Town and Country Planning in Turkey."

31. Ibid.

32. Ergun Özbudun, *Social Change and Political Participation in Turkey* (Princeton, N.J.: Princeton University Press, 1976), p. 210.

33. Ismet Kılıncaslan, "Governmental Programs Affecting Internal Migration in Turkey," in İbrahim Şanlı, Yücel Ünal, and İsmet Kılıncaşlan, *Internal Migration and Metropolitan Development in Turkey* (Istanbul: Reyo, 1976), p. 197.

34. Law 486 of 1924, Law Concerning Penal Provisions for Municipal Affairs.

35. Law 5431 of 1949, Law Concerning Demolishing of Buildings without Construction Permits and Amending Article 13 of the Municipal Construction and Roads Law.

36. See Heper, *Gecekondu Policy in Turkey,* p. 19.

37. Keleş and Payne, "Town and Country Planning in Turkey."

38. Sewell, "Squatter Settlements in Turkey," pp. 43–44.

39. Ibid., p. 73.

40. Keleş and Payne, "Town and Country Planning in Turkey."

41. Sewell, "Squatter Settlements in Turkey," p. 72.

42. Sewell calculates that "industry would have to almost double wages" had inexpensive gecekondu housing not been available; ibid., pp. 183–184.

43. Aksoy, "The Housing Problems of Istanbul and the Gecekondu Phenomenon," p. 47.

44. See Law 5218 of 1948, Law Concerning the Authorization of the Municipality to Give Part of Its Own Land to Those Who Will Build Dwellings; and Law 5228 of 1948, Law on the Encouragement of Home Building.

45. See Law 6188 of 1953, Law on the Encouragement of Home Building and on Illegally Built Dwellings; and Law 7367 of 1959, Law Concerning Land to be

Transferred from the State to the Municipalities; and the discussion of these measures in Heper, *Gecekondu Policy in Turkey,* pp. 19–20.

46. Quoted in Karpat, *The Gecekondu,* p. 65.

47. See State Planning Organization, *Kalkınma Planı, Birinci Beş Yıl: 1963–1967* (Ankara, 1963), pp. 434–435.

48. Law 775 of 1966.

49. Aksoy, "The Housing Problems of Istanbul and the Gecekondu Phenomenon," p. 42.

50. Keleş and Payne, "Town and Country Planning in Turkey."

51. Heper, *Gecekondu Policy in Turkey,* p. 53.

52. These and other data in this paragraph are from Ergüden, "An Overview of the Housing Sector in Turkey," p. 10.

53. See Aksoy, "The Housing Problems of Istanbul and the Gecekondu Phenomenon," p. 47.

54. İbrahim Şanlı, "Internal Migration in Turkey," in İbrahim Şanlı, Yücel Ünal, and Ismet Kılıncaşlan, *Internal Migration and Metropolitan Development in Turkey* (Istanbul: Reyo, 1976), p. 89.

55. Keleş and Payne, "Town and Country Planning in Turkey."

56. See State Planning Organization, *Kalkınma Planı, Üçüncü Beş Yıl 1973–1977* (Ankara, 1973), pp. 828–841. The Second Five-Year Development Plan, for the period 1968–1972, did not alter significantly the priorities established in the First Five-Year Plan, stressing prevention and self-help; see State Planning Organization, *Kalkınma Planı, Ikinci Beş Yıl: 1968–1972* (Ankara, 1969), pp. 273–287.

57. See State Planning Organization, *Dördüncü Beş Yıllık Kalkınma Planı: 1978–1983* (Ankara, 1978), pp. 470–477.

58. Ergüden, "An Overview of the Housing Sector in Turkey," p. 3.

59. Malcolm D. Rivkin, *Area Development for National Growth: The Turkish Precedent* (New York: Praeger, 1965), p. 119.

60. Law 6217 of 1954, Law Concerning the Modification of Article 26 of the Land Title Law.

61. Law 634 of 1965, Flat Law.

62. Ministry of Reconstruction and Settlement, *Turkish Monograph on Human Settlements Situation and Related Trends and Policies,* Economic Commission for Europe, Committee on Housing, Building and Planning (Ankara, July 1982), p. 64.

63. Ruşen Keleş, "Urbanization in Turkey," an International Urbanization Survey Report to the Ford Foundation, (New York, 1972) p. 86.

64. Law No. 5218 of 1948.

65. Malcolm D. Rivkin, *Land Use and the Intermediate-Size City in Developing Countries: With Case Studies of Turkey, Brazil, and Malaysia* (New York: Praeger, 1975), p. 63.

66. See Ministry of Reconstruction and Settlement, "Low Standard Housing with Special Reference to Squatter-Housing Problem in Turkey," Report to Committee on Housing, Building and Planning, Economic Commission for Europe.

67. Law 2487 of 1981, Collective Housing Law; see note 1 of this chapter for the text of Article 57 of the 1982 Constitution.

68. See Ministry of Reconstruction and Settlement, "Housing Sector in National Development Plans and the Prospects of the New Law on Collective Housing in Turkey," (Ankara, May 1982), p. 9.

69. Adnan Başer Kafaoğlu, Minister of Finance, quoted in *Tercüman,* January 23, 1983.

70. See Ministry of Reconstruction and Settlement, "Housing Sector in National Development Plans and the Prospects of the New Law on Collective Housing in Turkey," p. 9.

71. Türel and Altaban, "Urban Growth and the Role of the State in the Provision of Housing in Turkey," p. 12.

72. Suavi Akansel, "Batıkent New Settlement Project," paper presented to the 18th Congress of the International Society of City and Regional Planners, Istanbul, September 1–9, 1982, pp. 10–11.

73. Batıkent brochure prepared by Kent-Koop, Union of Housing Cooperatives in Batıkent, Ankara.

74. Mayor Ali Dinçer, press conference.

75. Batıkent brochure prepared by Kent-Koop.

Chapter 8

1. Istanbul Urban Development Project, General Urban Planning Study, "Draft Interim Report," Phase I (Istanbul, 1975), p. 24.

2. Ruşen Keleş and Geoffrey K. Payne, "Town and Country Planning in Turkey," in Martyn Wynn, ed., *Planning and Urban Growth in Southern Europe* (London: Mansell, in press).

3. A small amount of land also belonged to tribes.

4. Keleş and Payne, "Town and Country Planning in Turkey."

5. Under Article 38 of the Constitution of 1961, "State and public institutions are empowered to expropriate, totally or partially, land and buildings under private ownership in accordance with regulations and procedures defined by law in cases where the public interest requires it, provided that their real values are compensated for in advance." In other words, government must pay the fair market value of land and improvements acquired through condemnation.

6. Tax value was prescribed as the basis for compensation for expropriated private property in the Collective Housing Law of 1981 and in a tax law adopted the following year. A more complicated formula was adopted in Article 46 of the Constitution of 1982, involving tax value, unit prices, building costs, and other "objective criteria."

7. See Chamber of Architects, *Kent Toprakları Sorunu* (Ankara, 1973), p. 52.

8. See Kemal Kartal, "Kent Toprağında Mülkiyet," *Cumhuriyet,* December 23–26, 1978.

9. Ministry of Reconstruction and Settlement, *Turkish Monograph on Human Settlements Situation and Related Trends and Policies,* Economic Commission for Europe, Committee on Housing, Building and Planning (Ankara, July 1982), p. 26.

10. İbrahim Şanlı, "Internal Migration in Turkey," in İbrahim Şanlı, Yücel

Ünal, and İsmet Kılınçaslan, *Internal Migration and Metropolitan Development in Turkey* (Istanbul: Reyo, 1976), p. 85.

11. Metin Heper, *Gecekondu Policy in Turkey: An Evaluation with a Case Study of Rumelihisarustu Squatter Area in Istanbul*, assisted by Mark H. Butler and Nedret T. Butler, Boğaziçi University Publications no. 146 (Istanbul: Boğaziçi University Press, 1978), p. 42.

12. Şanlı, "Internal Migration in Turkey," p. 86.

13. Orhan Tuna, *İstanbul Gecekondu Önleme Bölgeleri Araştırması* (İstanbul: İktisat Fakültesi Yayını, 1977), p. 28.

14. Selman Ergüden, "An Overview of the Housing Sector in Turkey," paper presented to the 18th Congress of the International Society of City and Regional Planners, Istanbul, September 1–9, 1982, p. 15.

15. Keleş and Payne, "Town and Country Planning in Turkey."

16. See H. İnalcık, "Istanbul," in E. van Donzel, Bernard Lewis, and Charles Pallet, eds., *The Encyclopedia of Islam*, new edition, vol. 4. (Leiden: Brill, 1974), pp. 235–237.

17. Law 486 of 1924, Law Concerning Penal Provisions for Municipal Affairs.

18. Law 1593 of 1930.

19. Law 6785 of 1957.

20. Quoted in Steven V. Roberts, "Migration a Problem in Istanbul," *New York Times*, February 29, 1976.

21. Heper, *Gecekondu Policy in Turkey*, p. 17.

22. Mayor Ahmet İsvan, quoted in Roberts, "Migration a Problem in Istanbul."

23. Şerif Tüten, Minister of Reconstruction and Settlement, speech to Population and Environment Conference, Ankara, June 1982; see Environmental Problems Foundation of Turkey, *Population and Environment Conference* (Ankara, December 1982), p. 40.

24. Keleş and Payne, "Town and Country Planning in Turkey."

25. Istanbul Chamber of Industry, *İstanbul Metropolitan Alanında Sanayi Yerleşim Planlaması*. Research Section, Publication no. 10 (İstanbul, October 1981), p. 83.

26. Heper, *Gecekondu Policy in Turkey*, p. 39.

27. Institute of Local Government Studies, University of Birmingham, "Istanbul Municipality: Developing Capacity for Municipal Management," Consultants Report, Co-operative Action Programme, Turkey—Project (78)37, CT/5018, Technical Co-operation Service Organization for Economic Co-operation and Development (Paris, September 6, 1978), p. 64.

28. Jansen also prepared plans for Mersin, Adana, Ceyhan, Gaziantep, Tarsus, and Izmit. Proust did planning for Bursa, and other foreign specialists worked on plans for Trabzon, Erzurum, Çorum, Dikili, Niğde, Balıkesir, Zonguldak, and Menemen, including Le Corbusier in Izmir; see "Turkey: History, Geography and Planning," *ISOCARP Bulletin* (May 1982), p. 11.

29. Keleş and Payne, "Town and Country Planning in Turkey."

30. State Planning Organization, *Dördüncü Beş Yıllık Kalkınma Planı: 1978–1983* (Ankara, 1978), p. 77.

31. Law 1580 of 1930.

32. Law 2290 of 1933.

33. The Town Planning Law of 1957 was amended in 1972 to exempt most towns between 5,000 and 10,000; see Law 6785 of 1957 and Law 1605 of 1972, Law Concerning Modifications in the Town Planning Law.

34. Keleş and Payne, "Town and Country Planning in Turkey." Under the legislation currently in force, such matters are taken before regional administrative courts.

35. Institute of Local Government Studies, University of Birmingham, "Istanbul Municipality: Developing Capacity for Municipal Management," p. 60.

36. Keleş and Payne, "Town and Country Planning in Turkey."

37. Istanbul Urban Development Project, "Draft Interim Report," p. 38.

38. Keleş and Payne, "Town and Country Planning in Turkey."

39. See Lloyd Rodwin, Nations and Cities: A Comparison of Strategies for Urban Growth (Boston: Houghton Mifflin, 1970), pp. 81, 84–91.

40. The Greater Istanbul Master Plan Bureau was created in 1966 and reformulated in 1967 by the cabinet decree that established area-wide planning bodies for the three metropolitan areas. Izmir's agency was set up in 1968, and Ankara's in 1969. Metropolitan planning was undertaken in the 1970s for Adana, Bursa, Elâzığ, Erzurum, and Samsun.

41. Greater Istanbul Master Plan Bureau, 1980.

42. Institute of Local Government Studies, University of Birmingham, "Istanbul Municipality: Developing Capacity for Municipal Management," p. 60.

43. Istanbul Urban Development Project, "Draft Interim Report," p. 15.

44. Ayten Çetiner, "On Population, Growth and Development of Istanbul," Special Report 1 in H. İbrahim Şanlı, Dolmuş-Minibus System in Istanbul: A Case Study in Low-Cost Transportation (İstanbul: İstanbul Teknik Üniversitesi Matbaası—Gümüşsuyu, 1981), p. 199.

45. State Planning Organization, Kalkınma Planı, Ikinci Beş Yıl: 1968–1972 (Ankara, 1969), p. 270–273.

46. State Planning Organization, Kalkınma Planı, Birinci Beş Yıl: 1963–1967 (Ankara, 1963), p. 474.

47. State Planning Organization, Kalkınma Planı, Ikinci Beş Yıl: 1968–1972, p. 269.

48. Ibid., p. 263.

49. Ibid.

50. Yücel Ünal, "Migration in the Eastern Black Sea Region," in İbrahim Şanlı, Yücel Ünal, and İsmet Kılıncaşlan, Internal Migration and Metropolitan Development in Turkey (Istanbul: Reyo, 1976), p. 147.

51. Istanbul Urban Development Project, "Draft Interim Report," p. 26.

52. Malcolm D. Rivkin, Area Development for National Growth: The Turkish Precedent (New York: Praeger, 1965), p. 45.

53. Ali Türel and Özcan Altaban, "Urban Growth and the Role of the State in the Provision of Housing in Turkey," paper presented to the 18th Congress of the International Society of City and Regional Planners, Istanbul, September 1–9, 1982, p. 2.

54. Rivkin, Area Development for National Growth, p. 100.

55. World Bank, *Turkey: Prospects and Problems of an Expanding Economy.* A World Bank Country Report (Washington, 1975), p. 163.

56. Rivkin, *Area Development for National Growth,* p. 128.

57. Heper, *Gecekondu Policy in Turkey,* p. 22.

58. Hasan Gençağa, "Growth Determinants of Urban Centers of Different Sizes," Ph.D. thesis, Columbia University (New York, 1976), p. 20.

59. State Planning Organization, *Kalkınma Planı, Üçüncü Beş Yıl 1973–1977* (Ankara, 1973), pp. 947–949.

60. Rivkin, *Area Development for National Growth,* p. 92.

61. The number of priority development provinces was cut back to 25 by the military government in 1981.

62. The 1982 Constitution provided that "Regional organizations with broad authority comprising several provinces may be established to promote productivity and coordination of public services."

63. World Bank, *Turkey: Prospects for an Expanding Economy,* p. 167.

64. Ibid., p. 177.

65. Keleş and Payne, "Town and Country Planning in Turkey."

66. Ünal, "Migration in the Eastern Black Sea Region," p. 150.

67. Rivkin, *Area Development for National Growth,* p. 100.

68. Barlas Tolan, *Türkiye'de İller İtibariyle Sosyo-Ekonomik Gelişmişlik Endeksi,* State Planning Organization (Ankara, 1972); and unpublished data from the Turkish Union of Banks.

69. State Planning Organization, *Dördüncü Beş Yıllık Kalkınma Planı: 1978–1983,* p. 75.

70. Rodwin, *Nations and Cities,* p. 77.

71. Rivkin, *Area Development for National Growth,* p. 92.

72. Ibid.

Chapter 9

1. Andrew Finkel, "Community Power in Turkish Cities," in Korel Göymen, Hans F. Illy, and Winfried Veit, eds., *Local Administration: Democracy versus Efficiency?* Analysen no. 103/104 (Bonn: Friedrich Ebert Stiftung, 1982), p. 93.

2. Sevim Aksoy, "The Housing Problems of Istanbul and the Gecekondu Phenomenon," *Planning and Administration,* no. 1 (1980), p. 39.

3. State Planning Organization, *Urban Public Finance Policies,* Country Report II, SPO. Pub. no. 1760, Social Planning Department Pub. no. 333 (Ankara, April 1981), p. 35.

4. Ministry of Reconstruction and Settlement, *Turkish Monograph on Human Settlements Situation and Related Trends and Policies,* Economic Commission for Europe, Committee on Housing, Building and Planning (Ankara, July 1982), p. 23.

5. Suavi Akansel, "Habitat for All: What Is the Solution," paper presented to the 18th Congress of the International Society of City and Regional Planners, Istanbul, September 1–7, 1982, p. 9.

BIBLIOGRAPHY

This listing is limited to source material dealing directly with Turkey. Other references are provided in the notes.

GENERAL ECONOMIC, SOCIAL, AND POLITICAL DEVELOPMENT

Akarlı, Engin D., and Gabriel Ben-Dor, eds. *Political Participation in Turkey*. Istanbul: Boğaziçi University Publications, 1975.

Aker, Ahmet. *İşçi Göçü* [Labor Migration]. İstanbul: Sander Yay, 1972.

Association of Turkish Businessmen and Industrialists. *1977 Yılı Programı ve 1977 Yılı Bütçesi Üzerine Görüşler* [Comments and Proposals on the 1977 Program and 1977 Budget]. İstanbul, 1977.

———. *Turkey 1976*.Istanbul, 1976.

Baer, Gabriel. "The Administrative, Economic and Social Functions of Turkish Guilds." *International Journal of Middle East Studies*, vol. 1, no. 1 (1970), 28–50.

Benedict, Peter, Fatma Mansur, and Erol Tümertekin, eds. *Turkey: Geographic and Social Perspectives*. Leiden: Brill, 1974.

Berger, Morroe. *The Arab World Today*. New York: Doubleday, 1964.

Bulutay, Tuncer, Serim Timur, and Hasan Ersel. *Türkiye'de Gelir Dağılımı: 1968* [Income Distribution in Turkey: 1968]. Ankara: Siyasal Bilgiler Fakültesi Yayınları, 1971.

Derviş, Kemal, and Sherman Robinson. "The Structure of Income Inequality in Turkey: 1950–1973." In Ergun Özbudun and Aydın Ulusan, eds., *The Political Economy of Income Distribution in Turkey.* New York: Holmes & Meier, 1980, 83–122.

Dodd, Clement H. *Democracy and Development in Turkey.* North Humberside: Eothen Press, 1979.

Kili, Suna. *1960–1975 Döneminde Cumhuriyet Halk Partisinde Gelişmeler* [Developments in the Republican People's Party during 1960–1975]. Istanbul: Boğaziçi Üniversitesi Yayınları, 1976.

Mardin, Şerif. "Turkey: The Transformation of an Economic Code." In Ergun Özbudun and Aydın Ulusan, eds., *The Political Economy of Income Distribution in Turkey.* New York: Holmes & Meier, 1980, 23–53.

Ministry of Public Works, State Highways General Directorate. *Cumhuriyetin 50. Yılında Karayolları* [Highways in the 50th Year of the Republic]. Publication no. 213. Ankara, 1973.

Öncü, Ayşe. "Chambers of Industry in Turkey: An Inquiry into State-Industry Relations as a Distributive Domain." In Ergun Özbudun and Aydın Ulusan, eds., *The Political Economy of Income Distribution in Turkey.* New York: Holmes & Meier, 1980, 455–480.

Özbudun, Ergun. "Income Distribution as an Issue in Turkish Politics." In Ergun Özbudun and Aydın Ulusan, eds., *The Political Economy of Income Distribution in Turkey.* New York: Holmes & Meier, 1980, 55–82.

———. *Social Change and Political Participation in Turkey.* Princeton, N.J.: Princeton University Press, 1976.

———. "Voting Behaviour: Turkey." In Jacob M. Landau, Ergun Özbudun, and Frank Tachau, eds., *Electoral Politics in the Middle East: Issues, Voters and Elites.* London: Croom Helm, 1980, 107–143.

Özbudun, Ergun, and Aydın Ulusan, eds. *The Political Economy of Income Distribution in Turkey.* New York: Holmes & Meier, 1980.

Özötün, Erdoğan. *Türkiye Gayri Safî Yurt İçi Hâsılası.* [Gross National Product of Turkey by Provinces]. İller İtibariyle. Ankara: State Institute of Statistics, 1980.

Paine, Suzanne. *Exporting Workers: The Turkish Case.* Cambridge: Cambridge University Press, 1975.

Roberts, Steven V. "Modernization Leaves Turkey's Culture in Disorder and Its People Seeking an Identity." *New York Times,* May 23, 1977.

———. "Turks Are Moving Toward the Left as New Jobs in Industry Lure Them from the Land," *New York Times,* May 31, 1977.

State Planning Organization. *Gelir Dağılımı Araştırması—1973* [Income Distribution—1973]. Ankara, 1976.

———. *Türk Köylerinde Modernleşme Eğilimileri Araştırması* [A Study on Modernization of Turkish Villages]. Social Planning Department, Pub. no. 198. Ankara, 1970.

Tezel, Yahya Sezai. "Turkish Economic Development, 1923–1950: Policy and Achievements." Ph.D. thesis, Cambridge University, Cambridge, 1975.

Timur, Serim. "Socio-Economic Determinants of Differential Fertility in Turkey." Paper presented at the Second European Population Conference, Council of Europe, Strasbourg, August 31–September 7, 1971.

Tuncer, Baran. "A Study of the Socio-Economic Determinants of Fertility in Turkey." Discussion Paper no. 121, Economic Growth Center, Yale University. New Haven, 1971.

"Turkey: How Sick a Man?" *Economist,* September 12, 1981.

Weiker, Walter F. *The Modernization of Turkey: From Atatürk to the Present Day.* New York: Holmes & Meier, 1981.

World Bank. *Turkey: Prospects and Problems of an Expanding Economy.* A World Bank Country Report. Washington, 1975.

GENERAL URBANIZATION

Ankara Chamber of Architects. *Türkiye'de Kentleşme* [Urbanization in Turkey]. Ankara: Mimarlar Odası Yayını, 1971.

Danielson, Michael N., and Ruşen Keleş. "Urbanization and Income Distribution in Turkey." In Ergun Özbudun and Aydın Ulusan, eds., *The Political Economy of Income Distribution in Turkey.* New York: Holmes & Meier, 1980, 269–309.

Environmental Problems Foundation of Turkey. *Environmental Profile of Turkey.* Ankara, 1981.

———. *Population and Environment Conference.* Ankara, December, 1982.

Gökçe, Birsen. *Gecekondu Gençliği* [Gecekondu Youth]. Ankara: Hacettepe Üniversitesi, 1971.

Irmak, Y. *Türkiye'de Kentleşme* [Urbanization in Turkey]. Kültür Bakanlığı Yayını, no. 345. Ankara, 1979.

Kartal, Kemal. *Kentleşme ve İnsan* [Urbanization and the Human Being]. Ankara: Türkiye ve Orta Doğu Amme İdaresi Enstitüsü, 1978.

Keleş, Ruşen. "Alternatif Şehirleşme Hareketlerinin Maliyeti Hakkında Ön Rapor" [Preliminary Report on the Cost of Alternative Urbanization Policies]. State Planning Organization. Ankara, 1967.

———. "Urbanization in Turkey." An International Urbanization Survey Report to the Ford Foundation. New York, 1972.

———. "Urbanization, Population and the Environment." In Environmental Problems Foundation of Turkey, *Population and Environment Conference.* Ankara, December 1982.

Keleş, Ruşen, and Orhan Türkay. *Köylü Gözü ile Türkiye Köylerinde*

İktisadî ve Toplumsal Değişme [Economic and Social Change in Turkey's Villages as Perceived by the Villagers]. Türk İktisadî Gelişmesi Araştırma Projesi no. 13. Ankara: Siyasal Bilgiler Fakültesi, Maliyi Enstitüsü, 1962.

Keleş, Ruşen, and Artun Ünsal. *Kent ve Siyasal Şiddet* [Urbanization and Political Violence]. Ankara: Siyasal Bilgiler Fakültesi, 1982.

Kılınçaslan, İsmet. "Governmental Programs Affecting Internal Migration in Turkey." In İbrahim Şanlı, Yücel Ünal, and İsmet Kılınçaslan, *Internal Migration and Metropolitan Development in Turkey*. Istanbul: Reyo, 1976, 155–201.

Kuran, Timur. "Internal Migration: The Unorganized Urban Sector and Income Distribution in Turkey, 1963–1973." In Ergun Özbudun and Aydın Ulusan, eds., *The Political Economy of Income Distribution in Turkey*. New York: Holmes & Meier, 1980, 349–375.

Levine, Ned. "Old Culture–New Culture: A Study of Migrants in Ankara, Turkey." *Social Forces*, vol. 51, no. 3 (March 1973), 355–368.

Rivkin, Malcolm D. *Land Use and the Intermediate-Size City in Developing Countries: With Case Studies of Turkey, Brazil, and Malaysia*. New York: Praeger, 1975.

Şanlı, İbrahim. "Internal Migration in Turkey." In İbrahim Şanlı, Yücel Ünal, and İsmet Kılınçaslan, *Internal Migration and Metropolitan Development in Turkey*. Istanbul: Reyo, 1976, 17–98.

Şenyapılı, O. *Kentlileşen Köylüler* [The Urbanizing Peasants]. Ankara: Karacan Armağanı 77, Milliyet Yayınları, 1978.

State Planning Organization. *Kent Eşiği Araştırması* [Research into Urban Thresholds]. SPO Pub. no. 1838, Social Planning Department, Pub. no. 350. Ankara, 1982.

———. *Kentleşme, Yerleşme Sektör Raporu* [Urbanization and Settlement Sector Report]. SPO Pub. no. 1851, Social Planning Department, Pub. no. 357. Ankara, 1982.

Tekeli, İlhan. *Bağımlı Kentleşme: Kırda ve Kentte Dönüşüm Süreci* [Dependent Urbanization: Process of Transformation in Rural and Urban Areas]. Ankara: Mimarlar Odası, 1977.

Tekeli, İlhan, Yiğit Gülöksüz, and Tarık Okyay. *Gecekondulu, Dolmuşlu, İşportalı Şehir* [The City with the Gecekondu, the Dolmuş, and the Peddler]. İstanbul: Cem Yayınevi, 1976.

Tümertekin, Erol. *Türkiye'de Şehirleşme ve Şehirsel Fonksiyonlar* [Urbanization and Urban Functions in Turkey]. Istanbul: Publications of Istanbul University, Faculty of Letters Press, Institute of Geography, 1973.

Turkish Association of Municipalities. *Büyük Belediyelerde Şehirleşme Sorunları Konferansı* [Conference on Urbanization Problems of Large Cities]. Ankara, 1968.

Ünal, Yücel. "Migration in the Eastern Black Sea Region." In İbrahim Şanlı, Yücel Ünal, and İsmet Kılınçaslan, *Internal Migration and Metropolitan Development in Turkey.* Istanbul: Reyo, 1976, 101–153.

INDIVIDUAL CITIES

Akçura, Tuğrul. *Ankara: Türkiye Cumhuriyetinin Başkenti Hakkında Monografik Bir Araştırma* [A Monograph on the Capital of the Turkish Republic]. Ankara: Orta Doğu Teknik Üniversitesi, 1971.

Ankara Metropolitan Area Master Plan Bureau. "Summary: Environmental and Urban Service Standards in Ankara," Publication no. 3. Ankara, 1970.

Ankara Municipality. *Ankara Kent İçi Ulaşım Etüdü Ulaşım Modeli.* [Transportation Model for Intracity Transportation in Ankara] Ankara, 1979.

————. *Birinci Toplutaşım Kongresi (Bildiriler)* [First Congress on Mass Transportation]. Ankara, 1978.

————. *İkinci Toplutaşım Kongresi (Bildiriler)* [Second Congress on Mass Transportation]. Ankara, 1979.

Ankara Municipality, Mayor's Office. *1976 Malî Yılı Çalışma Raporu* [Mayor of Ankara's Report on 1976 Activities]. Ankara: June, 1977.

Arı, Oğuz. "Ankara'da Yetenekli Devamlı Endüstri İşçileri Sorununun İncelenmesi."]A Study on the Question of Permanent Industrial Workers in Ankara] *Boğaziçi Üniversitesi Dergisi—Soyval Bilimer,* vol. 1 (1973), 9–32.

Beyru, Rauf. *İzmir Şehri Üzerinde Bir İnceleme* [A Study on the City of Izmir]. Ankara: Orta Doğu Teknik Üniversitesi, 1969.

Çetiner, Ayten. "On Population, Growth, and Development of Istanbul." Special Report 1 in H. İbrahim Şanlı, *Dolmuş-Minibus System in Istanbul: A Case Study in Low-Cost Transportation.* Istanbul: Istanbul Teknik Üniversitesi Matbaası—Gümüşsuyu, 1981.

Clark, John. "The Growth of Ankara, 1961–1969." *Review of the Geographical Institute of the University of Istanbul,* International Edition, no. 13, (1970–1971), 119–139.

Drakakis-Smith, David W. *Housing Problems in Ankara.* University of Durham, Department of Geography. Durham, 1975.

————. "Slums and Squatters in Ankara." *Town Planning Review,* vol. 47, no. 3 (July 1976), 225–240.

Görgün, Sevim. "İstanbul Belediyesinin Finansal Durumu ve Sorunları" [Financial State and Problems of the Municipality of Istanbul]. Istanbul, 1977.

Göymen, Korel, ed. *Bir Yerel Yönetim Öyküsü: 1977–80 Ankara Belediy-*

esi Deneyimi [Local Government Story: Experiences in the City of Ankara during 1977–1980]. Ankara: Ozgün Matbaacılık Sanayi, 1983.

Güzelsu, Kutlu. "Metropolitan Istanbul 1982." Paper presented to the 18th Congress of the International Society of City and Regional Planners, Istanbul, September 1–9, 1982.

İnalcık, H. "Istanbul." In E. van Donzel, Bernard Lewis, and Charles Patter, eds., *The Encyclopedia of Islam*, new edition, vol. 4. Leiden: Brill, 1974, 224–248.

Institute of Local Government Studies, University of Birmingham. "Istanbul Municipality: Developing Capacity for Municipal Management." Consultant's Report, Co-operative Action Programme, Turkey—Project (78)37, CT/5018, Technical Co-operation Service Organization for Economic Co-operation and Development. Paris, September 6, 1978.

Istanbul Chamber of Industry. *İstanbul Metropolitan Alanında Sanayi Yerleşim Planlaması* [Planning Industrial Location in the Istanbul Metropolitan Area]. İstanbul, 1982.

Istanbul Governor's Office, Planning and Coordination Department. *1. İstanbul Sempozyumu* [First Istanbul Symposium]. İstanbul: 1982.

Istanbul Metropolitan Plan Bureau. *Büyük İstanbul Nazim Plan Raporu* [Report of the Greater Istanbul Metropolitan Plan]. Istanbul, November, 1970.

———. *Income and Income Distribution: Annex to Socio-Economic Issues*, Annex 2:4. Istanbul, 1975.

———. "The Provision of Local Services and the Problem of Municipal Finance." *Socio-Economic Issues*, Annex 2–6. Istanbul, July, 1976.

Istanbul Technical University, Institute of Planning. *2000 Yılında İstanbul* [Istanbul in the Year 2000]. İstanbul, 1975.

Istanbul Urban Development Project. General Urban Planning Study. "Draft Interim Report," Phase I. Istanbul, 1975.

Keleş, Ruşen. *İzmir'in Mahalleleri* [Districts of Izmir]. Ankara: Sosyal Bilimler Derneği Yayını, 1973.

Keskin, Ahmet. "Urban Transportation in Istanbul: An Overview." Special Report 2 in H. İbrahim Şanlı, *Dolmuş-Minibus System in Istanbul: A Case Study in Low-Cost Transportation*. Istanbul: İstanbul Teknik Üniversitesi Matbaası—Gümüşsuyu, 1981.

Kıray, Mübeccel. *İzmir: Örgütleşmeyen Kent* [Izmir: The Unorganized City]. Ankara: Sosyal Bilimler Derneği, 1972.

Özmucur, Süleyman. "Distribution of Income in Istanbul." Istanbul Metropolitan Planning Bureau, Technical Memorandum no. 117. Istanbul, January 1975.

———. "İstanbul Gayrisafâ Hâsılası: 1950–1974" [Gross Product of Istanbul]. İstanbul Şehirsel Gelişme Projesi, Istanbul Metropolitan Planning Bureau, Technical Memorandum no. 211. İstanbul, May 1975.

Payne, Geoffrey K. "Ankara: Housing and Planning in an Expanding City." A research report submitted to the Social Science Research Council. London, 1977.

————. "The Gecekondus of Ankara." *Process Architecture,* no. 15 (May 1980), 71–82.

Roberts, Steven V. "Migration a Problem in Istanbul." *New York Times,* February 29, 1976.

Şanlı, H. İbrahim. *Dolmuş-Minibus System in Istanbul: A Case Study in Low-Cost Transportation.* Istanbul: İstanbul Teknik Üniversitesi Matbaası—Gümüşsuyu, 1981.

Suzuki, Peter. "Peasants Without Plows: Some Anatolians in Istanbul." *Rural Sociology,* vol. 31, no. 4 (December 1966), 428–438.

Turkish Union of Chambers for Architects and Engineers, Chamber of Land Survey. *Kentleşme Sorunlari ve İstanbul* [Urbanization Problems and Istanbul]. Ankara: Pelin Offset Basımevi, 1980.

Ünal, Yücel. "Legal and Administrative Aspects of Transportation and the Dolmuş-Minibus System in Istanbul." Special Report 3 in H. İbrahim Şanlı, *Dolmuş-Minibus System in Istanbul: A Case Study in Low-Cost Transportation.* Istanbul: İstanbul Teknik Üniversitesi Matbaası—Gümüşsuyu, 1981.

HOUSING AND GECEKONDUS

Abadan-Unat, Nermin et al. *Migration and Development.* Ankara: Ajans-Türk Press, 1976.

Aksoy, Sevim. "The Housing Problems of Istanbul and the Gecekondu Phenomenon." *Planning and Administration* no. 1 (1980), 39–48.

Ankansel, Suavi. "Batıkent New Settlement Project." Paper presented to the 18th Congress of the International Society of City and Regional Planners, Istanbul, September 1–9, 1982.

————. "Habitat for All: What Is the Solution." Paper presented to the 18th Congress of the International Society of City and Regional Planners, Istanbul, September 1–9, 1982.

Bulca, A. "Toplu Konut Üretiminde Yerel Yönetim Öncülüğü" [Municipal Leadership in Mass Housing Production]. *Mimarlık,* no. 3 (1978).

Eke, Feral. "Absorption of Low-Income Groups in Ankara," in *Progress in Planning,* D. Diamond and J. B. McLoughlin, eds., Vol. 19, Part 1 (1982), pp. 1–88.

Ergüden, Selman. "An Overview of the Housing Sector in Turkey." Paper presented to the 18th Congress of the International Society of City and Regional Planners, Istanbul, September 1–9, 1982.

Geray, Cevat. "Gecekondu Sorununa Toplu Bakiş" [A General View of the Squatting Problem]. *Amme İdaresi Dergisi,* vol. 1, no. 2 (September 1968), 11–28.

———. "Konut Gereksinmesi ve Karşılanması." *Amme İdaresi Dergisi,* vol. 14, no. 2 (June 1981).

Hart, Charles W. M. *Zeytinburnu Gecekondu Bölgesi* [Zeytinburnu Squatter Settlement]. İstanbul: İstanbul Ticaret Odası Yayınları, 1969.

Heper, Metin. *Gecekondu Policy in Turkey: An Evaluation with a Case Study of Rumelihisarüstü Squatter Area in Istanbul.* Assisted by Mark H. Butler and Nedret T. Butler. Boğaziçi University Publications no. 146. Istanbul: Boğaziçi University Press, 1978.

Karpat, Kemal H. *The Gecekondu: Rural Migration and Urbanization.* Cambridge: Cambridge University Press, 1976.

———. "The Politics of Transition: Political Attitudes and Party Affiliation in the Turkish Gecekondu." In Engin D. Akarlı and Gabriel Ben-Dor, eds., *Political Participation in Turkey.* Istanbul: Boğaziçi University Publications, 1975.

Keleş, Ruşen. *100 Soruda Türkiye'de Kentleşme, Konut ve Gecekondu* [Turkish Urbanization, Housing, and Squatting in 100 Questions]. 3rd ed. İstanbul: Gerçek, 1983.

———. "Lower Income Urban Settlements in Turkey." Paper Presented to the Expert Group Meeting on Strategies for the Improvement of Different Types of Lower-Income Settlements, United Nations Center for Housing, Building and Planning, November 28–December 2, 1977.

Kent-Koop. *Feasibility Study: A Summary.* Ankara, 1980.

———. *Konut 81* [Housing 81]. Ankara, 1982.

Kongar, Emre. "Altındağ Gecekondu Bölgesi ve Altındağ'da Kentle Bütünleşme." *Amme İdaresi Dergisi,* vol. 6, no. 3–4 (1973).

Ministry of Reconstruction and Settlement. "Housing Sector in National Development Plans and the Prospects of the New Law on Collective Housing in Turkey." Ankara, May 1982.

———. "Low Standard Housing with Special Reference to Squatter-Housing Problem in Turkey." Report to Committee on Housing, Building and Planning, Economic Commission for Europe.

———. *13 Büyük Şehirde Gecekondu* [Squatter Housing in 13 Large Cities]. Ankara, 1968.

———. *Turkish Monograph on Human Settlements Situation and Related Trends and Policies.* Economic Commission for Europe, Committee on Housing, Building and Planning. Ankara, July 1982.

Öğretmen, İbrahim. *Ankara'da 158 Gecekondu* [158 Gecekondus in Ankara]. Ankara: Siyasal Bilgiler Fakültesi Yayınları, 1957.

Saran, Nephan. "Squatter Settlement Programs in Istanbul." In Peter Benedict, Fatma Mansur and Erol Tümertekin, eds., *Turkey: Geographic and Social Perspectives.* Leiden: Brill, 1974.

Şenyapılı, Tansı. *Bütünleşmemiş Kentli Nüfus Sorunu* [The Unintegrated Urban Population Issue]. Ankara: Orta Doğu Teknik Üniversitesi, 1978.

———. *Gecekondu: Çevre İşçilerin Mekânı* [Gecekondu: The Habitat of Marginal Workers]. Ankara: Orta Doğu Teknik Üniversitesi, 1982.

Sewell, Granville H. "Squatter Settlements in Turkey: Analysis of a Social, Political and Economic Problem," Ph.D. thesis, Massachusetts Institute of Technology, Cambridge, Mass., 1966.

State Planning Organization. *Konut Sektörü Raporu* [Housing Sector Report]. SPO Pub. no. 1870, Social Planning Department Pub. no. 365. Ankara, 1982.

Tankut, Gönül. "Ankara'da Gecekondu Problemi." *Mimarlık ve Sanat,* no. 7–8 (1963).

Tuna, Orhan. *İstanbul Gecekondu Önleme Bölgeleri Araştırması* [Research on Rehabilitation Areas in Istanbul Squatter Settlements]. İstanbul: İktisat Fakültesi Yayını, 1977.

Türel, Ali, and Özcan Altaban. "Urban Growth and the Role of the State in the Provision of Housing in Turkey." Paper presented to the 18th Congress of the International Society of City and Regional Planners, Istanbul, September 1–9, 1982.

Turkish Society for Housing and Planning. *Türkiye'de Bölge Planlaması Alanındaki Gelişmeler* [Progress in Regional Planning in Turkey]. Publication no. 2. Ankara, 1964.

Yasa, İbrahim. *Ankara'da Gecekondu Aileleri* [Squatter Families in Ankara]. Ankara: Sağlık ve Sosyal Yardım Bakanlığı, Soysal Hizmetler Genel Müdürlügü, 1966.

———. "Types of Occupations and Economic Order in Gecekondu Communities." *8th Seminar on Housing and Planning.* Ankara: Faculty of Political Science, 1964.

Yörükan, Turhan. *Gecekondular ve Gecekondu Bölgelerinin Sosyo-Kültürel Özellikleri, İmar ve İskân Bakanlığı* [Squatter Houses and Socio-Cultural Characteristics of Squatter Areas]. Ankara: Ministry of Reconstruction and Settlement, 1968.

URBAN GOVERNMENT

Akalın, Muzaffer. *Bir Olayın Hikâyesi* [Story of a Political Affair]. İstanbul: M. Sucuoğlu Matbaası, 1961.

Ankara Belediyesi Başkanlık Uzmanları. *Toplumcu Belediye* [Peoples' Municipality]. Ankara, 1977.

Ceyhun, Demirtaş. *Bir Yeni Dev* [A New Giant]. İstanbul: Tekin Yayınevi, 1977.

Chamber of Architects. "Yerel Yönetim Uygulamaları Üzerine Tartışmalar" [A Discussion on Local Administration Activities]. *Mimarlık*, no. 2 (1977).

Dalokay, Vedat. *06 Dalokay* [Mayor of Ankara: Dalokay]. Ankara, 1977.

Danielson, Michael N., and Ruşen Keleş. "Allocating Public Resources in Urban Turkey." In Ergun Özbudun and Aydın Ulusan, eds.,*The Political Economy of Income Distribution in Turkey*. New York: Holmes & Meier, 1980, 311–348.

Ergin, Osman Nuri. *Mecelle-i Umur-u Belediye* [Code of Municipal Affairs]. İstanbul, 1922.

————. *Türk Şehirciliğinin Tarihi İnkişafı* [Historical Development of Turkish Urbanism]. İstanbul: Cumhuriyet Gazetesi ve Matabaası, 1944.

Finkel, Andrew. "Community Power in Turkish Cities." In Korel Göymen, Hans F. Illy, and Winfried Veit, eds., *Local Administration: Democracy versus Efficiency?* Analysen no. 103/104. Bonn: Friedrich Ebert Stiftung, 1982.

Geray, Cevat, and Ruşen Keleş. *Personelinin Gözüyle Küçük Belediyelerin Sorunları* [Problems of Smaller Municipalities]. Ankara: Türkiye ve Orta Doğu Amme İdaresi Enstitüsü, 1969.

Gökçeer, Fikri. *Atatürk Yılında Belediyelerimiz* [Our Municipalities in Atatürk's Year]. Ankara: Türk Belediyecilik Derneği, 1981.

Gönül, Mustafa. *Yerel Yönetim Birlikleri* [Union of Local Authorities]. Ankara: Türkiye ve Orta Doğu Amme İidaresi Enstitüsü, 1976.

Gorvine, Albert. *An Outline of Turkish Provincial and Local Government*. Ankara: Faculty of Political Sciences, 1956.

Göymen, Korel. "The Restructuring of Local Administrations in Turkey." In Korel Göymen, Hans F. Illy, and Winfried Veit, eds., *Local Administration: Democracy versus Efficiency?* Analysen no. 103/104. Bonn: Friedrich Ebert Stiftung, 1982, 137–152.

Gözübüyük, Şeref. *Türkiye'de Mahallî İdareler* [Local Administration in Turkey]. Ankara: Türkiye ve Orta Doğu Amme İdaresi Enstitüsü, 1967.

İller Bankası Dergisi [Journal of the Bank of Local Authorities].

İsvan, Ahmet. "Halkın Belediyesi Olmak" [To Be the People's Municipality]. *Mimarlık*, no. 2 (1977).

Keleş, Ruşen. "Belediye Gelirleri ve Malî Denkleşme" [Municipal Revenues and Intergovernmental Fiscal Relations]. *Amme İdaresi Dergisi*, vol. 5 (March, 1972).

————. "Decentralization: Experience and Prerequisites." In Korel Göymen, Hans F. Illy, and Winfried Veit, eds., *Local Administration: Democracy versus Efficiency?* Analysen no. 103/104 (Bonn: Friedrich Ebert Stiftung, 1982, 117–130.

————. "Yerel Yönetimlerde Güncel Oluşumlar" [Present Developments in Local Government]. *Tütengil'e Saygı*. İstanbul: İstanbul Matbaası, 1981.

————. "Yerel Yönetimlerin Özerkliği ve Bir Örnekolay" [Local Autonomy and a Relevant Case]. *Seha L. Meray Armağanı* vol. 2. Ankara: Siyasal Bilgeler Fakültesi, 1982.

Keleş, Ruşen, and Cevat Geray. *Türk Belediye Başkanları: 1958–1964* [Turkey's Mayors: 1958–1964]. Ankara: Türk Belediyecilik Derneği, 1964.

Keleş, Ruşen, and Fehmi Yavuz. *Yerel Yönetimler* [Local Government]. Ankara: Turhan Kitabevi, 1983.

Kılınçaslan, İsmet. *Büyük İstanbul Şehrinde Hizmetler ve Belediye Giderleri Analizi Uzerine Bir Deneme* [An Essay on the Analysis of Municipal Services and Expenditures in Greater Istanbul]. İstanbul: İstanbul Teknik Üniversitesi, 1974.

Koc, Yıldırım. "1974–1980 Döneminde Belediyelerde İşçi-İşveren İlişkileri" [Employer-Employee Relations in Municipalities during 1974–1980]. *Toplum ve Bilim*, no. 17 (Spring 1982), 88–115.

Lewis, Bernard. "Balladiyya" [Municipality]. In E. van Donzal, Bernard Lewis, and Charles Pallet, eds., *The Encyclopedia of Islam*, new edition, vol. 1. Leiden: Brill, 1959, 972–977.

Nadaroğlu, H. *Mahalli İdareler: Felsefesi, Ekonomisi, Uygulaması* [Local Administration: Its Philosophy, Economics, and Practice]. İstanbul: Sermet Matbaası, 1978.

Ortaylı, İlber. *Tanzimattan Sonra Mahallî İdareler* [Local Government after Tanzimat]. Ankara, 1974.

Payaslıoğlu, Arif T. *Merkezî İdarenin Taşra Teşkilâtı Üzerinde bir İnceleme* [A Study of the Provincial Organization of Central Administration]. Ankara: Türkiye ve Orta Doğu Amme İdaresi Enstitüsü, 1965).

Saral, Talât. "Türk Belediyeciliğinin Genel Görünümü" [A General View of Turkish Municipalities]. *Maliye Dergisi* (March–April 1980).

Soysal, Mümtaz. *Local Government in Turkey*. Ankara: Institute of Public Administration for Turkey and the Middle East, 1967.

State Planning Organization. *Belediye Hizmetleri Sektör Raporu* [Sector Report on Municipal Services]. SPO Pub. no. 1852, Social Planning Department Pub. no. 359. Ankara, 1982.

————. *Şehir Altyapısı* [Municipal Infrastructure]. SPO Pub. no. 1850, Social Planning Department Pub. no. 356. Ankara, 1982.

————. *Urban Public Finance Policies*. Country Report II, SPO Pub. no. 1760, Social Planning Department Pub. no. 333. Ankara, April 1981.

Tekeli, İlhan. "Belediyeler ve Kent Yönetiminin Sınıfsal Yapısı" [The Municipalities and the Class Composition of City Administration]. *Mimarlık*, no. 1 (1977).

————. "Belediyeler ve Merkezi İdare Çelişkisi" [The Conflict between Municipalities and the Central Government]. *Mimarlık*, nos. 8–9 (1975).

————. "Can Municipalities in Turkey Be Considered as Institutions of a Civic Society with a Broad Social Base?" in Korel Göymen, Hans F. Illy, and Winfried Veit, eds., *Local Administration: Democracy versus Efficiency?* Analysen no. 103/104. Bonn: Friedrich Ebert Stiftung, 1982, 69–81.

Tezel, Yahya. "Demokrasi ve Belediyeler" [Democracy and Municipalities]. *Toplumcu Düşün*, no. 8 (1979), 185–198.

Trak, Ayşe. "Belediyeler ve İşsizlik Sorunu" [Municipalities and Unemployment]. Union of Mediterranean Towns, Papers of the Conference, Istanbul, May 12–15, 1980.

Türkcan, Ergun, ed. *Belediye İslevlerine Nicel bir Yaklaşım* [A Quantitative Approach to Municipal Functions]. Ankara: Türk İdareciler Derneği, 1981.

————. *Türkiye'de Belediyeciliğin Evrimi* [The Evolution of Municipalities in Turkey]. Belediyecilik Araştırma Projesi 1. Ankara: Türk İdareciler Derneği, 1978.

————. *Yeni Bir Belediyeciliğe Doğru* [Towards a New Municipal Administration]. Belediyecilik Araştırması III. Ankara: Türk İdareciler Derneği, 1982.

Turkish Labor Party. *Yerel Yönetimler Demokratikleştirilmelidir* [Local Government Should Be Democratized]. Ankara, 1977.

Turkish Municipal Association. *Belediye Gelirleri Semineri* [Seminar on Municipal Revenues] Ankara, 1972.

————. İller ve Belediyeler Dergisi [Review of Provinces and Municipalities].

————. *"Türkiye'de Metropolitan İdareler* [Metropolitan Administrations in Turkey]. Ankara, 1969.

Union of Administrators. *Büyük Kent Belediyeleri ve Sorunları Sempozyumu* [Symposium on Large City Municipalities and Their Problems]. Ankara, 1977.

Yavuz, Fehmi. *Tük Mahallî İdarelerinin Yeniden Düzenlenmesi Üzerinde bir Araştirma* [A Study on the Reorganization of Turkish Local Governments]. Ankara: Türkiye ve Orta Doğu Amme İdaresi Enstitüsü, 1966.

URBAN PLANNING AND DEVELOPMENT

Gök, T., ed. *Türkiye'de İmar Planlaması* [Urban Planning in Turkey]. Ankara: Orta Doğu Teknik Üniversitesi, Şehir ve Bölge Planlama Bölümü, 1980.

Istanbul Chamber of Industry. *İstanbul Metropolitan Alanında Sanayi Yerleşim Planlaması* [Planning Industrial Location in the Istanbul Metropolitan Area]. Research Section, Publication no. 10. İstanbul, October 1981.

Kartal, Kemal. "Kent Toprağında Mülkiyet" [Urban Land Ownership]. *Cumhuriyet,* December 23–26, 1978.

Keleş, Ruşen, and Geoffrey K. Payne. "Town and Country Planning in Turkey." In Martyn Wynn, ed., *Planning and Urban Growth in Southern Europe.* London: Mansell, in press.

Ministry of Reconstruction and Settlement. *Büyük İstanbul Bölgesi Kent İşletmesi Sorunları Uluslararası Semineri* [Seminar on Urban Management Problems in the Greater Istanbul Area]. İstanbul: Aralık, 1974.

"Turkey: History, Geography and Planning." *ISOCARP Bulletin,* May 1982.

Turkish Union of Chambers for Architects and Engineers. *Kent Toprakları Sorunu* [The Problem of Urban Land]. Ankara, 1973.

United Nations Development Programme. Project of the Government of Turkey, Project Document, "International Drinking Water Supply and Sanitation Decade Technical (TST) Support." TUR/81/012/A/01/14, in *Resmi Gazete,* no. 17813 (September 15, 1982).

Yavuz, Fehmi. "Planning Turkish Cities." In Arnold Whittick, ed., *Encyclopedia of Urban Planning.* New York: McGraw-Hill, 1974, 1014–1029.

———. *Kentsel Topraklar* [Urban Land]. Ankara: Siyasal Bilgiler Fakültesi, 1980.

Yavuz, Fehmi, Ruşen Keleş, and Cevat Geray. *Şehircilik: Sorunlar, Uygulama ve Politika* [Urbanization: Problems, Implementation and Policy]. 2d ed. Ankara: Siyasal Bilgiler Fakültesi, 1978.

REGIONAL DEVELOPMENT AND PLANNING

Albaum, Melvin, and Christopher S. Davies. "The Spatial Structure of Socio-Economic Attributes of Turkish Provinces." *International Journal of Middle East Studies,* vol. 4, no. 3 (July 1973), 288–310.

Gençağa, Hasan. "Growth Determinants of Urban Centers of Different Sizes," Ph.D. thesis, Columbia University, New York, 1976.

Keleş, Ruşen. "The Effects of External Migration on Regional Development in Turkey." Paper presented to the conference on National and Regional Development in the Mediterranean Basin, St. Aidan's College, University of Durham, April 13–17, 1982.

———. "The National Settlement Patterns and Policies of Turkey." Paper presented at Expert Group Meeting on National Settlement Policies, United Nations Center for Housing, Building and Planning, New York, November 14–18, 1977.

———. "Regional Disparities in Turkey." In Turkish Society for Housing and Planning, *Turkiye'de Bölge Planlamasi Alanındakı Gelişmeler* [Recent Developments in Regional Planning in Turkey]. Publication no. 2 (Ankara, 1964).

Rivkin, Malcolm D. *Area Development for National Growth: The Turkish Precedent.* New York: Praeger, 1965.

Rodwin, Lloyd. *Nations and Cities: A Comparison of Strategies for Urban Growth.* Boston: Houghton Mifflin, 1970.

Srikantan, K. S. "Regional and Rural-Urban Socio-Demographic Differences in Turkey." *Middle East Journal,* vol. 27, no. 3 (Summer 1973), 275–300.

State Planning Organization. *Bölgesel Gelişme Sektör Raporu* [Sector Report on Regional Development]. SPO Pub. no. 1854, Social Planning Department Pub. no. 360. Ankara, 1982.

———. *Planlı Dönemde Toplam Mevduat ve Toplam Kredilerin Bölgesel Dağılımı* [Total Bank Deposits and Total Credits by Geographical Regions]. SPO Pub. no. 17. Ankara, 1982.

———. *Türkiye'de Organize Sanayi Bölgeleri (1961–1981)* [Organized Industrial Districts in Turkey]. SPO Pub. no. 1839, Social Planning Department Pub. no. 351. Ankara, 1982.

———. *Türkiye'de Yerleşme Merkezlerinin Kademelenmesi* [Hierarchy of Settlements in Turkey]. Ankara, 1982.

Tolan, Barlas. *Türkiye'de İller İtibariyle Sosyo-Ekonomik Gelişmişlik Endeksi.* [Socio-Economic Development Studies in Turkey by Provinces] State Planning Organization. Ankara, 1972.

NATIONAL DEVELOPMENT PLANS

State Planning Organization. *Kalkınma Planı, Birinci Beş Yıl: 1963–1967* [First Five-Year Development Plan]. Ankara, 1963.

———. *Kalkınma Planı, Ikinci Beş Yıl: 1968–1972* [Second Five-Year Development Plan]. Ankara, 1969.

———. *Kalkınma Planı, Üçüncü Beş Yıl 1973–1977* [Third Five-Year Development Plan]. Ankara, 1973.

———. *Yeni Strateji ve Kalkınma Planı Ücüncü Beş Yıl (1973–1977)* [Strategy and Basic Targets of Long-Term Development and the Third Five-Year Plan]. Ankara, 1973.

———. *Dördüncü Beş Yıllık Kalkınma Planı: 1978–1983* [Fourth Five-Year Development Plan]. Ankara, 1978.

LAWS RELATING TO URBAN DEVELOPMENT

Law 486 of 1924. Umur-u Belediyeye Müteallik Ahkâm-ı Cezaiye Hakkinda Kanum [Law Concerning Penal Provisions for Municipal Affairs].

Law 583 of 1925. Ankara'da İnşası Mukarrer Yenimahalle için Muktazi Yerler ile Bataklık ve Merzagi Arazinin Şehremanetince İstimlâki Hakkında Kanun [Law Concerning the Expropriation of Land Required for the Construction of a New Quarter in Ankara and of Marshy Lands].

Law 1351 of 1928. Ankara Şehri İmar Müdürlüğü Teşkilât ve Vezaifine Dair Kanun [Law Concerning the Organization and Functions of the Development Directorate of the City of Ankara].

Law 1580 of 1930. Belediye Kanunu [Municipal Law].

Law 1593 of 1930. Umumî Hıfzıssıhha Kanunu [Public Hygiene Law].

Law 2290 of 1933. Belediye Yapı ve Yollar Kanunu [Law on Municipal Roads and Buildings].

Law 5218 of 1948. Ankara Belediyesine Arsa ve Arazisinden Belli Bir Kısmını Mesken Yapacaklara Tahsis ve Temlik Yetkisi Verilmesi Hakkında Kanun [Law Concerning the Authorization of the Municipality to Give Part of Its Own Land to Those Who Will Build Dwellings].

Law 5228 of 1948. Bina Yapımını Teşvik Kanunu [Law on the Encouragement of Home Building].

Law 5431 of 1949. Ruhsatsız Yapıların Yıktırılmasına ve Belediye Yapı ve Yollar Kanununun 13. Maddesinin Değiştirilmesine Dair Kanun [Law Concerning Demolishing of Buildings Without Construction Permits and Amending Article 13 of the Municipal Construction and Roads Law].

Law 6188 of 1953. Bina Yapımını Teşvik ve İzinsiz Yapılan Binalar Hakkında Kanun [Law on the Encouragement of Home Building and on Illegally Built Dwellings].

Law 6217 of 1954. Tapu Kanununun 26. Maddesinin Değiştirilmesi Hakkında Kanun [Law Concerning the Modification of Article 26 of the Land Title Law].

Law 6785 of 1957. İmar Kanunu [Town Planning Law].

Law 7367 of 1959. Hazıneden Belediyelere Verilecek Arazi ve Ansalar Hakkında Kanun [Law Concerning Land to be Transferred from the State to the Municipalities].

Law 634 of 1965. Kat Mülkiyeti Kanunu [Flat Law].

Law 775 of 1966. Gecekendu Kanunu [Gecekondu Law].

Law 1605 of 1972. 6785 Sayılı İmar Kanununda Bazı Değişiklikler Yapılması Hakkında Kanun [Law Concerning Modifications in the Town Planning Law].

Law 2380 of 1981. Belediyelere ve İl Özel İdarelerine Genel Bütçe Vergi

Gelirlerinden Pay Verilmesi Hakkında Kanun [Law Concerning Giving Shares to Municipalities and Provincial Local Administrations out of the General Tax Revenues].

Law 2464 of 1981. Belediye Gelirleri Kanunu [Municipal Revenues Law].

Law 2487 of 1981. Toplu Konut Kanunu [Collective Housing Law].

Law 2561 of 1981. Büyük Şehirlerin Yakın Çevresindeki Yerleşim Yerlerinin Anabelediyelere Bağlanmaları Hakkında Kanun [Law on the Amalgamation of Small Localities Surrounding Larger Cities with These Larger Cities].

Law 2805 of 1983. İmar ve Gecekondu Mevzuatına Aykırı Olarak Yapılan Yapılara Uygulanacak İşlemer ve 6785 Sayılı İmar Kanununun Bir Maddesinin Değiştirilmesi Hakkında Kanun [Law on the Procedures Concerning the Illegally Erected Buildings and Gecekondus and Modification of Law 6785].

Law 2814 of 1983. 23 Haziran 1965 Tarihli ve 634 Sayılı Kat Mülkiyeti Kanununun Bazı Maddelerinin Değiştirilmesine ve Bu Kanuna Bazı Maddeler Eklenmesine Dair Kanun [Law on Modifications and Additions to the Flat Law of 1965].

INDEX

Adana, 35
  industrialization in, 38, 39
  population, 50
  satisfaction with life in, 69
  squatter settlements in, 41–42
Administrative agencies, of city govern-
    ments, 78, 80–81
Administrative tutelage, 82–83, 96–97
  conflict over, 116
  political parties and, 102
Aegean regions, 37, 209, 228
Agriculture
  government price subsidies for, 47
  migration to cities due to modernization
    of, 33, 34, 213
  regional differences in, 34
Air pollution, 69, 133–34
Altaban, Özcan, 157
Anatolia
  colonialism and, 14
  growth of, 210
  modernization of. See Ankara
  See also Central Anatolia; Eastern
    Anatolia
Angora, 59
Ankara, 3, 59–63
  central government and, 118
    conflict with, 92
    master plans, 16, 95
    support from, 68
  colonialism and, 14
  development of, 6, 230
    industrialization, 38, 39, 209
    metropolitan planning bureau for,
      201–2, 203
    modernization, 69, 217
    outward spread, 64–65
    plans for, 10, 198, 200
    rapid urbanization, 28
    unplanned, 23
  economic and political advantages of,
    50–52, 114

elections in, 101, 106, 107, 108, 109, 110
family income in, 53
government of, 80, 81, 82
  budget, 85
  central aid to, 87
  central government conflict and, 92
  mayoral skill in, 22–23
  revenues, 84
history of, 59–60
housing in, 158, 160, 161, 180, 182, 186–
    90, 225–26, 227–28, 230, 231, 232.
  See also Squatter settlements in, be-
    low
labor in, 122
land use and costs in, 163, 193–94, 198
merchants associations in, 118
middle class and, 124
as national capital, 37, 59–61, 73, 74,
    205, 208, 215, 227
political influence in, 221
population, 3, 35, 49, 50, 58, 59, 61–62,
    150, 151, 228
public services in, 52, 136
  electricity, 116
  transportation, 149, 150, 151, 153–54,
    155, 156
  water, 135
satisfaction with life in, 69
space in the markets and, 118–19
squatter settlements in, 3, 7, 39, 41, 44,
    59, 62, 63, 105, 139, 164, 165, 166,
    167, 173, 179
violence in, 219
Ankara Electricity and Gas and Bus
    Agency, 18, 19
Ankara Electricity and Gas Establish-
    ment, 146
Ankara Planning Commission, 60–61, 74
Antalya, 212
Areal scope, governmental units classified
    by, 18–19, 20
Assimilation, politics of in cities, 128–30

Assistant mayors, 80–81, 82, 112
Association of Progressive Municipalities
    (Devrimci Belediyeler Derneği), 114
Association of Taxi and Minibus Drivers,
    119
Ataturk, Kemal Mustafa, 3, 10, 14, 15,
    27, 56, 59–60, 73, 74, 103, 205, 208,
    209, 230
Ataturk bridge, 155

Bank of Local Authorities (İller Bankası),
    87, 89, 90–91, 143–45, 199
Bank of Municipalities (Belediyeler Bank-
    ası), 143
Bank of the Provinces, 18
Batıkent, 187–90, 203, 225, 227–28, 230,
    231, 232
Beyoğlu, 73
Birthrate, migration to cities and, 33
Black Sea, 37
Bridges, 155
    Bosphorus, 52, 57, 134, 152, 155, 156,
    217
Building Encouragement Law of 1948,
    182
Building regulations, 195–98
Bureaucrats, political influence of, 220.
    See also Government
Bursa
    industrialization in, 38, 39
    population, 50
    private sector and, 15
    satisfaction with life in, 69
    squatter settlements in, 41
Buses, 156
    minibuses, 149, 150, 151
Byzantine Empire, 53, 54
Byzantium, 53

Cabinet, 19
Capital. See Ankara
Cars, private, 150, 151–52
Central Anatolia, 35, 37
Centralized political system, 9, 12, 72–75,
    231–32
    See also Government
Central Traffic Committee, 152
Chambers of commerce and industry, 120
Cities
    central government and, 71, 73, 74–75,
    77, 79, 82, 83–88, 89–95, 222. See
    also Politics
    economic adversity in, 46–47
    family income, 31–32
    government of, 11–12, 18, 71, 77–81,
    103. See also Mayors; Politics; Ur-
    ban development, government and

council of, 19, 78, 79, 96, 103, 111–
    12, 113
elections, 103–4
employees of, 121–23
European models for, 73
housing and, 185, 186–90
metropolitan planning and, 202
municipal planning and, 199–201
Ottoman Empire and, 72–73
squatter settlements and, 176–77,
    178, 179
Standing Committees of, 78, 79–80,
    118
subdistricts, 78, 81
taxes, 83–84, 85–86
Turkish Republic and, 74–75
urban development and, 196–97
large, 49–70. See also Ankara; Istanbul;
    Izmir
    advantages of, 50–52
    concentrated development in, 68, 69–
    70
    costs of, 69–70
    population, 49–50, 51
    pressures on national government
    from, 113
    public services in, 69
    rapid outward growth of, 63–65
    satisfaction with life in, 69
    socioeconomic differences in, 65–68
    unemployment in, 6, 39, 40, 41
    military government and, 114
    unions of, 110–11
    violence in, 130–31, 219
    See also Political parties; Population;
    Public services; specific cities; Squat-
    ter settlements; urban development,
    government and; Urbanization
City Development Law, 119–20
City (urban) planning. See Urban devel-
    opment, government and
Civil servants, of cities, 121–23
Collective housing program, 184–86, 189
Colonialism, urbanization and, 14
Communication, modernization and, 10
Concentrated development, in large
    cities, 68, 69–70
Concentration of resources
    central government and, 231
    metropolitan plans and, 202–3
    transportation and, 155–56
    urban development and, 21–24, 192,
    229–30
Constantine the Great, 53
Constantinople, 53–54. See also Istanbul
Constituencies
    national politics and urban, 104–5
    resource concentration and, 21–22

Constitutional Court, 119–20
  electricity agency and, 146
  land use and, 193
Constitutions
  housing needs and, 157, 184
  land use and, 193
  military and, 95, 96
  1961, 11, 31, 78
  1982, 31, 96–97, 184
Council
  of city government, 19, 78, 79, 96, 103, 111–12, 113
  of provinces, 73, 77
Council of Ministers, 76, 97
Council of State, 116, 199
Counties (ilce), 75
Craftsmen (esnaf), 117
Çukurova, 212, 228

Dalokay, Vedat, 108, 114, 117, 135, 187, 188, 190
Debts of cities, central government cancelling or postponing, 87–88
Demirel, Süleyman, 117
Democracy, 7, 8–9, 11, 31, 222–23, 226
Democratic Party, 102, 105, 106, 126, 158, 169, 180–81, 221
Denizli, 209
Dependency theorists, 14
Dinçer, Ali, 115, 153, 154, 187, 188, 232
Diyarbakir, 49
Dolmuş. See Group taxis
Drivers Association, 118
Duality, 40–43
  of the Turkish metropolis, 65–68

Eastern Anatolia, industrial development in, 35
Eastern Turkey, Western Turkey versus, 34–38
Ecevit, Bülent, 107, 108–9, 110, 114, 115
Economic development
  assimilation and, 129, 130
  migration and, 45, 46–48
  modernization and, 11
  See also Industrialization
Education
  inadequacy of, 135
  investment by central government in, 88
  modernization and, 10, 11
  regional disparities in, 32, 35, 213
  responsibility for, 144, 145
  squatter settlements and, 138, 139, 140, 141
Elections. See Political participation
Electricity
  adequacy of, 135

Ankara and, 116
  Bank of Local Authorities and, 143–45
  city size and, 52
  public investments in, 136
  regional disparities in, 32, 35
  responsibility for, 144, 146
  in squatter settlements, 138, 139, 140, 141
  Turkish Electricity Agency and, 18, 32, 88, 143, 146
  for urban housing units, 159, 160
Electricity, Tramway and Tunnel Authority of Istanbul, 154
Elgotz, Herman, 198
Employment
  in Instanbul, 15
  municipal, 121–23
  in services, 39, 40
  unions and, 120–21
  See also Unemployment
Energy, 88
  Minister of, 116, 146
Erzincan, 209
Erzurum, squatter settlements in, 41–42
Eskişehir, 38, 39, 41
Etatism, Ankara and, 60
European Resettlement Fund, 189

Factories, government's acceptance of, 16
  See also Industrialization
Family income
  in larger cities, 52, 53, 65, 66
  regional disparities in, 31–32, 35
Father state (devlet baba), 9
Federation of the Drivers and Automobile Operators of Turkey, 119
Ferry services, 152, 156
Fire-fighting, 73, 144
Fiscal resources, 22, 83–86
Five-Year Development Plans, 10, 12
  First (1963–1967), 158, 159, 175, 206, 210
  Second (1968–1972), 206–7, 210
  Third (1973–1977), 134, 179–80, 183, 207, 211
  Fourth (1978–1982), 180, 183
Foundations (vakıf), 73
Fourth Crusade, 54
Functional scope, governmental units classified by, 19–21
Future of the cities, 228–33

Galata bridge, 155
Garbage collection, 136, 144. See also Sewage disposal
Gas, responsibility for, 144
Gaziantep, 38, 39, 41, 49

Gecekondu. See Squatter settlements
Gecekondu Fund, 115
Gecekondu Improvement Act of 1966, 140
Gecekondu Law of 1966, 1975–79, 199
Gecekondu Law of 1976, 177
Golden Horn, 58, 155
Government, 71–97
  agriculture and, 47
  assistance and investments by, 86–88
  capital. *See* Ankara
  centralization and, 9, 12, 72–75, 231–32
  cities and, 71, 73, 74–75, 77, 79, 82, 83–88, 89–95, 222. *See also* Political parties; Politics
  conflict in, 89
  functional instruments of, 89–91
  industrialization and, 11, 38
  influence of, 12–15
  local, 75–76. *See also* Cities
  means of control of, 81–82
  migration policy and, 31
  provincial government and, 76–77
  revenues controlled by, 83–86
  squatter settlements and, 16, 42, 58, 87, 158, 159, 165–66, 167, 169, 170–80, 224, 225, 226–27
  structure, 17–18
    areal scope and, 18–19, 20
    functional scope and, 19–21
    resource concentration and, 21–24
  Turkish Republic and, 73–74
  two-tier for metropolitan areas, 232
  urbanization and, 7, 13–18, 224–33. *See also* Urban development, government and
  see also Administrative tutelage; Cities; Housing; Military government; Politics; Public services; Urban development, government and
Grand National Assembly, 104
Greater Istanbul Master Plan Bureau, 20–21, 154, 156, 203
Greater Istanbul sewerage project, 147
Grey Wolf, 130
Group taxis *(dolmuş)*, 42, 119, 134, 138, 149, 150, 151, 153–54
Guilds *(lonca)*, 72, 117–19

Headman *(muhtar)*, 81
Health services
  inadequacy of, 135
  investment by central government in, 88
  land use and, 196
  Ministry of Health and, 90
  modernization and, 11

regional disparities in, 32, 35–36, 213
responsibility for, 144, 145
Heussler, M., 60, 198
High Administrative Court *(Danıştay)*, 97
Highway Directorate, 153
Highways. *See* Roads and highways
Highway Traffic Law of 1953, 153
Housing
  duality in, 41–42
  future and, 228, 229
  government and, 19, 157–90, 225–26, 227–28, 230, 231, 232. *See also* Squatter settlements
    acceptance by, 15–16
    aid from, 87
    city government and, 186–90
    conventional housing, 159–60, 161
    electricity and, 159, 160
    Housing Law of 1981, 183–86, 189
    as low priority, 157–59
    for middle class, 180–83
    military, 96, 184–86
    mortgage-credit programs, 161
    policy on, 184
    private housing, 160–61, 162, 180–81, 182, 184
    standards, 42
    water supply and, 159, 160
  landowners' influence in policies on, 119–20
  large cities and, 69
  modernization and, 11
  municipal planning and, 200
  private investment in, 158–59
  responsibility for, 144. *See also* government and, *above*
  rural development and, 213
  slums, 162
  tenants' associations and, 124
  See also Squatter settlements
Housing and Squatting Division, 139
Housing cooperatives, in Batıkent, 188–90
Housing Law of 1981, 184–86, 189

İller Bankası, 231
Independence, resource concentration and, 21
Industrial Development Bank, 52, 57
Industrialization, 219
  government and, 11–12, 17, 38, 227
  modernization and, 10
  private investment in, 12
  public investment in, 205–6, 207
  regional development and, 35, 209, 210–11

rural areas and, 213, 219
urbanization and, 6, 38-40
Industry and Commodity Exchanges, 120
Inflation, cities and, 46-47
Informal sector, modern economy versus,
    40-43
Infrastructure
    Ministry of Reconstruction and Settle-
        ment and, 90
    modernization and, 10
    See also Bridges; Roads and highways
Inter-Ministerial Coordination Council for
    Development in Metropolitan Areas,
    203
International Bank for Reconstruction
    and Development, 95
International migration, 30-31
Isparta, 209
Istanbul, 3, 53-59
    amalgamation in, 232
    as capital, 72-73
    central government and, 68, 87, 95
    colonialism and, 14
    development of, 6, 225
        historical, 53-56
        industrialization, 35, 38, 39, 209
        metropolitan planning bureaus for,
            201-2, 203, 204
        modernization, 69
        plans for, 198
        rapid urbanization, 94
        suburban, 64
        urban planning, 208
    as economic center, 58
    economic and political advantages of,
        50-52, 114, 221
    elections in, 101, 106, 107, 108, 109, 110
    employment in, 15
    geographic setting, 53, 54
    government of, 81, 82, 94
        budget, 85
        employment in, 122
        mayoral skill, 22-23
    housing in, 66-68, 160, 161, 182, 187.
        See also squatter settlements in, be-
        low
    income distribution in, 53, 66
    inflation and, 47
    land use and cost in, 194, 196-97, 198
    modern, 58-59, 217
    population of, 3, 27, 35, 50, 54-55, 56,
        58, 228
    public services in, 52, 136
        sewage disposal, 96, 146-47
        transportation, 149, 153, 154, 155,
            156
        water, 135, 146-47

    satisfaction with life in, 69
    squatter settlements in, 7, 39, 40, 41-
        42, 44, 58-59, 105, 124, 126-27, 131,
        138, 139, 163, 165, 167, 169, 174, 179
    violence in, 47, 131, 219
Istanbul Bus Owners Association, 153
Istanbul Hilton, 57
Istanbul Metropolitan Planning Bureau,
    120
Istanbul Provincial Directorate, 18
Istanbul Taxi and Dolmuş Drivers' Asso-
    ciation, 153
Istanbul Technical University, 57
Istanbul Water and Sewerage Agency, 18,
    146-47, 232
İsvan, Ahmet, 116-17, 196
Izmir
    amalgamation in, 232
    central government and, 67, 87, 95
    colonialism and, 14
    development, 6
        industrialization, 38, 39
        master plans for, 95
        metropolitan planning bureaus for,
            201-2
        rapid urbanization, 94
        suburban, 64
    districts of, 66, 67
    economic and political advantages of,
        50-52, 114
    elections in, 106, 107, 108, 109, 110
    family income in, 53
    housing of, 66-68, 161, 182. See also
        squatter settlements of, below
    municipal labor in, 122
    population, 27, 50, 228
    private sector and, 15
    public services in, 53, 154
    satisfaction with life in, 69
    squatter settlements of, 7, 39, 41-42,
        105, 165
Izmit, 15

Jansen, Hermann, 60, 61, 198
Joint Municipal Fund, 115
Joint Traffic Fund, 90
Justice Party (JP), 102, 105, 106, 107, 108,
    109, 110, 111, 115, 116, 117, 118, 119,
    123, 129, 130, 184, 221

Karabük, 209
Kayseri, 38, 41
Keban, 212
Kent-Koop, 121
Kırıkkale, 49, 209
Konya, 38
Kütahya, 209

Labor Unions. *See* Unions
Land deed *(tapu),* for squatter housing,
      168–69, 176, 177–78
Land Law of 1858, 193
Land Office, 18
Landowners, political influence of, 119–
      20
Land use
   Ankara and, 61
   government and, 87, 22
   large cities and, 69
   Real Estate Bank and, 18, 87, 90, 158,
      180, 181
   standards, 192–98
      building and zoning controls, 195–98
      history of, 192–93, 195–96
      land prices and, 193–95
Law on Collective Housing (Law 2487 of
      1981), 184–86, 189
Law 486 of 1924, 196
Law 1580 of 1930. *See* Municipal Law of
      1930
Law 2380 of 1981, 85
Law 2464 of 1981, 85–86
Law 2487 of 1981. *See* Law on Collective
      Housing
Local government, 75–76. *See also* Cities

Mahalle. See Neighborhood organizations
Market forces, urban development and,
      14, 15
   See also Private sector
Marmara, 56, 201, 212, 214, 228
   industry in, 209
   population, 35, 37
Marmara Regional Planning Organization,
      201
Marshall Plan, 213
Marxists, urban development and, 14
Mayors, 78–79, 80
   functional jurisdictions, 19
   influence of, 114
   military rule and, 96
   political parties and, 103, 112, 113
   political skill of, 22–23
Menderes, Adnan, 57
Merchants, political influence of, 117–19,
      220
Merchants Associations, 117–19
Metropolitan planning, 95, 201–4. *See
      also* Urban development, govern-
      ment and
Middle class, 123–24, 180–83, 220
Migration, 3, 4, 5
   agriculture and, 33, 34, 213
   governmental agencies and, 18
   government control and, 204

highway and road improvements and,
      17, 34
housing for. *See* Squatter settlements
   international, 30–31
   to large cities, 49, 62
   middle class and, 123
   permanency of, 44–45
   political conflict and, 127–31
   public service needs resulting from, 135
   rapid urbanization and, 6, 29–31
   regional development and, 209
   rural development and, 212–13
   slowing of, 46–48
   success of, 43–46
   to Western Turkey, 35
Military government, 8, 85–86, 114, 223
   central planning and, 12
   cities and, 85–86, 95–97
      violence in, 130
   housing and, 90, 184–86
   land use and, 193
   municipal power agencies and, 146
   political parties and, 8, 233
   small business organizations and, 119
   squatter settlements and, 173
   transportation issues and, 154
Minibuses, 149, 150, 151
Minister of Interior, 82, 97, 112, 116, 147
Ministries of Reconstruction, Education
      and Agriculture, 153
Ministry of Commerce, 92
Ministry of Energy and Natural Re-
      sources, 116, 146
Ministry of Finance, 91–92, 116, 185, 187
Ministry of Health, 90
Ministry of Interior, 18, 74, 89–90, 96,
      152, 153
Ministry of Local Affairs, 18, 91, 92, 110,
      111, 114, 116, 143, 187
Ministry of Public Works, 18, 152
Ministry of Reconstruction and Settle-
      ment, 18, 19, 39, 87, 89, 90, 91, 92,
      95, 99, 143, 154, 175–76, 181, 183,
      184, 185, 187, 190, 195, 197, 199, 201,
      202, 203, 212, 231
Ministry of Transportation and Communi-
      cations, 90, 152
Mixed economy, 11–12, 13
Modern industrial economy, second econ-
      omy versus, 40–43
Modernization
   of agriculture, 33, 34, 213
   commitment to, 7, 10–11
   development of large cities and. *See*
      Ankara; Istanbul; Izmir
   national development plans and, 12
   of public transportation, 213

rural areas and, 34
strategies of, 205–8
urbanization as a corollary to, 31
Mohammed, Sultan, 54
Mohammed the Conqueror, 54
Moltke, Wilhelm von, 198
Muhtar, 126
Multiparty system, 102, 103. *See also*
    Political parties
Municipal council. *See* Council
Municipal debts, cancellation or post-
    ponement by central government,
    87–88
Municipal employees, political influence
    of, 121–23, 220
Municipal government. *See* Cities
Municipalities, 75. *See also* Cities
Municipal Law of 1930, 74, 77, 79, 153,
    195, 199
Municipal planning, 199–201. *See also*
    Urban development, government and
Municipal Roads and Buildings Act of
    1933, 199

National Action Party, 130
National assembly, 19
National development plans. *See* Five-
    Year Development Plans; Planning
National Fund for Gecekondus, 87, 99,
    102, 177, 178
National government. *See* Government
Nationalism, 10, 60
National Land Office, 195
National Salvation Party, 130
National Security Council, 96, 146
Neighborhood organizations *(mahalles)*
    of city governments, 73, 78, 81
    of squatter settlements, 100, 125–26
New settlements fund, 184

Oil prices, economy and, 46
One-party rule, 102, 103. *See also* Polit-
    ical parties
Osmaniye, 209
Ottoman Empire
    Ankara and, 59
    central government from, 9, 72–73
    Istanbul as capital of, 54–55
    land use and, 193, 195–96
    political power and, 15
Overurbanization, 39, 41

Parks, 138, 144
Pashas, 72
Planned city. *See* Ankara
Planning, 205
    State Planning Organization and, 18,

40, 92, 136, 159, 185, 198, 203, 208,
    212, 214–15
    See also Five-Year Development Plans;
    Regional development; Urban de-
    velopment, government and
Planning Council for Greater Istanbul,
    203
Police protection, 144
    squatter settlements and, 138, 139, 140
Political participation, 220
    by city dwellers, 105–9
    modernization and, 11
    in national elections, 100–101
    urbanization and, 100–102
Political parties, 8, 222–23
    centralized, 103–4
    cities and, 75, 102–12
        city-center conflict and, 114–17
        city influence and, 112–14
        city politics and, 111–12
        elections and, 103–4
        Republican People's Party and, 109–
            11
        squatters and, 125–26
        urban constituencies and, 104–5
        urban vote and, 105–9
    Democratic Party, 102, 105, 106, 126,
        158, 169, 180–81, 221
    Justice Party, 102, 105, 106, 107, 108,
        109, 110, 111, 115, 116, 117, 118, 119,
        123, 129, 130, 184, 221
    military government and, 8, 233
    as multiparty system, 102, 103
    National Action Party, 130
    National Salvation Party, 130
    one-party rule, 102, 103
    Republican People's Party, 8, 102, 103,
        105, 106, 107, 108, 109, 110, 115, 116,
        117, 118, 123, 129, 130, 183–84, 187,
        221
    urbanization and, 221
    see also Politics
Political skill, concentrating resources
    and, 22–23
Politics, 99–131
    assimilation and, 128–30
    city-central government relations and,
        112–17
    conflict in, 114–17
    influence of cities and, 113–14
    pressure from cities and, 112–13
    disorder and, 130–31
    dual development and, 43
    migration and, 127–31
    municipal planning and, 200
    public services and, 138–41
    urban groups and, 117–27. *See also*

Squatter settlements
chambers of commerce, 120
landowners, 119–20
merchants associations, 117–19
middle class, 123–24
municipal employees, 121–23
small merchants, 119
unions, 110–11, 120–21, 181–82
urbanization and, 100–102, 218–24
See also Government; Political parties
Pollution, 69, 133–34
Population
rural, 27, 28–29, 30
in squatter settlements, 41–42, 165
of Turkey, 6
urban, 6–7
future, 228
growth in, 27–28, 29, 30
large cities, 49–50, 51, 75. See also
Ankara; Istanbul; Izmir
regional differences in, 35, 37
Populism, in the cities, 108
Precinct organizations. See Neighborhood organizations
Primate city. See Istanbul
Prime minister, 19
Private cars, 150, 151–52
Private decisions, urban development
and, 15
Private industry, public versus, 12
Private sector
government's responsiveness to, 15–16
urban development and, 14, 15
Private transportation, cars for, 150, 151–
52. See also Public transportation
Producing municipality, 111
Property tax, 83, 85, 119–20
Prost, Henri, 198
Provinces (il), 75
councils of, 73, 77
government of, 18, 76–77. See also Pro-
vincial governors,
regional planning and, 211–12
Provincial councils, 73, 77
Provincial governors (vali), 76–77
Ataturk and, 74
coordination of government efforts by,
92–93
functional jurisdictions and, 19
military government and, 96
Ottomans and, 73, 74
Provincial Traffic Committee, 152–53
Public housing fund, 184, 186, 190
Public Hygiene Law, 196
Public industrial sector, 11–12
Public services, 32–33, 133–56
adequacy of, 135–36

centralizing, 145–47
city size and, 52
distribution, 137–41
employment in, 39, 40
government and, 87, 88, 141–47
in large cities, 69
migration and, 44
military government and, 96
organizing, 141–47
political pressures and, 138–41
regional differences in, 32, 33, 34
in squatter settlements, 134, 137–41,
149, 176, 178, 179
Turkish Republic and, 74
under Ottomans, 72, 73
urbanization and need for, 220
See also specific services
Public transportation, 147–56
buses, 156
central government and, 152
agencies, 18
Ministry of Transportation and, 90,
152
city government and, 152–55
ferry services, 152, 156
group taxis, 42, 119, 134, 138, 149, 150,
151, 153–54
inadequacy of, 135
large cities and, 69
migration to the cities and modernization of, 213
minibuses, 149, 150, 151
rail system, 10, 18, 152, 156
rapid transit, 154, 155
small merchants and, 119
squatter settlements and, 138, 139, 140
See also Roads and highways; Traffic

Rail system, 10, 18, 152, 156
Rapid-transit, 154, 155
Rapid urbanization. See Urbanization
Real Estate Bank (Emlâk Kredi Bankası),
18, 87, 90, 158, 180, 181
Regional development, 208–12, 214–15
migration and urban growth and, 34–38
planning for, 92, 201
See also Urban development, government and
Regional Planning Department, 92
Regional Planning Organization, 201
Republican People's Party (RPP), 8, 102,
103, 105, 106, 107, 108, 109, 110, 115,
116, 117, 118, 123, 129, 130, 183–84,
187, 221
Resources, urbanization and competition
for scarce, 4. See also Concentration
of resources

Revenues, central government and, 83–86
Roads and highways
    central government and, 17, 18, 34,
        152, 227
    inadequacy of, 135
    investments in, 155, 156
    large cities and, 51, 57
    regional disparities in, 35
    responsibility for, 144
    squatter settlements and, 139, 140, 141
    See also Public transportation; Traffic
Roman Empire, Constantinople and, 53–
    54
Rural areas, 7, 75
    agriculture and, 33, 34
    cities compared to, 31–34
    development of, 212–14
    family income and, 31–32
    governmental policies and, 33–34
    modernization and, 11
    number of, 213
    population, 27, 28–29, 30
    services, 32–33
    voter turnout in, 100–101
    See also Migration
Rural-urban migration. See Migration

St. Sophia, church of, 54
Samsun, 35, 41–42
School of Design, 57
Schools. See Education
Second economy, modern economy ver-
    sus, 40–43
Services. See Public services
Sewage disposal
    adequacy of, 135
    central aid for, 87
    future and, 228
    large cities and, 69, 146–47
    military government and, 96
    responsibility for, 144
    in squatter settlements, 138, 139, 168
Sheraton Hotel, 117
Slums, 162. See also Squatter settlements
Small business organizations, 117–19
Social factors, migration and, 33, 45–46
Social Insurance Agency, 158, 181
Social Security Agencies, 88
Southeastern Turkey, population of, 37
Southern Anatolia, population of, 35, 37
Squatter settlements (gecekondu), 7
    alternatives to, 174
    apartments replacing, 170
    assimilation of, 128–30
    description of, 165, 167–68
    development of, 165–67
    discontent among, 128, 130–31

employment and, 39–40, 41
father state concept and, 9
government and, 16, 42, 58, 87, 158,
    159, 165–66, 167, 169, 170–80, 224,
    225, 226–27
land deeds for, 168–69, 176, 177–78
land use for, 164, 165
in large cities, 66–68, 69. See also Ank-
    ara; Istanbul; Izmir
migration policy and, 31
modernization and, 11
National Fund for Gecekondus and, 87,
    99, 102, 177, 178
neighborhood organizations in, 100,
    125–26
origins of, 163
outward sprawl due to, 63
political system and, 8
    party support by, 106, 107, 108, 109,
        110
    political influence of, 22, 105, 124–27,
        220–21
    political participation by, 101, 102,
        113
population of, 41–42, 165
public services in, 134, 137–41, 149,
    176, 178, 179
union's influence on policies on, 120–21
See also under Gecekondu; Migration
Standing committees (Belediye Encü-
    meni), 78, 79–80, 118
State Housing Bank, 182
State Hydraulic Works, 143, 146
State Planning Office, 228
State Planning Organization, 18, 40, 92,
    136, 159, 185, 198, 203, 208, 212,
    214–15
State Railway, 152
State Water Works, 18
Street cleaning, 144
Subdistricts (Belediye Şubesi), 78, 81
Suburban areas
    building and land-use regulation in, 197
    of Istanbul and Izmir, 64
    metropolitan reform and, 94–95
Suleiman the Magnificent, 55

Tariff and Regulation Committee, 118
TARKO, 92
Taxation, 83–86
Telephone, responsibility for, 144
Tırtıl, Abdullah, 86, 146
Topkapı palace, 55
Town Planning Law of 1957, 196, 197,
    199, 200
Traditional sector, modern economy ver-
    sus, 40–43

Traffic
  central government and, 152
  conditions causing, 151–52
  Istanbul and, 153
  Ministry of Interior and, 90
  squatter settlements and, 140
  See also Public transportation
Traffic Directorate, 152, 153
Transportation
  duality of, 42
  modernization and, 10
  See also Public transportation; Traffic
Türel, Ali, 157
Turkish Electricity Agency, 18, 32, 88, 143, 146
Turkish Maritime Bank, 152
Turkish Municipal Association, 114
Turkish People's Liberation Army, 130
Turkish Railways Agency, 154
Turkish Republic, 73, 74, 193, 196
Turkish revolution, 10, 14
Tutelage. See Administrative tutelage
Two-tier government, for major metropolitan areas, 232

Unemployment, in cities, 6, 39, 40, 41
Union of Chambers of Commerce, 120
Unions
  housing and, 181–82
  in municipalities, 110–11
  political influence of, 120–21
Urban centers, large cities as. See Cities
Urban development, government and, 191–215, 225, 227
  constraints on, 191–92
  future and, 228–33
  reform and change and, 93–95
  policy on, 91–93
  urbanization and regional development strategies, 204–15
    industrialization and, 205–6, 207
    migration control, 204
    modernization and, 205–8
    regional development and, 208–12, 214–15
    rural development, 212–14
  urban planning and, 23–24, 198–204
    evaluation of, 230–31
    history of, 198
    metropolitan planning, 201–4
    municipal planning, 199–201
  See also Land use
Urbanization
  concentrating resources and, 21–24
  definition, 3–4

evaluation of, 217–33
government and, 7, 13–18, 224–33
industrialization and, 38–40
modernization and, 10
planning for, see Urban development government and
political participation and, 100–102
politics and, 218–24
rapid, 6–7, 27–48
  constitutional provision on, 31
  dual society created by, 40–43
  growth and, 6
  migration and, 29–31, 33, 34, 43–46
  population and, 27–28, 29, 30
  regional disparities and, 34–38
  rural areas compared to, 31–34
  slowing of, 46–48
regional development and, 208–9
similarities and differences of, 5–6
See also Cities; Industrialization
Urban planning. See Urban development, government and
Urban populism, 108–9

Violence, in cities, 47, 130–31, 219
Voting. See Political participation

Water service
  adequacy of, 135
  Bank of Local Authorities and, 143–45
  future and, 228
  large cities and, 52, 53, 69, 146–47
  military government and, 96
  public investments in, 88, 136
  regional disparities in, 35
  responsibility for, 144, 145–46
  in squatter settlements, 138, 139, 140, 141
  urban housing units and, 159, 160
Wealth
  in larger cities, 52, 53
regional differences in, 35
  See also Family income
Western Europe, workers migrating to, 30–31
Western Turkey, eastern Turkey versus, 34–38
World Bank, 37

Yenisehir, 60

Zonguldak, 212
Zoning controls, 195–98. See also Land use